At the back of this book:
Tennessee State Performance Indicators and Reading and Writing Accomplishments

Reading STREET

Tennessee

Program Authors

Peter Afflerbach

Camille Blachowicz

Candy Dawson Boyd

Wendy Cheyney

Connie Juel

Edward Kame'enui

Donald Leu

Jeanne Paratore

P. David Pearson

Sam Sebesta

Deborah Simmons

Sharon Vaughn

Susan Watts-Taffe

Karen Kring Wixson

PEARSON
Scott Foresman

Editorial Offices: Glenview, Illinois • Parsippany, New Jersey • New York, New York
Sales Offices: Boston, Massachusetts • Duluth, Georgia • Glenview, Illinois
Coppell, Texas • Sacramento, California • Mesa, Arizona

We dedicate Reading Street to
Peter Jovanovich.

His wisdom, courage,
and passion for education
are an inspiration to us all.

About the Cover Artist

Award-winning artist Greg Newbold began drawing and painting at age three—and never stopped. His illustrated books for children include *Spring Song and Winter Lullaby*. Mr. Newbold also does illustrations for magazines, motion pictures, and food products such as catsup and jelly. He creates his illustrations in a studio next to his house, snuggled in the Rocky Mountains of Utah.

ISBN: 0-328-26125-4

3 4 5 6 7 8 9 10 V057 15 14 13 12 11 10 09 08 07

Dear Tennessee Reader,

A new school year is beginning. Are you ready? You are about to take a trip along a famous street—*Scott Foresman Reading Street*. During this trip you will meet exciting people, such as Revolutionary War hero Paul Revere, a cowgirl who lassoes tornadoes, and a boy who creates his own world with its own language and customs. You will take real and imaginary journeys to the bottom of the sea and the center of the Earth.

As you read selections about ghost towns, blues singers, and insects that swell up to store food, you will gain exciting new information that will help you in science and social studies.

While you're enjoying these exciting pieces of literature, you will find that something else is going on—you are becoming a better reader, gaining new skills and polishing old ones.

Have a great trip—and send us a postcard!

Sincerely,
The Authors

Meeting Challenges

What kinds of challenges do people face and how do they meet them?

Read It
ONLINE
sfsuccessnet.com

Doing the Right Thing

What makes people want to do the right thing?

Read It
ONLINE
sfsuccessnet.com

Inventors and Artists

Read It ONLINE
sfsuccessnet.com

What do people gain from the work of inventors and artists?

Adapting

How do people and animals adapt to different situations?

Adventurers

Who goes seeking
adventure and why?

Read It
ONLINE
sfsuccessnet.com

13

The unexpected

Read It

ONLINE

sfsuccessnet.com

What can we learn from encounters with the unexpected?

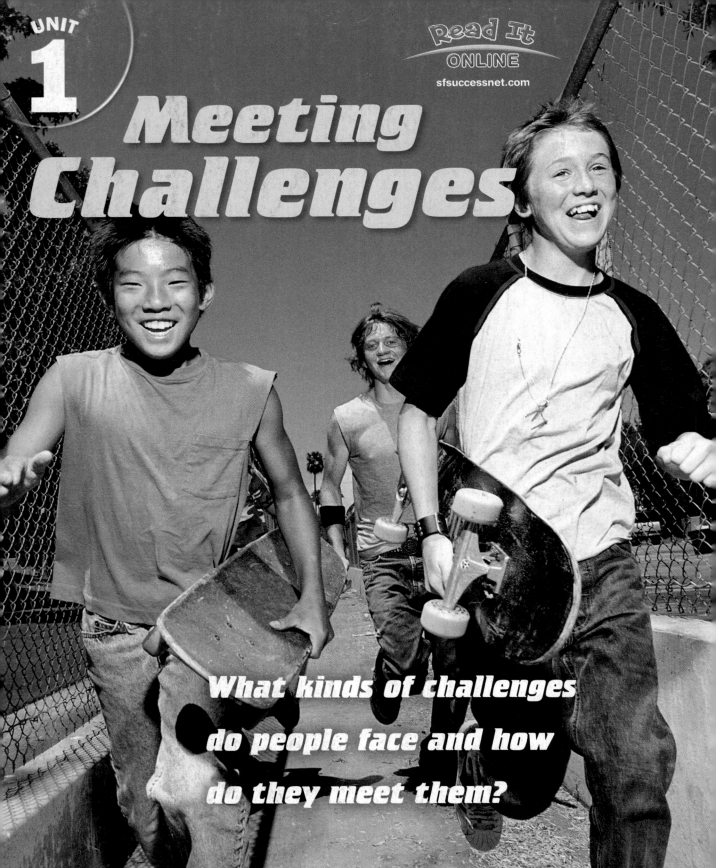

Read It
ONLINE
sfsuccessnet.com

Meeting Challenges

What kinds of challenges do people face and how do they meet them?

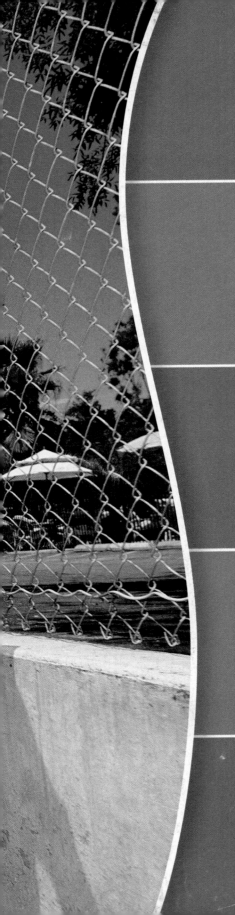

Comprehension

Skill
Plot and Character

Strategy
Prior Knowledge

Plot and Character

- The plot is the pattern of events in a story.

- A plot includes (1) a problem or conflict, (2) rising action, as the conflict builds, (3) a climax, when the problem or conflict is faced, and (4) a resolution, when the problem or conflict is solved. See the story map below.

- Characters are people or animals in a story.

- Characters show you what they're like by what they say and do and how they treat each other.

Strategy: Prior Knowledge

Good readers use what they already know to help them follow a story. Before you read, look at the title, illustrations, and author. Have you read stories by this author before? Remember that you will read about characters, a problem, and how that problem is resolved.

1. Read "Homework Help." As you read, make a story map like the one above.

2. Write a new resolution for "Homework Help." Use your story map and your own knowledge of homework to help you.

Homework Help

Anna was rushing to get to school. Her mom exclaimed, "I see the bus!" Anna stuffed toast in her mouth and gathered up her homework from the table.

She darted outside and hopped onto the bus. Her history report was due today. She decided to examine it one last time. Anna searched her backpack, but there was no report. She groaned and thought, *I can't believe I forgot my report! What am I going to do?*

Anna began to imagine how she could get that report. Her dog was always snorting around the table looking for scraps from a meal. Maybe he would snatch her report, sprint to school, and slide it under her locker door. Well, Max was smart, but not THAT smart.

Another idea came to Anna. Perhaps a hurricane-force wind would blow through the kitchen window. It would carry her report to school and drop it on Mr. Mulligan's desk. Hmm, that idea was unlikely too.

As Anna got off the bus, she realized that the only solution was to be honest and tell Mr. Mulligan what happened. Suddenly, Anna heard a blaring horn. There was her mom, waving her report out their car window. Anna dashed over to the car. "Thanks, Mom," she sighed. "You're the greatest!"

Skill Who is the main character in this story? What is the problem?

Strategy Ask: "Has this ever happened to me?" If so, how did you deal with the problem? What do you think Anna will do?

Skill What kind of person is Anna? How can you tell?

Strategy Based on other stories you have read, did you expect this story to end this way? Why or why not?

19

reputation

worshipped

essential

acquainted

assignment

expanded

procedures

guaranteed

Remember

Try the strategy. Then, if you need more help, use your glossary or dictionary.

Vocabulary Strategy
for Suffixes

Word Structure When you come to a longer word you don't know, see if it ends with *-tion*, *-ation*, or *-ment*. These suffixes are added to verbs to turn them into nouns that mean "the act or state of _____" or "the result of _____." For example, *development* means "the act of developing" or "the result of developing." You may be able to use the suffix to help figure out the unknown word's meaning.

1. Cover the suffix *-tion*, *-ation*, or *-ment*.

2. Look at the base word. Do you know what it means? (Try this with *assignment*.)

3. Add the meaning of the suffix. Remember, the part of speech will change.

4. Reread the sentence to see if your meaning makes sense.

As you read "Becoming a Word Wizard," look for base words that end in *-tion*, *-ation*, or *-ment*. Use the suffixes to help you figure out the meanings of the words.

Becoming a Word Wizard

Would you like to build a powerful reputation as a word wizard? You may have seen that some people have a strong command of words. They always seem to know the perfect word to use at just the right time. If you have worshipped these people from afar, do not fear. You too can become one of them. However, it is essential that you study the dictionary. You will need to find a dictionary you like and make it your close personal friend.

To get acquainted with your dictionary, read the explanation in the front. It will explain the parts and organization of the word entries and tell you how to use the book.

As you find new words, make it your assignment to look them up. Learn their pronunciations, meanings, and histories. Make it a point to use them as you speak and write. Before you know it, your vocabulary will be expanded many times. These procedures are guaranteed to help you sound smarter and understand what you read better.

Write an article explaining how to become a better student. Use as many words in the Words to Know list as you can.

Frin·dle

by Andrew Clements
illustrated by James Bernardin

How do Nick and Mrs. Granger meet the challenge of getting to know each other?

Fifth grade was different. That was the year to get ready for middle school. Fifth grade meant passing classes. It meant no morning recess. It meant real letter grades on your report cards. But most of all, it meant Mrs. Granger.

There were about one hundred fifty kids in fifth grade. And there were seven fifth-grade teachers: two math, two science, two social studies, but only one language arts teacher. In language arts, Mrs. Granger had a monopoly—and a reputation.

Mrs. Granger lived alone in a tidy little house in the older part of town. She drove an old, pale blue car to school every morning, rain or shine, snow or sleet, hail or wind. She had a perfect attendance record that stretched back farther than anyone could remember.

Her hair was almost white, swept away from her face and up into something like a nest on the back of her head. Unlike some of the younger women teachers, she never wore pants to school. She had two skirt-and-jacket outfits, her gray uniform and her blue uniform, which she always wore over a white shirt with a little cameo pin at the neck. And Mrs. Granger was one of those people who never sweats. It had to be over ninety degrees before she even took off her jacket.

She was small, as teachers go. There were even some fifth graders who were taller. But Mrs. Granger seemed like a giant. It was her eyes that did it. They were dark gray, and if she turned them on full power, they could make you feel like a speck of dust. Her eyes could twinkle and laugh, too, and kids said she could crack really funny jokes. But it wasn't the jokes that made her famous.

Everyone was sure that Mrs. Granger had X-ray vision. Don't even think about chewing a piece of gum within fifty feet of her. If you did, Mrs. Granger would see you and catch you and make you stick the gum onto a bright yellow index card. Then she would safety-pin the card to the front of your shirt, and you'd have to wear it for the rest of the school day. After that, you had to take it home and have your mom or dad sign the card, and bring it back to Mrs. Granger the next day. And it didn't matter to Mrs. Granger if you weren't in fifth grade, because the way she saw it, sooner or later, you would be.

All the kids at Lincoln Elementary School knew that at the end of the line—fifth grade—Mrs. Granger would be the one grading their spelling tests and their reading tests, and worst of all, their vocabulary tests—week after week, month after month.

Every language arts teacher in the world enjoys making kids use the dictionary: "Check your spelling. Check that definition. Check those syllable breaks."

But Mrs. Granger didn't just enjoy the dictionary. She *loved* the dictionary—almost worshipped it. Her weekly vocabulary list was thirty-five words long, sometimes longer.

As if that wasn't bad enough, there was a "Word for the Day" on the blackboard every morning. If you gave yourself a day off and didn't write one down and look it up and learn the definition—sooner or later Mrs. Granger would find out, and then, just for you, there would be two Words for the Day for a whole week.

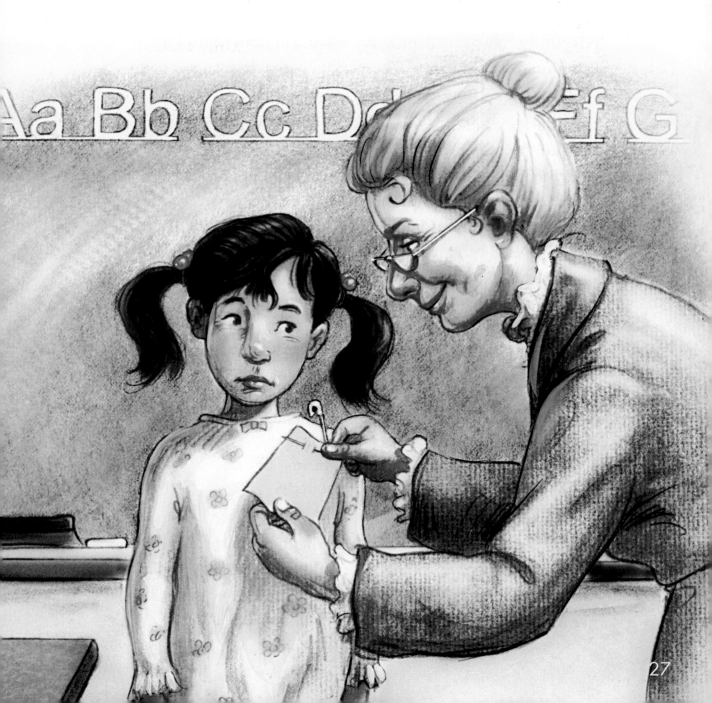

Mrs. Granger kept a full set of thirty dictionaries on a shelf at the back of the room. But her pride and joy was one of those huge dictionaries with every word in the universe in it, the kind of book it takes two kids to carry. It sat on its own little table at the front of her classroom, sort of like the altar at the front of a church.

Every graduate of Lincoln Elementary School for the past thirty-five years could remember standing at that table listening to Mrs. Granger's battle cry: "Look it up! That's why we have the dictionary."

Even before the school year started, when it was still the summer before fifth grade for Nick and his friends, Mrs. Granger was already busy. Every parent of every new fifth grader got a letter from her.

Nick's mom read part of it out loud during dinner one night in August.

Every home is expected to have a good dictionary in it so that each student can do his or her homework properly. Good spelling and good grammar and good word skills are essential for every student. Clear thinking requires a command of the English language, and fifth grade is the ideal time for every girl and boy to acquire an expanded vocabulary.

And then there was a list of the dictionaries that Mrs. Granger thought would be "acceptable for home study."

Mrs. Allen said, "It's so nice to have a teacher who takes her work this seriously."

Nick groaned and tried to enjoy the rest of his hamburger. But even watermelon for dessert didn't cheer him up much.

Nick had no particular use for the dictionary. He liked words a lot, and he was good at using them. But he figured that he got all the words he needed just by reading, and he read all the time.

When Nick ran into a word he didn't know, he asked his brother or his dad or whoever was handy what it meant, and if they knew, they'd tell him. But not Mrs. Granger. He had heard all about her, and he had seen fifth graders in the library last year, noses stuck in their dictionaries, frantically trying to finish their vocabulary sheets before English class.

It was still a week before school and Nick already felt like fifth grade was going to be a very long year.

The first day of school was always a get-acquainted day. Books were passed out, and there was a lot of chatter. Everyone asked, "What did *you* do over the summer?"

Periods one through six went by very smoothly for Nick.

But then came period seven. Mrs. Granger's class was all business.

The first thing they did was take a vocabulary pretest to see how many of the thirty-five words for the week the kids already knew. *Tremble, circular, orchestra*—the list went on and on. Nick knew most of them.

Then there was a handout about class procedures. After that there was a review paper about cursive writing, and then there was a sample sheet showing how the heading should look on every assignment. No letup for thirty-seven minutes straight.

Nick was an expert at asking the delaying question—
also known as the teacher-stopper, or the guaranteed-time-
waster. At three minutes before the bell, in that split second
between the end of today's class work and the announcement
of tomorrow's homework, Nick could launch a question
guaranteed to sidetrack the teacher long enough to delay
or even wipe out the homework assignment.

Timing was important, but asking the right question—
that was the hard part. Questions about stuff in the news,
questions about the college the teacher went to, questions
about the teacher's favorite book or sport or hobby—
Nick knew all the tricks, and he had been very
successful in the past.

Here he was in fifth grade, near the
end of his very first language arts class
with Mrs. Granger, and Nick could feel
a homework assignment coming the
way a farmer can feel a rainstorm.

Mrs. Granger paused to catch her breath, and Nick's hand shot up. She glanced down at her seating chart and then up at him. Her sharp gray eyes were not even turned up to half power.

"Yes, Nicholas?"

"Mrs. Granger, you have so many dictionaries in this room, and that huge one especially . . . where did all those words come from? Did they just get copied from other dictionaries? It sure is a big book."

It was a perfect thought-grenade—KaPow!

Several kids smiled, and a few peeked at the clock. Nick was famous for this, and the whole class knew what he was doing.

Unfortunately, so did Mrs. Granger. She hesitated a moment and gave Nick a smile that was just a little too sweet to be real. Her eyes were the color of a thundercloud.

"Why, what an interesting question, Nicholas. I could talk about it for hours, I bet." She glanced around the classroom.

"Do the rest of you want to know too?" Everyone nodded yes. "Very well then. Nicholas, will you do some research on that

subject and give a little oral report to the class? If you find out the answer yourself, it will mean so much more than if I just told you. Please have your report ready for our next class."

Mrs. Granger smiled at him again. Very sweetly. Then it was back to business. "Now, the homework for tomorrow can be found on page twelve of your *Words Alive* book. . . ."

Nick barely heard the assignment. His heart was pounding, and he felt small, very small. He could feel the tops of his ears glowing red. A complete shutdown. An extra assignment. And probably a little black mark next to his name on the seating chart.

Everything he had heard about this teacher was true— don't mess around with The Lone Granger.

Reader Response

Open for Discussion Nick's plan to sidetrack Mrs. Granger backfires. Have you or someone you know ever had a plan that didn't work out as planned? Tell about it.

1. The author uses many details about school life. Give some examples of these details. Why do you think he has put all those details in this story?

2. Reread the author's description of his character, Mrs. Granger, on pages 25–26. What three adjectives would you use to describe her?

3. Think about what you know about fifth grade. Does Nick's description of fifth grade match your prior knowledge? Why or why not?

4. The story says that "Mrs. Granger loved the dictionary— almost worshipped it." Make a web with *dictionary* at the center. Add to the web with words from the Words to Know list and from the story.

Test Practice

Look Back and Write
How does Mrs. Granger meet Nick's challenge at the end of the story? Use details from the story to support your answer.

How did the book *Frindle* get its name? While visiting a school in Rhode Island, Andrew Clements talked to a class about the way words work. He pulled a pen from his pocket and said that if everyone in the classroom agreed to always call a pen a "frindle" from then on, other people might start to use the new word. Then "frindle" might become a real word in the dictionary one day. Later he wondered, *What would happen if a kid started using a new word, and other kids really liked it, but his English teacher didn't?* The result was *Frindle*.

About his book, Mr. Clements says, "*Frindle* includes a lot of material drawn from my own experiences as a kid and a teacher and a parent.

The School Story

The Landry News

One of the things I love about Nick is that he's right on the edge—he's what a good friend of mine calls 'Very Nearly Naughty.' But Nick is so smart and funny, and he has such a good heart and such good ideas that you have to forgive him."

35

Fantasy

Genre

- A fantasy is a make-believe story that could never happen in the real world.

- Some characters and plot situations may be realistic, while others are exaggerated and even silly.

- The author uses a realistic classroom setting but then introduces fantastic characters who do impossible things.

- Preview the story. What is it about the title and art that make you think, "This is a fantasy"?

Link to Writing

Write another postcard to the vacationing punctuation marks. Try to convince them to return to the classroom. This time, use correct punctuation marks.

Punctuation Takes a Vacation

by Robin Pulver

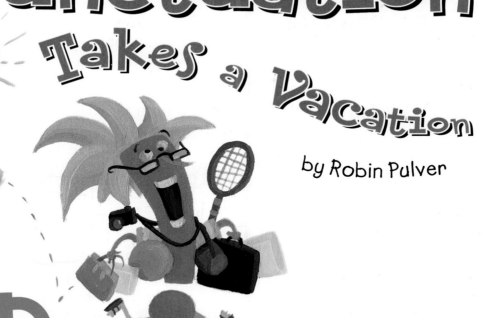

Day after day, the punctuation marks showed up in Mr. Wright's classroom. Day after day, they did their jobs. They put up with being erased and replaced and corrected and ignored and moved around.

Then on the hottest, stickiest day the class had ever seen, right in the middle of a lesson about commas, Mr. Wright mopped his forehead and said, "Let's give punctuation a vacation."

As the kids cheered and headed for the playground to cool off, the punctuation marks stared at one another in disbelief.

"Is this the thanks we get?" asked a question mark.

"Well!" huffed an exclamation point.

"Now, now," said a comma.

"We *should* take a vacation," said a period. "They'll soon learn how much they need us."

Character   What is bothering Mr. Wright? Why?

"It's 11:00 now," said a colon. "Let's leave at 11:02."

"Great!" said an exclamation point.

"Don't leave without us!" yelled the apostrophes.

Whoosh! Punctuation rushed out the door.

Whoosh! They rushed back in to grab the quotation marks, who were too busy talking to pay attention.

When Mr. Wright's class returned from the playground, they couldn't wait to find out what happened in Chapter 4 of their book, *Ace Scooper, Dog Detective*.

Mr. Wright opened his mouth to read aloud, but then he stopped and stared.

THIS IS WEIRD THE PUNCTUATION IS MISSING UH OH WHERE COULD IT BE YIKES MAYBE PUNCTUATION TOOK A VACATION WE ARE IN BIG TROUBLE NOW

Mr. Wright was right. Nothing made sense without punctuation.

A couple days later, the school secretary delivered a small bundle of postcards to Mr. Wright's class. They were postmarked "Take-a-Break Lake."

The kids guessed who wrote the postcards, and they wanted to write back. But they couldn't write without punctuation. The best they could do was borrow some from Mr. Rongo's class next door, where punctuation seemed to be running wild.

Wow! What a ride! You should try tubing! Scary! Fun! Yikes! Hold on! We want Mommmmmeeeeeeee!

Emotional Us

Do you miss us? How much? Why couldn't we take a vacation sooner?

Guess who?

We flop. We plop. We stop. We stay put in our lounge chairs. We are happy thinking our complete thoughts.

Thoughtfully yours, Sentence Stoppers

Dear Friends, Swimming, sailing, sunning, soaring, waterskiing. Next time we must remember bug spray, toothpaste, flashlight, water shoes.

Mr. Wright's class Hometown

A big "hello" from vacation paradise, "where the water is as clear as a well-punctuated sentence." We talk all day. We talk all night. Too busy talking to write any more.

The Yackity Yaks

Mr. Wright's class Hometown USA 46738

 Plot Who is upset and why?

Dear, Punctuation

Please come! back We need you? We, miss, you, too. Life at? School is! "difficult" without, you?

We can?t do reading writing or riddles? without punctuation Chapter 4 of our book <u>Ace, Scooper,</u> does,nt make sense We, will, never? take punctuation for! granted again. Wont you please come back before 10 00 on Friday:

Mr. Wright says.
Punctuation, please come home

Sincerely

Mr' Wright.s Class

40

So the punctuation marks returned to Mr. Wright's classroom to do the jobs only they could do. Mr. Rongo's unruly punctuation scrambled back to their own classroom.

We have so much to tell you.

Who did you miss the most?

It's good to be back in Mr. Wright's class!

COMMAS, PERIODS, EXCLAMATION POINTS, QUESTION MARKS, COLONS, APOSTROPHES, QUOTATION MARKS: TAKE YOUR PLACES 10:00 A.M. TIME TO STUDY US.

Reading Across Texts

Which character do you think is a stronger, more confident person, Mrs. Granger in *Frindle* or Mr. Wright in *Puctuation Takes a Vacation?*

Writing Across Texts Draw pictures of the two characters and write your answer below them.

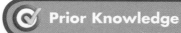 **Prior Knowledge** What makes this a happy ending?

Comprehension

Skill
Cause and Effect

Strategy
Monitor and
Fix Up

Skill

Cause and Effect

- An effect is what happened as the result of a cause. A cause is what made something happen.

- Words such as *why, because,* and *as a result* are clues to cause-and-effect relationships.

- If there are no clue words, ask yourself, "Why did this event happen? What happened as a result of this event?"

- An effect may become the cause of another effect.

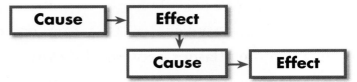

Strategy

Strategy: Monitor and Fix Up

Good readers make sure they understand what they are reading. If you don't understand how causes result in certain effects, pause. Ask yourself, "What don't I understand?" You might decide to review what you've read and *read on* to find out what happens.

Write

1. Read "The Real Thunder and Lightning." Make a graphic organizer like the one above to show the cause of lightning that flashes inside a cloud.

2. Use your graphic organizer to write a paragraph that explains the cause of thunder. If you have difficulty, reread the last paragraph to see if that helps.

The Real THUNDER and Lightning

Some tall tales and myths give fanciful explanations for things that happen in nature, such as thunder and lightning. These stories are fun to read, but the real explanations can also be interesting.

The real cause of lightning involves electrical charges. Inside a storm cloud, a strong positive electrical charge may form near the top of the cloud, and a strong negative charge near the bottom. When these opposite charges flow toward each other, lightning flashes inside the cloud. When opposite charges flow from one cloud to another, lightning flashes between the clouds. When negative charges at the bottom of a cloud move down toward positive charges on Earth, lightning flashes from the cloud to the ground. Watch out!

Thunder happens only when there is lightning because lightning causes it. Thunder results from the rapid heating of the air along a lightning flash. The heated air expands. As a result, it creates a sound wave. Then the claps and rumbles of thunder are heard.

Skill Look at the clue word *cause* here. It tells you that you will read about the cause of lightning. Get ready to start a graphic organizer.

Strategy Do you feel you understand what causes lightning inside a cloud? If not, reread the first part of the second paragraph.

Skill What causes lightning that flashes from a cloud to the ground? Make a graphic organizer, such as a drawing, if you need help.

Strategy Do you feel you understand what causes lightning and what causes thunder? If not, which parts of the article should you reread?

43

Vocabulary Strategy
for Homonyms

Words to Know

pitch
veins
daintily
thieving
devastation
branded
constructed
resourceful
lullaby

Remember

Try the strategy. Then, if you need more help, use your glossary or dictionary.

Context Clues When you are reading, you may come across a familiar word used in an unfamiliar way. The word may be a homonym. Homonyms are spelled the same, but they have different meanings. For example, *feet* can be units of measurement or the end parts of the legs. You can use the context—the words and sentences around the word—to figure out which meaning is being used.

1. Reread the sentence in which the homonym appears.

2. Look for clues to the homonym's meaning.

3. If you need more help, read the sentences around the sentence with the homonym. Look for clues or additional information that suggests the homonym's meaning.

4. Try the meaning in the sentence. Does it make sense?

As you read "The Tale of Carrie the Calf," look for homonyms. Use the context to determine the meanings of the homonyms.

44

The Tale of Carrie the Calf

From the moment she was born, we knew Carrie the calf was different. Her eyes were black as pitch, and she was strong as a bull. Instead of blood, she seemed to have a magic potion in her veins. Overnight, she grew fifty feet tall. Morning found her daintily eating the tops of trees.

It was hard finding enough for her to eat! We would give her a hundred bales of hay for breakfast, but by lunch she would be over at the next ranch, happily eating its trees and anything else in sight. This thieving did not make her too popular. It also caused considerable devastation around the country.

Then the time came to brand the calves! How could a hundred-and-fifty-foot-tall calf be branded? We quickly constructed a two-hundred-foot-tall fence to hold her in. She just smiled and hopped over it, and then ambled off to find another forest to eat. To catch Carrie, we were going to have to be more resourceful.

Next, we made a set of speakers big as a house. We broadcast a soothing lullaby that could be heard over three states. Soon Carrie was sleeping without a care.

Look at the pictures in the story. Choose one to write about. Use as many words in the Words to Know list as you can.

by Jerdine Nolen • illustrated by Kadir Nelson

THUNDER Rose

What challenges does Rose set up
for herself and how does she
meet them?

ose was the first child born free and easy to Jackson and Millicent MacGruder. I recall most vividly the night she came into this world. Hailing rain, flashing lightning, and booming thunder pounded the door, inviting themselves in for the blessed event.

Taking in her first breath of life, the infant did not cry out. Rather, she sat up and looked around. She took ahold of that lightning, rolled it into a ball, and set it above her shoulder, while the thunder echoed out over the other. They say this just accentuated the fact that the child had the power of thunder and lightning coursing through her veins.

"She's going to grow up to be good and strong, all right," Doc Hollerday said.

The child turned to the good doctor with a thoughtful glance and replied, "I reckon I will want to do more than that. Thank you very kindly!"

Shifting her gaze to the two loving lights shining on her, which were her ma and pa, she remarked, "Much obliged to you both for this chance to make my way in the world!" Then she announced to no one in particular, "I am right partial to the name Rose."

So much in love with this gift of their lives, her ma and pa hovered over her in watchful splendor. Overcome with that love, they lifted their voices in song, an old song and a melody so sweet and true—a lullaby passed down from the ages, echoing since the beginning of time.

49

"There is a music ringing so sweetly in my ears," the new-born exclaimed. "It's giving me a fortunate feeling rumbling deep in the pit of me. I'll register it here at the bull's-eye set in the center of my heart, and see what I can do with it one day!"

Rose snored up plenty that first night breathing on her own, rattling the rafters on the roof right along with the booming thunder. There was nothing quiet about her slumber. She seemed determined to be just as forceful as that storm. With the thunder and lightning keeping watch over her the rest of the night, her ma and pa just took to calling her Thunder Rose.

The next morning, when the sun was high yellow in that billowy blue sky, Rose woke up hungry as a bear in spring, but not the least bit ornery. Minding her manners, she politely thanked her ma for the milk, but it was not enough to quench her hungry thirst. Rose preferred, instead to drink her milk straight from the cow.

Her ma was right grateful to have such a resourceful child. No other newborn had the utter strength to lift a whole cow clear over her head and almost drink it dry. In a moment's time, Rose did, and quite daintily so. She was as pretty as a picture, had the sweetest disposition, but don't let yourself be misled, that child was full of lightning *and* thunder.

Out on that paper-bag brown, dusty dry, wide-open space, Rose often was found humming a sweet little tune as she did her chores. And true to her word, Rose did *more* than grow good and strong.

The two-year-old became quite curious about the pile of scrap iron lying next to the barn. Rose took a good-sized

piece, stretched it here, bent and twisted it there. She constructed a thunderbolt as black as pitch to punctuate her name. She called it Cole. Wherever she went, Cole was always by her side. Noticing how skilled Rose was with the metal, her pa made sure there was an extra supply of it always around.

At the age of five, Rose did a commendable job of staking the fence without a bit of help. During her eighth and ninth years, Rose assembled some iron beams together with the wood blocks she used to play with and constructed a building tall enough to scrape the sky, always humming as she worked.

By the time she turned twelve, Rose had perfected her metal-bending practices. She formed delicately shaped alphabet letters to help the young ones learn to read. For his birthday, Rose presented her pa with a branding iron, a circle with a big *M-A-C* for MacGruder in the middle, just in time, too, because a herd of quick-tempered longhorn steer was stampeding its way up from the Rio Grande. They were plowing a path straight toward her front door.

Rose performed an eye-catching wonder, the likes of which was something to see. Running lightning-fast toward the herd, using Cole for support, Rose vaulted into the air and landed on the back of the

biggest lead steer like he was a merry-go-round pony. Grabbing a horn in each hand, Rose twisted that varmint to a complete halt. It was just enough to restrain that top bull and the rest of the herd.

But I believe what touched that critter's heart was when Rose began humming her little tune. That cantankerous ton of beef was restless no more. He became as playful as a kitten and even tried to purr. Rose named him Tater on account of that was his favorite vegetable. Hearing Rose's lullaby put that considerable creature to sleep was the sweetest thing I had witnessed in a long, long time.

After the dust had settled, Ma and Pa counted twenty-seven hundred head of cattle, after they added in the five hundred they already had. Using the scrap iron, Rose had to add a new section to the bull pen to hold them all.

"What did you do to the wire, Rose?" Ma asked, surprised and pleased at her daughter's latest creation.

"Oh, that," she said. "While I was staking the fence, Pa asked me to keep little Barbara Jay company. That little twisty pattern seemed to make the baby laugh. So I like to think of it as a Barbara's Wire."

"That was right clever of you to be so entertaining to the little one like that!" her ma said. Rose just blushed. Over the years, that twisty wire caught on, and folks just called it barbed wire.

Rose and her pa spent the whole next day sorting the animals that had not been branded. "One day soon, before the cold weather gets in," she told her pa, "I'll have to get this herd up the Chisholm Trail and to market in Abilene. I suspect Tater is the right kind of horse for the long drive northward."

On Rose's first trip to Abilene, while right outside of Caldwell, that irascible, full-of-outrage-and-ire outlaw Jesse Baines and his gang of desperadoes tried to rustle that herd away from Rose.

Using the spare metal rods she always carried with her, Rose lassoed those hot-tempered hooligans up good and tight. She dropped them all off to jail, tied up in a nice neat iron bow. "It wasn't any trouble at all," she told Sheriff Weaver. "Somebody had to put a stop to their thieving ways."

But that wasn't the only thieving going on. The mighty sun was draining the moisture out of every living thing it touched. Even the rocks were crying out. Those clouds stood by and watched it all happen. They weren't even trying to be helpful.

Why, the air had turned so dry and sour, time seemed to all but stand still. And there was not a drop of water in sight. Steer will not move without water. And that was making those bulls mad, real mad. And when a bull gets angry, it's like a disease that's catching, making the rest of the herd mad, too. Tater was looking parched and mighty thirsty.

"I've got to do something about this!" Rose declared.

Stretching out several iron rods lasso-fashion, then launching Cole high in the air, Rose hoped she could get the heavens to yield forth. She caught hold of a mass of clouds and squeezed them hard, real hard, all the while humming her song. Gentle rain began to fall. But anyone looking could see there was not enough moisture to refresh two ants, let alone a herd of wild cows.

Suddenly a rotating column of air came whirling and swirling around, picking up everything in its path. It sneaked up on Rose. "Whoa, there, now just hold on a minute," Rose called out to the storm. Tater was helpless to do anything about that sort of wind. Those meddlesome clouds caused it. They didn't take kindly to someone telling them what to do. And they were set on creating a riotous rampage all on their own.

Oh, this riled Rose so much, she became the only two-legged

tempest to walk the western plains. "You don't know who you're fooling with," Rose called out to the storm. Her eyes flashed lightning. She bit down and gnashed thunder from her teeth. I don't know why anyone would want to mess with a pretty young woman who had the power of thunder and lightning coursing through her veins. But, pity for them, the clouds did!

Rose reached for her iron rod. But there was only one piece left. She did not know which way to turn. She knew Cole alone

was not enough to do the job right. Unarmed against her own growing thirst and the might of the elements, Rose felt weighted down. Then that churning column split, and now there were two. They were coming at her from opposite directions. Rose had some fast thinking to do. Never being one to bow down under pressure, she considered her options, for she was not sure how this would all come out in the end.

"Is this the fork in the road with which I have my final supper? Will this be my first and my last ride of the roundup?" she queried herself in the depths of her heart. Her contemplations brought her little relief as she witnessed the merciless, the cataclysmic efforts of a windstorm bent on her disaster. Then the winds joined hands and cranked and churned a path heading straight toward her! Calmly Rose spoke out loud to the storm as she stood alone to face the wrack and ruin, the multiplying devastation. "I *could* ride at least *one* of you out to the end of time! But I've got this fortunate feeling rumbling deep in the pit of me, and I see what I am to do with it this day!" Rose said, smiling.

The winds belted at a rumbling pitch. Rose squarely faced that storm. "Come and join me, winds!" She opened her arms wide as if to embrace the torrent. She opened her mouth as if she were planning to take a good long drink. But from deep inside her, she heard a melody so real and sweet and true. And when she lifted her heart, she unleashed *her* song of thunder. It was a sight to see: Rose making thunder and lightning rise and fall to the ground at her command, at the sound of *her song*. Oh, how her voice rang out so clear and real and true. It rang from the mountaintops. It filled up the valleys. It flowed like a healing river in the breathing air around her.

Those tornadoes, calmed by her song, stopped their churning masses and raged no more. And, gentle as a baby's bath, a soft, drenching-and-soaking rain fell.

And Rose realized that by reaching into her own heart to bring forth the music that was there, she had even touched the hearts of the clouds.

The stories of Rose's amazing abilities spread like wildfire, far and wide. And as sure as thunder follows lightning, and sun follows rain, whenever you see a spark of light flash across a heavy steel gray sky, listen to the sound of the thunder and think of Thunder Rose and *her* song. That mighty, mighty song pressing on the bull's-eye that was set at the center of her heart.

Reader Response

Open for Discussion An old timer says, "What? You've never heard of Thunder Rose? Didn't you see her TV interview last night?" Now you take the old timer's role. Tell the tall tale of Thunder Rose, based on what you've just read, as the old timer would tell it.

1. Thunder Rose meets the challenge of the twin tornadoes. How? Her solution may seem unusual, but the author has prepared you for it. You got a preview of Rose's unusual talent early in the story. How does this preview make the ending more believable?

2. What caused Rose to question her survival? What effect did her *song* have on the storm?

3. Think about the thunder and lightning storms you have been in or watched outside. Compare what you have heard and seen to the storms in "Thunder Rose."

4. The author uses colorful vocabulary to describe objects and events in the story. Which words from the Words to Know list did he use instead of *song, clever, built, stealing, mess,* and *tar?*

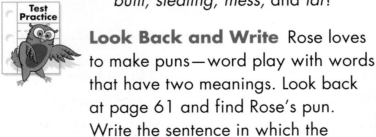

Look Back and Write Rose loves to make puns—word play with words that have two meanings. Look back at page 61 and find Rose's pun. Write the sentence in which the pun appears and explain it.

Meet the Author and the Illustrator
Jerdine Nolen and Kadir Nelson

Read other books illustrated by Kadir Nelson.

Jerdine Nolen says that as a child she was never bored. There was always something to do with her five sisters and two brothers. Since there wasn't much space in their house, she had to have a sense of humor. Despite all the distractions, Ms. Nolen says she can't remember a time when she wasn't writing and collecting words. "My mother encouraged me to do that. She was always eager to hear my new list of 'favorite words.'"

Once you have a story, Ms. Nolen says, it's important to keep revising and reworking it. "It is like sculpting or wiring the pieces together in a way, so the words on the page have enough life—they could stand up and walk around all on their own."

Kadir Nelson says that as a child, "I always knew I'd be an artist. My mother was so supportive, and she never talked me out of it. I was also fortunate that I had an uncle who was an art teacher. He introduced me to the seriousness of taking care of my gift."

In addition to the award-winning children's books he has illustrated, Mr. Nelson has created artwork for *Vibe Magazine*, *The New Yorker*, *Sports Illustrated*, *The New York Times*, and Nike. His paintings can be found in the private collections of famous actors, sports figures, and musicians.

Big Jabe

Ellington Was Not a Street

Expository Nonfiction

Genre

- **Expository nonfiction may include graphic sources, such as charts and photos, that show information.**

- **A chart is a sheet of information.**

- **Facts are arranged in an easy-to-read form.**

Text Features

- **The facts in a chart are listed in rows and columns.**

- **Readers read down the column and across the row to find the cell—the rectangle—that has the information they want.**

- **Preview the text and chart. Look at the headings at the top of the chart.**

Link to Science

Use reference sources to find what you should do if a tornado strikes near you. Make a list of Tornado Safety Tips.

Measuring Tornadoes

BY TRUDI STRAIN TRUEIT

About 800 tornadoes strike the United States each year, resulting in an average of 80 deaths and 1,500 injuries.

It is difficult to accurately measure the high winds inside a tornado, so scientists rely on the Fujita Scale, or F-scale, for help. Created by Theodore Fujita, the F-scale looks at the damage a tornado causes to figure out its wind speed. Nearly 70 percent of the twisters that hit the United States fall into the F-0 and F-1 categories. These weak tornadoes are typically less than 3 miles (5km) long and no wider than 50 yards (45m). They usually do little damage— unless they strike without warning.

About 30 percent of tornadoes are strong tornadoes, rating F-2 or F-3 on the scale. Those reaching F-4 or above are called violent tornadoes. Fewer than one in fifty twisters ever become violent, but the most violent tornadoes cause almost two-thirds of tornado-related deaths.

FUJITA SCALE		
RATING	**ESTIMATED WIND SPEED**	**DAMAGE**
F-0 (weak)	**40–72 mph** (64–116 kph)	**Light:** Damage to TV antennae, chimneys, and small trees (about 3 of 10 tornadoes are F-0)
F-1 (weak)	**73–112 mph** (117–180 kph)	**Moderate:** Broken windows, mobile homes overturned, moving cars pushed off roads (about 4 of 10 tornadoes)
F-2 (strong)	**113–157 mph** (181–253 kph)	**Considerable:** Roofs torn off, mobile homes and large trees destroyed (about 2 of 10 tornadoes)
F-3 (strong)	**158–206 mph** (254–331 kph)	**Severe:** Cars lifted off the ground, trains overturned (about 6 of 100 tornadoes)
F-4 (violent)	**207–260 mph** (332–418 kph)	**Devastating:** Solid walls torn apart, cars tossed, large objects become missiles (about 2 of 100 tornadoes)
F-5 (violent)	**261–318 mph** (419–511 kph)	**Incredible:** Homes lifted off their foundations and thrown, straw and grass able to pierce tree trunks (fewer than 1 of 100 tornadoes)
F-6 to **F-12** (violent)	**319–700 mph** (512–1,126 kph) or Mach 1, the speed of sound	**Inconceivable:** Though it was once thought tornadoes could reach the speed of sound, scientists now believe F-5 is the top of the scale

Reading Across Texts

Look back at the drawings of the twin tornadoes that Thunder Rose lassoed. Where do you think they would be listed on the Fujita Scale?

Writing Across Texts Describe what you think Thunder Rose's tornadoes did to the farms in her area.

Cause & Effect Why are the F-6 to F-12 tornadoes called "inconceivable"?

Theme and Setting

- The theme is the underlying meaning of a story.

- The theme is often not stated. You can figure out a theme when you have finished reading from events and other evidence in the story.

- The setting is where and when the story takes place. Writers use details, such as sights and sounds, to describe it.

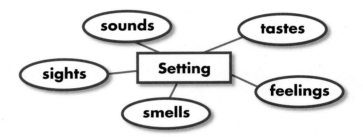

Strategy: Visualize

Active readers create pictures of the story in their minds as they read. The sights, smells, sounds, tastes, and feelings described by the author all help you visualize the setting, the characters, and the events.

1. Read "Alone." Make a graphic organizer like the one above about the story's setting.

2. Make pictures and write captions for chores Jesse does in the story. Use your graphic organizer to help you.

ALONE

Jesse heard the horses trotting and the wagon wheels creaking even after the wagon disappeared into the thick forest. Soon, those familiar sounds faded. Then he heard nothing but the summer wind rustling the tall prairie grass surrounding his family's log cabin. Jesse was all alone.

Jesse's parents had gone to town to buy supplies for the winter. They would be gone several days. His father insisted Jesse was old enough to stay alone and manage the work on the farm, but Jesse wasn't so sure. Even so, he set about doing his chores.

Jesse milked the cow, weeded the vegetable garden, and fixed the latch on the barn door. He cooked his own potato soup and sliced some bread for dinner. That night, alone, Jesse had a hard time sleeping. Wolves were howling in the distance. He was trained to use his father's musket and kept it nearby just in case.

Each day Jesse was too busy to think of anything but farm chores. Each night, he lay in bed, nervous.

On the sixth day, Jesse had just heard the first cry of a wolf at dusk when he noticed an even more familiar sound. It was the wagon coming down the trail. His parents were home!

Skill After reading the title and first paragraph, what do you think the theme might be?
a) the beauty of nature
b) love of animals
c) surviving by yourself

Strategy Visualize: Hear the horses clip-clop and the wagon wheels creak. See the tall prairie grass and a log cabin.

Skill What are some events in the story that would happen only in this setting, not in your community today?

Strategy How might Jesse look at the beginning of the final paragraph? How might he look at the end?

Words to Know

lair
ravine
gnawed
sinew
shellfish
kelp
headland

Vocabulary Strategy
for Unfamiliar Words

Dictionary/Glossary Sometimes when you read, you come across a word you do not know. You can use a glossary or dictionary to find out the meaning of the word. A glossary is a list of important words in a book and their meanings. A dictionary lists all words, in alphabetical order, and gives their meanings, pronunciations, and other helpful information.

1. Check the back of your book for a glossary. If there is no glossary, look up the word in a dictionary.

2. Find the entry for the word. Dictionary entries are in alphabetical order.

3. Read the pronunciation to yourself. Saying the word may help you recognize it.

4. Read all the meanings given for the word.

5. Choose the one that makes sense in your sentence.

As you read "Island Survival," use the glossary or a dictionary to find out the meanings of the vocabulary words.

Island Survival

Have you ever imagined being shipwrecked on an island? What would you do to survive? First, you would take a look around to see how you could get food, water, and shelter. A lot would depend on what kind of land your island had.

A rocky, hilly island might have a cave you could use as your home—unless it was already a lair for a wild animal. As you explored, you would keep an eye out for things you could use for building or for hunting. Small trees growing in a ravine might be cut down to build a lean-to.

If you were able to hunt game, you might save parts of animals to use in your home. After you gnawed the flesh, you would have hides to make a blanket. Sinew could serve as a kind of rope. In shallow waters you would find shellfish to eat. The kelp floating there could be used as "wallpaper" or even as food.

If your island had a headland, it would provide a good high point from which to look out for rescue. You might build a fire there to draw the attention of passing ships.

Write

Write a story about a wild animal that lives on an island. Use as many words in the Words to Know list as you can.

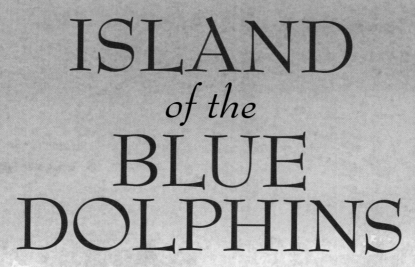

ISLAND
of the
BLUE
DOLPHINS

by Scott O'Dell   *illustrated by* E. B. Lewis

How will Karana meet the physical
challenges that face her?

Genre

Historical fiction is realistic fiction that takes place
in the past and is often full of adventure. As you read,
keep asking yourself what might happen next.

From 1835 to 1853, a young Native American girl named Karana lived alone on a rugged island seventy-five miles off the coast of California. The author has fashioned this story out of the few facts known about her.

Karana and her people lived on the island until Aleut hunters killed some of the men. A friendly ship later took her people off the island, but she stayed there to be with her brother, who was left behind by the ship's crew. After her brother was killed by wild dogs, Karana faced the challenge of living alone on the island.

The Island of the Blue Dolphins was my home; I had no other. It would be my home until the white men returned in their ship. But even if they came soon, before next summer, I could not live without a roof or a place to store my food. I would have to build a house. But where?

That night I slept on the rock, and the next day I began the search. The morning was clear, but to the north, banks of clouds hung low. Before long they would move in across the island, and behind them many other storms were waiting. I had no time to waste.

I needed a place that was sheltered from the wind, not too far from Coral Cove, and close to a good spring. There were two such places on the island—one on the headland and the other less than a league to the west. The headland seemed to be the more favorable of the two, but since I had not been to the other for a long time, I decided to go there and make certain.

The first thing I found, which I had forgotten, was that this place was near the wild dogs' lair. As soon as I drew near to it the leader came to the opening of the cave and watched me with his yellow eyes. If I built a hut here I would have to kill him and his pack. I planned to do this anyway, but it would take much time.

The spring was better than the one near the headland, being less brackish and having a steadier flow of water. Besides it was much easier to reach, since it came from the side of a hill and not from a ravine as the other one did. It was also close to the cliff and a ridge of rocks which would shelter my house.

The rocks were not so high as those on the headland and therefore would give me less protection from the wind, yet they were high enough, and from them I could see the north coast and Coral Cove.

The thing that made me decide on the place to build my house was the sea elephants.

The cliffs here fell away easily to a wide shelf that was partly covered when the tide came in. It was a good place for sea elephants because they could crawl halfway up the cliff if the day were stormy. On fair days they could fish among the pools or lie on the rocks.

The bull is very large and often weighs as much as thirty men. The cows are much smaller, but they make more noise than the bulls, screaming and barking through the whole day and sometimes at night. The babies are noisy too.

On this morning the tide was low and most of the animals were far out, just hundreds of specks against the waves, yet the noise they made was deafening. I stayed there the rest of the day, looking around, and that night. At dawn when the clamor started again I left and went back to the headland.

There was another place to the south where I could have built my house, near the destroyed village of Ghalas-at, but I did not want to go there because it would remind me of the people who were gone. Also the wind blew strong in this place, blowing against the dunes which cover the middle part of the island so that most of the time sand is moving everywhere.

Rain fell that night and lasted for two days. I made a shelter of brush at the foot of the rock, which kept off some of the water, and ate the food I had stored in the basket. I could not build a fire because of the rain and I was very cold.

On the third day the rain ceased and I went out to look for things which I would need in building the house. I likewise needed poles for a fence. I would soon kill the wild dogs, but there were many small red foxes on the island. They were so numerous that I could never hope to get rid of them either by traps or with arrows. They were clever thieves and nothing I stored would be safe until I had built a fence.

The morning was fresh from the rain. The smell of the tide pools was strong. Sweet odors came from the wild grasses in the ravines and from the sand plants on the dunes. I sang as I went down the trail to the beach and along the beach to the sandspit. I felt that the day was an omen of good fortune.

It was a good day to begin my new home.

Many years before, two whales had washed up on the sandspit. Most of the bones had been taken away to make ornaments, but the ribs were still there, half-buried in the sand.

These I used in making the fence. One by one I dug them up and carried them to the headland. They were long and curved, and when I had scooped out holes and set them in the earth they stood taller than I did.

I put the ribs together with their edges almost touching, and standing so that they curved outward, which made them impossible to climb. Between them I wove many strands of bull kelp, which shrinks as it dries and pulls very tight. I would have used seal sinew to bind the ribs together, for this is stronger than kelp, but wild animals like it and soon would have gnawed the fence down. Much time went into its building. It would have taken me longer except that the rock made one end of the fence and part of a side.

For a place to go in and out, I dug a hole under the fence just wide and deep enough to crawl through. The bottom and sides I lined with stones. On the outside I covered the hole with a mat woven of brush to shed the rain, and on the inside with a flat rock which I was strong enough to move.

I was able to take eight steps between the sides of the fence, which gave me all the room I would need to store the things I gathered and wished to protect.

I built the fence first because it was too cold to sleep on the rock, and I did not like to sleep in the shelter I had made until I was safe from the wild dogs.

The house took longer to build than the fence because it rained many days and because the wood I needed was scarce.

There was a legend among our people that the island had once been covered with tall trees. This was a long time ago, at the beginning of the world when Tumaiyowit and Mukat ruled. The two gods quarreled about many things. Tumaiyowit wished people to die. Mukat did not. Tumaiyowit angrily went down, down to another world under this world, taking his belongings with him, so people die because he did.

In that time there were tall trees, but now there were only a few in the ravines and these were small and crooked. It was very hard to find one that would make a good pole. I searched many days, going out early in the morning and coming back at night, before I found enough for a house.

I used the rock for the back of the house and the front I left open since the wind did not blow from this direction. The poles I made of equal length, using fire to cut them as well as a stone knife which caused me much difficulty because I had never made such a tool before. There were four poles on each side, set in the earth, and twice that many for the roof. These I bound together with sinew and covered with female kelp, which has broad leaves.

The winter was half over before I finished the house, but I slept there every night and felt secure because of the strong fence. The foxes came when I was cooking my food and stood outside gazing through the cracks, and the wild dogs also came, gnawing at the whale ribs, growling because they could not get in.

I shot two of them, but not the leader.

While I was building the fence and the house, I ate shellfish and perch which I cooked on a flat rock. Afterwards I made two utensils. Along the shore there were stones that the sea had worn smooth. Most of them were round, but I found two with hollow places in the center which I deepened and broadened by rubbing them with sand. Using these to cook in, I saved the juices of the fish which are good and were wasted before.

For cooking seeds and roots I wove a tight basket of fine reeds, which was easy because I had learned how to do it from my sister Ulape. After the basket had dried in the sun, I gathered lumps of pitch on the shore, softened them over the fire, and rubbed them on the inside of the basket so that it would hold water. By heating small stones and dropping them into a mixture of water and seeds in the basket I could make gruel.

I made a place for fire in the floor of my house, hollowing it out and lining it with rocks. In the village of Ghalas-at we made new fires every night, but now I made one fire which I covered with ashes when I went to bed. The next night I would remove the ashes and blow on the embers. In this way I saved myself much work.

There were many gray mice on the island and now that I had food to keep from one meal to other, I needed a safe place to put it. On the face of the rock, which was the back wall of my house, were several cracks as high as my shoulder. These I cut out and smoothed to make shelves where I could store my food and the mice could not reach it.

By the time winter was over and grass began to show green on the hills, my house was comfortable. I was sheltered from the wind and rain and prowling animals. I could cook anything I wished to eat. Everything I wanted was there at hand.

Reader Response

Open for Discussion For a little while, you watched Karana, all alone on the island. Now report back: What do you think are her chances for survival? What is your evidence?

1. The author wrote *Island of the Blue Dolphins* in the first person, as if Karana is speaking to the reader. Why do you think he chose to tell the story in this way?

2. Write a sentence that states the theme of the story. What evidence can you find to support your theme?

3. Visualize the house Karana builds. Describe her house using details from the story.

4. Words from the Words to Know list, such as *lair, ravine,* and *headland,* give you a sense of place. Find other words from the story that add to your understanding of Karana's island.

Look Back and Write What is the most important physical challenge that Karana faces? How does she meet this challenge? Use story details to support your answer.

Scott O'Dell

Read other books by Scott O'Dell.

Island of the Blue Dolphins was Scott O'Dell's first book for young people. It won the Newbery Medal and became a best seller. The idea for the book came when he found an article about a young girl, Karana, who lived alone for eighteen years on an island off the California coast. "*Island of the Blue Dolphins* began in anger, anger at the hunters who invade the mountains where I live and who slaughter everything that creeps or walks or flies," Mr. O'Dell wrote.

After *Island of the Blue Dolphins,* Mr. O'Dell wrote another twenty-five books for young people. He believed that writing stories for young readers was more rewarding than writing for adults. His young readers wrote him letters and asked many questions. One of the frequent questions was, "What's the most important thing a writer should do?" His answer was to stick with it. "Writing is hard, harder than digging a ditch, and it requires patience," he said.

Mr. O'Dell died in 1989.

The Black Pearl

Carlota

Interview

Genre

- In an interview the interviewer asks questions. The other person, the subject, answers.

- Interviews usually appear in magazines or newspapers.

Text Features

- An interview first introduces the subject, or the person being interviewed.

- Questions and answers begin with a name in bold type followed by a colon.

- The words on the page are the actual words spoken by the subject and the interviewer.

- Preview the interview. How do you think reading it might help you out some day?

Link to Reading

Do research to find state and national parks in your area. What safety rules help keep visitors from getting lost?

SEVEN SURVIVAL QUESTIONS

by Buck Tilton
from Boys' Life *Magazine*

When you're lost, being a good leader can mean the difference between life and death. John Gookin, an authority on wilderness survival at the National Outdoor Leadership School (NOLS), shares his expert advice:

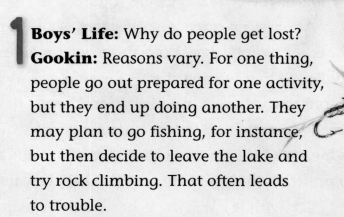

1 Boys' Life: Why do people get lost?
Gookin: Reasons vary. For one thing, people go out prepared for one activity, but they end up doing another. They may plan to go fishing, for instance, but then decide to leave the lake and try rock climbing. That often leads to trouble.

The other big mistake is over-correcting for minor navigation errors. Instead of calmly retracing their steps, people head off in the wrong direction at a fast pace.

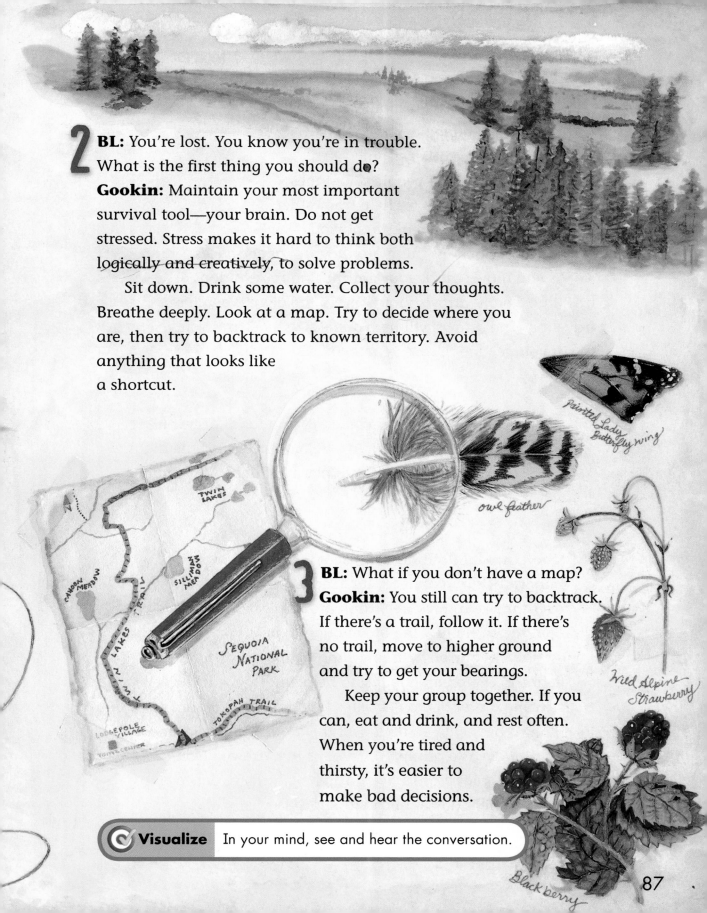

2 **BL:** You're lost. You know you're in trouble. What is the first thing you should do?

Gookin: Maintain your most important survival tool—your brain. Do not get stressed. Stress makes it hard to think both logically and creatively, to solve problems.

Sit down. Drink some water. Collect your thoughts. Breathe deeply. Look at a map. Try to decide where you are, then try to backtrack to known territory. Avoid anything that looks like a shortcut.

Painted Lady Butterfly wing

owl feather

3 **BL:** What if you don't have a map?

Gookin: You still can try to backtrack. If there's a trail, follow it. If there's no trail, move to higher ground and try to get your bearings.

Keep your group together. If you can, eat and drink, and rest often. When you're tired and thirsty, it's easier to make bad decisions.

Wild Alpine Strawberry

Blackberry

Visualize In your mind, see and hear the conversation.

87

4 **BL:** Are there things you should do while you're trying to backtrack?

Gookin: If you see other people, ask for directions. Lost people sometimes are embarrassed to ask for help from others.

Stay visible. Take breaks in obvious places such as trail junctions, high ground, and open spaces.

As you move, mark your path. Using rocks or logs or tree limbs, build arrows that point in the direction you're traveling. The arrows will help guide searchers and you, too, if you need to retrace your steps.

5 **BL:** What if you can't find familiar terrain?

Gookin: Find a safe place to spend the night while there is still plenty of light. Stay calm.

6 **BL:** What makes a place safe?

Gookin: Maintaining body heat is often the most important survival necessity. Find shelter such as a rock overhang or a thick tree. High ground is best. If you can do it safely, build a fire big enough to help you stay warm.

Cover yourself with anything available, from forest debris to evergreen boughs, to help you stay warm. Even wearing a pair of glasses helps hold in a little bit of heat. Make a bed of green boughs if the ground is cold or snowy.

Huddle as a group, like spoons in a drawer. Don't expect a great night's sleep. You'll be lucky to get catnaps. Stay near a trail in case others pass by.

Ponderosa Pine Needles

7 **BL:** What about the next day?

Gookin: Make yourself easy to find. Stay put, and sit in open spaces or on high points.

Searchers most easily spot geometric shapes (like a triangle or SOS) from the sky. Build one or more using your gear or anything else available, including people. Keep any reflective material out in the open. Signal mirrors are excellent survival tools. Used correctly, they can be seen for 20 miles. If you don't have a mirror, improvise with glass or even eyeglass lenses. A smoky fire can also be seen from far away in calm conditions.

Acorn

Fir

TOP SURVIVAL DOS:

- Stay calm.
- Be methodical.
- Drink water.
- Keep warm.
- Build a fire—it's good for signaling and warmth.

TOP SURVIVAL DON'TS:

- Don't take risks, or shortcuts.
- Don't act impulsively.
- Don't hike after dark.
- Don't avoid people. Ask for help.
- Don't lose your spirit. Think positive thoughts.

pine nuts

Reading Across Texts

If Karana listed survival tips for life on her island, what might they be?

Writing Across Texts Make a list of Karana's top five tips.

Bob Cat Tracks

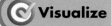 **Visualize** Can you see yourself lost but remaining calm?

89

Sequence

Skill

- Sequence is the order that events happen in a selection. When you read, think about what comes first, next, and last.

- Several events can occur at the same time. Words such as *meanwhile* and *during* give clues that two events are happening at the same time.

- You can remember sequence by making a time line.

First Event	Second Event	Third Event	Fourth Event

Strategy: Ask Questions

Strategy

Good readers ask themselves *good* questions about *important* information, such as the sequence of events. Asking questions *before* you read helps you connect what you will read to what you already know. Asking questions *as* you read helps you understand what you are reading. Asking questions *after* you read helps you remember important information.

1. Read "A Special League." As you read, make a time line like the one above to track sequence.

2. Write the questions you had as you read. Then write the answers if the article gave them.

A Special League

African Americans have been among those playing baseball since the sport began. Sadly, for many years black players were not allowed to play on the same teams as white players.

In 1882 the first professional African American teams were formed. Unlike earlier players, these players were paid to play.

The first long-lasting league for black teams was the Negro National League (NNL). It was founded in 1920. Another league, the Eastern Colored League, was founded in 1923. These leagues gave talented black players the chance to play the game they loved. They also gave fans the chance to see great baseball.

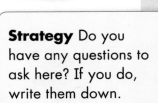

The NNL became very popular in the 1930s. From then until 1950, the East-West All-Star game was played every year. Between 30,000 and 40,000 fans attended! Yet things were not as easy for black players as for white players. Black players had to travel more often and play more games. They made less money. In some places they were refused rooms in hotels.

In 1947 professional baseball became integrated. That year, blacks were allowed to play with whites on Major League teams. Meanwhile, television was starting to show baseball games. These events led to the end of the Negro National League.

Strategy Look at the title and scan the article. Ask, "What is this article about? What do I already know about it?"

Skill The sequence clue "In 1882" is a good place to start a time line.

Strategy Do you have any questions to ask here? If you do, write them down.

Skill What clue word tells you that two events happened at the same time?

Satchel Paige

Words to Know

confidence

windup

fastball

outfield

mocking

weakness

unique

Remember

Try the strategy. Then, if you need more help, use your glossary or dictionary.

Vocabulary Strategy
for Antonyms

Context Clues When you read, you may come to a word you do not know. You may find a clue about the word's meaning in the words near the unknown word. For example, you may find an antonym, or a word with the opposite meaning of the unknown word. You can use the antonym to figure out the unknown word's meaning.

1. Reread the sentence with the unknown word.

2. Look at the words nearby for words that signal opposites, such as *unlike, but,* and *on the other hand.* They may point to an antonym.

3. Decide what the antonym means.

4. Give the unknown word the opposite meaning. Does this meaning make sense in the sentence?

As you read "Play Ball!" check the context of words you don't know. See if an antonym gives you a clue to meaning.

Play Ball!

Many young people dream of becoming a great baseball player. Only a few will be able to do this. One reason is that you must first have a lot of talent. Another is that you must be willing to work very hard. With work comes skill. With skill comes the confidence a great player needs.

For a pitcher, every windup and throw of the ball helps him or her learn something. Whether learning to deliver a smoking fastball or a dancing curve, the pitcher must master difficult moves. A hitter learns with every at-bat which pitch should go by and which should be slammed into the outfield. Even the mocking "Heybatterbatterbatter" of the other team can help build a hitter's concentration.

Being dedicated, the great player of tomorrow is willing to work on a weakness until it finally becomes a strength. The really great player is unique. He or she has passed the common level of play expected and has invented a style that stands out. Every player who tries hard and loves the game, though, is a winner, no matter what.

Write

Look at the pictures in *Satchel Paige.* Choose one to write about. Use as many words in the Words to Know list as you can.

Satchel Paige

by Lesa Cline-Ransome
paintings by James E. Ransome

Besides athletic ability, what makes an athlete great?

Genre A **biography** tells about a person's life. Look for how Satchel Paige handled the challenges in his life.

Leroy "Satchel" Paige earned his nickname as a young man. He carried suitcases—satchels—for passengers at Union Station in Mobile, Alabama. Satchel was a natural athlete. People said that by the age of ten he could outpitch grown men. So in 1923, at the age of 19, he decided to earn his living as a baseball player. In those days baseball was a segregated sport. African Americans were forced to play in their own leagues, separate from whites.

As a semipro pitcher, Satchel developed his own unique style. He'd pick up a tip here and there, put his Satchel spin on it, and polish it off with a brand-new name. Got so Satch began to think of his pitches as his children. The "hesitation" was his magic slow ball. The "trouble ball" caused all sorts of havoc. And then there was the "bee ball," which, according to Satch, would "always be where I want it to be."

97

There was an odd way about his pitching. He would stand tall and straight as an oak tree on the mound. His foot looked to be about a mile long, and when he shot it into the air, it seemed to block out the sun. Satch's arm seemed to stretch on forever, winding, bending, twisting. And then there was that grin he flashed just as he released the ball. It seemed to say, "Go ahead, just try and get a hit off of that."

"Strike one!"

And you never saw it coming. I mean, one minute it was there, plain as day in his hand, and then, all of a sudden . . .

"Strike two!"

It was in the catcher's mitt. The batter would strain his eyes, squint a little.

Here it comes, got it now.

"Strike three!"

Just like that. All over.

"Next batter up!"

"Give it to 'em, Satch. Show your stuff," fans and teammates would shout. And he did. Every time. Folks would pack the stands to see how many Satchel could strike out in one game. He made the crowds laugh with his fast talking and slow walking ("A man's got to go slow to go long and far," he'd say), but mostly he made them cheer. Never in his nineteen years had he heard a sweeter sound. The more cheers he heard, the more his confidence grew. A kind of confidence that made him call to the outfield with the bases loaded and the last hitter up to bat, "Why don't you all have a seat. Won't be needing you on this one."

Wherever the crowds went, a good paycheck followed, so he made sure to keep them coming. After just one year he was playing in the Negro major leagues for the Chattanooga Black Lookouts, and the folks were still cheering and shouting, "Give it to 'em, Satch. Show your stuff."

There were two major leagues back in 1924, when Satchel was called up. Because the white major-league ball clubs wouldn't allow blacks to play in their leagues, blacks had created their own in 1920 and named them the Negro Leagues. The white major-league players enjoyed trains, hotels, hot meals, and short seasons.

Negro League players were often refused meals in restaurants and rooms in hotels. They ate on the road and slept where they could—in train depots or on baseball fields. They played two, sometimes three games a day, nearly every day, in a season as long as the weather would hold. And when the season ended in America, Satch went right on playing and traveling in other parts of the world.

Life in the Negro Leagues suited Satchel. He was a traveling man. One city could never hold him for long. He moved from Alabama, where he played with the Birmingham Black Barons, to Tennessee, where he played with the Nashville Elite Giants, and to Pennsylvania, where he played with the Pittsburgh Crawfords.

From the first breath of spring till the cool rush of fall he would ride. Sometimes he joined his teammates on rickety old buses, bumping along on back roads studded with potholes so deep, players would have to hold on to their seats (and stomachs) just to keep from spilling into the aisles. But mostly he drove alone, in cars that would take him wherever he wanted to go. The fans would always be waiting in the next town. Their wait could be a long one—he was never much for keeping anyone's time but his own.

Once he reached his mid-thirties, the joys of traveling began to wear thin for Satchel. He found himself longing for a more settled life and the comforts of a home. In 1941 he finally found it in the warm smile and tender heart of Lahoma Brown. Satch rested his travel-weary legs and happily began his second career as husband and father. But even though he had finally found what he thought he'd been searching for, it was only a year before he took to the road again with his first and only true love—baseball. His family would have to wait.

Satchel's teammates were in love with the game, too. And out of that love grew players better than anyone could ever dream. His teammates included "Cool Papa" Bell, a hitter who ran bases so fast, if you blinked you'd swear he'd never left home plate. Oscar Charleston was an outfielder who could tell just where a ball would land as soon as it hit the bat. And then there was Josh Gibson, who some said could hit a ball so hard and so far, it would land somewhere in the middle of next week. Because of his powerful hitting and home run record, Josh was sometimes called "the black Babe Ruth," but many wondered if the Babe should have been called "the white Josh Gibson."

Back in 1923, when Gibson and Satch were teammates on the Pittsburgh Crawfords, they were considered a mighty powerful duo. Posters for the Crawfords read,

Josh Gibson and Satchel Paige
THE GREATEST BATTERY IN BASEBALL
Gibson guaranteed to hit two home runs and
Paige guaranteed to strike out the first nine men.

"Someday we'll meet up and see who's best," they would often joke with each other. In 1942, soon after Satchel's return to the road, they got their chance.

Josh Gibson of the Homestead Grays

It was September 10, 1942, the second game of the Negro
World Series. Satch's team, the Kansas City Monarchs, was in
a heated best-of-seven matchup against the Homestead Grays,
led by Josh Gibson. Toward the end of the game, Satch decided
to raise the stakes. With two outs in the inning and one man
on base, he walked two players so the bases would be loaded
when Josh Gibson came up to bat. "Someday we'll meet up and

see who's best" rang in Satch's ears as he prepared to face the man who would now determine the fate of his team and Satch's reputation. Satchel called to Josh, "Remember back when we were playing with the Crawfords and you said you was the best hitter in the world and I was the best pitcher?"

"Yeah, I remember," Josh called back.

"Well, now we're going to see what's what," Satch said.

With a ball in hand and a grin on his face, Satch told Josh, "I'm gonna throw a fastball letter high."

"Strike one!"

Josh shook his head, tightened his grip on the bat, and resumed his position as he tried to stare into Satchel's eyes.

But Satch stared straight ahead at Josh's knees. His coach back at the Mount Meigs School had always told him,

"Look at the knees, Satch. Every weakness a batter has, you can spot in the knees."

"Now I'm gonna throw this one a little faster and belt high," Satch said during the windup.

"Strike two!"

In typical Satch style, he called in a mocking voice, "Now I got you oh-and-two and I'm supposed to knock you down, but instead I'm gonna throw a pea at your knee."

"Strike three!"

Josh never moved the bat. Satch slowly exhaled the breath he'd been holding since the windup. It was over. He'd done what he'd come to do.

"Nobody hits Satchel's fastball," he said through a smile as bright as the sun. "And nobody ever will."

Reader Response

Open for Discussion A good biography helps you, the reader, see and hear the person the book is about. It brings that person to life. Reread aloud the part of *Satchel Paige* that did the most to bring him alive for you.

1. A good biographer must select which details to include about the subject's life. How do you think Lesa Cline-Ransome decided what to include about the life of Satchel Paige?

2. Reread pages 104–106. In your own words, describe how Satchel Paige defeated Josh Gibson, in sequence from start to finish.

3. Ask yourself this question: How did fans feel about Satchel Paige? Look back at page 99 and answer it.

4. To understand the story of Satchel Paige, it helps to know the game of baseball. Which words on the Words to Know list are baseball terms? Find three other words in the text that could be used to talk about baseball.

Look Back and Write From the information in the selection, describe what kind of person Satchel Paige was. Use details from the text to support your answer.

James E. Ransome, the illustrator of *Satchel Paige*, has won many awards for his work. He and his wife Lesa Cline-Ransome, who wrote *Satchel Paige*, live in upstate New York with their four children.

Mr. Ransome says that he did not have the opportunity to meet artists or visit art galleries while growing up. "I do not remember how my interest in art began," he writes, "but I do remember that some of my first drawings were of hot-rod cars and images copied from the pages of comic books and the Bible." Mr. Ransome says, "What makes illustrating books so exciting is that not only am I learning about the characters, the environment they live in, and the history of the period, but I can also allow the story to dictate the palette and design that I use to illustrate it, thus giving each book an original, different look and feel."

Lesa Cline-Ransome was working in the fashion world in New York City when she became interested in education. She started teaching and then turned to writing for children. Ms. Cline-Ransome says she is comfortable working with her husband. She says that she trusts completely his artistic judgments, and that he sometimes comes to her for ideas about how to illustrate a story.

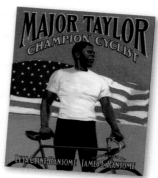

Major Taylor, Champion Cyclist

The Wagon

ALL-STARS

Lesa Cline-Ransome & James E. Ransome

109

Expository Nonfiction

Genre
- **Expository nonfiction deals with real people and events.**
- **Expository articles often appear in magazines.**

Text Features
- **Some articles deal with how things were different in the past.**
- **Expository articles about the past often include pictures that show what people and places looked like.**

Link to Social Studies
Women couldn't vote in the 1870s, but they could play baseball. Do some research in books or on the Internet to find out when women finally did gain the right to vote and how they gained that right.

THE GIRLS of SUMMER

by Ellen Klages

Baseball is largely considered a man's game. But what if you take a closer look at its history?

The first team of professional baseball players, the Cincinnati Red Stockings, took the field in 1869. They were all male—the first boys of summer. The first girls of summer, women who were paid to play baseball, competed in their first game in 1875.

In the 1870s, an American woman could not vote. She could not own property in her own name after marriage. But she could play ball—as well as it could be played in an outfit that weighed as much as thirty pounds and included a floor-length skirt, underskirts, a long-sleeved, high-necked blouse, and high button shoes.

Amelia Bloomer designed and wore the loose-fitting, Turkish-style trousers that carried her name and made sports more practical for women athletes. In the 1890s, scores of "Bloomer Girls" baseball teams were formed all over the country.

The Bloomer Girls era lasted from the 1890s until 1934. Hundreds of teams—All Star Ranger Girls, Philadelphia Bobbies, New York Bloomer Girls—offered employment, travel, and adventure for young women who could hit, field, slide, or catch.

The Bloomer Girls teams dwindled as more and more minor league teams—farm clubs—were formed to provide experience for young men on their climb up to the majors. A few women were signed, briefly, to minor league contracts, but they were exceptions.

Although women had been playing pro ball on Bloomer Girls teams for more than forty years, in the 1930s public opinion was that they had inferior abilities when it came to sports. Women's professional baseball disappeared when the last of the Bloomer Girls teams disbanded in 1934.

Briefly, in the late 1940s and early 1950s, women played again. But in 1952 they were banned from professional baseball. The ban still holds today.

Reading Across Texts

This selection and *Satchel Paige* show how two groups of people had difficulties playing professional baseball for different reasons. What were those reasons?

Writing Across Texts Present your response in a two-column chart.

 **Sequence** How do the dates help you with the sequence of events?

Comprehension

Skill
Cause and Effect

Strategy
Summarize

 # Cause and Effect

- The cause is what made something happen. The effect is what happened as the result of a cause.

- Sometimes an author will use clue words such as *so* and *because* to show a cause-and-effect relationship, but not always.

- An effect may have more than one cause, and a cause may have more than one effect.

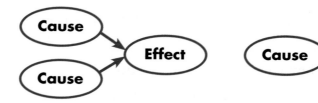

Strategy: Summarize

In a summary, you state main ideas and leave out unimportant details. Summarizing helps you make sure you understand and remember what you read. Summarizing is especially helpful when you read about a cause with several effects or an effect with several causes.

1. Read "Coming to the United States." Make a graphic organizer to show the causes of immigration.

2. Use information from your graphic organizer to help you write a brief summary about why many people have immigrated to the United States.

COMING TO THE UNITED STATES

Imagine getting on a boat and leaving your homeland. You cross miles and miles of ocean to go live in a country you have never been to before. The people speak a different language, eat different foods, wear different clothes.

If you did this, you would be an immigrant. Throughout U.S. history, many people have immigrated to this country. In fact, between 1880 and 1930, about 27 million people came to the United States. Why?

In some cases, people came for freedom of religion. Many Jewish people came from Eastern Europe and Russia, where they were persecuted because of their faith. Some people came to escape wars in their homelands. Many immigrants came to the United States from Mexico, where a revolution was being fought. Other people came to escape famine. Thousands left Ireland, where people were starving because of lack of food.

A great many immigrants came to make money. They left countries that had far fewer jobs to offer than the United States. These immigrants were willing to work hard to make better lives for themselves and their families.

Skill This sentence names an effect— millions of immigrants—caused by other events.

Skill *Why* is a clue word asking for causes, so look for causes to follow.

Strategy Only one item below should be used in a summary of immigration causes. Which item is that?
a) Many immigrants came by boat.
b) Many Jewish people lived in Europe and Russia.
c) Many people came for freedom of religion.

Strategy Which causes of immigration will you include in your written summary?

immigrants

circumstances

newcomer

advised

peddler

hustled

elbow

advice

luxury

Remember

Try the strategy. Then, if you need more help, use your glossary or dictionary.

Vocabulary Strategy
for Multiple-Meaning Words

Context Clues Some words have more than one meaning. You can find clues in nearby words to decide which meaning the author is using.

1. Think about different meanings the word can have.

2. Reread the sentence where the word appears. Which meaning fits in the sentence?

3. If you can't tell, then look for more clues in nearby sentences.

4. Put the clues together and decide which meaning works best.

As you read "A New Job in America," use the context and what you know about the vocabulary words to decide their meanings. For example, does *hustled* mean "hurried along" or "sold in a hurried way"?

A NEW JOB IN AMERICA

As immigrants came to America in the 1800s, many found themselves in difficult circumstances. What could a newcomer do to earn money? Often business owners would hire new immigrants only for low-paying jobs. Many immigrants must have worried that their decision to come here was not well advised.

However, there was one job that was wide open. They could peddle, or sell, goods in the streets. The peddler became a colorful figure in American history. On the crowded streets of cities, peddlers hustled items of every sort to people passing by. They would elbow their way into the crowd and announce their wares in a loud voice. Others packed things to sell on a horse or wagon and traveled West. Most settlers lived far from any town or store. They were happy to see someone coming with things they needed.

Picture the peddler with his odd mixture of goods spread out on a blanket. He gives advice to the women looking at his wares. This kind of needle is best. That sort of pot will last. He tries to convince them to buy some little luxury, such as a shiny set of combs for their hair. After the sale and maybe a meal, he goes on his way.

Write

Pretend you are an immigrant who has just arrived in New York in 1900. Write a journal entry about what you see and how you feel. Use as many words from the Words to Know list as you can.

SHUTTING OUT THE SKY

BY DEBORAH HOPKINSON

How does Marcus manage to meet the challenge of making a place for himself in a new country?

Genre

Expository nonfiction explains a person, a thing, or an idea. Notice how the author explains what life was like for a young man coming to the United States at the beginning of the twentieth century.

At the end of the nineteenth century, 23 million immigrants came to New York City from Europe. Marcus Ravage was one of them. Like many new immigrants, Marcus thought that he would soon be rich. He was about to learn that life in New York would be a lot harder than he thought.

RICH, OR POOR?

One early morning in December 1900, a sixteen-year-old boy left Ellis Island and made his way alone into New York City. Struggling with his heavy bundles, Marcus Ravage elbowed his way through the crowded streets of the Lower East Side.

Marcus shivered in the bitter cold. If only he'd followed his mother's advice and brought his heavy coat to America. He'd been so sure he wouldn't need it. After all, he'd argued, why should he bother carrying old clothes when he'd soon be rich enough to buy new ones!

But Marcus had brought something almost as precious as a warm coat, and with cold fingers he dug into his bundles to find it. It was just a crumpled bit of paper, but it was a link between his old life in Romania and his new one. On the paper was scribbled the New York address of distant relatives from back home.

Before long, Marcus found himself in the apartment of the Segal family, who had arrived from Romania just three months before. Mrs. Segal, along with her son and five daughters, lived in a five-room apartment on the third floor of a Rivington Street tenement. Looking around at the sofa, kitchen table, and ever so many chairs, Marcus felt sure that the Segals were already rich. And he wouldn't be far behind.

Mrs. Segal told Marcus he could stay for free for a few days. After that, he would be expected to find a job and pay fifty cents a week for his bed. With seven members of the Segal family plus him, the apartment would be crowded, Marcus thought, but it was better than being out on the street.

That evening, people Marcus had never seen before began
to stream into the apartment, tired from a long day of work.
Who were all these strangers? Marcus thought. As the hours ticked
by and the strangers didn't leave, Marcus realized they were
boarders—they lived there too! They paid Mrs. Segal for a bed,
and perhaps for meals and laundry. *Where would everyone sleep?*
he wondered.

Marcus soon found out. It wasn't long before everyone began
to rush about, lining up chairs in rows to make beds. Marcus and
three other young men shared the sofa, sleeping with their heads
on the cushions and feet propped awkwardly on chairs. Nine bodies
pressed together on the floor, huddling like seals on a rock. In the
kitchen, Mrs. Segal and one child cuddled on top of the washtubs
while the rest of the children slept on the floor. And the room
Marcus thought was the children's bedroom? A family of five
had taken it over.

*Immigrant family
in a crowded
apartment*

Soon the rooms were filled with deep breathing, dreadful snoring, and smells of all kinds. Yet despite his new, strange circumstances, Marcus fell asleep right away. Next morning he woke to the puffing of steam engines and clatter of wheels outside the windows. Once again the rooms hummed with activity. People raced to put the furniture back into place; the men scrambled to get dressed before the girls awoke. Mrs. Segal crammed extra feather beds into nooks and crannies and made coffee.

After everyone else had hurried off to work or school, Marcus and Mrs. Segal were left alone in the now neat and tidy apartment. Since Marcus was still considered a guest, Mrs. Segal wouldn't hear of him helping with the housework or marketing. He was thoroughly surprised to see Mrs. Segal clean the kitchen floor with precious soap rather than sand, as his mother would have back home.

When Mrs. Segal came back from the market, Marcus felt more confused then ever. She'd brought the largest eggplant (which some immigrants called a "blue tomato") he'd ever seen, as well as an

Fruit and vegetable stand in New York City

Customers inspecting baskets of produce

Street peddler in New York City

exotic yellow fruit in the shape of a cucumber—a banana. And then there was a cauliflower, a vegetable his father had eaten only once in a big city and had talked about ever since. To say nothing of meat— which she cooked for lunch!

Back home in his village only rich people could indulge in the luxury of meat in the middle of the day, eat such extraordinary vegetables, use soap instead of sand to clean floors, or live on the second floor of such a nice apartment.

But, Marcus puzzled, if the Segals were rich, if they had *already* made their million dollars in three months, why did they share their fine apartment with so many borders?

To a newcomer, or "greenhorn" like Marcus, it was all very confusing.

MARCUS THE PEDDLER

Sixteen-year-old Marcus Ravage was in trouble. No matter how he tried, he couldn't find a job. But Mrs. Segal, his relative (and now landlady), didn't seem to think he was trying quite hard enough. It was time he began to earn his keep, she told him firmly. After all, he was sleeping in her apartment and eating her food.

Mrs. Segal gave Marcus a dollar and pushed him out onto the street to get started as a peddler. This was America, she reminded him, where "everyone hustled, and nearly everybody peddled."

Marcus was ashamed and nervous at the same time. A lowly peddler! This certainly wasn't the way he'd imagined his start in America. He'd been so sure he could get rich right away. But what other choice did he have?

So Marcus took Mrs. Segal's dollar and one of her nice brass trays to Orchard Street. There he bought two boxes of chocolates. Opening the boxes, he arranged the candy pieces on the tray. Now he was in business.

Marcus stood on a busy corner trying to catch the attention of the crowds rushing off to work. Marcus shivered. More than ever, he wished he'd brought his heavy winter coat.

A busy market

Boys selling newspapers (right)

A policeman and a dog

A policeman chased him to another corner, where a boy ran by and tried to spill all his chocolates as a joke. And still, every person brushed by him without buying a thing. As the minutes went by, Marcus became even more cold and miserable. How could he face Mrs. Segal? Would she kick him out?

After about two hours, Marcus noticed the streets beginning to fill with pushcarts and other peddlers. Marcus later remembered "peddlers with pushcarts and peddlers with boxes, peddlers with movable stands and peddlers with baskets, peddlers with bundles, with pails, with satchels and suitcases and trunks. . . . They came pouring in from all directions—men with white beards, old women draped in fantastic shawls, boys with piping voices, young mothers with babes in their arms."

A man selling tablecloths nearby called out, "How is business?"

Marcus shook his head sadly. He hadn't made a single sale. As it happened, the man was also from Romania, and he took Marcus under his wing, "Move along, elbow your way through the crowds in front of the stores, seek out the women with kids; shove your tray into their faces," the older man advised. "Don't be timid. . . . And yell, never stop yelling: 'Candy, ladies! Finest in America. Only a nickel, a half-a-dime, five cents.'"

Then it was Marcus's turn to try. To his astonishment and delight, it began to work. His candy started to sell! By the end of the day, Marcus was glowing with pride.

That night Marcus went to a Romanian restaurant on Allen Street. For ten cents, he ordered the first meal he'd ever paid for in America: pot roast with mashed potatoes and gravy and a dish of chopped eggplant with olive oil. While he ate, Marcus counted his earnings: seventy cents, not counting the chocolates he had eaten himself.

Marcus was on his way.

Boys playing marbles

Marcus Ravage quickly made friends with other Romanian immigrants and started feeling at home in the United States. Later, he got a better job at a tailor shop and went to school at night. Nine years after coming to America, Marcus graduated from the University of Missouri and became a journalist and writer. He died in 1965 at the age of 81.

Reader Response

Open for Discussion   If Marcus wrote home to Romania, what would he say? Would he tell all or only the bright side? If you were Marcus, what would you write?

1. The author isn't making up Marcus; he really lived. How do you think the author got her information about him? List three possible ways.

2. Several surprises greet Marcus on his arrival in New York City. What are three things that surprise him and why? Look back at pages 119–123 to find answers.

3. What steps does Marcus take to start earning a living? Look back at pages 124–127 to summarize his progress.

4. What advice did Marcus's mother give him when he came to America? What other advice do you think he might have for newcomers? Use words from the Words to Know list to tell about it.

Look Back and Write
Marcus the peddler got some advice. What was it, who gave it, and how did it work? After rereading page 124, write the answer in your own words.

Deborah Hopkinson

Read more books by Deborah Hopkinson.

Deborah Hopkinson spent three years doing research for *Shutting Out the Sky,* a nonfiction book. While she is interested in nonfiction, she also loves historical fiction, and she likes to write about girls. She says that "when I was a girl, there weren't many stories about the exciting things that girls can do!"

Many of Ms. Hopkinson's award-winning books are about a woman or girl who has led an unusual life. Among them are the woman who invented exact measurements for recipes, and a seventeen-year-old girl who pitched for a semipro baseball team.

Ms. Hopkinson knew she wanted to be a writer, but she didn't know what she wanted to write. She says, "Then, when my daughter Rebekah was about three, we were reading a lot of children's books. Having a full-time career and a child, I was very busy. But I thought, 'Maybe I'll try writing for children. At least the books are short!' I have since found out that because a story is short doesn't mean that it is easy to write."

Deborah Hopkinson lives with her family in Walla Walla, Washington. The family also includes her husband and son, and a whole menagerie of pets, including ducks named George and Martha.

A Band of Angels

Girl Wonder

E-mail

Genre

- E-mail is short for "electronic mail"— messages sent over the Internet from one computer user to another.

- You can e-mail certain Web sites to gather information for school projects.

Text Features

- The address box gives vital information.

- The message looks like the body of a friendly letter.

Link to Social Studies

Imagine that you want to contact the tenement museum for information about a school project. Think of what this project might be, and make up an e-mail you might send.

The Immigrant Experience

To gather facts for a school report, Rachel gets on the Internet and visits the Web site of the Lower East Side Tenement Museum in New York City. At the site, she finds an e-mail address to contact for more information.

130

Take It to the NET
ONLINE
more activities sfsuccessnet.com

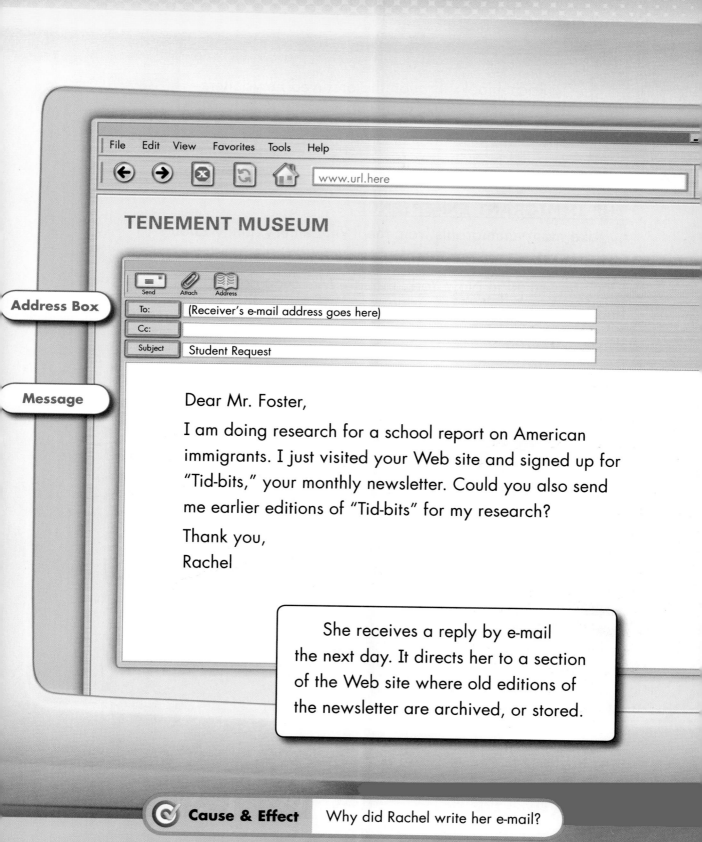

TENEMENT MUSEUM

Address Box

To: (Receiver's e-mail address goes here)
Cc:
Subject: Student Request

Message

Dear Mr. Foster,

I am doing research for a school report on American immigrants. I just visited your Web site and signed up for "Tid-bits," your monthly newsletter. Could you also send me earlier editions of "Tid-bits" for my research?

Thank you,
Rachel

She receives a reply by e-mail the next day. It directs her to a section of the Web site where old editions of the newsletter are archived, or stored.

Cause & Effect Why did Rachel write her e-mail?

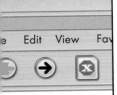

Rachel looks through the archived newsletters and sees this article. She finds it useful for her report. She also finds it surprising.

THE IMMIGRANT EXPERIENCE

Like many immigrants from the 19th century, Emily Zhou's father left his home and family to seek prosperity in America. Once he settled in New York, though, Mr. Zhou could only find low-paying, menial jobs: he worked twelve hour days for $20 in the basement of a Chinese restaurant.

Though he longed to return home, Mr. Zhou was deeply in debt and could not leave America. So, Mrs. Zhou joined her husband in New York City, leaving young Emily in the care of her grandparents. Emily did not see her parents for nearly a decade, finally reuniting with her family in New York when she was eighteen.

However, the Zhous are not immigrants from the 19th or early 20th centuries: Emily and her family are part of the recent surge of immigrants to New York City. Indeed, 37% of New Yorkers were born in another country.

Reading Across Texts

Compare this newsletter article with what you read in *Shutting Out the Sky*. How are the situations of Mr. Zhou today and Marcus Savage one-hundred plus years ago similar?

Writing Across Texts Write your response in a paragraph.

 Summarize What steps did Rachel follow to get her information?

The Microscope

by Maxine W. Kumin

Anton Leeuwenhoek was Dutch.
He sold pincushions, cloth, and such.
The waiting townsfolk fumed and fussed
As Anton's dry goods gathered dust.

He worked, instead of tending store,
At grinding special lenses for
A microscope. Some of the things
He looked at were:
    mosquitoes' wings,
the hairs of sheep, the legs of lice,
the skin of people, dogs, and mice;
ox eyes, spiders' spinning gear,
fishes' scales, a little smear
of his own blood,
    and best of all,
the unknown, busy, very small
bugs that swim and bump and hop
inside a simple water drop.

Impossible! Most Dutchmen said.
This Anton's crazy in the head.
We ought to ship him off to Spain.
He says he's seen a housefly's brain.
He says the water that we drink
Is full of bugs. He's mad, we think!

They called him *dumkopf,* which means dope.
That's how we got the microscope.

135

Full Day

by Naomi Shihab Nye

The pilot on the plane says:
In one minute and fifty seconds
we're going as far
as the covered wagon went
in a full day.

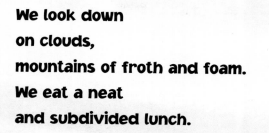

We look down
on clouds,
mountains of froth and foam.
We eat a neat
and subdivided lunch.

How was it for the people in
the covered wagon?
They bumped and jostled.
Their wheels broke.
Their biscuits were tough.
They got hot and cold and old.
Their shirts tore on the branches
they passed.

But they saw the pebbles
and the long grass
and the sweet shine of evening
settling on the fields.
They knew the ruts and the rocks.
They threw their furniture out
to make the wagons lighter.
They carried their treasures
in a crooked box.

Wrap-Up

Challenge Guide

Some of the people in Unit 1 met challenges successfully. Make a chart showing the person, the challenge, and what the person might say about meeting challenges. Then make a list of ideas called "When Facing a Challenge."

Unit 1 Person	The Challenge	Advice About Meeting Challenges

What kinds of challenges do people face and how do they meet them?

Let Me Introduce . . .

connect to
DRAMA

Choose your favorite person from Unit 1. Imagine that this person will give a speech about meeting challenges. With a partner, plan what you would say to introduce this person. Then dramatize introducing the person and giving the speech to a group as this person might give it.

Tall-Tale Action Hero

connect to
WRITING

In a tall tale, the hero's actions and other details may be wildly exaggerated, as in *Thunder Rose*. Choose one of the other selections in Unit 1 and rewrite it as a tall tale. Add some illustrations when your tale is complete.

Super Satchel

Doing the Right Thing

What makes people want to do the right thing?

Comprehension

Skill
Compare
and Contrast

Strategy
Answer Questions

Compare and Contrast

- When writers compare and contrast things, they tell how those things are alike or different.

- Words such as *same*, *also*, *before*, *although*, and *however* are clues that things are being compared and contrasted.

- Sometimes writers do not use clue words when they compare and contrast things.

Before	After

Strategy: Answer Questions

Good readers know how to find the answers to questions such as, "How would you compare and contrast _____ and _____ ?" Sometimes you can find an answer in just one place. Other times you must search in several places to find all the information to answer a question.

1. Read "A New Home." Make a graphic organizer like the one above to compare and contrast life for some Mexican people before and after they come to the United States.

2. Write a comparison of how Mexicans celebrate holidays in Mexico and in the United States. Use information from your graphic organizer to help you.

A NEW HOME

Thousands of people move from Mexico to the United States each year. Many come to find better-paying jobs and to provide better homes for their families.

The language of Mexico is Spanish. When adults move from Mexico to the United States, many continue to speak Spanish. Although learning a new language can be hard, their children usually learn English as well. They often speak Spanish at home and English at school. So, many Mexican American children speak two languages!

Some Mexican families come to towns where few other Mexicans live. However, many move to Mexican American neighborhoods. Some cities have large Mexican communities. In these communities, stores and restaurants have Spanish names and sell Mexican food, books, and clothing, the same as they do in Mexico. These neighborhoods can help make newcomers feel comfortable in their new country.

On May 5, Mexican Americans celebrate a Mexican holiday called Cinco de Mayo. On September 16, they celebrate Mexican Independence Day. Many Mexican Americans continue celebrating these holidays with parades, costumes, and special food. Of course they also enjoy celebrating American holidays, like the Fourth of July!

Skill There is no clue word here, but you can figure out a difference between life in Mexico and life in the United States for many people. Why would people come to the United States for jobs?

Strategy One sentence in this paragraph answers this question: How do many children's lives change when they come to the United States from Mexico?

Skill Which clue words in this paragraph call attention to a contrast and a comparison?

Strategy If someone asked you about the days on which Mexican and American holidays were celebrated, where would you find the answer?

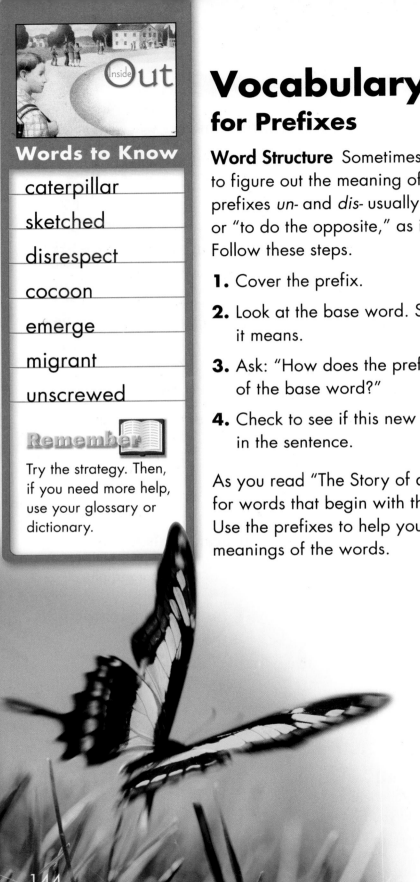

Words to Know

caterpillar

sketched

disrespect

cocoon

emerge

migrant

unscrewed

Remember

Try the strategy. Then, if you need more help, use your glossary or dictionary.

Vocabulary Strategy
for Prefixes

Word Structure Sometimes you can use prefixes to figure out the meaning of an unfamiliar word. The prefixes *un-* and *dis-* usually mean "the opposite of" or "to do the opposite," as in *untie* and *disappear*. Follow these steps.

1. Cover the prefix.

2. Look at the base word. See if you know what it means.

3. Ask: "How does the prefix change the meaning of the base word?"

4. Check to see if this new meaning makes sense in the sentence.

As you read "The Story of a Caterpillar," look for words that begin with the prefix *un-* or *dis-*. Use the prefixes to help you figure out the meanings of the words.

The Story of a Caterpillar

During recess I like to poke around and see the finer details up close and personal. One day I discovered a caterpillar munching leaves on a bush. It had blue spots and yellowish lines and many stubby little legs. It moved by rippling its whole body along in waves. It looked so interesting that I sketched it in my notebook. I thought my teacher, who loves science, would be intrigued.

She said I could put it in a jar with air holes and lots of leaves to eat, but to do this carefully. "We must not hurt the caterpillar or make it suffer," she said. "We don't want to disrespect nature." We watched to see what would happen, but after many weeks, we wondered if anything ever would. Then one day we spied a white cocoon hanging from a twig! The caterpillar had wrapped itself up for a long nap.

For weeks we checked the jar every morning until the cocoon opened and a beautiful moth began to emerge. It sat on a twig opening and closing its wings. We looked up the moth in an insect book. It had come from an eastern tent caterpillar. The book also said that like a migrant worker, some moths and butterflies travel thousands of miles in a year. I unscrewed the jar so the moth's trip could begin.

Write

Be a science reporter. Write about the life cycle of a butterfly. Use as many words from the Words to Know list as you can.

by Francisco Jiménez

Inside Out

illustrated by Raul Colon

Why does Francisco do what he does at the end of the story?

Francisco has come with his family from Mexico and speaks only Spanish. This is his first year in school in the United States. His parents are migrant workers. While Francisco is at school, they are out in the farm fields picking strawberries. Miss Scalapino is Francisco's teacher, and Roberto is his big brother. Right next to Francisco's desk is a caterpillar in a jar.

In time I learned some of my classmates' names. The one I heard the most and therefore learned first was Curtis. Curtis was the biggest, strongest, and most popular kid in the class. Everyone wanted to be his friend and to play with him. He was always chosen captain when the kids formed teams. Since I was the smallest kid in the class and did not know English, I was chosen last.

I preferred to hang around Arthur, one of the boys who knew a little Spanish. During recess, he and I played on the swings and I pretended to be a Mexican movie star, like Jorge Negrete or Pedro Infante, riding a horse and singing the *corridos* we often heard on the car radio. I sang them to Arthur as we swung back and forth, going as high as we could.

But when I spoke to Arthur in Spanish and Miss Scalapino heard me, she said "No!" with body and soul. Her head turned left and right a hundred times a second, and her index finger moved from side to side as fast as a windshield wiper on a rainy day. "English, English," she repeated. Arthur avoided me whenever she was around.

Often during recess I stayed with the caterpillar. Sometimes it was hard to spot him because he blended in with the green leaves and twigs. Every day I brought him leaves from the pepper and cypress trees that grew on the playground.

Just in front of the caterpillar, lying on top of the cabinet, was a picture book of caterpillars and butterflies. I went through it, page by page, studying all the pictures and running my fingers lightly over the caterpillars and the bright wings of the butterflies and the many patterns on them. I knew caterpillars turned into butterflies because Roberto had told me, but I wanted to know more. I was sure information was in the words written underneath each picture in large black letters. I tried to figure them out by looking at the pictures. I did this so many times that I could close my eyes and see the words, but I could not understand what they meant.

My favorite time in school was when we did art, which was every afternoon, after the teacher had read to us. Since I did not understand Miss Scalapino when she explained the art lesson, she let me do whatever I wanted. I drew all kinds of animals but mostly birds and butterflies. I sketched them in pencil and then colored them using every color in my crayon box. Miss Scalapino even tacked one of my drawings up on the board for everyone to see. After a couple of weeks it disappeared, and I did not know how to ask where it had gone.

One cold Thursday morning, during recess, I was the only kid on the playground without a jacket. Mr. Sims must have noticed I was shivering because that afternoon, after school, he took me to his office and pulled out a green jacket from a large cardboard box that was full of used clothes and toys. He handed it to me and gestured for me to try it on. It smelled like graham crackers. I put it on, but it was too big, so he rolled up the sleeves about two inches to make it fit. I took it home and showed it off to my parents. They smiled. I liked it because it was green, and it hid my suspenders.

The next day I was on the playground wearing my new jacket and waiting for the first bell to ring when I saw Curtis coming at me like an angry bull. Aiming his head directly at me, and pulling his arms straight back with his hands clenched, he stomped up to me and started yelling. I did not understand him, but I knew it had something to do with the jacket because he began to pull on it, trying to take it off of me. The next thing I knew, he and I were on the ground wrestling. Kids circled us. I could hear them yelling Curtis's name and something else. He pulled on one of the sleeves so hard that it ripped at the shoulder. He pulled on the right pocket and it ripped. Then Miss Scalapino's face appeared above. She pushed Curtis off of me and grabbed me by the back of the collar and picked me up off the ground. It took all the power I had not to cry.

On the way to the classroom Arthur told me that Curtis claimed the jacket was his, that he had lost it at the beginning of the year. He also said that the teacher told Curtis and me that we were being punished. We had to sit on the bench during recess for the rest of the week. I did not see the jacket again. Curtis got it but I never saw him wear it.

For the rest of the day, I could not even pretend I was paying attention to Miss Scalapino; I was so embarrassed. I laid my head on the top of my desk and closed my eyes. I kept thinking about what had happened that morning. I wanted to fall asleep and wake up to find it was only a dream. The teacher called my name but I did not answer. I heard her walk up to me. I did not know what to expect. She gently shook me by the shoulders. Again, I did not respond. Miss Scalapino must have thought I was asleep because she left me alone, even when it was time for recess and everyone left the room.

153

Once the room was quiet, I slowly opened my eyes. I had them closed for so long that the sunlight coming through the windows blinded me. I rubbed my eyes with the back of my hands and then looked to my left at the jar. I looked for the caterpillar but could not see it. Thinking it might be hidden, I put my hand in the jar and lightly stirred the leaves. To my surprise, the caterpillar had spun itself into a cocoon and had attached itself to a small twig. It looked like a tiny cotton bulb, just like Roberto had said it would. I gently stroked it with my index finger, picturing it asleep and peaceful.

At the end of the school day, Miss Scalapino gave me a note to take home to my parents. Papa and Mama did not know how to read, but they did not have to. As soon as they saw my swollen upper lip and the scratches on my left cheek, they knew what the note had said. When I told them what happened, they were very upset but relieved that I did not disrespect the teacher.

For the next several days, going to school and facing Miss Scalapino was harder than ever. However, I slowly began to get over what happened that Friday. Once I got used to the routine in school and I picked up some English words, I felt more comfortable in class.

On Wednesday, May 23, a few days before the end of the school year, Miss Scalapino took me by surprise. After we were all sitting down and she had taken roll, she called for everyone's attention. I did not understand what she said, but I heard her say my name as she held up a blue ribbon. She then picked up my drawing of the butterfly that had disappeared weeks before and held it up for everyone to see. She walked up to me and handed me the drawing and the silk blue ribbon that had the number one printed on it in gold. I knew then I had received first prize for my drawing. I was so proud I felt like bursting out of my skin. My classmates, including Curtis, stretched their necks to see the ribbon.

That afternoon, during our free period, I went over to check on the caterpillar. I turned the jar around, trying to see the cocoon. It was beginning to crack open. I excitedly cried out, "Look, look," pointing to it. The whole class, like a swarm of bees, rushed over to the counter. Miss Scalapino took the jar and placed it on top of a desk in the middle of the classroom so everyone could see it. For the next several minutes we all stood there watching the butterfly emerge from its cocoon, in slow motion.

At the end of the day, just before the last bell, Miss Scalapino picked up the jar and took the class outside to the playground. She placed the jar on the ground and we all circled around her. I had a hard time seeing over the other kids, so Miss Scalapino called me over and motioned for

me to open the jar. I broke through the circle, knelt on the ground, and unscrewed the top. Like magic, the butterfly flew into the air, fluttering its wings up and down.

After school I waited in line for my bus in front of the playground. I proudly carried the blue ribbon in my right hand and the drawing in the other. Arthur and Curtis came up and stood behind me to wait for their bus. Curtis motioned for me to show him the drawing again. I held it up so he could see it.

"He really likes it, Francisco," Arthur said to me in Spanish.

"*¿Como se dice 'es tuyo' en inglés?*" I asked.

"It's yours," answered Arthur.

"It's yours," I repeated, handing the drawing to Curtis.

Reader Response

Open for Discussion Imagine you are helping Miss Scalapino in her classroom. Your job is to help a new Spanish-speaking student named Francisco. Tell your plan.

1. Reread the descriptions of Miss Scalapino's movements at the top of page 150 and the green jacket on page 151. Why are they so specific? What do you think this author would say if you asked him this question?

2. Compare and contrast how Curtis treats Francisco on page 153 with how Francisco treats Curtis on page 157. Which character do you admire and why?

3. Why does Mr. Sims give Francisco the jacket? Include details from page 151 in your answer.

4. How does the caterpillar help Francisco adjust to his new school? Tell about it using words from the Words to Know list and the story.

Test Practice

Look Back and Write Francisco and the caterpillar seem to have something in common. Look back at page 152, where Francisco receives first prize, and read on about the caterpillar. Then write a comparison of what happens to the two of them.

Francisco Jiménez

Read more stories by Francisco Jiménez.

Francisco Jiménez once said, "I write in both English and Spanish. The language I use is determined by what period in my life I write about. Since Spanish was the dominant language during my childhood, I generally write about those experiences in Spanish."

Mr. Jiménez was born in Mexico. He came to the United States with his parents and older brother Roberto when he was four years old. His parents were looking for a better life for their family. They followed the crops from place to place in California, picking strawberries in the summer, grapes in the fall, and cotton in the winter. They often lived in tents or one-room shacks.

At first, school was a challenge for Mr. Jiménez. He didn't know much English, and he always missed the beginning of the school year because he was picking grapes. Yet school was the only stable thing in his life. He knew that what he learned in school would stay with him no matter how often he moved.

"Inside Out" is one of eleven stories in *The Circuit: Stories from the Life of a Migrant Child*. This book comes from his childhood experiences and has won numerous awards.

The Christmas Gift

The Circuit: Stories from the Life of a Migrant Child

E-mails

Genre

- E-mail is short for "electronic mail."

- E-mails are messages sent on a computer over the Internet. They travel from sender to receiver in a matter of moments.

Text Features

- Each e-mail has a heading that tells who submitted it when.

- These e-mails are for a general audience. The sender is writing to anyone who visits the Web site to read about random acts of kindness.

Link to Social Studies

With your teacher's help, begin a Random Acts of Kindness File for your classroom. Think of times when you practiced kindness and write about them.

Random Acts of Kindness

These e-mails are from the Random Acts of Kindness Foundation Web site. This nonprofit organization encourages people to practice kindness whenever and wherever they can.

A Mother's Appreciation

SUBMITTED BY: HAYLEY'S MOTHER / DATE SUBMITTED: 3/10/2004

I want to acknowledge the kindness of Madison. She was so sweet to my daughter, Hayley, who is a kindergartener.

Hayley was having a very difficult morning after being dropped off at school. Madison, who is in the same class as Hayley's brother, saw Hayley crying and generously walked her to her class. She took her to her teacher and made her feel better by doing so.

A Student's Random Act of Kindness

SUBMITTED BY: FAITH / DATE SUBMITTED: 12/4/2003

A friend of mine seemed to be having a hard time, so I wrote her a note that told her how much of an inspiration she has been to me. I also told her to always follow her dreams and never give up hope.

I then decided to do this for others in my classes. Most of them I had never even talked to before, but they just looked lonely or sad.

I didn't sign my name, so it was really special watching as they smiled and looked around, wondering who could have written it. I know it wasn't much, but it made their day.

Just a Pencil

SUBMITTED BY: JIM / DATE SUBMITTED: 9/26/2003

On the first day of school, Mario said, "I have no pencil." The math teacher told him to use the one on the chalk tray. On the second day of school, Mario repeated his statement, and the teacher just pointed to the chalk tray.

The scenario went on until the first school day after the winter break. On that day Mario met with the teacher at the door, smiled, and said, "Mr. C., I now have a pencil for YOU." The teacher took the new pencil and read the inscription: "Thank you for being kind."

The teacher never hassled Mario about not having a pencil because he, too, came from a poor background and never forgot how embarrassing it was to be laughed at in school for not having school supplies.

At first, the pencil represented a small symbol of kindness, but soon it evolved into Mario's determination to pass math class. He voluntarily spent extra time in class. He always arrived early each morning to get a head start on his assignment.

Just a pencil?—not really. To Mario, the pencil meant someone cared, and this feeling gave him the desire to succeed in math class and be successful in his new American school.

Reading Across Texts

What was Francisco's random act of kindness?

Writing Across Texts Write a letter from Francisco to Curtis, explaining Francisco's random act of kindness.

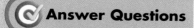 **Answer Questions** Reread any e-mails you have questions about.

Comprehension

Skill
Author's Purpose

Strategy
Monitor
and Fix Up

Author's Purpose

- An author may write to persuade, to inform, to entertain, or to express himself or herself.

- You can infer an author's purpose from the text features and specific language the author chose.

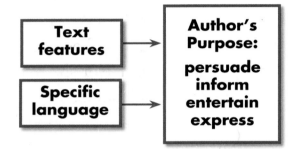

Strategy: Monitor and Fix Up

Good readers check their understanding as they read. Pace your reading depending on the author's purpose. If the author is informing you and you want to understand every detail, slow down. If the author is entertaining you, you can read a little faster.

1. Before you read "The Job of a Diplomat," preview the article. Make a graphic organizer like the one above to predict the author's purpose.

2. As you read, check your understanding. Make a second graphic organizer to see if the author's purpose is the same as you predicted.

162

The Job of a DIPLOMAT

The world has nearly 200 countries. How can we keep peace among so many groups? One way is through persons called diplomats. A country sends diplomats to foreign countries to speak for it.

Ambassadors The chief diplomat is often the ambassador. An ambassador is chosen by the president or other government leader. He or she lives in a foreign country and meets with its leaders. The spaces where ambassadors live and work are protected. The police or army of the foreign country may not enter these spaces.

Other diplomats Besides the ambassador, other diplomats serve in foreign countries. They must pass a government test to become a diplomat. In college they study subjects such as languages and world history that will help them understand other nations. They speak the language of the country where they are sent.

Diplomats report to their home government about the country in which they serve. They help travelers from their home country. They issue papers that allow people to come to their home country. In all these ways, diplomats help the countries of the world get along.

Skill Look at the title, headings, and some of the language. Is the author writing to persuade, inform, entertain, or express?

Strategy Pause after this first paragraph to check your understanding. Do you need to read more slowly? More quickly?

Strategy Check your understanding of the author's purpose. Has your understanding changed?

Skill Do you think the author achieved her purpose? Why or why not?

diplomat

representatives

visa

issue

refugees

agreement

superiors

cable

Vocabulary Strategy
for Unfamiliar Words

Dictionary/Glossary Sometimes the sentences around an unfamiliar word don't have context clues to help you find its meaning. Then you should look up the word in a dictionary or glossary. Follow these steps.

1. Look to see whether the book has a glossary. If not, then use a dictionary.

2. Find the word entry. If the pronunciation is given, read it aloud. You may recognize the word when you hear yourself say it.

3. Look over all the meanings listed in the entry. Try each meaning in the sentence with the unfamiliar word.

4. Choose the meaning that makes sense in your sentence.

As you read "Foreign Service," follow the steps above to help you find the meanings of unfamiliar words.

FOREIGN SERVICE

A U.S. diplomat works for the United States government in another country, the host country. He or she must be able to talk to the people of this country in their own language. Diplomats must know this language well. Imagine all the time diplomats would waste if they had to wait for everyone's words to be translated.

As representatives of the United States, diplomats have important duties. They may have to help Americans who want to travel to the host country or who are already there. For example, if visitors need a visa to enter the country, government officials may make certain demands before they issue this paper. In that case, a diplomat could help clear up any problems.

Refugees from the host country may want to live in the United States. Generally, there is an agreement between the two countries about refugees. This agreement outlines what the diplomat can and cannot do to help. If there is a question, the diplomat will call his or her superiors back in the United States for advice. Years ago, this meant sending a wire, or cable. Getting an answer could take hours, or even days. Today, a cell phone means instant contact.

Write

Look at the pictures in *Passage to Freedom*. Choose one to describe in words. Use as many words from the Words to Know list as you can.

PASSAGE TO FREEDOM

The Sugihara Story

by Ken Mochizuki   illustrated by Dom Lee

Afterword by Hiroki Sugihara

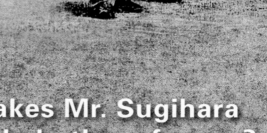

What makes Mr. Sugihara decide to help the refugees?

167

THERE IS A SAYING THAT THE EYES TELL EVERYTHING ABOUT A PERSON.

At a store, my father saw a young Jewish boy who didn't have enough money to buy what he wanted. So my father gave the boy some of his. That boy looked into my father's eyes and, to thank him, invited my father to his home.

That is when my family and I went to a Hanukkah celebration for the first time. I was five years old.

In 1940, my father was a diplomat, representing the country of Japan. Our family lived in a small town in the small country called Lithuania. There was my father and mother, my Auntie Setsuko, my younger brother Chiaki, and my three-month-old baby brother, Haruki. My father worked in his office downstairs.

In the mornings, birds sang in the trees. We played with girls and boys from the neighborhood at a huge park near our home. Houses and churches around us were hundreds of years old. In our room, Chiaki and I played with toy German soldiers, tanks, and planes. Little did we know that the real soldiers were coming our way.

Then one early morning in late July, my life changed forever.

My mother and Auntie Setsuko woke Chiaki and me up, telling us to get dressed quickly. My father ran upstairs from his office.

"There are a lot of people outside," my mother said. "We don't know what is going to happen."

In the living room, my parents told my brother and me not to let anybody see us looking through the window. So, I parted the curtains a tiny bit. Outside, I saw hundreds of people crowded around the gate in front of our house.

The grown-ups shouted in Polish, a language I did not understand. Then I saw the children. They stared at our house through the iron bars of the gate. Some of them were my age. Like the grown-ups, their eyes were red from not having slept for days. They wore heavy winter coats—some wore more than one coat, even though it was warm outside. These children looked as though they had dressed in a hurry. But if they came from somewhere else, where were their suitcases?

"What do they want?" I asked my mother.

"They have come to ask for your father's help," she replied. "Unless we help, they may be killed or taken away by some bad men."

Some of the children held on tightly to the hands of their fathers, some clung to their mothers. One little girl sat on the ground crying.

I felt like crying too. "Father," I said, "please help them."

My father stood quietly next to me, but I knew he saw the children. Then some of the men in the crowd began climbing over the fence, Borislav and Gudje, two young men who worked for my father, tried to keep the crowd calm.

My father walked outside. Peering through the curtains, I saw him standing on the steps. Borislav translated what my father said: He asked the crowd to choose five people to come inside and talk.

My father met downstairs with the five men. My father could speak Japanese, Chinese, Russian, German, French, and English. At this meeting, everyone spoke Russian.

I couldn't help but stare out the window and watch the crowd, while downstairs, for two hours, my father listened to frightening stories. These people were refugees—people who ran away from their homes because, if they stayed, they would be killed. They were Jews from Poland, escaping from the Nazi soldiers who had taken over their country.

The five men had heard my father could give them visas—official written permission to travel through another country. The hundreds of Jewish refugees outside hoped to travel east through the Soviet Union and end up in Japan. Once in Japan, they could go to another country. Was it true? the men asked. Could my father give them visas? If he did not, the Nazis would soon catch up with them.

My father answered that he could issue a few, but not hundreds. To do that, he would have to ask for permission from his government in Japan.

That night, the crowd stayed outside our house. Exhausted from the day's excitement, I slept soundly. But it was one of the worst nights of my father's life. He had to make a decision. If he helped these people, would he put our family in danger? If the Nazis found out, what would they do?

But if he did not help these people, they could all die.

My mother listened to the bed squeak as my father tossed and turned all night.

The next day, my father said he was going to ask his government about the visas. My mother agreed it was the right thing to do. My father sent his message by cable. Gudje took my father's written message down to the telegraph office.

I watched the crowd as they waited for the Japanese government's reply. The five representatives came into our house several times that day to ask if an answer had been received. Any time the gate opened, the crowd tried to charge inside.

Finally, the answer came from the Japanese government. It was "no." My father could not issue that many visas to Japan. For the next two days, he thought about what to do.

Hundreds more Jewish refugees joined the crowd. My father sent a second message to his government, and again the answer was "no." We still couldn't go outside. My little brother Haruki cried often because we were running out of milk.

I grew tired of staying indoors. I asked my father constantly, "Why are these people here? What do they want? Why do they have to be here? Who are they?"

My father always took the time to explain everything to me. He said the refugees needed his help, that they needed permission from him to go to another part of the world where they would be safe.

"I cannot help these people yet," he calmly told me. "But when the time comes, I will help them all that I can."

My father cabled his superiors yet a third time, and I knew the answer by the look in his eyes. That night, he said to my mother, "I have to do something. I may have to disobey my government, but if I don't, I will be disobeying my conscience."

The next morning, he brought the family together and asked what he should do. This was the first time he ever asked all of us to help him with anything.

My mother and Auntie Setsuko had already made up their minds. They said we had to think about the people outside before we thought about ourselves. And that is what my parents had always told me—that I must think as if I were in someone else's place. If I were one of those children out there, what would I want someone to do for me?

I said to my father, "If we don't help them, won't they die?"

With the entire family in agreement, I could tell a huge weight was lifted off my father's shoulders. His voice was firm as he told us, "I will start helping these people."

Outside, the crowd went quiet as my father spoke, with Borislav translating.

"I will issue visas to each and every one of you to the last. So, please wait patiently."

The crowd stood frozen for a second. Then the refugees burst into cheers. Grown-ups embraced each other, and some reached to the sky. Fathers and mothers hugged their children. I was especially glad for the children.

My father opened the garage door and the crowd tried to rush in. To keep order, Borislav handed out cards with numbers. My father wrote out each visa by hand. After he finished each one, he looked into the eyes of the person receiving the visa and said, "Good luck."

Refugees camped out at our favorite park, waiting to see my father. I was finally able to go outside.

Chiaki and I played with the other children in our toy car. They pushed as we rode, and they rode as we pushed. We chased each other around the big trees. We did not speak the same language, but that didn't stop us.

For about a month, there was always a line leading to the garage. Every day, from early in the morning till late at night, my father tried to write three hundred visas. He watered down the ink to make it last. Gudje and a young Jewish man helped out by stamping my father's name on the visas.

My mother offered to help write the visas, but my father insisted he be the only one, so no one else could get into trouble. So my mother watched the crowd and told my father how many were still in line.

One day, my father pressed down so hard on his fountain pen, the tip broke off. During that month, I only saw him late at night. His eyes were always red and he could hardly talk. While he slept, my mother massaged his arm, stiff and cramped from writing all day.

Soon my father grew so tired, he wanted to quit writing the visas. But my mother encouraged him to continue. "Many people are still waiting," she said. "Let's issue some more visas and save as many lives as we can."

While the Germans approached from the west, the Soviets came from the east and took over Lithuania. They ordered my father to leave. So did the Japanese government, which re-assigned him to Germany. Still, my father wrote the visas until we absolutely had to move out of our home. We stayed at a hotel for two days, where my father still wrote visas for the many refugees who followed him there.

Then it was time to leave Lithuania. Refugees who had slept at the train station crowded around my father. Some refugee men surrounded my father to protect him. He now just issued permission papers—blank pieces of paper with his signature.

As the train pulled away, refugees ran alongside. My father still handed permission papers out the window. As the train picked up speed, he threw them out to waiting hands. The people in the front of the crowd looked into my father's eyes and cried, "We will never forget you! We will see you again!"

I gazed out the train window, watching Lithuania and the crowd of refugees fade away. I wondered if we would ever see them again.

"Where are we going?" I asked my father.

"We are going to Berlin," he replied.

Chiaki and I became very excited about going to the big city. I had so many questions for my father. But he fell asleep as soon as he settled into his seat. My mother and Auntie Setsuko looked really tired too.

Back then, I did not fully understand what the three of them had done, or why it was so important.

I do now.

AFTERWORD

Each time that I think about what my father did at Kaunas, Lithuania, in 1940, my appreciation and understanding of the incident continues to grow. In fact, it makes me very emotional to realize that his deed saved thousands of lives, and that I had the opportunity to be a part of it.

I am proud that my father had the courage to do the right thing. Yet, his superiors in the Japanese government did not agree. The years after my family left Kaunas were difficult ones. We were imprisoned for eighteen months in a Soviet internment camp; and when we finally returned to Japan, my father was asked to resign from diplomatic service. After holding several different jobs, my father joined an export company, where he worked until his retirement in 1976.

My father remained concerned about the fate of the refugees, and at one point left his address at the Israeli Embassy in Japan. Finally, in the 1960s, he started hearing from "Sugihara survivors," many of whom had kept their visas, and considered the worn pieces of paper to be family treasures.

In 1969, my father was invited to Israel, where he was taken to the famous Holocaust memorial, Yad Vashem. In 1985, he was chosen to receive the "Righteous Among Nations" Award from Yad Vashem. He was the first and only Asian to have been given this great honor.

In 1992, six years after his death, a monument to my father was dedicated in his birthplace of Yaotsu, Japan, on a hill that is now known as the Hill of Humanity. In 1994, a group of Sugihara survivors traveled to Japan to rededicate the monument in a ceremony that was attended by several high officials of the Japanese government.

The story of what my father and my family experienced in 1940 is an important one for young people today. It is a story that I believe will inspire you to care for all people and to respect life. It is a story that proves that one person can make a difference.

Thank you. *Hiroki Sugihara*

Reader Response

Open for Discussion Sometimes it is hard to figure out the right thing to do. What was Mr. Sugihara's difficulty in deciding what to do? How did he make his decision? What would you have done?

1. *Passage to Freedom* is told through the eyes of a child. Find examples to show how this point of view adds to the report of events.

2. Is the purpose of the author to entertain the reader, inform the reader, or express how he felt? Find examples from pages 168–169 to justify your answer.

3. How hard did Mr. Sugihara have to work to help the refugees? Reread page 174 and discuss all the things he had to do.

4. Mr. Sugihara was a diplomat. Make a web with *diplomat* in the center. Add words from the Words to Know list and the selection that tell more about the life of a diplomat.

Test Practice

Look Back and Write Mr. Sugihara was honored for his work in several ways. Look back at page 177 to write about how he was honored.

Ken Mochizuki and Dom Lee

Ken Mochizuki

Passage to Freedom is Mr. Mochizuki's first children's nonfiction book. He approached the story as a journalist, gathering whatever information he could. He decided to tell the story from the point of view of Chiune Sugihara's son. But Hiroki Sugihara was only five years old at the time. Mr. Mochizuki says, "Having someone recall specific incidents that occurred over fifty years ago is no easy task." Fortunately Hiroki was able to remember many details.

Chiune Sugihara is one of Mr. Mochizuki's personal heroes. "He was a man willing to suffer the consequences and risk his life and career to save the lives of others."

Baseball Saved Us

Heroes

Dom Lee

Passage to Freedom is the third book Dom Lee has illustrated for Ken Mochizuki. Before Mr. Lee began working on the illustrations, he researched the time period to make sure the details he used were accurate. "When I first began my research for *Passage to Freedom,* I only knew a few facts about the Holocaust. But after visiting the Holocaust Museum at Washington D.C., I was shocked by what I saw. I will never forget the impact that museum left on me."

179

Autobiography

Genre

- An autobiography is the story of a person's life, or a single incident in it, told by that person.

- An autobiography tells about real places, people, and events in the author's life and how the author feels about them.

Text Features

- An autobiography is written from the first-person point of view, so the narrator refers to herself as *I*.

- Events in an autobiography are usually presented in chronological order.

- Scan the first few words of the paragraphs. Some begin with a phrase such as "by now" to show that time is passing.

Link to Social Studies

Read other autobiographies of people who lived in Europe during World War II. How were their experiences like Debora Biron's? How were they different?

180

I Wanted my Mother

BY DEBORA BIRON

During World War II, Debora Biron lived in Lithuania. Her family was Jewish, and the invading Germans were killing Jews. So Debora, about seven at this time, and her mother went to live with the Karashkas, a non–Jewish family who hid them on their farm. Natasha, a friend of the Karashkas, also helped. They also hid Herman, a friend of Debora's mother. Then one day the Germans began closing in.

By now the Germans were everywhere. It got so dangerous, we could no longer live upstairs and instead moved into the cellar under the kitchen. But Herman thought that wasn't safe either and decided we should build a bunker next to the cellar, where the Germans were less likely to look. He and Mr. Karashka designed the room.

It was seven feet long and very narrow. To get in and out, they made a trap door that opened into the hallway. It had wooden planks on top that matched the flooring. Underneath it was insulated with blankets and cotton so it wouldn't sound hollow when someone walked on it.

Author's Purpose   Is the author trying to inform you or entertain you?

For one week we all helped build the bunker, sleeping in the day and digging at night. Hour after hour we shoveled earth into bags which Mr. Karashka emptied onto his field. Finally the bunker was finished. It was tiny, dark, and uncomfortable. Although we each had a quilt and a wooden board to sleep on, the earthen floor was always damp, so our clothing and blankets smelled musty.

Because there was hardly any fresh air in the bunker, we kept the trap door braced open with a forked stick. At night the adults took turns being on guard to alert us if there was trouble.

Once we moved into the bunker, the Karashkas said we could go upstairs only to use the bathroom. But since they had told people I was their cousin and had an excuse for my living with the family, they said I could also go up to the kitchen to get food for myself and the others. I was proud that they trusted me. And I was happy to get away from the cramped, smelly bunker, even if only for a little while.

I hated living so tightly together with grown-ups who were irritable and constantly arguing. They fought if someone snored too loud, and they fussed over who should sleep in which bed. It got so bad, they began to tell one another to leave.

The worst was when they started talking about what they thought was happening to the Jews. That scared me. All I wanted was to lie in my mother's arms and listen to her read to me by the kerosene lamp.

Soon the Russians were bombing our area, always in the middle of the night. There was shelling in the forest next to our house. I was terrified, but I never complained. I didn't want to cause any extra problems. Besides, I thought this was what life was supposed to be like.

By then the Germans were searching for men to send to labor camps. Mr. Karashka moved into the bunker with us while Mrs. Karashka and Gruzia, the Karashkas' daughter, slept in the cellar under the kitchen to escape the bombing.

One hot summer night we all woke up to the sound of thumping on the floor above. I recognized that sound from the ghetto. It was the boots of German soldiers, and it meant something bad.

Herman, who had been on guard, heard it first and quickly started to close the trap door. With each step above, he carefully moved the forked stick a tiny bit, not wanting to grab it fast, or the door would have slammed shut. Each second the tramping upstairs came nearer. If the trap door didn't close soon the soldiers would find us.

 **Monitor & Fix Up** You may have to reread paragraphs carefully.

Suddenly the house was silent. The soldiers were standing right above us. A moment before, the trap door had closed.

"Who's down there?" a soldier shouted.

"It's only my child and me," Mrs. Karashka called from the cellar under the kitchen.

"Where is your husband?" he yelled.

"He's at the front," she said.

The soldier went downstairs and took a look for himself. None of us dared to breathe. When the soldier was satisfied with what he saw, he and the others left.

Afterward that's all we talked about. Over and over we relived what had happened. We couldn't believe we had survived to tell the story.

Now I could better understand how the Karashkas were protecting us. All along Natasha and my mother told me what wonderful people they were, and although I liked them a lot, I didn't realize until that night how they were risking their lives for us.

We stayed in the bunker for one more month. Then in August 1944 Russian troops marched through our village, and the Germans were finally gone. When it seemed safe, we crawled out of the bunker. A few days later we said good-bye to the Karashkas. After being in their house for a year, I was so happy to leave it. I wanted to get as far away from that place as possible.

Reading Across Texts

How do the Karashkas and Mr. Sugihara feel about helping people in trouble?

Writing Across Texts Make a list of reasons why a person should help someone in trouble.

 Monitor & Fix Up Where do you learn the Karashkas are risking their lives?

Skill

Compare and Contrast

- When you compare and contrast things you tell how they are alike or different.

- Sometimes clue words point out comparisons and contrasts, but not always.

- You can compare and contrast different things you read about with one another, and also with what you already know.

Similarities in Text	Differences in Text	Compared with What I Know

Strategy

Strategy: Predict

Good readers predict what will come next in a story or article. You can use the author's ideas and clue words to predict what the author will write about next. For example, if you have read an author's comparisons of things, you might predict you will next read about contrasts.

Write

1. Read "Wedding Traditions." Make a graphic organizer like the one above to compare and contrast the wedding traditions in the article.

2. Write about two wedding traditions you know of. Tell how they are similar to and different from the traditions in the article.

Wedding Traditions

Every day, all around the world, people get married. Marriage is special, so couples in different countries follow special wedding traditions.

One common tradition is to give money. In England a bride may receive a coin to put in her shoe on her wedding day. In Jordan and some other Muslim countries, the bride and her family get money or other gifts from the groom himself.

However, in many countries, the bride's family must pay money to the groom's family. This payment is called a dowry. In Greece, the dowry is often a piece of land.

Another common tradition is for the bride to wear something special for good luck. In Germany a bride may wear a gown that has been in her family for years, as well as a special wedding crown. In Ireland a bride may wear lace at the bottom of her dress, but in England, she might carry a lace handkerchief.

What about the United States? Perhaps you have heard this advice, which many brides follow: "Wear something old, something new, something borrowed, and something blue."

Strategy The word *different* can be a clue. What do you predict the author will compare and contrast?

Skill The word *common* can be a clue. Look for one similar wedding tradition in many countries described in the text. As you read, compare and contrast what you know about weddings with what you are reading.

Skill What contrast is signaled by the word *however*?

Strategy What do you predict the author will compare and contrast in this paragraph?

The Chi-lin Purse

Words to Know

traditions

behavior

sacred

benefactor

astonished

gratitude

procession

distribution

recommend

Remember

Try the strategy. Then, if you need more help, use your glossary or dictionary.

Vocabulary Strategy
for Greek and Latin Roots

Word Structure When you find a word you cannot read, see if there is a familiar root within it. Greek and Latin roots are used in many English words. For example, the Latin root *bene-* means "well" or "good." This root is used in *benefit*, *benefactor*, and *beneficial*. You can use roots to figure out the meaning of an unknown word.

1. See if you recognize a root in an unknown word. If you do, think about the words you know that also have this root.

2. See whether the root meaning of the known words gives you a clue about the meaning of the unknown word.

3. Then check to see if this meaning makes sense in the sentence.

As you read "The Meaning of Tales," look for roots in unfamiliar words to try and figure out their meaning.

The Meaning of Tales

Myths, fairy tales, and folk tales are time-honored traditions in many countries. Before people could write, they told stories to make each other laugh, cry, or shake with fear. These stories do more than just entertain. They preserve the earliest ideas and imaginings of a people. A myth may explain why something happens in nature. It may tell what causes the seasons, for example. A tale may show us the rewards for our behavior and teach us a lesson. Often, both myths and tales are tied to what people in earlier times found sacred and mysterious.

Fairy tales reach into the world of fancy. A poor girl finds a benefactor, such as a fairy godmother. A handsome prince discovers the girl and is astonished by her beauty. They fall in love. Someone evil tears them apart, and they suffer great misery. A magic being helps them defeat the evil. They feel a joyful gratitude. They celebrate their triumph in a grand procession through the kingdom.

The distribution of these stories all over the world shows how important they are to all people. Do you want to understand the nature of people? I recommend that you study tales.

Write

Write a myth or tale of your own that explains something or teaches a lesson about life. Use as many of the words from the Words to Know list as you can.

The Ch'i-lin Purse

RETOLD BY LINDA FANG

ILLUSTRATED BY ED YOUNG

Genre

Folk tales are stories or legends that are told over and over from one generation to the next. As you read, imagine that someone is sitting next to you telling you the story.

How does the story
show that one good deed
deserves another?

It is said that many years ago in China, in a small town called Teng-chou, there lived a wealthy widow, Mrs. Hsüeh. She had only one daughter, Hsüeh Hsiang-ling. Hsiang-ling was beautiful and intelligent, and her mother loved her dearly. But since everything Hsiang-ling wanted was given to her, she became rather spoiled.

When Hsiang-ling was sixteen years old, her mother decided that it was time for her to marry. Through a matchmaker, Hsiang-ling was engaged to a young man from a wealthy family in a neighboring town.

Mrs. Hsüeh wanted to prepare a dowry for Hsiang-ling that no girl in town could match. But Hsiang-ling was hard to please. Almost everything her mother bought for her was returned or exchanged at least two or three times.

When the dowry was finally complete, Mrs. Hsüeh decided to add one more item to it. It was the Ch'i-lin Purse, a red satin bag embroidered on both sides with a *ch'i-lin*, a legendary animal from ancient times. The *ch'i-lin* had scales all over its body and a single horn on its head. In the old Chinese tradition, the *ch'i-lin* is the symbol of a promising male offspring. Mrs. Hsüeh wanted to give Hsiang-ling the purse because she hoped that her daughter would give birth to a talented son.

When the purse Mrs. Hsüeh had ordered was ready, a family servant brought it home. But Hsiang-ling was not satisfied at all. "I don't like the pattern, take it back!" she said.

The servant returned to the store and ordered another. But when it was brought home, Hsiang-ling merely glanced at it and said, "The colors of the *ch'i-lin* are too dark, take it back!"

The servant went to place another order, but the new purse still did not please her. This time the servant broke down in tears.

"I won't go back again, young mistress. The people in the store laugh at me. They say I am hard to please. This is not true. You are the one who is hard to please. If you don't want this purse, I am going to leave you and work for someone else."

Although Hsiang-ling was spoiled, she was not a mean-spirited person. She somehow began to feel sorry for the old man, who had been with her family for more than forty years. So she looked at the purse and said, "All right, I will have this one. You may go and pay for it." The servant went back to the store, paid for the purse, and gave it to Mrs. Hsüeh.

Hsiang-ling's wedding fell on the eighteenth day of the sixth month according to the lunar calendar. It was the day Hsiang-ling had longed for since her engagement. She was very excited and yet a bit sad, because she knew she was leaving her mother and the home she had lived in for sixteen years.

Hsiang-ling wore a red silk dress and a red silk veil over her head. As she sat in her *hua-chiao,* a sedan chair draped with red satin, and waited to be carried to her new home, her mother came to present her with the Ch'i-lin Purse.

"My dear child," she said as she lifted up the satin curtain in front, "this is your *ta-hsi-jih-tzu,* your big, happy day. I am delighted to see you get married even though I will miss you terribly. Here is the Ch'i-lin Purse. I have put some wonderful things in it. But don't open it now. Wait until you are in your new home, and you will feel that I am with you."

Hsiang-ling was hardly listening. She was thinking about the wedding and wondering about her husband-to-be, whom she had never met. She took the purse and laid it on her lap. A few minutes later, four footmen came. Picking up the *hua-chiao*, they placed it on their shoulders, and the wedding procession began.

As the procession reached the road, it started to rain. Soon it was pouring so heavily that the footmen could not see well enough to continue. The wedding procession came to a halt, and the *hua-chiao* was carried into a pavilion that stood alongside the road.

There was another *hua-chiao* in the pavilion. It was shabby, with holes in the drapes. Hsiang-ling could hear a girl sobbing inside. This annoyed her, because she believed that a person crying on her wedding day could bring bad luck. So she told her maid to go and find out what was wrong.

"The bride is very sad," the maid said when she returned. "She is poor and has nothing to take to her new home."

Hsiang-ling couldn't help feeling sorry for the girl. Then her eyes fell on the Ch'i-lin Purse in her lap. She realized that she was lucky to have so many things, while this girl had nothing. Since she wasn't carrying any money with her, she handed the Ch'i-lin Purse to her maid. "Give this to the girl, but don't mention my name."

So the maid went over and gave the purse to the other bride. The girl stopped crying at once. Hsiang-ling had given away her mother's wedding gift without ever finding out what was inside.

A few minutes later, the rain stopped, the footmen picked up Hsiang-ling's *hua-chiao*, and the procession continued on its way. In an hour, Hsiang-ling arrived at her new home. She was happily married that evening, and to her delight she found her husband to be a wonderful and handsome young man. In a year's time, when she became the mother of a little boy, she felt she was the happiest woman in the world.

But six years later, there came a terrible flood. Hsiang-ling and her family lost their home and everything they owned. When they were fleeing their town, Hsiang-ling became separated from her husband and young son in the crowds of other townspeople. After searching for them in vain, Hsiang-ling followed a group of people to another town called Lai-chou. She had given up hope that she would ever see her husband and child again.

As Hsiang-ling sat, exhausted and alone, at the side of the road leading to Lai-chou, a woman came up to her and said, "You must be hungry. Don't you know that a *li* (one-third of a mile) down the road there is a food-distribution shack? Yüan-wai Lu has opened it to help the flood victims. Talk to his butler. I am sure you can get something to eat there."

Hsiang-ling thanked the woman, followed her directions, and found the place. A long line of people with bowls in their hands was waiting to get a ration of porridge. Hsiang-ling had never done such a thing in her life. As she stood in line holding a bowl and waiting her turn, she felt distraught enough to cry, but she forced herself to hold back the tears.

Finally, when it was her turn, Yüan-wai Lu's butler scooped the last portion of porridge into her bowl and said to the rest of the people in line, "Sorry, no more porridge left. Come back early tomorrow."

The person behind Hsiang-ling began to sob. Hsiang-ling turned around and saw a woman who reminded her of her mother, except that she was much older. Without a word, she emptied her porridge into the woman's bowl and walked away.

The butler was surprised at what Hsiang-ling had done. Just as she had made her way back to the road, he caught up with her and said, "Young lady, I don't understand. Why did you give away your porridge—are you not hungry?"

"I am hungry," said Hsiang-ling, "but I am young and I can stand hunger a bit longer."

"You are very unselfish," said the man. "I would like to help you. My master, Yüan-wai Lu, is looking for someone to take care of his little boy. If you are interested, I would be happy to recommend you."

Hsiang-ling gratefully accepted his offer and was brought to the house where Yüan-wai Lu and his wife lived.

Yüan-wai Lu, a man in his early thirties, was impressed by Hsiang-ling's graceful bearing, and he agreed to hire her. "My wife's health is very delicate and she seldom leaves her room. Your job is to take care of our son. You may play with him anywhere in the garden, but there is one place you must never go. That is the Pearl Hall, the house that stands by itself on the east side of the garden. It is a sacred place, and if you ever go in there, you will be dismissed immediately."

So Hsiang-ling began her life as a governess. The little boy in her care was very spoiled. Whenever he wanted anything, he wanted it right away, and if he didn't get it, he would cry and cry until he got it. Hsiang-ling was saddened by his behavior; it reminded her of how spoiled she had been as a child.

One day, Hsiang-ling and the little boy were in the garden. Suddenly, the ball they were playing with disappeared through the window of the Pearl Hall. The boy began to wail, "I want my ball, I want my ball! Go and get my ball."

"Young Master, I cannot go into the Pearl Hall," said Hsiang-ling. "Your father doesn't allow it. I will be dismissed if I do."

But the little boy only cried louder, and finally Hsiang-ling decided that she had no choice. She walked over to the east side of the garden and looked around. No one was in sight. She quickly walked up the steps that led to the Pearl Hall and again made sure that no one was watching. Then she opened the door and stepped in.

She found herself standing in front of an altar, where two candles and some incense sticks were burning. But in the place where people usually put the wooden name-tablets of their ancestors was a Ch'i-lin Purse! Instantly she recalled the events of her wedding day and how happy she had been. She thought of her wonderful husband and her own son and how much she missed them. She had everything then, and now she had nothing! Hsiang-ling burst into tears.

Suddenly, she felt a hand on her shoulder. When she turned around she found herself face-to-face with Mrs. Lu, her mistress, and a young maid.

"What are you doing here?" Mrs. Lu asked angrily.

"Young Master told me to come here and pick up his ball," Hsiang-ling replied.

"Then why are you weeping at the altar?"

"Because I saw the purse which once belonged to me."

Mrs. Lu looked startled. "Where are you from?" she asked, as she took the purse from the altar and sat down on a chair that leaned against a long table. There was a tremble in her voice.

"I am from Teng-chou."

"Bring her a stool," said Mrs. Lu, motioning to her maid. Not wanting to wait on another servant, the maid grudgingly brought a stool and put it to Mrs. Lu's right. "You may sit down," said Mrs. Lu. Somewhat confused, Hsiang-ling sat down.

"What was your maiden name?"

"Hsüeh Hsiang-ling."

"When were you married?"

"On the eighteenth day of the sixth moon, six years ago."

"Bring her a chair and put it to my left," Mrs. Lu ordered the maid. Hsiang-ling was told to move to the chair. She was surprised to see herself treated as a guest of honor.

"Tell me how you lost the purse," said Mrs. Lu.

"It was a gift from my mother. My wedding procession was stopped on the road because of a storm, and my *hua-chiao* was carried into a pavilion. There was another *hua-chiao* in it, and the bride was crying."

"Move her chair to the middle and move mine to the right side," ordered Mrs. Lu. The chairs were switched, and once again Hsiang-ling was told to sit down. She was astonished to find herself sitting in the middle seat—the place of the highest honor.

"Please continue," said Mrs. Lu.

"I gave the bride my purse. I never saw it again, and I have no idea how it got here."

Mrs. Lu dropped to her knees in front of Hsiang-ling and cried, "You are my benefactor! All these years I have been praying here for your well-being. When I got to my new home, I opened the purse and found it full of valuables, including this." She opened the purse and took out a piece of jade. "My husband and I were able to pawn it for a large sum of money. Using the money, we started a business and have now become very wealthy. So I reclaimed the jade and have kept it here in the purse since. We also built the Pearl Hall to house the purse and to honor you.

"I knew that you lived in the Teng-chou area, so when I heard about the flood I prayed day and night in that direction, begging Buddha to protect you from harm. I was hoping that one day I would find you and show you my gratitude. And here you are, taking care of my son! I know what we must do. We shall divide our property and give you half of it. That will make us all very happy."

Hsiang-ling was speechless as Mrs. Lu placed the purse in her hands. That same day, Yüan-wai Lu sent out servants in all directions to look for Hsiang-ling's husband and son. Soon they were found, in a village not far from Teng-chou.

A great friendship developed between the two families. Later, whenever Hsiang-ling told people about her purse, she would always end the tale by saying, "If you have a chance to do something good, be sure to do it. Happiness will come back to you."

Reader Response

Open for Discussion Tell about all the changes that happen in this story. Don't forget the changes in Hsiang-ling herself.

1. In ancient times, someone told or wrote or painted this story. Then it was handed down for generations. Why? What do you find in "The Ch'i-lin Purse" to explain its long life?

2. Look back at pages 194–195 and 202–203. Compare and contrast what the two women did for one another and why they did it.

3. Find clues on page 197 that lead you to predict that Hsiang-ling's life is going to get better.

4. This story is called an ancient Chinese story. What traditions of ancient China did you read about? Make a list, using some of the Words to Know list words and words from the story.

Look Back and Write Early in the story there is a clue that Hsiang-ling is not as selfish as she seems. Look back at page 193 to find that clue. Write what the clue is and why it is important.

Test Practice

Read more stories about China in these books.

As a ten-year-old girl living in Shanghai, China, Linda Fang was too shy to speak up in class. So one day her teacher handed her a picture book, told her to read it that night, and said, "Come back tomorrow and see if you can tell it to me." The teacher's goal was to help her student overcome her shyness.

The teacher's plan must have worked, because today Ms. Fang is a professional storyteller and the winner of the 1998 Storyteller of the Year Award.

She credits the start of her professional career, however, to good luck. She was working for a television station in Washington, D.C., in 1987. "They had a storytelling show. I saw that they didn't have Chinese stories, so I sent them one." The station liked the story, but they didn't have the right person to tell it. "They tried me on camera and thought I did well."

Fang first heard "The Ch'i-lin Purse" from her mother. As a little girl, she was fascinated that you could do something that might change someone's life without your ever knowing it.

Fa Mulan
by Robert D. San Souci

Da Wei's Treasure: A Chinese Tale
by Margaret and Raymond Chang

205

Fable

Genre

- A fable is a brief story that states a moral or lesson at the end. The action in the story shows the moral in action.

- Many fables have been passed by word of mouth from generation to generation until someone has written them down.

- Characters in fables are often animals.

- Animals in fables usually talk and behave like humans.

Link to Writing

Read other fables and make a list of the morals from each one. In your own words, write what each moral means.

The Lion and the Mouse

BY AESOP

A lion was sleeping in his lair one hot afternoon when a mouse ran over his nose and woke him up. The lion snarled and was just about to crush the mouse with his huge paw when:

"Oh spare me, my lord," cried the mouse. "I am really not worth killing. I mean you no harm—and I don't even taste nice."

The lion snarled sleepily.

"Besides," the mouse squeaked, "perhaps I can do something for you one day if you spare me now."

The lion gave a great roar of laughter, but he lifted his paw, and the mouse skipped out of reach. Still laughing, the lion sank back to his dreams.

Not long after, the lion was hunting in the woods when he fell into a trap. Some hunters had stretched a trip rope across one of his favorite paths. They had suspended a huge net above the path and had fixed it so that when the lion fell over the rope, the net would fall down and cover him, holding him prisoner until morning.

The lion twisted and turned and scratched and bit, but the more he struggled the more tightly he seemed to be held in the net. Soon he could not move at all. With no hope of escape, he began to roar, and his mighty voice echoed through every corner of the forest.

Now it happened that the mouse was also out hunting that night. Of course he quickly recognized the lion's voice, and he ran as fast as he could to the spot. He saw at a glance what the situation was and pausing only to say "Don't worry, sir, I'll have you out in no time," and "Keep still, sir, please," he began to gnaw and nibble the thick cords of the net. In a very short time the lion's front paws were free; then his head and mane; then his back legs and finally his tail.

The little mouse had done something for the great lion, just as he had promised.

In fact, he had saved his life.

Do not judge people's abilities by their appearance.

Reading Across Texts

How are the actions of the main characters in "The Ch'i-lin Purse" and "The Lion and the Mouse" alike?

Writing Across Texts Make a list of how the characters' actions are alike.

 Predict   Do the illustrations help you predict what will happen?

Fact and Opinion

- A statement of fact can be proved true or false. A statement of opinion tells what someone thinks or feels.

- Statements of opinion often contain words that make judgments, such as *interesting* or *beautiful*.

- A single sentence might contain both a statement of fact and a statement of opinion.

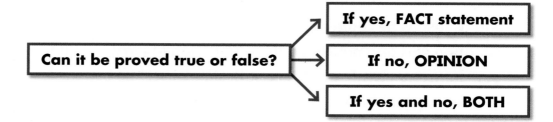

	If yes, FACT statement
Can it be proved true or false? →	**If no, OPINION**
	If yes and no, BOTH

Strategy: Ask Questions

Good readers ask themselves questions. As you read statements, ask yourself, "Is this a statement of fact? If so, how do I know whether it's true or false? Or is it a statement of opinion? Is the author trying to convince me of something?"

1. Make a graphic organizer like the one above. As you read "Chimps," write three sentences in the correct boxes: a statement of fact, a statement of opinion, and one with both.

2. Using a graphic organizer, find another statement of opinion. Write about why it is a statement of opinion, whether or not you agree with it, and why.

Chimps

Chimpanzees, or "chimps" for short, are amazing animals. They look and act in ways that sometimes remind us of ourselves.

Chimpanzees are hairy animals. Long dark hair covers most of their bodies, except their faces, which are bald. They grow to be from 3 to 5.5 feet tall and can weigh as much as 130 pounds. Chimpanzees have long arms and large ears, and they can make the funniest faces you've ever seen.

Chimpanzees spend time on the ground but are often in trees. It must be fun to swing from branch to branch the way they do. They also like to eat and sleep in trees, building nests from branches and leaves.

Chimpanzees are social animals. They live in groups. Chimps regularly groom each other's fur. They communicate using facial expressions, gestures, screams, hoots, and even roars.

Unfortunately, many chimpanzees are dying because people hunt them or destroy the forests where they live. It is important for us to learn as much as we can about these fascinating animals. We must make sure this endangered species does not become extinct.

Skill A word in this first sentence gives a clue about whether it is a statement of fact or opinion.

Strategy Here's a good place to ask yourself, "Which sentences in this paragraph contain facts? Which contain opinions?"

Skill Remember that a sentence can contain both a statement of fact and of opinion. One sentence in this paragraph has both.

Strategy What questions could you ask yourself about the statements in this paragraph to help you decide whether they are facts or opinions?

environment

contribute

conservation

enthusiastic

investigation

Remember

Try the strategy. Then, if you need more help, use your glossary or dictionary.

Vocabulary Strategy
for Unfamiliar Words

Context Clues As you read, you will find unfamiliar words. See if you can use context to figure out the meaning of a new word. *Context* means the words and sentences near the unfamiliar word.

1. Reread the sentence with the unfamiliar word. The author may include a synonym or other context clue to the word's meaning.

2. If you need more help, read the surrounding sentences. You may spot examples or explanations that give you clues to the word's meaning.

3. Add up the clues and decide on the meaning of the word.

4. Check to see that this meaning makes sense in the sentence.

As you read "Young People Helping the Environment," look for context clues to help you figure out the meanings of unfamiliar words.

YOUNG PEOPLE
Helping the Environment

This well-known line first appeared in a comic strip called *Pogo:* "We have met the enemy and he is us." Let's face it. When it comes to the environment, people are the enemy! Pollution has become a problem that worries people all over the world. Plants and animals do not contribute to the problem in any way. A migrating bird is not like a vacationing family. Birds do not send exhaust into the air or throw out bags full of trash. A growing number of people understand that conservation is necessary. We must protect our air, water, soil, plants, and animals.

We have no other home but Earth, so we had better make it last. Once young people understand this, they become enthusiastic about cleaning up. They will work long, hard, and cheerfully to help. They begin all sorts of projects, such as recycling paper and picking up trash. They may call attention to a problem so that a news station begins an investigation.

Young people like action. They like the feeling of accomplishing something good. The successes of young people can be inspirational. If you inspire adults to act in favor of the environment, think how much help the Earth can get.

Write

Be a reporter. Write a news story about a group of young people who are helping the environment. Use the photos on pages 212 to 223 for ideas. Use as many words from the Words to Know list as you can.

from
National Geographic for Kids

Jane Goodall's

10 Ways to Help Save Wildlife

by Jane Goodall

How does Jane
Goodall feel about
wild animals?

Chimpanzees are our closest living relatives. I have been lucky enough to spend most of my life studying these fascinating creatures. Now I travel the world teaching about wildlife conservation. Along the way, I've met thousands of caring young people who are enthusiastic about helping protect animals and who want to know what they can do to help. Here are ten suggestions:

1 Respect all life.

It's true that bees sting and sharks bite, so it's smart to be cautious. And tapeworms are simply too revolting to love. But we don't need to love a creature to respect it. And you can control your fear by learning about an animal's habits and staying out of its way. In all my years in the forest, not once did any leopard, buffalo, snake, or scorpion hurt me.

2 Think of animals as individuals.

When I first began writing reports about my "study subjects" and referred to them by name, scientists were shocked! They thought I should give chimpanzees like Flo and David Greybeard identifying numbers instead of names. But names are important; they make animals special. Once I was giving a speech and a fly flew into the room. I had just been talking about the need to respect all life. Oh, no, I thought. Somebody is going to swat that fly. So I said, "Do you see that fly who has come in through the window? I think her name is Elizabeth." And nobody swatted that fly! By naming the fly Elizabeth, I helped people see her as more than just another insect. Elizabeth had become an individual.

3 Dare to admit that humans aren't the only thinking, feeling beings on the planet.

How do I know? When I was 12 years old, I had a marvelous teacher—a small black dog named Rusty. Rusty was so intelligent that if I caught him stealing food off the table, he'd roll over on his back and act guilty. But if I scolded him for doing something he didn't realize was bad, he sulked! Rusty would go over to the wall and sit with his nose almost touching it. Even if I offered him walks or nibbles, he wouldn't budge. Only when I went down on my knees and apologized to him would Rusty stop sulking.

4 Get to know animals.

Avoid taming any creature (such as a deer) that might later be captured or shot because you've made it trust people. But if it (and you!) will be safe, try setting out food for the animal to eat. Then sit quietly a little distance away and observe. Take notes and try to imagine what the animal's life is like. You can do the same with a pet—yours or someone else's.

5 Be willing to learn from animals.

Many possess mysterious powers that humans lack. I am in awe of migrating birds, butterflies, and salmon, which all manage to navigate across thousands of miles of unfamiliar territory. And I am amazed when I hear about pets like Ninja, a tomcat who traveled 850 miles to get to his old home. Soon after moving with his owners from Utah to Washington State, Ninja disappeared. He showed up again a year later—back at their old house in Utah! How did he find it?

6 Speak up for what you believe.

Caitlin Alegre, 13, of Oakland, California, hated how some cosmetic companies put guinea pigs, rabbits, and mice through misery in order to test the safety of their products. So she pinned posters to trees and handed out informational leaflets. Now 16, she writes inspirational songs for her band, the Envirochicks. Once people know which companies are humane and which are not, Caitlin feels sure that most will buy only from humane companies. Then the other companies will change their ways.

7 Use less paper, gasoline, and red meat.

These are three products that contribute to reasons the rain forest homes of many animals are being destroyed. And it's easy to conserve. Simply reusing, recycling, and using less paper means loggers will cut down fewer trees. You can even help preserve rain forests by riding bikes, walking, and eating more veggie burritos than hamburgers. Saving gas and eating less beef can help reduce the need to clear rain forest land for oil production and grazing cattle.

8 Be inspired by the work of others.

Not many of us could bear to do what 16-year-old Lisa Thomas does. There are so many stray dogs in her hometown of Johannesburg, South Africa, that the local animal shelter regularly puts some to sleep. On those difficult days, Lisa visits the shelter and spends ten minutes petting and talking to each doomed animal. That way every dog experiences at least some love in its life and dies knowing human caring.

9 Join Roots and Shoots.

This is a program I started to help young people learn about animals and nature. As of today, groups have sprung up in more than 70 countries, and they're accomplishing wonderful things. One group, in Chicago, launched an investigation when a water bottling company suggested building a new plant at the head of a stream. The group's research showed that the factory would cause serious environmental harm, so the entire project was put on hold!

10 Have hope.

Believe that what you do matters. Yes, you're only one person out of more than six billion people living on this planet. And yes, a lot of damage has been done. But just think. If you and I and everyone else who reads this takes care not to harm the environment, animals, or each other—what a difference it will make! Together we can change the world.

Reader Response

Open for Discussion If you were introducing Jane Goodall to an audience, what would you say to help prepare them to listen to her message? What would you say or do afterwards to help make the message effective?

1. Jane Goodall numbers her points and discusses each one before moving on to the next. Do you find this a useful way of organizing? When might it be most useful?

2. Look back at the section called "Respect Life" on page 214. What are some facts you see there? What are some opinions?

3. Write two test questions about this selection. What are the answers and on which pages would you find them?

4. Create a way of your own to help save wildlife or protect the environment. Plan a poster. Use words from the Words to Know list or the selection.

Look Back and Write Look at page 216 to learn Jane Goodall's reason for giving personal names to wildlife. Write her reason. Then write about whether she has convinced you to think in the same way.

Meet the Author

Jane Goodall

Read more books by Jane Goodall.

"It's quite possible that today's teenagers will raise their children in a world with no wild chimpanzees, gorillas, orangutans, and bonobos," Dr. Jane Goodall said on a lecture tour. "It's a tragic prospect, but there is still time to act."

Dr. Goodall's interest in animals began at an early age when she dreamed of living with them in Africa. As a young woman, she traveled to Olduvai Gorge. "I always remember the first time I held in my hand the bone of a creature that had walked the earth millions of years before," she has said. "I had dug it up myself. A feeling of awe crept over me. I thought, 'Once this creature stood here. It was alive, had flesh and hair. It had its own smell. It could feel hunger and thirst and pain. It could enjoy the morning sun.'"

Dr. Goodall lived at the Gombe Game Reserve in Tanzania for many years. She spent her days following chimpanzees through the forest to record their habits. Her research gave the world a wealth of knowledge about chimpanzees.

Today, Dr. Goodall travels around the world speaking about the need to protect animals and the environment.

With Love: Ten Heartwarming Stories of Chimpanzees in the Wild

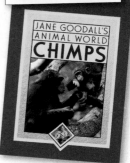

Jane Goodall's Animal World: Chimps

Expository Nonfiction

Genre

- Expository nonfiction gives you facts and, sometimes, opinions about real-life people, places, and things.

- Some expository non-fiction focuses on a single topic about those people, places, and things.

Text Features

- Sometimes the title gives the reader a hint about the topic of the selection. Here the title states the topic directly.

- Pictures show what the selection is about.

- Read the first paragraph. Notice the questions the selection will answer.

Link to Science

Choose one of the animals in the selection and research more about it. Then write an explanation telling a small child why he or she should not be afraid of that animal.

from Sandiegozoo.org

Why Some Animals Are Considered BAD or SCARY

illustrated by John Manders

You've heard the stories and seen the movies. Wolves gather in the woods to attack helpless people, especially girls (remember Little Red Riding Hood?). Bats with huge fangs seek you out to suck your blood. Snakes deliberately find people to attack. Toads give you warts. Actually, none of these things are true. So why do humans have so many fears and superstitions about certain animals? Why do people think some animals are evil?

Most of the time it's because of ignorance, not knowing the facts about an animal or not understanding what its behavior is for. Humans tend to fear what they don't know or understand. So if someone sees a vampire bat sucking a cow's blood, he might assume that all bats do that, and that they will do it to anything they can. Stories are made up and rumors start, and the next thing you know, people believe that all bats attack deliberately and suck blood. But this isn't based on fact. There are thousands of bat species, and most of them eat fruit or insects and are very important to the environment. Only a few bats suck blood—they are small and not aggressive, and they hang around livestock and nip at their heels to get blood. They don't ravenously attack, and they are just an annoyance to the cows and horses— they don't kill them.

Ask Questions What additional questions are you asking yourself?

Sometimes people's fears about animals are based on instinctive reactions from a long time ago. Thousands of years ago when humans didn't have houses and roads and cars, they did have reason to be frightened of some animals, especially big carnivores, because people could be hunted for dinner just like other prey animals. That's why the roar of a lion, the snarl of a jaguar, or the howl of wolves can send chills up our spines—instinctively, we remember when we were prey. And we still can be frightened—a tiger or a killer whale could certainly decide to eat you if it wanted to. But that's where knowledge comes in. If you researched the animal's behavior, you'd find out it probably wouldn't want to eat you. Humans are not a "natural" prey source for any of the top carnivores. They have many other regular sources of food that they'd rather eat. If they can't find their regular food and they are starving, or if a human intrudes upon them and makes them defensive, they will kill people, but it's not a common occurrence.

Some people believe that animals think the same way some people do, and that they are deliberately trying to hurt us or hunt us down—that they have evil intentions. That just isn't the case. Animals behave the way they do to survive. If a carnivore is hungry, it will kill something—but not because it is "evil," just because it will die if it doesn't eat. Venomous snakes don't hunt people down to bite them just because they feel like it—they only strike in order to defend themselves. Animals are wonderfully adapted to look and act the way they need to in order to live in their habitat and circumstances. They're just being themselves and going about their business. It's up to us to learn about them and understand them, rather than just thinking they are "bad."

So the next time you hear something strange about an animal, such as bats who zero in on you to get tangled in your hair, or hyenas who eat young children for fun, don't assume it's true. Do some research and find out what that animal is really like!

Reading Across Texts

Look over Jane Goodall's 10 points. What is another point that could be added to that list, based on "Why Some Animals Are Considered Bad or Scary"?

Writing Across Texts Write your point #11 and explain it.

 Fact & Opinion | How can you tell the author's opinions?

Comprehension

Skill
Sequence

Strategy
Graphic Organizers

Sequence

- The sequence of events is the order in which they take place, from first to last.

- Clue words such as *first*, *next*, and *then* may show sequence in a story or article, but not always. Other clues are dates and time of day.

- Two events can happen at the same time. *While* and *at the same time* are clue words.

Strategy: Graphic Organizers

Active readers often create graphic organizers to help them understand and remember what they read. A time line like the one below can help you keep track of the sequence of events.

Date .... **Date**

| First Event | Second Event | Third Event | Final Event |

1. Read "Before the Midnight Ride." Make a graphic organizer like the one above to show the sequence of events in the article.

2. Jot down three questions about the sequence of events. Look for answers in the article and do library research. Write your questions and answers.

Before the Midnight Ride

Paul Revere was born in December of 1734 in Boston, Massachusetts. He went to school at the North Writing School. His childhood was much like that of other boys at the time.

Skill What should be the first event on a time line about Paul Revere?

When Paul was a teenager, he was paid to ring the bells at a church. At the same time, his father was teaching him to work with silver. Paul was a silversmith until he joined the army in 1756. After his army service, Paul married Sarah Orne and returned to silverworking. He became one of the best-known silversmiths in America.

Strategy Here's a good spot to ask yourself: "What two things were going on in Paul's life when he was a teenager?"

In the 1760s and 1770s, trouble arose between the American colonies and England, and Paul became involved. He joined a group called the Sons of Liberty. They believed that the colonies should be free from England. In December of 1773 he helped throw tea into the harbor because the tea was taxed by England. This protest became known as the Boston Tea Party.

Skill Dates in this paragraph are clues to events you can put on your time line.

After that, Paul Revere became an express rider for the Massachusetts government. He rode a horse to bring news from Boston to the other colonies. He was at this job on that day in 1775, when his most famous ride took place.

Strategy Ask yourself: "What were all the important events in Paul Revere's life? Which events were happening at the same time as others?"

Words to Know

somber

fate

steed

fearless

magnified

glimmer

lingers

Try the strategy. Then, if you need more help, use your glossary or dictionary.

Vocabulary Strategy
for Endings

Word Structure The endings *-s, -ed,* and *-ing* may be added to verbs to change the tense, person, or usage of the verbs. You can use these endings to help you figure out the meanings of unfamiliar verbs.

1. Cover the ending and read the base form of the word.

2. Reread the sentence and make sure the word is a verb, that it shows action. (Nouns can also end in *-s.*)

3. Now look in the sentence for clues about what the word may mean.

4. See if your meaning makes sense in the sentence.

As you read "War Heroes in Stone," look for verbs that end with *-s, -ed, or -ing.* Think about the endings and the way the words are used to help you figure out their meanings.

War Heroes in Stone

Monuments to war heroes have a noble feeling. Artists who make statues to honor the war dead seem to understand their job. Soldiers who died in battle gave their lives for country and freedom. The somber job of the artist is to honor these heroes. Artists also want us to feel proud of what these heroes did. The artists' work is one way of giving thanks to those who met their fate on the field of battle.

Often the statue shows a general sitting on his steed, sword raised overhead. The marble forms are beautiful, powerful, and larger than life. In addition, the statue sits high on a pedestal so that visitors must look up. Both horse and man are a study in fearless forward motion. In this way, their bravery and patriotism are magnified and set in stone.

Have you ever seen such a statue at night? Imagine the white stone looming in the dark. Then a glimmer of moonlight brings it to life. The effect is strange to see. You feel you can almost hear the tread of troops marching down a dusty road. The distant sound of marching lingers in the air. You send a silent word of thanks to those who fought to keep your country free.

Choose one of the illustrations from the next selection. Write a paragraph describing it. Use as many words from the Words to Know list as you can.

How does Paul Revere
feel during his ride?

A **poem** is a composition arranged in lines. Some poems have rhyme, some have rhythm, and some have both. As you read this narrative poem—a long poem that tells a story—notice the rhyme and rhythm.

234

THE MIDNIGHT RIDE OF
PAUL REVERE

by

Henry
Wadsworth
Longfellow

graved and painted by

Christopher Bing

LISTEN, MY CHILDREN,
AND YOU SHALL HEAR

Of the midnight ride of Paul Revere,
On the eighteenth of April, in Seventy-Five,
Hardly a man is now alive
Who remembers that famous day and year.

He said to his friend, "If the British march
By land or sea from the town tonight,
Hang a lantern aloft in the belfry arch
Of the North Church tower as a signal light—
One, if by land, and two, if by sea;
And I on the opposite shore will be,
Ready to ride and spread the alarm
Through every Middlesex village and farm,
For the country folk to be up and to arm."

Then he said, "Good night!"
    and with muffled oar
Silently rowed to the Charlestown shore,
Just as the moon rose over the bay,
Where swinging wide at her moorings lay
The *Somerset*, British man-of-war;
A phantom ship, with each mast and spar
Across the moon like a prison bar,
And a huge black hulk, that was magnified
By its own reflection in the tide.

Meanwhile, his friend, through alley and street,
Wanders and watches, with eager ears,
Till in the silence around him he hears
The muster of men at the barrack door,
The sound of arms, and the tramp of feet,
And the measured tread of the grenadiers,
Marching down to their boats on the shore.

Then he climbed the tower
   of the Old North Church,
By the wooden stairs, with stealthy tread,
To the belfry-chamber overhead,
And startled the pigeons from their perch
On the somber rafters, that round him made
Masses and moving shapes of shade—
By the trembling ladder, steep and tall,
To the highest window in the wall,
Where he paused to listen and look down
A moment on the roofs of the town,
And the moonlight flowing over all.

Beneath the churchyard, lay the dead,
In the night-encampment on the hill,
Wrapped in silence so deep and still
That he could hear, like a sentinel's tread,
The watchful night-wind, as it went
Creeping along from tent to tent,
And seeming to whisper, "All is well!"
A moment only he feels the spell
Of the place and the hour, the secret dread
Of the lonely belfry and the dead;
For suddenly all his thoughts are bent
On a shadowy something far away,

Where the river widens to meet the bay—
A line of black that bends and floats
On the rising tide, like a bridge of boats.

Meanwhile, impatient to mount and ride,
Booted and spurred, with a heavy stride
On the opposite shore walked Paul Revere.
Now he patted his horse's side,
Now gazed on the landscape far and near,
Then, impetuous, stamped the earth,
And turned and tightened his saddle girth;
But mostly he watched with eager search
The belfry tower of the Old North Church,
As it rose above the graves on the hill,
Lonely and spectral and somber and still.

And lo! as he looks, on the belfry's height
A glimmer, and then a gleam of light!
He springs to the saddle, the bridle he turns,
But lingers and gazes, till full on his sight
A second lamp in the belfry burns!

A hurry of hoofs in a village street,
A shape in the moonlight, a bulk in the dark,
And beneath, from the pebbles,
    in passing, a spark
Struck out by a steed flying fearless and fleet:
That was all! And yet,
    through the gloom and the light,
The fate of a nation was riding that night;
And the spark struck out
    by that steed, in his flight,
Kindled the land into flame with its heat.

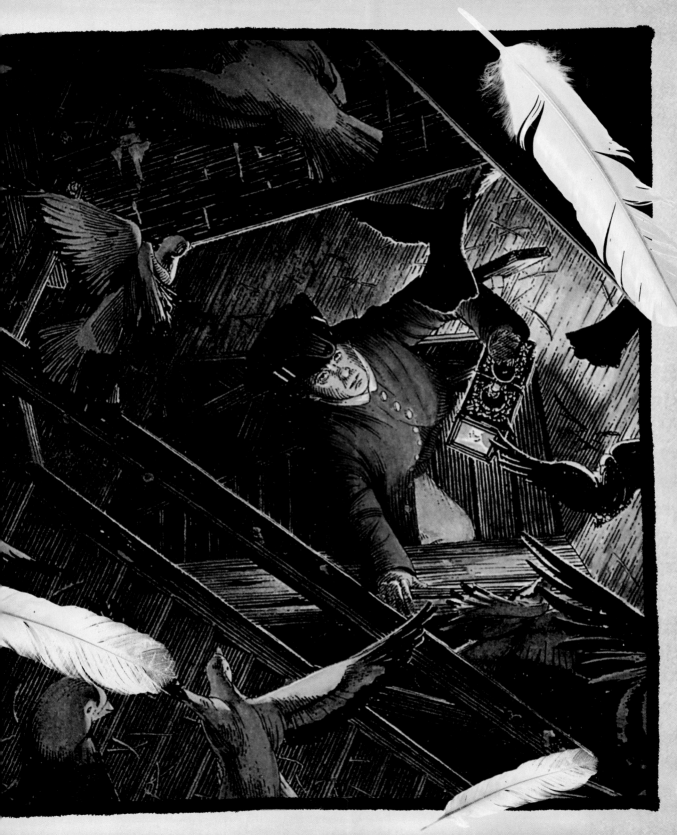

He has left the village and mounted the steep,
And beneath him, tranquil and broad and deep,
Is the Mystic, meeting the ocean tides;
And under the alders that skirt its edge,
Now soft on the sand, now loud on the ledge,
Is heard the tramp of his steed as he rides.

It was twelve by the village clock,
When he crossed the bridge
    into Medford town.
He heard the crowing of the cock,
And the barking of the farmer's dog,
And felt the damp of the river fog,
That rises after the sun goes down.

It was one by the village clock,
When he galloped into Lexington.
He saw the gilded weathercock
Swim in the moonlight as he passed,
And the meeting-house windows,
  blank and bare,
Gaze at him with a spectral glare,
As if they already stood aghast
At the bloody work they would look upon.

It was two by the village clock,
When he came to the bridge in Concord town.
He heard the bleating of the flock,
And the twitter of birds among the trees,
And felt the breath of the morning breeze
Blowing over the meadows brown.
And one was safe and asleep in his bed
Who at the bridge would be first to fall,
Who that day would be lying dead,
Pierced by a British musket-ball.

You know the rest. In the books you have read
How the British Regulars fired and fled—
How the farmers gave them ball for ball,
From behind each fence and farmyard wall,
Chasing the red-coats down the lane,
Then crossing the fields to emerge again
Under the trees at the turn of the road
And only pausing to fire and load.

So through the night rode Paul Revere,
And so through the night went his cry of alarm
To every Middlesex village and farm—
A cry of defiance and not of fear,
A voice in the darkness, a knock at the door,
And a word that shall echo for evermore!
For, borne on the night-wind of the Past,
Through all our history, to the last,
In the hour of darkness and peril and need,
The people will waken and listen to hear
The hurrying hoof-beats of that steed,
And the midnight message of Paul Revere.

Reader Response

Open for Discussion What if *The Midnight Ride of Paul Revere* were a movie? Imagine that you saw it. Tell about it, scene by scene, to your best friend. Remember, this is a spy movie with a stealthy, fast ride.

1. Read your favorite stanza aloud. Get the gallop into the rhythm as you read. Make the spoken words reveal the scene. Report your results.

2. Find clue words and phrases in the poem that signal the sequence of events. Make a list.

3. What makes the ride a dangerous one? Make a graphic organizer, a web with the word *danger* in the center, to answer the question.

4. Longfellow's descriptions help us see and hear this historic ride. What do *somber* and *fearless* describe? Find other examples of adjectives the poet uses to describe things.

Look Back and Write Who is the audience for this poem? Look back at the first stanza for clues. Based on those clues, who seems to be the speaker of the poem? Write your answers to these questions.

Henry Wadsworth Longfellow became the most popular poet of his day. Longfellow was one of the first American poets to write about people, traditions, and events with American themes.

Longfellow climbed the steps of the Old North Church and visited an inn in New England. These experiences probably inspired him to write *The Midnight Ride of Paul Revere.*

Chistopher Bing has said, "When people pick up one of my books, I want them to become absorbed into the work and feel like they are experiencing the time and the period of the event that they're looking at or reading about." He uses maps and re-created documents to make characters and settings come alive.

In the illustrations for *The Midnight Ride of Paul Revere*, Mr. Bing used a pen, ink, and a brush on white scratchboard to create the look of an old book. Mr. Bing has contributed editorial and political cartoons to the *New York Times*, *Washington Post*, and other newspapers. His illustrations for *Casey at the Bat* won a Caldecott Honor Book award.

Casey at the Bat: A Ballad of the Republic Sung in the Year 1888
by Ernest L. Thayer, illustrated by Christopher Bing

Paul Revere's Ride by Henry Wadsworth Longfellow, illustrated by Ted Rand

249

Revolutionary War Women

Web Site

Genre

- Web pages are found on Internet Web sites.

- A Web page contains information about a topic or topics.

Text Features

- Often this information is broken down into subtopics. Each subtopic is a link.

- The links on this page are in blue and underlined. When you click on a link, you move to another page.

Link to Social Studies

Do research to find out more about women in the Revolutionary War. Share what you find with the class.

Let's say you want to learn about women in the Revolutionary War. You find this page at a Web site created by a fifth-grade social studies class:

250

Take It to the NET
ONLINE
more activities sfsuccessnet.com

WOMEN IN THE REVOLUTION

Men alone did not win the American Revolution. Women helped make life easier for soldiers, and some of them even fought on the front lines. Many women stayed with their husbands during the American Revolution. Some women even brought their children.

We had fun researching women of this time period. We hope you enjoy our reports and illustrations.

- <u>Deborah Sampson</u>
- <u>Betsy Ross</u>
- <u>Phillis Wheatley</u>
- <u>Nancy Morgan Hart</u>
- <u>Molly Pitcher</u>
- <u>Abigail Adams</u>

You click your mouse on the link for <u>Deborah Sampson</u>, and a new page pops up on your computer screen:

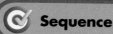 **Sequence** What steps has the writer taken so far?

<u>Deborah Sampson</u> By Michael Z.

Deborah Sampson was born in Plypton, Massachusetts. She was born on December 17, 1760. She died in 1827. She read a copy of Tom Paine's *Common Sense*, and decided to make herself some men's clothing and disguise herself as a man and fight in the Revolutionary War as a soldier. She went to Medway, Massachusetts, and enlisted in the army as Robert Shirtliff.

It is not certain how long Deborah served in the army, but she was wounded twice. The first time she got a sword slash on her head during a skirmish with Loyalist soldiers near Tarrytown, New York. A few months later she was shot in the shoulder with a musket ball. It was not discovered that she was a woman when she got medical help.

Her true identity was not revealed until she got sick with yellow fever in Philadelphia. When she rejoined her troop, her doctor gave her commanding officer a letter telling them the truth. The officers were shocked, but Deborah had earned their respect. Instead of the punishment she expected, she received an honorable discharge from the army.

Reading Across Texts

Think about the two selections and what lessons you learn from reading about Paul Revere and Deborah Sampson.

Writing Across Texts Imagine that you are explaining the lessons you learned to a friend. Write down what you would say.

 **Graphic Organizers**   What organizer would best show facts about Sampson?

For Peace Sake

by Cedric McClester

For peace sake
we need to do our best.
For peace sake
let's put the hate to rest.
For peace sake
it never is too late.
For peace sake
let's rid our lives of hate.

I believe that we can
build a bridge to understand,
we're all in this together.
It never ever is too late,
together let's rid our lives of hate.
Let's do it for peace sake.

For peace sake
we need to do our best.
For peace sake
let's put love to the test.

Love is really what we need;
together we can plant the seed.
For peace sake let's work in harmony.
For peace sake,
for love and happiness,
for peace sake
and for all the rest.

I believe that we can
build a bridge to understand,
we're all in this together.
It never ever is too late,
together let's rid our lives of hate.
Let's do it, let's do it
for peace sake.

For peace sake
we can make it right.
For peace sake
it can happen overnight.

It's time to take a break
from bigotry and hate—
we have an equal place
within the human race.
Love is really what we need,
together we can plant the seed.
For peace sake let's work in harmony.

For peace sake
examine how you feel.
For peace sake
how much of it is real?
For peace sake,
if you only knew
what hate can do to you.

I believe that we can
build a bridge to understand,
we're all in this together.
It never ever is too late,
together let's rid our lives of hate.
Let's do, let's do,
for peace sake.

Two People I Want to Be Like

by Eve Merriam

That man
stuck in traffic
not pounding his fists against the steering
wheel
not trying to shift to the next lane
just
using the time
for a slow steady grin
of remembering
all the good unstuck times

and that woman
clerking in the supermarket
at rush hour
bagging bottles and cartons and boxes and
    jars and cans
punching it all out
slapping it all along
and leveling a smile
at everyone in the line.

I wish they were married to each other.

Maybe it's better they're not,
so they can pass their sweet harmony around.

Not in Vain

by Emily Dickinson

If I can stop one heart from breaking,
I shall not live in vain:
If I can ease one life the aching,
Or cool one pain,
Or help one fainting robin
Unto his nest again,
I shall not live in vain.

STRANGERS

by Janet S. Wong

Sometimes strangers talk so fast,
                           so rough,
                           so big—
you wonder if it's just a bluff.

They can make you feel so weak,
                           so small,
                           so dumb—
you wonder if they know it all.

But maybe they're the ones who need
someone to follow. Take the lead.

Ten Steps to a Better World

connect to
WRITING

In a selection in this unit, Jane Goodall identifies ten things you can do to help save wildlife. Think about what you learned from the other selections in this unit. Write a list of ten things you could do to make life better for the people who live around you.

10 things I can do to make life better for people around me.

1. Recycle
2. Mow Mrs. Lee's lawn
3.

5.
6.
7.
8.
9.
10.

What makes people want to do the right thing?

Press Conference

connect to
SOCIAL
STUDIES

Imagine that Francisco, Mr. Sugihara, Hsiang-ling, and Paul Revere had a press conference. Work with a group to stage it. The reporters will ask the four people about the events in which they chose a difficult course of action. The characters should respond by telling why they chose to do what they thought was the right thing.

Difficult Decisions

connect to
ART

Think about a real-life person who made a difficult choice in order to do the right thing. Find out more about this person. Then create a collage with drawings, poems, photographs, newspaper headlines, captions, and so on. Your collage should help viewers understand the choice the person made and the impact it had on others.

What do people gain from the work of inventors and artists?

Read It
ONLINE
sfsuccessnet.com

 # Author's Purpose

- The author's purpose is the reason or reasons an author has for writing. The purpose may change during a selection, but most selections have one main purpose.

- An author may write to persuade you, to inform you, to entertain you, or to express ideas or feelings. The kinds of ideas and the way the author states them help you see the author's purpose.

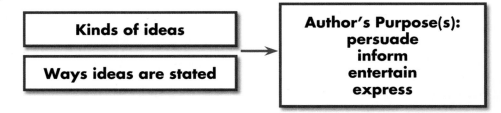

| Kinds of ideas | → | **Author's Purpose(s):** persuade inform entertain express |

| Ways ideas are stated |

Strategy: Story Structure

Active readers pay attention to story structure for clues about the author's main purpose. Generally, authors identify the problem of the main character at the start. They work through the problem as the action rises in the middle, and then solve it with the climax and outcome.

Write

1. Read "Minnie Miller, Millionaire." Use the graphic organizer above to give the author's *main* purpose for writing and two ideas from the story that support your answer.

2. Write a paragraph telling what you think the author's main purpose was for writing "Minnie Miller, Millionaire" and how the author achieved that purpose.

Minnie Miller, Millionaire

Minnie Miller was a six-year-old with a grown-up's goal. She would make herself a millionaire. How would Minnie reach this grand goal? It was August, and what did people crave when the air sweltered and sizzled? Minnie Miller would make her million selling lemonade.

Building the stand was easy. Two sawhorses and a slab of plywood from the basement did the trick. Then there was a quick trip to the QuickMart with Mom for lemons and sugar. Soon it was all ready, but Minnie scrunched up her freckled face. "Boring," she said. "My stand totally lacks pizazz. I must spice it up. But how?"

"I got it!" Minnie cried. Minnie's mom was an artist. Together, they got a huge sheet of paper and began painting. Soon they had a colossal collage of glistening lemons, sparkling ice, and a mammoth mouth with the tongue eagerly licking the lips. All day long people streamed in from all around for a cool, refreshing drink.

Did Minnie Miller make her million? Not quite. She still had $999,984.17 to go. Her next brilliant brainstorm? We'll have to wait and see.

Skill What is the author's purpose so far? Has this first paragraph persuaded, informed, entertained, or expressed feelings?

Strategy What new problem shows up here?
a) The lemons are sour.
b) The stand is ordinary.
c) Minnie needs spices.

Strategy How is the problem solved?

Skill How has the author used words with similar sounds to create humor? Look for examples in the story.

263

Words to Know

permit

subject

worthless

scoundrel

admiringly

Remember

Try the strategy. Then, if you need more help, use your glossary or dictionary.

Vocabulary Strategy
for Multiple-Meaning Words

Context Clues Some words have more than one meaning. Use words and sentences around the word with multiple meanings to figure out which meaning the author is using.

1. When you are puzzled by a multiple-meaning word, read the words and sentences around it to get the context for the word.

2. Then think about the different meanings the word has. For example, *direct* can mean "to manage," "to command," and "to show the way."

3. Reread the sentence, replacing the word with one of the meanings.

4. If this meaning does not work, try another one.

As you read "Heroes and Dragons," use the context and your knowledge of the word to decide which meaning a multiple-meaning word has. For example, does *permit* mean "to allow" or does it mean "a license"?

HEROES AND DRAGONS

Reading is sometimes compared to a magic carpet ride. It takes you to new places on a moment's notice. The magic can be even stronger when you read a fairy tale, but there is a secret. You must not hesitate to believe in the unbelievable. You must permit your fancy to run wild.

Your destination is a kingdom in which royalty and fairies hold every power. Some heroic deed must be performed, and a poor but loyal subject always comes forward to get it done. Maybe our young hero must slay a dragon that breathes fire. Along the way, he or she must seek help and decide which advice is helpful and which is worthless. He or she may run into an awful scoundrel and have to solve another problem or two. At last our hero faces the dragon! The deed is done, with the help of magic and a strong, true heart.

We nod our heads admiringly at the hero's victory. It isn't because the characters are true to life. It's because the story echoes the truth of values that are important to every person— faith, love, courage, hope. This is what we believe in.

Write

Write a letter to a friend telling what you love about reading. Use as many of the words in the Words to Know list as you can.

WINGS
for the KING

by Anne Sroda
illustrated by Franklin Hammond

Who will show the King
the secret of flying?

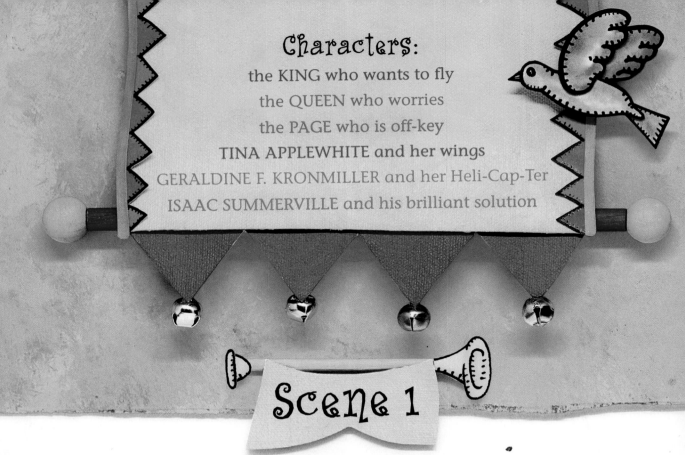

Characters:

the KING who wants to fly

the QUEEN who worries

the PAGE who is off-key

TINA APPLEWHITE and her wings

GERALDINE F. KRONMILLER and her Heli-Cap-Ter

ISAAC SUMMERVILLE and his brilliant solution

Scene 1

SETTING: *Main hall of the castle. Two thrones are center.*

AT RISE: *KING and QUEEN are on thrones. QUEEN is crocheting. KING restlessly changes his position three or four times until QUEEN turns to look at him.*

QUEEN: Your Highness, my dear, whatever is the matter?

KING: My darling, my life lacks adventure. I want to have more fun. To put it simply, I am bored. I need a change of scene. *(He stands and crosses to imaginary window, center. He peers out over the audience.)* It even depresses me to look out the window.

QUEEN: But why?

KING: Because everything out there has something to do. The sun and the clouds and the birds are busy in the air. *(He stops and moves head as though watching. He smiles and points finger.)* There! That's what can cure my boredom!

QUEEN *(Running to stand next to him; peering out):* What? Where?

KING *(Pointing out):* Up there!

QUEEN: The birds? What do you want with a sparrow?

KING: Not the whole bird, just his wings. His lovely, feathery wings. I want to travel to distant lands. I want to fly! There must be someone in my kingdom who can make me a pair of wings. *(He crosses to side of stage and calls.)* Page! *(He calls again, more loudly.)* Page! *(He turns to QUEEN.)* Where is that boy? *(PAGE enters behind KING, holding horn. He bows, unseen by KING.)*

PAGE *(Loudly):* Sire! *(KING jumps in surprise and whirls to face him.)*

KING: Go to the royal treasure chest and fetch me a bag of gold. I will give that bag of gold to the person who brings me a pair of wings that will help me fly. *(Curtain falls.)*

Scene 2

TIME: *A few hours later.*

SETTING: *Same as Scene 1.*

AT RISE: *KING and QUEEN are sitting on their thrones. PAGE enters and blows a fanfare on his horn, off-key.*

KING *(Covering his ears with his hands):* I thought you said you had practiced. Oh, well, get on with it.

PAGE: Sire, may I present your loyal subject, Tina Applewhite, and her, uh, wings. *(TINA APPLEWHITE enters, carrying large wings. She trips over them as she bows.)*

TINA: Not my wings, Your Majesty, but yours. Your wings to lift you above the treetops, to let you soar among the clouds. I used only the finest imported balsa wood for the frame. The lining is pure Oriental silk. And the feathers—well, the feathers are. . . .

KING *(Interrupting):* Do they fly?

TINA: I beg your pardon?

KING: Do they fly? Even if they're solid gold, they are worthless to me if they do not fly.

TINA: *(Reproachfully):* Your Majesty, do they fly? Do fish swim? Do lions roar? Do elephants have trunks?

KING *(Interrupting):* All right, all right, let's get on with it. How do I wear them?

TINA: Oh, it's very simple, Your Majesty. Put your arms through here and hold onto these. *(She helps KING put on wings.)*

KING *(Running about stage, flapping wings):* These are wonderful wings! I just know they will work. *(He jumps up and down.)* Look! I feel lighter already! I shall take off from the parapet! *(He runs off.)*

QUEEN *(Calling after him):* Please be careful!

PAGE *(Looking out window):* He's on the parapet now. What courage! He doesn't even hesitate! He's off!

QUEEN: I hope he doesn't fly too far and get lost.

PAGE *(Admiringly):* Look at those wings flap! It doesn't seem to be doing him much good, though. Uh-oh. I wouldn't worry about his getting lost, Your Majesty. *(A loud crash is heard.)* He's landed.

TINA: Maybe I'm the one who'd better worry. *(KING reenters, limping, with wings broken and crown askew.)*

QUEEN *(Running to him):* What happened, my darling?

KING *(In a daze):* These wings did not take me up. These wings took me down. Do you suppose I am wearing them upside-down? *(He turns toward TINA angrily.)* I thought you said they would fly!

QUEEN *(Wringing her hands):* I knew it wouldn't work. This whole idea was a mistake.

TINA: But, Your Majesty, they do. I tied a string to them and took them out in the wind, and they flew beautifully.

KING: Out in the wind, eh? And were you wearing them at the time?

TINA: Oh, no. I was on the ground holding on to the other end of the string.

KING *(Angrily):* This is not a set of wings. This is a kite! *(To PAGE)* Take this imposter away to the dungeon. And off with her wings. *(PAGE helps KING remove the wings from his back. PAGE carries wings as he shoves TINA off. KING limps to the throne. KING and QUEEN sit.)*

QUEEN: My beloved, will you please give up this dangerous business before you get yourself killed?

KING: Don't be absurd. Flying is no more dangerous than anything else. I could fall off a horse, you know.

QUEEN: Yes, but you would be a great deal closer to the ground.

KING: Balderdash! *(PAGE enters and blows horn, still off-key. KING covers his ears.)*

PAGE: Sire, may I present your loyal subject, Geraldine F. Kronmiller, and her *(Sighs)* wings. *(GERALDINE F. KRONMILLER enters, carrying a hat with a propeller attached.)*

GERALDINE *(Bowing):* Your Highness, I offer you my ingenious invention, the Heli-Cap-Ter. *(She holds hat forward.)*

KING *(Skeptically):* The Heli-Cap-Ter, eh. How does it work?

GERALDINE: Well, Sire, these things on top are called rotors. You wind the rotors to the left as far as they will go, and release them.

KING: And that's all there is to it?

GERALDINE: That's all, Your Highness. The spinning rotors lift you, and you tilt your head in the direction you want to go. Then, as the rotors wind down, they lower you gently back to the ground.

KING: Gently?

GERALDINE: Gently.

QUEEN *(Worried; to KING):* Don't do it. It doesn't look safe to me.

KING: My dear, a child's hobbyhorse doesn't look safe to you. *(He removes his crown, crosses to GERALDINE, takes hat and puts it on.)* Just wind it up and let it go?

GERALDINE: That's all, Your Highness, except for one thing.

273

KING *(Interrupting):* Just a minute, my good woman. Tell me, have you tried the Heli-Cap-Ter yourself? I mean, really tried it?

GERALDINE: Oh, yes. Yes, indeed. It works. I guarantee it.

KING: That's good enough for me. *(He runs out.)*

GERALDINE: But Your Highness, wait!

PAGE *(Looking out "window"):* How dauntless is Our Majesty! There he goes! *(Pauses)* There he goes—down. *(Loud crash is heard.)*

GERALDINE: But the Heli-Cap-Ter works! It's been laboratory tested. *(KING reenters, without Heli-Cap-Ter.)*

QUEEN *(Running up to KING):* My poor baby! Didn't it work?

KING: Oh, it worked, all right. The Heli-Cap-Ter went up, up, up. *(He points up.)* But I went down, down, down. *(He points down.)*

GERALDINE: Does this mean I'm not going to get the bag of gold?

KING *(Angrily):* Take her to the dungeon! *(PAGE grabs GERALDINE's arm and leads her off. KING limps to throne, puts crown back on and sits, as does QUEEN.)*

QUEEN: My dear, I hate to say I told you so, but. . . .

KING *(Interrupting):* If you hate to say it, then don't say it.

QUEEN *(Haughtily):* Well. *(PAGE enters and raises horn to his lips, but before he can blow, KING motions for him to stop.)*

KING: Please. Let's just skip the fanfare. What have you got now?

PAGE *(Lowering horn and clearing throat):* Sire, may I present your loyal subject, Isaac Summerville, and his . . . wings? *(ISAAC SUMMERVILLE enters, carrying an armload of at least eight books.)*

ISAAC *(Bowing awkwardly):* Your Majesties, may I present the best wings of all! *(Holds out books)*

KING: Funny, those don't look like wings. How do you wear them?

ISAAC: You don't wear them, Your Majesty, you look at them. They are called books.

KING: Oh, I see. They're magic. You look at them, say a few words like abracadabra or fiddle-dee-faddle, and they take you wherever you want to go.

ISAAC: Well, not exactly.

KING (*Losing patience*): Well, then how do they work?

ISAAC: Permit me. (*He crosses to KING and hands him a book.*) Open it. (*KING opens book.*)

KING: Here's a picture. (*Reads*) The pyramids of Egypt. So that's what they look like! (*QUEEN looks over his shoulder as he turns pages.*)

QUEEN: Look, my dear, a picture of Paris. There's the River Seine.

KING: What a good picture! I feel as if I'm really there.

ISAAC: Now you see what I mean. Books are wings to the land of knowledge. And they are also wings to the land of fun. Look at these. (*He gives three books to QUEEN. She opens one. KING looks over her shoulder.*)

QUEEN: Why, it's a story about a little girl and a talking rabbit! It's called *Alice's Adventures in Wonderland.*

KING (*Scratching his head*): Wonderland. Is that north or south of here?

ISAAC: It's not north or south. Or east or west either. The only way you can visit Wonderland is by reading that book.

KING: Let's see the rest of these. (*He takes the rest of the books from ISAAC and looks at the titles.*) Hm-m-m. Here's one that will take me to China, and another about Africa.

QUEEN (*Taking another book from pile and leafing through it*): I could go to Switzerland with Heidi. I've always wanted to see the Alps.

KING: This is very exciting, indeed. (*Pauses thoughtfully*) But I had hoped to discover something.

ISAAC: Reading is discovering, Your Highness. There's something new on every page.

KING (*Still looking at the titles*): Wait a minute! Here's a book called *The Principles of Aeronautics*. (*Calls*) Page! Take this book down to the dungeon. Make sure those two scoundrels read it, and then let them go free.

PAGE (*Crossing and taking book*): Yes, Sire.

KING (*Reaching beside his throne to get the bag of gold; to ISAAC*): Here, my good man, take your bag of gold. You have earned it. With books around, I don't think I'll ever be bored again.

ISAAC (*Taking gold and bowing*): I thank you, Your Highness.

KING: Now, both of you leave us alone so we can do some reading. (*ISAAC bows again and exits. PAGE bows and exits.*)

KING (*To QUEEN*): All right, my jewel, where do you want to go?

QUEEN: I can't decide. (*She looks at two open books in her lap.*) Should I visit the land of Oz with Dorothy in *The Wizard of Oz* or Never-Never Land with Peter Pan and Wendy?

KING (*Eagerly*): Never-Never Land! I would choose that one.

QUEEN: You'd like it, my darling. It's about a boy who really can fly. His name is Peter Pan.

KING: That sounds perfect!

QUEEN: All right. You read *Peter Pan* (*She hands him a book.*), I'll read *The Wizard of Oz*, and then we'll trade.

KING: Good idea! (*He opens the book.*) Well, bon voyage, your Highness. Have a nice trip.

QUEEN: You, too, Your Highness. I'm so glad we found out about books.

KING: So am I. It's the only way to fly! (*Both bury their noses in books as the curtain falls.*)

279

Reader Response

Open for Discussion What might happen next? Plan a third scene for this play in which you show the impact of books on the Queen and King.

1. In certain places, the author has the characters describe action taking place offstage. How do these descriptions help make the play better?

2. The author's purpose is to entertain. Look back at pages 270 and 271 and find examples of how the author uses humor to entertain.

3. Many stories use a text structure with three events. The first two events fail in some way, and the third succeeds. Look back at the play and identify these three events.

4. The words *subject* and *permit*, from the play, are multiple-meaning words. Use both meanings of each word in separate sentences that sound as if they might fit into the play.

Look Back and Write On page 277, Isaac suggests two ways that books are like wings. Write the two ways. Then add one more way, based on your own experience.

Meet the Illustrator

Franklin Hammond

Read more books with plays you can perform.

Growing up in Canada, Franklin Hammond had asthma. Back then, doctors didn't let kids with asthma play sports, so Mr. Hammond explored art instead. He wasn't a great student, but he worked hard so that he could one day attend his dream school, the Ontario College of Art and Design.

As a professional artist, Mr. Hammond says he especially loves working on children's books "because they allow me to be truly creative." He is well known for his unique three-dimensional art, which includes real-life objects and materials.

He had a great opportunity to experiment in three dimensions when he created the flying machine in *Wings for the King.* He carefully assembled this fantastic structure using wood, wire, and metal. He says, "There are lots of small details in my work, so I hope kids look closely and find them."

In his spare time, Hammond helps run a gallery where he sells his art, including his work from children's books. Maybe someday someone will buy the flying machine that the King rejected!

Folktales on Stage: Scripts for Reader's Theater
by Aaron Shepard

Cinderella Outgrows the Glass Slipper and Other Zany Fractured Fairy Tale Plays
by J.M. Wolf

Narrative Nonfiction

Genre
- **Narrative nonfiction tells the true story of an event that takes place over a certain period of time, anywhere from minutes to years.**

- **This event may come from one person's life, or it may involve several people, places, and things.**

Text Features
- **The event is usually told in chronological order, from start to finish.**

- **Narrative nonfiction sometimes contains quotes from the people involved.**

- **Look at the title and illustrations to get an idea of who and what this selection deals with.**

Link to Social Studies
Look for other books and articles about young inventors. Find one invention of special interest. Share what you find with the class.

from *Brainstorm!* by Tom Tucker

Becky Schroeder

ENLIGHTENED THINKER

Rebecca Schroeder entered the world of invention at the age of ten, while a pupil at Ladyfield Academy in Toledo, Ohio. One October evening, she had gone with her mother to a shopping center and was waiting in the car, poring over her studies, while her mother hurried in for some groceries.

BECKY'S MOM

"I was in the car doing my homework when it started to get dark," she told reporters later. "I kept thinking WHAT A GOOD THING IT WOULD BE IF PEOPLE COULD WRITE IN THE DARK."

Her father encouraged her to pursue her inspirations. "I'm always coming up with ideas," explained Becky when the media thronged around her. "It happens when you least expect it."

At first, she kept the idea to herself. The homework arrived on the teacher's desk the next day, but the idea of writing in the dark glimmered in her mind for many days, until she went to the library to find out what kinds of things GLOW in the dark.

Author's Purpose Is the author trying to inform or entertain?

GLOW WORM

LANTERNFISH

FIREFLY

GLOW STICK

ELECTRIC EEL

"FLUORESCENCE" was the word she had in mind. Wrong—fluorescent compounds fade just after they're removed from the light. Next she considered "bioluminescence," meaning the emission of light by organisms. Glowworms? Fireflies? Would some living creature light her inspiration?

When that didn't seem promising, Becky discovered "PHOSPHORESCENCE," the action of certain substances that produce a glow after exposure to light.

At first, she thought of an ink that would glow in the dark, but then she had another idea: what about coating the surface of something like a clipboard with phosphorescent material? Then, if she set writing paper on top, the board would glow through, silhouetting any letters on the paper, thereby making them visible in the dark.

Charles Schroeder describes it this way: "She came home. She said, 'I HAVE AN INVENTION.' I said, 'Oh.' Then her mother said, 'I think she really does.'"

The next step? A trip to a hobby shop to get phosphorescent paint. Then she needed a room with no windows, so she commandeered one of the family's bathrooms for her laboratory. And one evening, after her first experiments, Becky Schroeder ran into the family room, shouting, "It works! It works!"

A ROOM WITH NO WINDOWS?

LABORATOR

PHOSPHOR

HOBBY SHOPS

Charles Schroeder was impressed. "The thing worked better than I thought it could have worked," he says. In the blackness, his daughter held up a glowing rectangle on which he could read her message: "I CAN WRITE IN THE DARK."

I can write in the dark.

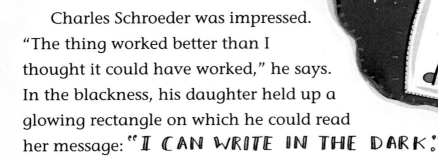

PATENT #3,832,556

① A TABLET OF WRITING PAPER

② LIFTED + TURNED BACK TOP SHEET OF WRITING TABLET

③ INSERTION OF "PHOSPHORESCENCE" "BACKING" "SHEET"

Two years later, on August 27, 1974, the U.S. Patent and Trademark Office awarded Becky patent #3,832,556 for a "LUMINESCENT Backing Sheet for Writing in the Dark." Newspapers and magazines rushed to tell her story; she appeared on a number of television shows and won several awards.

In the years that followed, Becky has been granted almost a dozen patents that stake out improvements on her basic idea. Becky formed a company called BJ Products (BJ stands for Becky Jane), and now she calls her product Glo-Sheet.

Text Structure What clues tell you that sequence is the text structure?

285

Who are the potential customers for **Glo-Sheet**? At various times, both the U.S. Navy and NASA have taken a serious look at the invention. Becky sees many uses for it, for people such as pilots in darkened cockpits; policemen filling out forms and soldiers in war zones at night; doctors, nurses, and other medical personnel making their evening rounds; and movie and theater critics who need to jot notes during shows. But to date, although many **Glo-Sheets** have been sold directly, Becky has found no distributor.

POLICE

DOCTOR

DIVERS

ASTRONAUTS

AIRPLANE PILOTS

MOVIE CRITICS

For her brainstorm, Becky was named an Ohio Inventor of the Year, and was inducted into the **OHIO INVENTORS HALL OF FAME.** Today, more than twenty years later, she is in demand to speak about invention at state and national meetings, and at schools and universities. Now married, she assists her husband in running his own insurance agency, and she also uses her creativity in designing jewelry for a local store.

OHIO

HALL OF FAME

To kids, her message is: "Childhood? That's where you start inventing." And she warns them against listening to nay-sayers, those people, sometimes friends or family, who may unconsciously discourage kid inventors because they themselves do not believe. Becky says, "KEEP AN OPEN MIND — things could come up."

Today, when people hear about Glo-Sheet, they are still intrigued. Kids get excited about writing letters at summer camp after lights-out, for example—or other everyday applications. And they like Becky's story, too, the story of a little girl who conquered the dark with a bright idea.

Reading Across Texts

Compare the King and Becky Schroeder. Were they both inventors? What goals did they have in mind? What methods did they use for achieving them?

Writing Across Texts Present your answers in two separate paragraphs.

Text Structure   How do the illustrations help make things clearer?

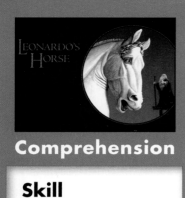
Skill
Main Idea
and Details

Strategy
Summarize

 Strategy

Main Idea
and Details

- The main idea is the most important idea about a topic. Details are small pieces of information that tell more about the main idea.

- Sometimes the author states the main idea of a paragraph or an entire article in a single sentence at the beginning, middle, or end. Other times the author leaves the main idea unstated, so readers must put it into their own words.

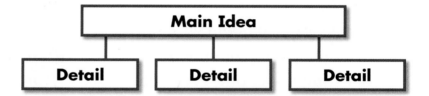

 Strategy

Strategy: Summarize

Active readers summarize to help them understand the most important information they read. Summarizing can help you find the main idea of a selection. Writing a summary can help you organize the information.

1. Read "Bronze." Make a graphic organizer like the one above to show the main idea and the details that support it.

2. Use information from your graphic organizer to help you write a summary of "Bronze."

Bronze

People have used bronze for thousands of years to make many things. Bronze is a soft metal made from copper and tin. It cannot be hammered or bent, so it is not a good material for making tools. However, in molten or liquid form it can be shaped into things such as statues, pots, and bowls.

Thousands of years ago, bronze was shaped using the "lost-wax method." In this method, a model was made using plaster or clay. Then it was coated in wax followed by another layer of plaster or clay. When heated, the wax melted away, leaving a space. The bronze was melted and poured into the space. When it cooled, the plaster or clay was taken off. Using this method, only one item could be made from the model.

In time, molds were formed out of other materials, such as wood. A wooden mold could be used again and again. It was pressed into sand, and when it was removed, the impression was left in the sand. Bronze was poured into the sand. Later, it was removed, and the surface was smoothed.

Bronze is still used today. You may even have some items made from bronze in your home!

Skill Notice the first sentence of this paragraph is basically telling what it is all about.

Strategy This is a good place to summarize. What two or three most important ideas have you read so far?

Skill Did one sentence seem to tell what this article was basically about? Hint: Look early on in the article.

Strategy How will summarizing help you remember important ideas?

depressed

achieved

philosopher

architect

fashioned

midst

bronze

cannon

rival

Remember

Try the strategy. Then, if you need more help, use your glossary or dictionary.

Vocabulary Strategy
for Greek and Latin Roots

Word Structure Many words in English are based on Greek and Latin roots. For example, *bio-* means "life." It is found in words such as *biography* and *biology*. When you see a longer word you cannot read, look for a root that can help you figure out the word's meaning.

1. Look at the unfamiliar word. Try to identify a root word within it.

2. Think of words you know where this same root appears.

3. What does the root mean in these words?

4. Try the meaning in the unfamiliar word and see if it makes sense in the sentence.

As you read "They Called It the Renaissance," look for Greek and Latin roots to help you figure out the meanings of unknown words. (Hint: The Greek root *arch-* means "chief, ruler." The Greek root *philo-* means "loving.")

290

They Called It the RENAISSANCE

The Middle Ages ran from about A.D. 500 to about 1450. This was a time that might have depressed anyone. People in Europe looked back at the past instead of forward to the future.

But by 1450, people had stopped thinking only about the past and started looking ahead to what might be achieved in the future. This new age was known as the Renaissance.

Inventors started coming up with exciting new inventions. The title philosopher became important again, as thinkers explored new ways to enrich people's lives. The architect became an important figure as beautiful new buildings took shape in cities and towns across Europe. Artists fashioned powerful sculptures and painted vivid paintings that looked natural and real.

In the midst of all this growth and change, of course, there was still fighting. Art was the glory of the age, but war was the harsh reality. Bronze might be used to make a beautiful statue or a deadly cannon. People were sailing off to find new lands. A nation might become a rival of another nation, fighting for land in the Americas. In so many ways, people in the Renaissance were preparing for the modern world.

Write

Leonardo da Vinci did many things during the Renaissance. Look at the illustrations in *Leonardo's Horse*. Write a paragraph about what you think he might have achieved. Use as many of the words from the Words to Know list as you can.

BY JEAN FRITZ

ILLUSTRATED BY HUDSON TALBOTT

LEONARDO'S HORSE

Will Leonardo's greatest dream ever come true?

Genre   A **biography** is a story of a person's life written by another person. As you read, notice all the ups and downs in Leonardo da Vinci's life.

Anyone who watched the young Leonardo wander
the countryside around his home in Vinci might have guessed
that he would be an artist. He stopped to examine everything.
He looked at the landscape as if he were memorizing it. So it
was no surprise when his father took him as a young teenager
to Florence to study art.

295

People noticed that Leonardo was different.

He dressed differently. While other young men wore long togas, Leonardo wore short, rose-colored velvet togas.

He wrote differently. Backwards. From the right side of the paper to the left. A person would have to use a mirror to read his writing.

And he wouldn't eat meat. He liked animals too much to eat anything that had once been alive. Nor could he stand the sight of caged birds. If he saw a man selling birds, he would buy them all. Then he would open the cages and watch the birds fly away. What a flurry they made! How did they do it? All his life Leonardo tried to discover their secret of flying so he could make a flying machine for himself.

For a man who liked to ask questions, Leonardo da Vinci was born at the right time—April 15, 1452. Everybody was asking questions then. The age was called the Renaissance, a time of rebirth when people who had forgotten how to be curious became curious again. They were exploring new countries, discovering, inventing, looking at old things in new ways. What was the point, Leonardo asked, in copying what had already been done? He had to bring his own experience into whatever he painted. You wouldn't catch him putting a halo around the head of a saint. How could he? He had never seen a halo.

Leonardo da Vinci turned out to be a famous artist; still, he was not just an artist. He could never be just one thing. He was an engineer, an architect, a musician, a philosopher, an astronomer. Once he fashioned a special kind of flute made of silver in the shape of a horse's head. The ruler of Florence, Lorenzo de' Medici, asked him to deliver it as a gift to the duke of Milan. This was lucky for Leonardo. He had heard that the duke of Milan wanted to honor his father with a bronze horse in front of his palace. And Leonardo wanted to be the one to make it.

Temporary bridge

Eight-gun cannon

Armored Tank

This would be his mark on history. Hundreds of years later people would point to the horse. "Leonardo made that," they would say.

So he wrote to the duke, listing all the things that he could do. He could make cannon, lightweight bridges, and covered chariots that couldn't be broken or harmed. On and on he went, but he saved the most important point for the last. He could make a bronze horse. In the end, he didn't send the letter. He simply left for Milan. Never mind that he was in the midst of painting a large religious picture in Florence. Let someone else finish it. He had planned the picture and that was the important part.

War chariot

Exploding
cannonballs

Cannon

Parachute

Catapult

Leonardo was thirty years old now, handsome with curly blond hair. The duke gave him the job of working on the horse, but at the same time he was expected to take charge of entertainment in the palace. He had a beautiful singing voice, he could play musical instruments, he could juggle and ask riddles, and he was also asked to stage elaborate plays for special occasions. Whenever he had a chance, he went back to the horse.

He visited the stables, studying how a horse was put together.

He needed to understand everything about his subject. He measured and drew pictures until he knew where all the bones and muscles of a horse were. But you couldn't show all the muscles on a statue, he said, or the horse would look like a bag of turnips. You should show only those muscles the horse was using or getting ready to use.

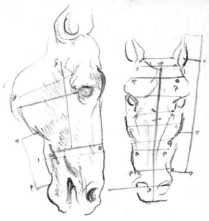

He visited statues of horses. Many were shown in an amble—left front leg moving at the same time as the left back leg. This was not easy for a horse; he had to be taught to do it. Leonardo saw one horse, however, that he described as free—left front leg and right back leg moving together, in a trot. Moreover, both ears were pointed forward. (Some horses pointed one ear back to hear the rider's orders.)

Leonardo was ready to begin.

But the duke wasn't quite ready. He wanted a much bigger horse than the one he had originally planned. One three times larger than life. Could Leonardo manage anything that large? the duke wondered. He wrote to Lorenzo, asking him to recommend someone who could do the job.

Lorenzo replied: Leonardo da Vinci was the only one.

On April 23, 1490, Leonardo wrote in his notebook: "I resumed work on the horse." The hardest part would be the casting. He collected 58,000 pounds of metal—tin and copper—which would be heated until it was fluid. This would be turned into bronze and used to cast the horse. But should he pour the bronze all at once? No one had tried a single pouring of anything this large.

In November 1493, he had completed the clay model—twenty-four feet high. It was shown off at one of the duke's special occasions, and it was a sensation.

But Leonardo seemed to be in no hurry to start casting. Perhaps he wasn't sure how he'd do it. Besides, he was planning a new project.

Later, in 1498, there were rumors that the French were preparing to invade Milan, and the duke wanted to be ready. And there was all the metal that Leonardo had collected. Just what the duke needed. So he sent it off to be made into cannon. Well, this is war, Leonardo reasoned. What else could they do?

When the French came in 1499, Leonardo and the duke fled. But the horse couldn't leave. There he was when the French arrived. The archers laughed. Never would they find as perfect a target, they said. Pulling back the strings on their bows, they let their arrows fly. Ping! Ping! Ping! The horse sagged. Ping!

Then it rained. And the horse became smaller and smaller. At last it was nothing but a pile of mud stuck with arrows.

Leonardo went back to inventing and painting, but he never forgot his horse.

He still wanted to invent a flying machine. But he still couldn't do it.

His greatest disappointment, however, was his horse.

As Leonardo became older, his hair turned white and grew down to his shoulders. His beard reached to his waist.

And he became depressed. What had he achieved? he asked himself. He complained to his notebook: "Tell me," he asked, "if anything has been achieved by me. Tell me. Tell me." It was especially hard when his rival, Michelangelo, taunted him.

"You," Michelangelo said, "who made a model of a horse you could never cast in bronze and which you gave up, to your shame."

In his notebook Leonardo mourned, "I have wasted my hours."

On May 2, 1519, Leonardo da Vinci died. It was said that even on his deathbed, Leonardo wept for his horse.

In 1977 Charles Dent, an American and a big fan of Leonardo, saw a magazine article about him. When he read that Leonardo died grieving for his horse, Charles said, "Let's give Leonardo his horse."

But Charles Dent died before work was finished. Later, a sculptor from New York City, Nina Akamu, carried on with Charles's dream. Many people contributed money to help her finish. Finally, on September 10, 1999, in Milan, Italy, in front of huge crowds, the horse was unveiled.

At last Leonardo's horse was home.

Reader Response

Open for Discussion Remember that Leonardo da Vinci died mourning the things he had left unfinished. If he could glance over your shoulder and read about himself now, what would he say?

1. Jean Fritz's biographies put the reader right there alongside the subject of the book. Find examples that seem to put you right there, beside Leonardo.

2. What is Jean Fritz's main idea in this book? She shows how Leonardo was brilliant, but what else does she show about his character, about the kind of person he is? Look back at page 298 to answer the question.

3. Look back through the selection and think about the major events. Discuss which events you would use to summarize Leonardo's life.

4. The words *architect* and *philosopher* describe two of da Vinci's talents. What other talents were mentioned in the selection?

Look Back and Write Leonardo da Vinci was a man of many talents. To prove this, write a list of his accomplishments, beginning with the professions that are mentioned on page 297.

Jean Fritz

Read more books by Jean Fritz.

Jean Fritz writes books about history because she enjoys doing research. She says, "For every book I write, I have to read a great deal and usually travel to the place where that person lived. It's like being a detective. I want to find the truth, so I never make up anything in these books, not even conversation. If you see quotation marks, you can be sure I have a source for them."

While writing *Leonardo's Horse*, Ms. Fritz went to Italy. She was there when the 24-foot bronze horse was presented as a gift from the American people to the Italian people. She says, "It was one of my most exciting adventures."

Although Ms. Fritz today lives along the Hudson River in New York, she spent her childhood in China. She heard her parents' stories about America and felt a need to know all she could about America, both past and present. Many of her biographies are about people important in American history, such as George Washington, Benjamin Franklin, and Harriet Beecher Stowe.

Ms. Fritz says, "I get letters from readers sometimes who say they like the way I add 'fun' to history. I don't add anything. It's all true, because past times were just as filled with exciting events and 'fun' stories as are present times."

Bully for You, Teddy Roosevelt

Can't You Make Them Behave, King George?

Narrative Nonfiction

Genre

- **Some narrative nonfiction explains the history of something.**

- **Sometimes this history shows how one invention led to another.**

Text Features

- **Some narrative nonfiction uses a time line to help organize events in history.**

- **Usually, events are presented in time order, from first to last.**

- **Take a look at the illustrations and time line to see what this article is about.**

Link to Social Studies

Look for other books and articles about flight. Share what you learn with the class.

BY ROGER YEPSEN

HUMANS WITH WINGS

Daedalus watches Icarus' wings fall apart as Icarus falls from the sky.

Icarus and Daedalus

John Damian

When you were younger, you probably ran around flapping your arms and pretending you could fly. Many adults have dreamed of being free from Earth's gravity too. They've been building machines designed to fly by human power for centuries. They've also been crashing for centuries. The best-known crash of all was supposed to have happened around 3500 B.C. in the Mediterranean Sea. An inventor, Daedalus, and his son, Icarus, escaped from an island prison on wings that Daedalus had made of feathers and wax. But young Icarus flew higher and higher, in spite of his father's warnings that the sun's heat would melt the wax and loosen the feathers. Icarus fell into the sea and drowned.

That story is just a fable. But throughout history, people have built contraptions made of feathers, silk, and wood in attempts to fly with their own power. Unlike Icarus, they didn't get very far from the ground. Even Leonardo da Vinci, the brilliant Italian artist and inventor, could do no better. Five hundred years ago, he sketched designs for humanpowered planes and a helicopter. But it seems that they never got off the drawing board.

Sketch of da Vinci's wing

Main Idea How can you figure out the main ideas in this article?

313

John Baptist Danti with his winged oars

Countless others have tried and failed. Some broke bones, and some lost their lives. Several years before Columbus set off for America, another bold Italian, John Baptist Danti, climbed a tower and set off through the air with winged oars. He crashed on a church roof and was seriously injured.

In the 1500s, John Damian attempted to race a sailing ship from Scotland to France. Needless to say, he lost. Flapping a pair of wings made from chicken feathers, he leaped from a castle wall and went straight down, breaking his thigh bone.

In Germany in the 1600s, a cautious man named Bernier tested his flying machine by jumping first from a stool, then a table, a first-floor window, and a second-floor window. He should have stopped there. His last leap, from a third-floor window, resulted in several broken bones.

John Damian jumps from a castle wall with his chicken feather wings.

Bernier in his flying machine

Vincent de Groof

In the 1800s, Belgian shoemaker Vincent de Groof used his skills to make an ornithopter—an airplane that flies like a bird. The wings were operated by his arms, while his legs flapped a tail. He launched himself from a balloon and fell to his death.

Were these people foolish to try such stunts? Or would you call them brave pioneers? Today, when men and women are killed in attempts to explore space, we consider them heroes, not fools.

Vincent de Groof jumps from a balloon in his ornithopter flying machine.

Reading Across Texts

Look back at *Leonardo's Horse* and "Humans with Wings" and make a list of Triumphs and a list of Tragedies.

Writing Across Texts Use your lists to write a paragraph about either the joy or the pain of being an inventor.

 **Summarize** What does this article tell you about attempts to fly?

 Skill

Fact and Opinion

- You can prove a statement of fact true or false. You can do this by using your own knowledge, asking an expert, or checking a reference source such as an encyclopedia, a nonfiction text, or a dictionary.

- A statement of opinion gives ideas or feelings, not facts. It cannot be proved true or false.

- A sentence may contain both a statement of fact and a statement of opinion.

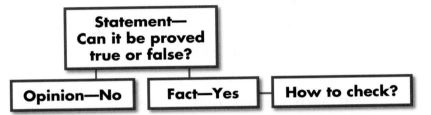

Statement— Can it be proved true or false?

| Opinion—No | Fact—Yes | How to check? |

 Strategy

Strategy: Predict

Active readers try to predict what they will learn when they read a nonfiction article. Preview the article. Predict whether you will read mostly statements of fact or statements of opinion. This will help focus your reading. After you read, see whether your prediction was correct.

1. Read "Dinosaurs." Use the graphic organizer above to find two opinions and three facts. For each fact you write, explain how you could check it.

2. Write two facts you know about dinosaurs and one opinion you have about them.

DINOSAURS

By far the most fascinating creatures ever to walk the earth were the dinosaurs. Dinosaurs lived from about 215 million years ago until about 65 million years ago. Their name comes from two Greek words that mean "terrible lizard." When you see drawings or models of certain dinosaurs, it is very easy to understand how they got their name.

Types of dinosaurs Some dinosaurs were herbivores, meaning that they ate only plants. Apatosaurus and Iguanodon were herbivores. Other dinosaurs were carnivores, or meat eaters. The most feared dinosaur of all, Tyrannosaurus, was a carnivore.

Dinosaur characteristics Dinosaurs were marked by special body features. Stegosaurus had armor that it used for protection. Pterosaur had wings like a bat's. Tyrannosaurus had strong back legs but short, weak front ones.

What happened to the dinosaurs? No one knows for sure, though there are several ideas about why they disappeared. Some of these ideas are as interesting as the dinosaurs themselves.

Strategy Consider the title and the headings. Scan the article. Do you predict that the statements you will read will be mostly fact or opinion?

Skill Clue words can help you find two opinions in this first paragraph.

Skill Which statements were facts in the section you just read? What could you use to check whether they are true or false?

Strategy What about the prediction you made at the beginning of the article? Was it correct?

Words to Know

workshop

proportion

mold

tidied

foundations

erected

occasion

Remember

Try the strategy. Then, if you need more help, use your glossary or dictionary.

Vocabulary Strategy
for Homonyms

Context Clues Homonyms are words with the same spelling but different histories and meanings. Sometimes an unfamiliar word is a homonym. You can use context to help figure out its meaning. The words and sentences around the homonym offer clues.

1. Read the words and sentences around the homonym to find clues.

2. Think about the different meanings the homonym might have. For example, the word *bill* can mean "a statement of money owed" or "the beak of a bird."

3. Try each meaning in the sentence.

4. Decide which meaning makes sense in the sentence.

As you read "The Artist of the Hour," look for words that are homonyms. Decide which meaning the author is using.

THE ARTIST OF THE HOUR

Imagine that you are an artist at work in your workshop. You have been asked to make a sculpture for the new hospital. When people look at this sculpture, they are supposed to think about freedom and hope. You have decided to make a group of birds in flight.

First, you make a clay shape of each bird. You must measure carefully to be sure the proportion of the wings to the body is just right. Then you cover the shapes with melted plastic and let it get hard. Each mold has the exact shape of the bird you made. Next, you pour cement into each mold. After it hardens, any crumbs of cement and plastic must be tidied up. Then you have a whole bird shape.

Meanwhile, you have to build foundations for the birds. These are bases made of wood or cement, with iron pipes sticking up. When they are fastened to the rods, the birds will look as though they are sailing into the sky.

You hope your work of art will be erected in the flower garden at the hospital. When it is put in place, you will be honored for your work. There will be a party to celebrate the occasion.

Write

How would you make a model of a dinosaur? Write an explanation and the steps in your plan. Use as many of the words in the Words to Know list as you can.

THE DINO OF WATER

By **BARBARA KERLEY**
With drawings by **BRIAN SELZNICK**

How does Waterhouse Hawkins
introduce the world to a new
kind of creature?

SAURS
HOUSE
HAWKINS

A **biography** is a story of a person's life written by another person. As you read, notice how Waterhouse Hawkins is a combination artist/scientist.

321

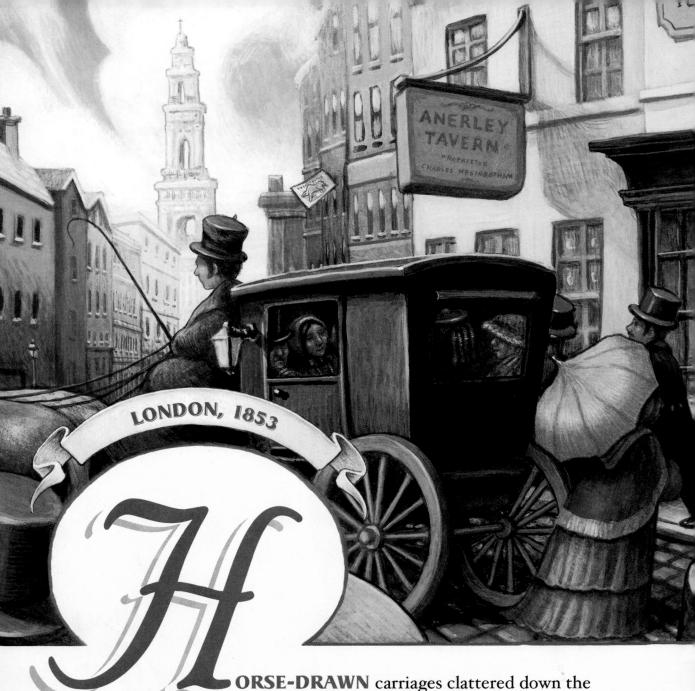

LONDON, 1853

*H*ORSE-DRAWN carriages clattered down the
streets of London in 1853. Gentlemen tipped their hats to ladies
passing by. Children ducked and dodged on their way to school.

But Benjamin Waterhouse Hawkins had no time to be out
and about. Waterhouse, as he liked to call himself, hurried
toward his workshop in a park south of town. He was expecting
some very important visitors. He didn't want to be late.

As he neared his workshop, Waterhouse thought of the hours he'd spent outside as a boy. Like many artists, he had grown up sketching the world around him. By the time he was a young man, he'd found his true passion: animals. He loved to draw and paint them. But what he really loved was sculpting models of them. Through his care and hard work, they seemed to come to life.

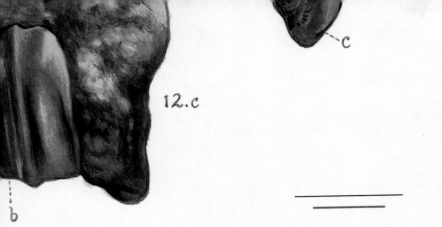

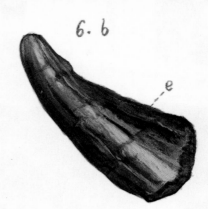

Now Waterhouse was busy with a most exciting project: He was building dinosaurs! His creations would prowl the grounds of Queen Victoria and Prince Albert's new art and science museum, the Crystal Palace.

Even though the English had found the first known dinosaur fossil many years before—and the bones of more dinosaurs had been unearthed in England since then—in 1853, most people had no idea what a dinosaur looked like.

Scientists weren't sure either, for the only fossils were some bits and pieces—a tooth here, a bone there. But they thought that if they studied a fossil and compared it to a living animal, they could fill in the blanks.

And so, with the help of scientist Richard Owen, who checked every muscle, bone, and spike, that's exactly what Waterhouse was doing. He wanted to create such perfect models that anyone—a crowd of curious children, England's leading scientists, even the Queen herself!—could gaze at his dinosaurs and see into the past.

325

Waterhouse threw open the doors to his workshop. Nervously, he tidied up here and there. His assistants came, then Richard Owen.

At last, the visitors arrived: Queen Victoria and Prince Albert!

The Queen's eyes grew wide in surprise. Waterhouse's creatures were extraordinary! How on earth had he made them?

He was happy to explain: The iguanodon, for instance, had teeth that were quite similar to the teeth of an iguana. The iguanodon, then, must surely have looked like a giant iguana. Waterhouse pointed out that the few iguanodon bones helped determine the model's size and proportion. And another bone—almost a spike—most likely sat on the nose, like a rhino's horn.

Just so for the megalosaurus. Start with its jawbone. Compare it to the anatomy of a lizard. Fill in the blanks. And voilà! A dinosaur more than forty feet long.

Waterhouse was also making ancient reptiles and amphibians. While Richard Owen could imagine their shapes, it took an artist to bring the animals to life.

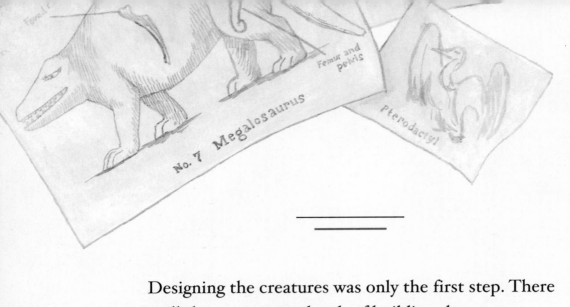

Designing the creatures was only the first step. There was still the monumental task of building them.

Waterhouse showed his guests the small models he'd made, correct in every detail, from scales on the nose to nails on the toes. With the help of his assistants, he had formed the life-size clay figures and created the molds from them. Then he erected iron skeletons, built brick foundations, and covered the whole thing with cement casts from the dinosaur-shaped molds.

"It is no less," Waterhouse concluded, "than building a house upon four columns."

4
Mold

5
Iron Skeleton
(must support tons
of dinosaur)

6
Finished Dinosaur
(bricks, tiles and broken
stones, all held together
with cement, covered with
casts and painted)

Tiles &
Broken
Stones

In the weeks to follow, Waterhouse basked in the glow of the Queen's approval. But he would soon face a much tougher set of critics: England's leading scientists. Waterhouse wanted to be accepted into this circle of eminent men. What would they think of his dinosaurs?

There was only one way to find out. Waterhouse would show them. But why not do it with a little style?

A dinner party. On New Year's Eve, no less. And not just any dinner party. Waterhouse would stage an event that no one would ever forget!

He sketched twenty-one invitations to the top scientists and supporters of the day, the words inscribed on a drawing of a pterodactyl wing. He pored over menus with the caterer.

The iguanodon mold was hauled outside. A platform was built. A tent erected.

As the hour drew near, the table was elegantly set, and names of famous scientists—the fathers of paleontology—were strung above the tent walls. All was ready.

With great anticipation, Waterhouse dressed for the occasion in his finest attire. He was ready to reveal his masterpiece!

When the guests arrived, they gasped with delight! Waterhouse smiled as he signaled for dinner to begin. With solemn formality, the footmen served course after course from silver platters. Up and down the steps of the platform they carried the lavish feast: rabbit soup, fish, ham, and even pigeon pie. For dessert, there were nuts, pastries, pudding, and plums.

For eight hours, the men rang in the New Year. They laughed and shouted. They made speech after speech, toasting Waterhouse Hawkins. All the guests agreed: The iguanodon was a marvelous success. By midnight they were belting out a song created especially for the occasion:

THE JOLLY OLD BEAST IS NOT DECEASED
THERE'S LIFE IN HIM AGAIN!

The next months passed by in concrete, stone, and iron, as Waterhouse put the finishing touches on his dinosaurs. Inside the iguanodon's lower jaw he signed the work: B. HAWKINS, BUILDER, 1854. The models were now ready for the grand opening of the Crystal Palace at Sydenham Park.

Forty thousand spectators attended the regal ceremony. In the sun-filled center court, Waterhouse mingled with scientists and foreign dignitaries. At last, the Queen arrived! The crowd cheered, "Hurrah!"

Cannons boomed, music swelled, and a choir of one thousand
voices sang. Waterhouse bowed before the Queen. Then she and
Prince Albert invited the spectators to enjoy the amazing sights.

Waterhouse hurried to the lake and waited for the crowd
to arrive.

First two, then ten, then a dozen more . . . Gasped! Shrieked!
Laughed and cried: So this was a dinosaur!

AFTERWORD

In 1868, Waterhouse traveled to the United States to create the first-ever model of a complete dinosaur skeleton. The model went on display to amazed visitors of Philadelphia's Academy of Natural Sciences. Waterhouse also worked on making more dinosaur sculptures for a museum in New York City's Central Park. But before he could finish, vandals broke into his workshop, smashed the models to pieces, and buried them in the park. Today, pieces of the dinosaurs of Waterhouse Hawkins are still buried somewhere in Central Park.

Reader Response

Open for Discussion Say you are Waterhouse Hawkins. You get a letter saying that miniature model dinosaurs are fine to play with but life-size dinosaur models are expensive and not useful. What would you reply?

1. This biography is about an artist and his art. It does not tell personal information, such as whether Waterhouse had children or liked to swim. Do you wish this information were in the book or are you happy with what's there? What needs to be told in a biography?

2. Look back at pages 332–335. What are people's opinions of the dinosaurs? Discuss the different ways the people express their opinions.

3. Look back at page 324. What would lead readers to predict that Waterhouse Hawkins would one day amaze the people of Victorian England?

4. Describe Waterhouse's plan for impressing England's leading scientists. Use words from the Words to Know list and other words from the selection.

Look Back and Write Look back at pages 328–329 for Waterhouse's six steps for building a dinosaur model. List them. Then write two questions you would need to ask to get more information before building your own model.

Meet the Author and the Illustrator

Barbara Kerley and Brian Selznick

Read another book by Barbara Kerley. Read another book illustrated by Brian Selznick.

BARBARA KERLEY

Barbara Kerley says she got the idea for writing *The Dinosaurs of Waterhouse Hawkins* when her daughter asked how big a T. rex was. "I had no idea, so we got a book on dinosaurs from the library. In it was this incredible drawing of a dinner party, with formal waiters, candlesticks on the table, and all these elegant gentlemen stuffed into a dinosaur. I was hooked—I just had to find out the story behind that picture."

BRIAN SELZNICK

Once Ms. Kerley had written the manuscript, Brian Selznick got a call from his editor. She described *The Dinosaurs of Waterhouse Hawkins*. Mr. Selznick said the story left his head spinning and all he could say was "I'll do it!" Mr. Selznick has also written and illustrated his own books.

Song of Papa's Island
by Barbara Kerley

A Week in the Woods
by Andrew Clements
illustrated by Brian Selznick

339

Interview

Genre

- In an interview, the interviewer asks questions and the subject answers them.

- Interviews are often found in magazines and newspapers.

Text Features

- The interview first introduces the subject, or the person being interviewed.

- An interview gives the actual words spoken by the subject and interviewer.

- Preview the questions in bold type. What do they tell you about the interview?

Link to Science

Research how scientists use other kinds of models in their work, such as computer models. Explain to a classmate what you have learned.

A Model SCIENTIST

FROM OWL MAGAZINE

Meet Garfield Minott. He's been making dinosaur models since he was seven years old. Back then, he made dinosaurs just for fun. Today, his passion for the prehistoric has turned into a cool and unusual dinosaur job.

Q: OWL: What exactly do you do?

A: **Garfield:** I'm a paleo-artist. I bring dinosaurs back to life!

Q: How do you do that?

A: I build real-life models of the dinosaurs scientists discover. My models help dinosaur scientists to gain a better understanding of these incredible creatures. I get bags of bones shipped to me from scientists, and I use these bones to plan my models. When it comes to learning about dino bones, nothing beats the real thing!

Q: What can you tell from a simple bone?

A: Lots of stuff! If you took all the muscles off of a bone, you'd be left with marks on the bone called "scarring." These marks tell me how the muscles were attached. Then, I can tell how the skin formed around the muscles. As I build up, layer after layer from the inside out, I can bring an animal back to life!

Q: How do you make your models?

A: Once I've researched in books and bones, I make a rough drawing. Then, I make a skeleton of the body out of welded steel. Next, I start layering on the muscles, which are made out of clay. When that's done, I start on the skin. If the dinosaur had scales, then I make the scales and layer them on one at a time. This could take three to five weeks. I want my dinosaur models to look as close as possible to the real thing.

 Predict   What will this be about? How quickly will you read it?

Q: When did you become interested in models?

A: I've been making models ever since I was a kid growing up in Jamaica. My mom used to bake a lot and whenever she did, she would teach me how to mold things out of flour. In those days, I was crazy about lizards so that's mostly the kind of models I made.

Q: When did you get hooked on dinosaurs?

A: When I was seven years old my family moved to Canada. Because I was in a new country, I became a pretty shy kid. One day my teacher asked me what kind of animals I liked. Of course I said, "Lizards." She said, "Well, if you like lizards you must like dinosaurs." I had no idea what a dinosaur was. She took me to the library, pulled a book off the shelf, and showed me my first dinosaur. I went totally bananas!

342

Q: And you've been crazy about dinos ever since?

A: Yes! And I especially loved hearing all those long and crazy dinosaur names. *Tyrannosaurus rex* is my favorite. That name still makes me flip out!

Q: Did you ever imagine a career with dinosaurs?

A: When I was a kid, I had a kit that came with tiny models of dinosaurs. I used these models to play "dinosaurs" with friends. But, after a while I learned about more kinds of dinosaurs than I had in my kit—so I made the ones I didn't have out of Plasticine™. And, if my *T. rex* got hungry and ate a whole herd of models, I had to make new dinosaurs very quickly! I did this so often that I became good at building models in no time at all. That's how I became a model expert.

Predict Did you predict accurately? Should you change your rate?

343

Q: How did model building become your job?

A: I found out about a paleo-artist who worked at the Royal Ontario Museum in Toronto. One day I went to meet him. He saw that I was interested in dinosaurs and a good model builder, so he suggested that I volunteer at the museum. I did, and I've been building models ever since.

Q: Do you wish dinosaurs still roamed Earth?

A: If they did, humans wouldn't be here. We'd be eaten! I'd like to see a live dinosaur on an island somewhere, and just observe it.

Q: **What's the coolest fact you've learned about dinosaurs?**

A: Dinosaurs never stopped growing the way humans do. Some were as long as a football field! That's unbelievable. To me, dinosaurs are amazing. Right now I'm working on a model of an Afro Titan. It's the biggest one I've ever made. I could lay down inside its head! If this dinosaur were alive, it could eat me whole in one bite.

Reading Across Texts

Both Waterhouse Hawkins and Garfield Minott enjoy what they do. Make notes on places in each selection that show this statement to be true.

Writing Across Texts Present your results in two paragraphs, one for each selection.

 Fact & Opinion On what facts does Garfield Minott base his opinions?

Skill
Main Idea
and Details

Strategy
Graphic
Organizers

Main Idea
and Details

- The main idea is the most important idea about the topic.

- Sometimes the author tells you the main idea. Sometimes you must figure it out for yourself.

- Supporting details are small pieces of information that tell more about the main idea.

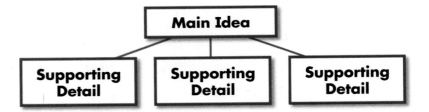

Strategy: Graphic Organizers

Active readers use graphic organizers to help them understand, organize, and remember what they read. Making a graphic organizer as you read can help you figure out the main idea and the details that support it.

1. Read "Aretha: An American Queen." Make a graphic organizer like the one above for the paragraphs.

2. Use your graphic organizers with main ideas to write a summary of this article.

Aretha

An American Queen

The United States is not ruled by a queen. There is a queen who rules in the hearts of American music lovers, though. That queen is Aretha Franklin.

Aretha Franklin was born in Memphis, Tennessee, in 1942. Both her parents were religious gospel music singers. Aretha grew up listening to gospel music. She also learned to sing it as a child.

Even when she was little, people saw that she was a talented singer. Aretha began singing on stage in her early teens. She sang with her father, and people took notice. Her first album, *The Gospel Sound of Aretha Franklin*, was released in 1956. She was only 14 years old!

When Aretha turned 18, she moved to New York. Soon, she was singing all types of music. Eventually, she developed her own style of singing. It came from deep inside her. It was a mixture of gospel and rhythm and blues. This music was called "soul music." Aretha sang it so well that she became known as "The Queen of Soul."

Aretha was voted into the Rock and Roll Hall of Fame in 1987. Her songs are still played on radio today. For many people, she still rules as queen.

Skill What is the main idea of the third paragraph?
a) Aretha's talent was obvious at an early age.
b) Aretha began singing on stage with her father.
c) Aretha's first album was released in 1956.

Strategy Create a graphic organizer to show the main idea and supporting details of the third paragraph. Use your main idea choice from above.

Skill What is the main idea of this paragraph?

Strategy Graphic organizers you create can help you with other tasks, such as summarizing.

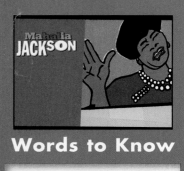

Words to Know

slavery

teenager

barber

religious

choir

appreciate

released

Remember

Try the strategy. Then, if you need more help, use your glossary or dictionary.

Vocabulary Strategy
for Antonyms

Context Clues An antonym is a word that has the opposite meaning of another word. For example, *cold* is an antonym for *hot*. An author may put an antonym near a difficult word to help you discover what it means.

1. Read the words and sentences around the unfamiliar word.

2. Look for antonyms that show contrast with the unfamiliar word. When things are contrasted, words such as *unlike*, *not*, *but*, or *on the other hand* may signal the contrast.

3. Give the unfamiliar word the opposite meaning of the antonym. Does this meaning make sense in the sentence?

As you read "Out of Great Pain, Great Music," check the words and sentences around any unfamiliar word. See if an antonym helps you figure out its meaning.

Out of Great Pain,
GREAT MUSIC

It is hard to understand how people in the United States ever put up with slavery, since Americans value freedom so highly. However, for some 250 years, some white people made slaves of African Americans. Every child of a slave, from infant to teenager, also became the owner's property. Slaves performed many jobs, from cook to field hand to barber. In fact, the rich economy of the South depended upon slave labor. Yet slaves were not paid wages for this valuable work.

Slavery caused great sorrow and pain, but it also gave rise to some of the world's most moving music. Spirituals are religious folk songs that began among slaves in the South. They would sing these songs to help raise their spirits. Church gave them a place to express their hope for a better life to come. The choir made powerful music about that hope.

Slavery ended for African Americans some 140 years ago. But spirituals remain an important part of life for many African Americans today. People of many races and backgrounds have come to appreciate spirituals. They also love blues music, which also originated from the African American experience of slavery. Many African American singers have released recordings of blues music and spirituals that have sold millions of copies all around the world.

Write

Look at the illustrations in "Mahalia Jackson." Choose an illustration to write about. Use as many words from the Words to Know list as you can..

from *The Blues Singers:*
Ten Who Rocked the World

Mahalia
JACKSON

by
Julius Lester

illustrated by
Lisa Cohen

How did
Mahalia Jackson
use the **blues**
in a **new** and
different way?

Expository nonfiction explains what certain things are and how they came to be. As you read, notice how the author explains a musical form known as the blues and how it came to be.

In this selection the author is talking to his granddaughter. He wants her to know about a kind of music that he loves, the blues.

First he explains that the blues is not just a feeling. It's a kind of music. Then he tells her about a great singer who knew all about the blues.

So what are the blues? Well, the blues are like having the flu in your feelings. But instead of your nose being stuffed up, it's your heart that feels like it needs blowing. Everybody gets the blues, even children.

But the blues is not only a feeling. It's also a kind of music that cures the blues. The words of a blues song might be sad, but the music and the beat wrap around your heart like one of your grandmother's hugs.

The roots of the blues go back to slavery. If anything would give you the blues, it was slavery. Imagine somebody owning you like I own my car. Just like I can sell my car to anybody who has the money, somebody could sell you and me the same way.

One of the ways black people fought against slavery was with the breath in their bodies. They wove hope on the air by singing songs called spirituals—songs for the spirit. Their bodies were in slavery, but it didn't mean their spirits had to be buried in sorrow as white as fog.

Slavery ended in 1865, but freedom didn't take its place. The people who had owned the slaves still owned the land. How could the slaves truly be free if they had to keep working for the same people who had owned them?

Blues music probably started something like this: Somebody was out in the field working one day. She knew she would be working from sunup to sundown on somebody's farm making fifty cents a day until the day she died. Thinking about it made her heart burn as if it had been struck by lightning. The pain was so bad she didn't know what to do, and suddenly she started singing.

Got a hurtin' in my heart, feels like I'm going to die,
Got a hurtin' in my heart, feels like I'm going to die,
I feel like a bird whose wings will never fly.

Singing just those few words made her feel a little better, and everybody who heard her felt a little better too.

The blues IS LIFE
And don't you forget it!

Ray Charles

They took
THE GOSPEL
FEELING
and put it into the
BLUES.

Mahalia Jackson (1911–1972) was not a blues singer. She sang church songs, gospel, but she knew blues and brought the blues feeling into church music. Other people, like Ray Charles and Aretha Franklin, grew up singing gospel, too, but they took the gospel feeling and put it into the blues. The words in a gospel song and the words in the blues will be different, but both can make you start moaning like you've just bitten into the best fried chicken anybody ever made. So that's why you have to know about Mahalia Jackson. Even if she didn't sing the blues, she learned a lot from listening to blues singers, and blues singers have learned a lot from listening to her sing gospel.

Mahalia grew up in New Orleans, Louisiana, the city where jazz was born and where there is still more good music and good food per block than anyplace in the world. Her father worked on the docks during the day loading bales of cotton on boats, was a barber at night and a preacher on Sundays. When Mahalia was five years old her mother died. Her father took her to live with Mahalia Paul, an aunt who lived nearby and the woman for whom Mahalia Jackson was named. Mahalia never lived with her father again, but she saw him almost every day at his barbershop.

Mahalia grew up loving music, and the person she wanted to sing like was none other than Bessie Smith. But Mahalia's aunt was very religious, and she took Mahalia to church every day. When talking about her childhood, Mahalia said that in her church, "everybody sang and clapped and stomped their feet, sang with their whole bodies! They had the beat, a powerful beat, a rhythm we held on to from slavery days, and [the] music was so strong and expressive, it used to bring the tears to my eyes." It was in church that Mahalia first started singing.

She dropped out of school after the eighth grade and went to work doing people's laundry. Mahalia began hearing stories from relatives and friends about how good life was in Chicago, Illinois. So when she was sixteen, another aunt, Hannah, took her to Chicago to live. Once there, Mahalia joined a gospel group and a church choir while working during the day as a maid in hotels.

It was in Chicago that Mahalia got the chance to see her idol, Bessie Smith, who came to town to put on a show. Years later Mahalia remembered that Bessie "filled the whole place with her voice [and] I never went home until they put us out and closed up for the night."

Mahalia's singing brought her to the attention of Thomas A. Dorsey, who directed a number of gospel choirs in Chicago. Dorsey was the father of gospel music, but earlier in his life he had been the pianist for Ma Rainey, the blues singer Bessie Smith had traveled with. He began taking her to out-of-town churches for concerts and her reputation began to grow almost as fast as you are.

In 1946, Mahalia's first record was released. She would go on to become the most famous gospel singer in the world, and in 1976 she received (posthumously) a Grammy Lifetime

"Bessie FILLED THE WHOLE PLACE with HER VOICE [and] I never went home UNTIL they put us out and closed up for the night."

Achievement Award. Mahalia was a close friend of Martin Luther King, Jr., and at the March on Washington, he asked her to sing right before he gave his famous "I Have a Dream" speech.

Mahalia Jackson had a big voice, and she could go from a high note to a low one as easily as you put one foot in front of the other. She could hold a note until you thought she should run out of breath, and she could put together a lot of notes in a line of music that would take your breath away. And she did it as easily as a cloud floats across the sky.

When I was a teenager, I was attending a meeting in Chicago with my church youth group. Mahalia came to our meeting and sang a few songs. I knew who she was, and I'm sorry now that I didn't have sense enough to appreciate listening to one of the greatest singers of the twentieth century. I hope you won't make the same mistake if you get a chance to hear some of the great singers of today.

Reader Response

Open for Discussion "So that's why you have to know about Mahalia Jackson," writes Julius Lester. Why does he write this? What does he tell you in the selection to convince you that he is right?

1. Imagine that you must describe your favorite singer's voice to a friend. Now read the paragraph on page 357 about Mahalia Jackson's voice. How well has the author described it?

2. This selection is about the blues. The main idea about the blues has to do with slavery and people's feelings. Look back at pages 352–353 and discuss exactly what this main idea is.

3. How are blues and gospel music similar and different from each other? Make a Venn diagram using your own knowledge and the information on page 355.

4. Which Word to Know list words describe major influences on Mahalia Jackson's life? Explain your answer.

Look Back and Write Music has to begin somewhere. Look back at the beginning of the selection to help you remember where music called the blues began. Then write a summary about the birth of the blues.

Julius Lester

Read more books by Julius Lester.

Julius Lester says, "I write because the lives of all of us are stories. If enough of those stories are told, then perhaps we will begin to see that our lives are the same story. The differences are merely in the details."

Mr. Lester has published more than thirty books and won many honors for his children's books, including the Newbery Honor Medal. When he was growing up in the 1940s and 1950s, he never dreamed he would one day become a writer. He wanted to be a musician. After recording two albums and hosting radio and television shows, he turned to writing. In addition to his work as a writer, he teaches at the University of Massachusetts. His photographs of the civil rights movement were part of an exhibition at the Smithsonian Institution.

Black Cowboy, Wild Horses

The Knee-High Man and Other Tales

It is important to Mr. Lester to help African American children become aware of their heritage. In his books for young people, he doesn't focus on the history of wars and politics, but rather on the lives and experiences of ordinary people.

Perfect Harmony

by Charles R. Smith, Jr.

Genre

- A poem is a composition arranged in lines. A line may be as short as a single word.

- Many poems are written in the first person, with the speaker serving as a character.

- Some poems have rhyme; others do not. The poet creates images through the rhyme and rhythm of language.

- The poet also uses images to express thoughts and feelings.

- Read the introduction and look at the titles of the poems and the photographs. What do you think the poems will be about?

Link to Reading

Think of something you do that involves intense physical activity, such as dancing, running, basketball, or gymnastics. Write a poem about how it feels to do this activity. Share your poem with the class.

The author's poems are inspired by his work with the Boy's Choir of Harlem, in New York City. This choir of young African American men performs for audiences around the world.

FOcus

Feet apart
arms at sides
chest puffed out
head held high

w a i t i n g

to release butterflies
inside.

Eyes focus
like
the calm
before the storm
ready to erupt
before I perform
toes tingle
feet quake
muscles twitch

hands shake
while
throat hums
hummmmmmms
hummmmmmmmmmmmmmms
so that
my voice may
awake.
Focus
I must
focus
to channel my
electricity
and relax

r e l a x
r e l a x

before I set
the butterflies
free.

 **Main Idea**   What parts of the body does the singer use to gain focus?

Deep Breaths

Ex-
hale
s l o w.
In-
hale
d e e p.
Thoughts focus.
Ready.
Release.

Breath
breathes life
into words
on a page
gives them
a stage
to showcase
sound

and express
rage
drown sorrows
and engage
ears
with musical
notes
that jump
leap
and
shout
from throats
voicing words
floating
on air
built up
in lungs
singing

singing
a song
that began
with a breath
transformed
from air
to notes
to words
in voice
waiting
to be
sung.

Energy spent.
Ex-
hale
and
done.

Reading Across Texts

Compare how Mahalia Jackson and the speaker of the poems use their bodies when they sing.

Writing Across Texts Make a list of tips that Mahalia and the speaker might give to people who want to sing with great energy and power. Share your tips with the class.

 Main Idea What does it mean to "breathe life into words"?

Comprehension

Skill
Graphic Sources

Strategy
Prior Knowledge

Graphic Sources

- Some graphic sources are maps, time lines, charts, diagrams, and pictures with captions.

- A graphic source makes information easy to see and understand.

- Preview graphic sources to help predict what an article or story may be about.

- As you read, compare the information in graphic sources with the information in the text.

Strategy: Prior Knowledge

Good readers use what they already know to help them understand what they read. Connect what you are reading with what you have read before and what you know from personal experience. Use what you already know to understand the information in graphic sources.

1. Read "Computer Art and What It Takes." As you read, make a list of computer graphics tools that are new to you.

2. Write down three things you learned as you read the article and studied the picture.

Computer Art
and What It Takes

What do all these things share: the characters you play with in video games, the weather maps you see on TV, and the cartoons you laugh at in modern movies? They have all been created on computers. They are all examples of computer graphics.

It does not take much to put together a computer graphics system. Graphics software allows you to create the pictures. A computer hard drive stores the graphics, or pictures, and lets you work with them. A monitor shows you the pictures.

Also necessary are a mouse and a keyboard to input commands. Some equipment to input pictures is needed as well. This could be a digital pad or camera, a scanner, or a light pen. If you want to make a copy of the pictures on paper, you'll need a printer too.

Skill Preview the picture below. What does it suggest this article will be about?

Strategy Which of the tools pictured below have you already used or seen someone else use?

Skill Which items that you are reading about are pictured here?

Strategy Did the text match what you already know about some of these items? Did you learn anything new about any of them? If so, you have just added to your prior knowledge.

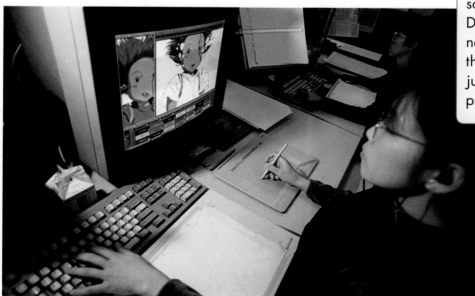

Words to Know

prehistoric

landscape

background

miniature

reassembled

Remember

Try the strategy. Then, if you need more help, use your glossary or dictionary.

Vocabulary Strategy
for Prefixes

Word Structure A prefix is a syllable added at the beginning of a base word that has a meaning of its own. Recognizing a prefix can help you figure out the word's meaning. For example, *pre-* means "before." If you *prearrange* something, you arrange it ahead of time. The prefix *re-* means "again." If you *reheat* soup, you warm it up again.

1. Look at an unfamiliar word to see if it has a base word you know.

2. Check to see if a prefix has been added to the base word.

3. Ask yourself how the prefix changes the meaning of the base word.

4. Try the meaning in the sentence. Does it make sense?

As you read "Visiting the Past," find words with prefixes. Use the prefixes to help you figure out the meanings of the words.

Visiting the Past

While we were on vacation, our family visited an incredible theme park. It had models that reproduce scenes from the past. Once we entered the park, we split up and went our own ways.

I went straight to the exhibit of prehistoric times. Paintings of huge, strange plants created the feeling of an ancient landscape. The model dinosaurs were life-sized, looked real, and even moved! A tape of background noises, such as animal cries and splashes, added to the realism. In one large room, artists had shaped a past world in miniature.

When we reassembled as a family for lunch, my brother described the Old West community he had visited. It had a whole street from a mining town—complete with general store, hotel, and jail. He rode a cart into a deep tunnel. Down there, the exhibit showed how miners worked. Occasionally, he said, you felt a tremor and heard a boom. Somehow they reproduced the explosions when ore was blasted from a mountain! We agreed that this was the best theme park we have ever visited.

Write

What place have you visited that uses special effects? Write an article about the place for the school newspaper. Use words from the Words to Know list.

SPECIAL EFFECTS

by Jake Hamilton

IN FILM AND TELEVISION

How do they make those fantastic movies look so realistic?

Genre

Expository nonfiction explains what certain things are and how they came to be. As you read, notice how the author explains how artists make miniature models for movie sets.

IN MINIATURE

Special effects (SFX) is the art of making the impossible
into a fantastic reality. Special effects has always pushed the
boundaries of human imagination. It keeps today's movie and
television audiences glued to their seats in starry-eyed wonder.

The art of miniature model-making has always been an
important part of special effects in movies. Some movie stories
have big, spectacular, action-filled scenes. They may call for fights
between dinosaurs, explosions on the Golden Gate Bridge, or
an armed force charging through the desert. Movie-
makers can save time and money by making
models for these scenes. This article
tells the story of the building of
a miniature landscape for
a television show.

*400-foot (120m)
film magazine
with running
time of $4\frac{1}{4}$
minutes at
normal speed*

*Prime lens interchangeable
with the zoom lens*

*Matte box reduces
lens flares.*

*Concept model is 1 ft x 1 ft
(0.3 meter x 0.3 meter)*

1 A General Idea

A special effects team must build a prehistoric world in a workshop. The team's first step is to make a "concept" model of this mini-world. The model will give a general view of what the finished product will look like. This model shows that the landscape will include a fallen tree and a circular lake.

2 Getting Larger

The movie-makers study this concept model to decide on the size and shape of the finished product. Then they make a larger and more detailed "prototype" model. This gives them a clearer picture of how the finished product will look. The prototype comes in sections that are fitted together like puzzle pieces. This 2 ft x 2 ft (0.6 m x 0.6 m) prototype is fully painted and fitted with bushes and trees. Now the team can work on the final product.

Cameraman's eyepiece

Camera door is opened to thread the film past the gate.

Final model landscape will be in three main sections—white areas show where the divides are between the main sections.

Cardboard representation of early reptile

Getting Started

The full-size miniature model will be 24 ft x 24 ft (7.2 m x 7.2 m). Building it will take real cooperation among all the SFX team members. The model's base is made of the kind of plastic used in fast food cups and boxes. Model-makers carve the plastic surface to make hills and valleys and rivers and lakes. They use references such as pictures of trees and rocks to guide them. These model-makers are using photographs of a dry riverbed as a guide.

3

Model-makers carve details in ground of model's front section.

Miniature trees and bushes are modeled with plastic and paint, as well as real pieces of greenery.

4 Carving It Out

Here, the model-makers are cutting out the area of the huge circular lake at the heart of the model. They will then add more surface detail and mark out other features in the landscape.

Rebuilding 5

The model is cut into sections so it can be taken on trucks to the television studio. Since the model is so large and detailed, each section is numbered. That way, when the pieces reach the studio they can be reassembled easily.

Rebuilding the landscape is just like putting a huge jigsaw puzzle together.

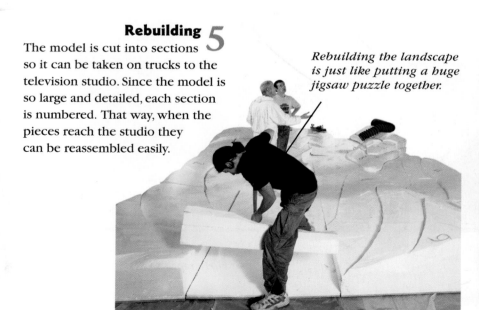

6 Foaming the Model

At the studio, the model is put back together, and the miniature trees, rocks, and other surface details are all put in place. Then a technician wearing a special protective suit sprays the model. He uses a light foam made from toxic chemicals. The foam gives the surface of the model a smooth, natural look. He also adds bumps and dips to the surface. This makes it look just like a real landscape.

To protect against toxic fumes, the technician wears a respirator.

7 In the Studio

Putting the miniature landscape back together takes a great deal of attention to detail. Every last tree, bush, and rock must be exactly in place. A huge painted backdrop of blue sky streaked with clouds has been placed on the far wall. Lights positioned overhead will give the landscape more texture and shadow.

Technician's head pops up between two of the main landscape sections.

Appropriate large potted plants are used for the foreground.

8 Fixing in Place

Model-makers use a special glue to make sure the sections will not come apart. The glue is carefully dried by hand. Technicians use the same kind of blow-dryer people use on their hair. That way they can aim the hot wind just right so it will not disturb any delicate details on the landscape's surface.

Computer Generated Imagery

Many future movies will be created or enhanced on screen, using computer generated imagery (CGI). This 3-D animated dragon has been created as a wire frame image before being fleshed out, enhanced, and lit carefully—all on a computer.

REPTILE MODELING

Early reptiles were needed to inhabit the prehistoric scene, so miniature models were prepared. After it was agreed which reptiles to model, including Moschops (left), each one was sculpted carefully in nondrying clay, which is easy to shape. The model is attached to metal leg stands, and the smallest details are added at this stage, including horned backbones, razor-sharp claws, and scaled reptile skin.

The model-maker sprays the model with plastic sealer to make it possible to release the fiberglass of the mold from the clay later on. A dividing wall of clay is then placed around the model (right) so that when the mold is made it can be split into two halves.

The mold is filled with foam latex and the result is this white-faced reptile. The model-makers can now paint its skin with different textures of green and yellow. The creature is hollow in the middle so that SFX technicians can get their arms up and inside to operate it without the viewer seeing.

Foam latex model of a Lystrosaur

Water makes Lystrosaur glisten on film.

The final image of one reptile perched on a fallen log in the miniature landscape looks incredibly realistic. The creature has also been given small eyes, pointed claws, and fanged teeth.

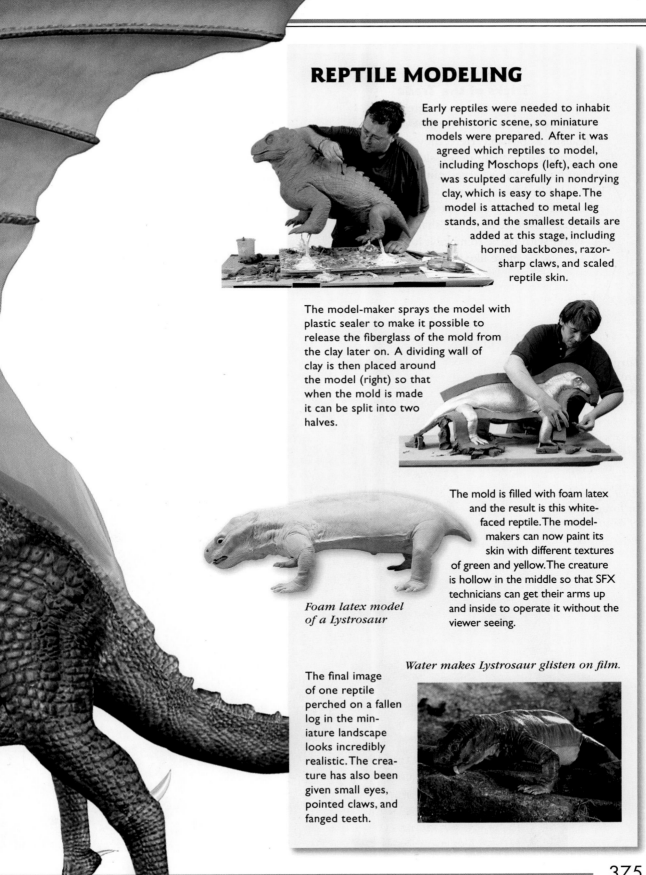

375

Tricks of the Trade

The model-makers go to great lengths to make a miniature look as realistic as possible. Here, they are working on a slight depression in the surface that was carved out for a lake. It is filled with water to a depth of just 1.5 in. (4 cm.). The model-makers are layering the shallow water with fabric to make it look more like a deep lake.

Model-makers refer to television monitor for camera's eye-view.

Large, potted trees are used for foreground section.

Real log is used in foreground of landscape.

Toy Soldiers

Director Steven Spielberg used a miniature model to plan shots for the film *Raiders of the Lost Ark.* Directors often use miniature models to plan the way a scene should look, including actors' movements, the scenery, and any special lighting or camera angles.

Spielberg decides where to position the camera for the desert shot.

Sand dunes are constructed from polystyrene and beach sand.

Miniature models of tents, tanks and other vehicles are used.

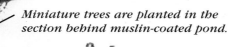

Miniature trees are planted in the section behind muslin-coated pond.

Landscape is supported on timber platform.

Sand used on ground of miniature and to cover cracks in model surface.

Finally Ready

It has taken most of the day to reassemble the entire miniature landscape. Now the scene is ready for filming. During filming, SFX team members beneath the platform can reach up and move the reptile models around from below. Notice how the trees in the background section of the landscape are much smaller than the trees in the foreground section. This makes the scene seem to roll back away rapidly into the distance. The large painted backdrop and studio lighting add to the effect of a vast prehistoric landscape roamed by early reptiles.

Reader Response

Open for Discussion The miniature landscape is being made for a TV show. What might that show be like? Use what you know from the selection to imagine different scenes and the sounds that would go with them.

1. The selection includes photographs to help you visualize the process that the author describes in words. What are some steps and tools that are not shown? Would showing them make the selection better?

2. Think up additional captions for the photographs.

3. Look back at the selection as you recall art projects you have done in school or at home. Which project does the selection most remind you of? Describe it.

4. What makes this prehistoric landscape look realistic? Use words from the Words to Know list in your answer.

Look Back and Write Imagine that you have the entire team of technicians from the selection in front of you. You are the boss, explaining in general what they must do. Write what you would say to them.

Jake Hamilton has always loved movies. As a boy, he saw every film he could and spent hours in movie theaters. Today, as a successful journalist, Mr. Hamilton gets to watch movies as part of his job. He is a film critic for newspapers and magazines. He also reviews movies for the BBC World Service. This is his first book for young people.

Many people working in the film industry helped Mr. Hamilton in the making of the book *Special Effects in Film and Television*. The special effects departments of major film studios allowed him behind the scenes to see how they work. They showed him how special effects are staged. He was able to photograph the equipment used to create those awesome effects.

Computer Animation From Start to Finish
by Samuel G. Woods

Virtual Reality
by Holly Cefrey

Searching For Animation

Search Engines

Genre

- A search engine is a tool that helps Internet users find the Web sites they need.

- It uses keywords — words you type in to pinpoint what you're looking for.

Text Features

- The search window is where you type in keywords. Then you click on a Search button.

- The search results are displayed in a list below the search window.

- Each item on the list leads to a Web site that contains the keywords.

Link to Social Studies

Do your own research on animation. Share fun facts with the class.

Matt does an Internet search to find out more about animation. He starts by typing the keyword "animation" into a search engine and then clicking on the SEARCH button.

380

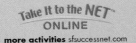
Take It to the NET™
ONLINE
more activities sfsuccessnet.com

Matt gets a long list of Web sites. He uses his mouse and the scroll bar to scroll through the results until he gets to the 27th item on the list.

File   Edit

     www.url.here

Search   "animation"   GO!

> **Search Results: "animation"**

25. <u>Animation World</u> - Site provides a look at the latest happenings in the world of animation.

26. <u>Animation Express</u> - We have dozens of Web-based animation shorts, updated twice-weekly.

27. <u>Drawn to be Wild</u> - Check out this information about animation and find out about its history, meet some famous animators, and learn the tricks of the trade.

Matt would like to learn tricks of the animation trade. So he clicks on the link <u>Drawn to be Wild</u>.

 Prior Knowledge   How does this search remind you of your own?

The next thing he sees on his computer screen is this:

THE UK'S ANIMATION CELEBRATION

Welcome to Drawn to be Wild. Here you can find a wealth of information about films and animators.

Learn to be Wild
Facts, figures and history about the world of animation

Ask Brian
Many children had questions for our Drawn to be Wild expert Brian Sibley. Read a selection of them here.

Other Web sites
Kids' sites on the Web that we think you'll like

Matt clicks on Learn to be Wild, and up pops an article about how animation tricks the eye. Read from the article that Matt found by searching the Internet.

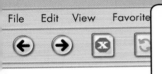

A Trick of the Eye
by Brian Sibley

No matter how they are made, all animated films work because of an optical illusion called "persistence of vision." The simplest example of this visual trick is the old-fashioned "flip-book." These books present a sequence of line illustrations, one after the other. Each one is slightly different, so that when the book is "flipped," the pictures

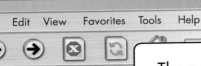

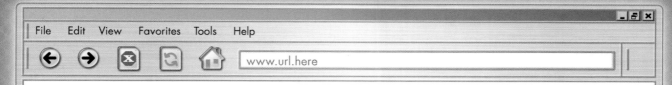

appear to move. What really happens is that the eye holds onto an image for a fraction of a second after seeing it. Then, when that image is replaced with another — and then another and another — the eye tells the brain that those drawings are moving.

Every movie ever made, whether animated or live-action, works in just this way. Film is really just a long strip of pictures, called frames. Like the drawings in a flip-book, each frame is slightly different from the one before and after. A motion picture camera is designed to photograph 24 still frames every second. Then, when developed and edited, that film is passed through a projector at the same speed. That way, what we see (or think we see) are moving pictures.

The difference with an animated film is that the camera works on a "stop-frame" system. It takes single static pictures. The animator has to provide the illusion of movement by drawing 24 separate pictures (or, in the case of model animation, by moving each puppet 24 times) for every single second of film.

Reading Across Texts

The selections about special effects and animation tell about tricking the eye. Make a list of the "tricks" in each selection.

Writing Across Texts Which "trick" do the filmmakers in both selections use? Expain it in your own words.

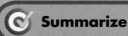 **Summarize** Can you summarize this animation trick?

Chemistry 101

by Marilyn Nelson

George Washington Carver
Inventor, Scientist, Teacher
1864?–1943

A canvas apron over his street clothes,
Carver leads his chemistry class into
the college dump. The students follow, a claque
of ducklings hatched by hens. Where he
sees a retort, a Bunsen burner,
a mortar, zinc sulfate, they see
a broken bowl, a broken lantern,
a rusty old flatiron, a fruit jar top.
Their tangle of twine, his lace.
He turns, a six-inch length of copper tubing
in one hand. "Now, what can we do with this?"
Two by two, little lights go on.
One by hesitant one, dark hands are raised.
The waters of imagining, their element.

The Bronze Horse

by Beverly McLoughland

The museum guard is fast asleep
Chin on his chest in his fold-up chair,
The bronze horse paws at the marble floor
His muscles quiver, his nostrils flare

His bronze mane flows as though a breeze
Has blown through the door, while the breath of sun
In the empty room holds summer fields
Of tender green, where the horses run.

And feeling his bronze soul come to life,
He lifts one foot from the marble floor,
Nuzzles the silence which stirs to hear
Hoofbeats echo through the open door.

The Termites

by Douglas Floriatt

Our
high and
mighty
termite
mound
arises
far above
the ground,
and just as
deep, grows
underground.
Our nest is
blessed to be
immense. It gives
us all a firm
defense, superior
to any fence. It
shields us from our
enemies. It keeps us
cooler, by degrees.
From floods and droughts
it guarantees. A prize
nobody will assign in
architectural design, but
still our hill suits us just fine.

Stairs

by Oliver Herford

Here's to the man who invented stairs
And taught our feet to soar!
He was the first who ever burst
Into a second floor.

The world would be downstairs today
Had he not found the key;
So let his name go down to fame,
Whatever it may be.

Invent It Yourself

connect to
SCIENCE

Think of the inventions in this unit. Each one was an attempt to make people's lives better. Make a chart like the one below and put each one on it. Then, plan and describe your own invention using the chart. Make a drawing of your invention.

What It Is Made Of	What It Is For	How It Works

What do people gain from the work of inventors and artists?

Inventors in the News

connect to
WRITING

Leonardo da Vinci looked ahead to a time when people would fly. Waterhouse Hawkins helped people visualize the dinosaurs of the distant past. Become a newspaper reporter at the time of one of these men. Write a news article on the man and his work. Include details on how people of the time feel about your subject.

Today's Times

Leonardo Tackles High and Mighty Problems

Creative Influences

connect to
SOCIAL STUDIES

Apart from the inventors and artists you met in this unit, whose creative work has been important in your life? Research and make notes on this person and his or her work. Then present an oral report from your notes. Describe this person's work, telling why it is important to you.

Sandra's Report on Monet

Claude Monet was a famous artist who painted pictures of beautiful flowers. He used a style called Impressionism. I like his flowers because they remind me of my mom's garden. She works in the garden all weekend. Sometimes she lets me help plant bulbs.

Read It
ONLINE
sfsuccessnet.com

Adapting

How do people and
animals adapt to
different situations?

Weslandia

Comprehension

Skill
Draw Conclusions

Strategy
Answer Questions

Skill

Draw Conclusions

- A conclusion is a decision you make after thinking about the details in what you read.

- Often your prior knowledge can help you draw, or make, a conclusion.

- When you draw a conclusion, be sure it makes sense and is supported by what you have read.

| Detail | + | Detail | + | What you know | → | Conclusion |

Strategy

Strategy: Answer Questions

Sometimes you must draw a conclusion to answer a question asked in a book, by a teacher, or on a test. The details you need for your answer may be in one place or in several places. Use those details plus what you already know to draw a conclusion that answers the question.

1. Read "The Go-Cart." Make two graphic organizers like the one above to help draw conclusions about why Jeff entered the go-cart race and how he felt about himself.

2. Answer this question and explain your answer: Was Jeff's family helpful and supporting?

The Go-Cart

The summer had been downright boring. Nothing extraordinary had occurred. Then one day Jeff read the announcement in the local newspaper: "Go-Cart Race Next Month! First Prize $1,000!" He decided that he *had* to enter that race.

"But Jeff, you don't own a go-cart," his father said.

The newspaper noted that the go-cart had to be homemade, not factory-manufactured and bought. Jeff had been saving his allowance for what seemed like an eternity, and he had enough money to buy the plans and parts for a go-cart.

"But Jeff, you've never built anything," his mother said.

Jeff set about his building task. He read the instructions that came with his go-cart kit carefully. If something was confusing or hard to understand, he called the hardware store and asked for a clerk to explain. Every day he toiled on his go-cart, and every night it was that much closer to being finished.

Finally, the day of the race arrived. Jeff put on his helmet and revved his engine. The announcer roared, "On your mark! Get set! Go!" And Jeff, who had never raced a go-cart before, was off!

Skill Why do you think Jeff *had* to enter the go-cart race?

Strategy To answer that question, you need to draw a conclusion. The details in the paragraph can help you.

Skill How do you think Jeff felt about himself as he revved his engine, waiting for the race to begin?

Strategy To answer that question, think of details from throughout the story. Also think how *you* would feel if you were in Jeff's place.

envy

fleeing

civilization

complex

strategy

blunders

inspired

rustling

Remember

Try the strategy. Then, if you need more help, use your glossary or dictionary.

Vocabulary Strategy
for Endings

Word Structure The endings *-ed*, *-ing*, and *-s* may be added to verbs to change the tense, person, or usage of the verbs. You can use endings to help you figure out the meaning of an unfamiliar word.

1. Examine the unfamiliar word to see if it has a base word you know.

2. Check to see if the ending *-s*, *-ed*, or *-ing* has been added to a base word. Remember that some base words drop the final *-e* before adding an ending. For example, *rustle* becomes *rustling*.

3. Reread the sentence and make sure the word shows action. (The ending *-s* may be added to nouns too.)

4. Decide how the ending changes the meaning of the base word.

5. Try the meaning in the sentence.

As you read "Long-Ago Lives," look for words that end with *-ed*, *-ing*, or *-s*. Use the endings to help figure out their meanings.

Long-Ago Lives

We do not tend to think with envy about the lives of people who lived thousands of years ago. We are likely to imagine them fleeing for their lives from enemies or wild beasts. Any civilization without excellent shopping, television, and computers seems far too primitive for us.

However, we have learned much about early cultures. What we have learned shows us that their world was often complex, not simple. They were not all that different from us. For example, two thousand years ago the Mayan people played a ball game. The game was played by teams on stone courts with special goals. Players needed great strength and skill. The strategy was to send a heavy ball through a high stone ring using only hips, knees, elbows, and buttocks. Kings might play this game, for which the stakes were very high. No one wanted to make any blunders because the loser might lose his head!

This game may have inspired our modern game of soccer. Stand on one of these ancient ball courts and you can almost hear the rustling of a feather headdress and the yelling of the crowd.

Write

Look at the pictures in *Weslandia*. Choose one to write about. Use as many words from the Words to Know list as you can.

Why does Wesley take up the challenge of creating his own world?

Genre **Fiction stories** are stories that the author has made up. As you read, notice how the character makes up his own world.

Weslandia

by PAUL FLEISCHMAN   illustrated by KEVIN HAWKES

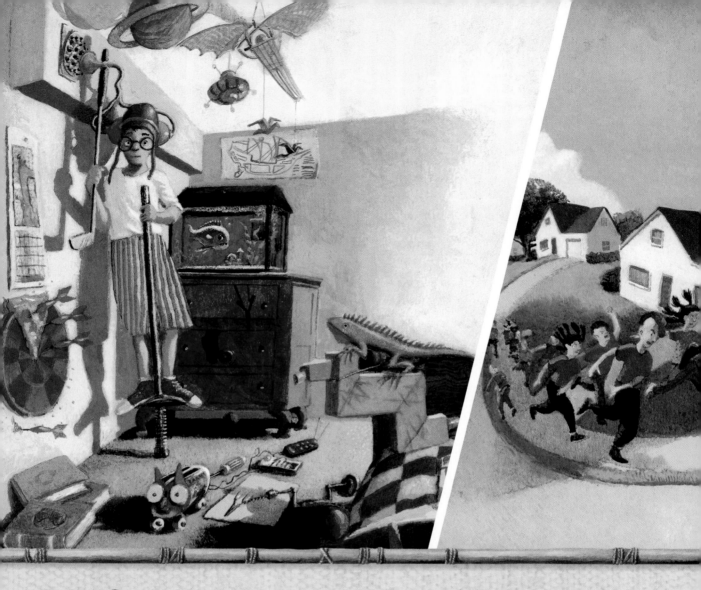

"Of course he's miserable," moaned Wesley's mother. "He sticks out."

"Like a nose," snapped his father.

Listening through the heating vent, Wesley knew they were right. He was an outcast from the civilization around him.

He alone in his town disliked pizza and soda, alarming his mother and the school nurse. He found professional football stupid. He'd refused to shave half his head, the hairstyle worn by all the other boys, despite his father's bribe of five dollars.

Passing his neighborhood's two styles of housing—garage on the

left and garage on the right—Wesley alone dreamed of more exciting forms of shelter. He had no friends, but plenty of tormentors.

Fleeing them was the only sport he was good at.

Each afternoon his mother asked him what he'd learned in
school that day.

"That seeds are carried great distances by the wind," he answered
on Wednesday.

"That each civilization has its staple food crop," he answered on
Thursday.

"That school's over and I should find a good summer project,"
he answered on Friday.

399

As always, his father mumbled, "I'm sure you'll use that knowledge often."

Suddenly, Wesley's thoughts shot sparks. His eyes blazed. His father was right! He could actually *use* what he'd learned that week for a summer project that would top all others. He would grow his own staple food crop—and found his own civilization!

The next morning he turned over a plot of ground in his yard. That night a wind blew in from the west. It raced through the trees and set his curtains snapping. Wesley lay awake, listening. His land was being planted.

Five days later the first seedlings appeared.

"You'll have almighty bedlam on your hands if you don't get those weeds out," warned his neighbor.

"Actually, that's my crop," replied Wesley. "In this type of garden there are no weeds."

Following ancient tradition, Wesley's fellow gardeners grew tomatoes, beans, Brussels sprouts, and nothing else. Wesley found it thrilling to open his land to chance, to invite the new and unknown.

The plants shot up past his knees, then his waist. They seemed to be all of the same sort. Wesley couldn't find them in any plant book.

"Are those tomatoes, beans, or Brussels sprouts?" asked Wesley's
neighbor.

"None of the above," replied Wesley.

Fruit appeared, yellow at first, then blushing to magenta.
Wesley picked one and sliced through the rind to the juicy purple
center. He took a bite and found the taste an entrancing blend of
peach, strawberry, pumpkin pie, and flavors he had no name for.

Ignoring the shelf of cereals in the kitchen, Wesley took
to breakfasting on the fruit. He dried half a rind to serve as a
cup, built his own squeezing device, and drank the fruit's juice
throughout the day.

Pulling up a plant, he found large tubers on the roots. These he boiled, fried, or roasted on the family barbecue, seasoning them with a pinch of the plant's highly aromatic leaves.

It was hot work tending to his crop. To keep off the sun, Wesley wove himself a hat from strips of the plant's woody bark. His success with the hat inspired him to devise a spinning wheel and loom on which he wove a loose-fitting robe from the stalks' soft inner fibers.

Unlike jeans, which he found scratchy and heavy, the robe was comfortable, reflected the sun, and offered myriad opportunities for pockets.

His schoolmates were scornful, then curious. Grudgingly, Wesley allowed them ten minutes apiece at his mortar, crushing the plant's seeds to collect the oil.

This oil had a tangy scent and served him both as suntan lotion and mosquito repellent. He rubbed it on his face each morning and sold small amounts to his former tormentors at the price of ten dollars per bottle.

"What's happened to your watch?" asked his mother one day.

Wesley admitted that he no longer wore it. He told time by

the stalk that he used as a sundial and had divided the day into eight segments—the number of petals on the plant's flowers.

He'd adopted a new counting system as well, based likewise upon the number eight. His domain, home to many such innovations, he named "Weslandia."

Uninterested in traditional sports, Wesley made up his own. These were designed for a single player and used many different parts of the plant. His spectators looked on with envy.

Realizing that more players would offer him more scope, Wesley invented other games that would include his schoolmates,

games rich with strategy and complex scoring systems. He tried to be patient with the other players' blunders.

August was unusually hot. Wesley built himself a platform and took to sleeping in the middle of Weslandia. He passed the evenings playing a flute he'd fashioned from a stalk or gazing up at the sky, renaming the constellations.

His parents noted Wesley's improved morale. "It's the first time in years he's looked happy," said his mother.

Wesley gave them a tour of Weslandia.

"What do you call this plant?" asked his father. Not knowing

its name, Wesley had begun calling it "swist," from the sound
of its leaves rustling in the breeze.

In like manner, he'd named his new fabrics, games, and foods,
until he'd created an entire language.

Mixing the plant's oil with soot, Wesley made a passable
ink. As the finale to his summer project, he used the ink and
his own eighty-letter alphabet to record the history of his
civilization's founding.

In September, Wesley returned to school . . .
He had no shortage of friends.

Reader Response

Open for Discussion Would you like to live in Weslandia or a land of your own making? What is your opinion about making a new civilization? Use *Weslandia* as support for your opinion.

1. *Weslandia* shows that you can find a fun idea for a fantasy tale just beyond your own back door. How can you tell that Paul Fleischman had fun inventing this story? Use examples from the text.

2. Pretend you have never read *Weslandia*. Look only at the illustrations, from start to finish. Then draw conclusions about the plot and characters. Use examples from the art to support those conclusions.

3. Would you say that Wesley is a person you could admire? Support your answer with details from the story.

4. Wesley sees himself as an outcast from civilization. What do you think he meant? What did he do to change his situation? Answer the questions using words from the Words to Know list.

Look Back and Write Look at the picture on pages 406–407 and read the story's final sentence. Explain how they make a surprise ending to *Weslandia*.

408

Paul Fleischman

Read more books by Paul Fleischman.

When he was asked if his childhood was like Wesley's in *Weslandia*, Paul Fleischman replied, "Yes and no. I felt different from my peers because I was so short—the shortest boy in my grade all the way through 10th grade. And like Wesley, my friends and I made up an alternate world—our own games, our own underground school newspaper." On the other hand, he says, "Unlike Wesley, I wasn't an outcast. I was president of my grammar school and had a great pack of friends."

Mr. Fleischman has received many awards for his books, including a Newbery Medal for *Joyful Noise: Poems for Two Voices*. He grew up in Santa Monica, California, where he listened to his father, well-known writer Sid Fleischman, read chapters of his books to the family. Paul Fleischman says, "We grew up knowing that words felt good in the ears and on the tongue, that they were as much fun to play with as toys."

Paul Fleischman's love for music has played a part in his writing. While growing up, he learned to play the piano. He also enjoyed listening to all kinds of music on the radio, from Beethoven symphonies to pop songs. Mr. Fleishman now lives on the coast in California with his wife, Patty. He has two grown sons.

Lost!
A Story in String

**Joyful Noise: Poems
for Two Voices**

Poetry

Under the Back Porch

BY VIRGINIA HAMILTON

Our house is two stories high
shaped like a white box.
There is a yard stretched around it
and in back
a wooden porch.

Under the back porch is my place.
I rest there.
I go there when I have to be alone.
It is always shaded and damp.
Sunlight only slants through the slats
in long strips of light,
and the smell of the damp
is moist green,
like the moss that grows here.

My sisters and brothers
can stand on the back porch
and never know
I am here
underneath.
It is my place.
All mine.

Keziah

BY GWENDOLYN BROOKS

I have a secret place to go.
Not anyone may know

And sometimes when the wind is rough
I cannot get there fast enough.

And sometimes when my mother
Is scolding my big brother,

My secret place, it seems to me,
Is quite the only place to be.

Reading Across Texts

Look back at *Weslandia* and ask yourself what kind of
poem Wesley might write about the world he created.

Writing Across Texts Write a poem about *Weslandia*
that you think Wesley might have written.

Draw Conclusions What makes the porch a secret place?

Generalize

- An author may write similar details about different things or people. You can use these similar details to make a general statement that covers all the things or people. This statement is called a generalization.

- A valid generalization can be supported by facts or details. A faulty generalization cannot.

- Sometimes an author makes a generalization and uses a clue word such as *all, many,* or *in general* to signal it.

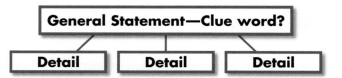

Strategy: Predict

Active readers try to predict what will happen next. When you read a generalization, be on the lookout for similar details that fit it. You can also use a generalization to predict other details that fit it.

1. Read *CP*. Using a graphic organizer like the one above, write the generalization that the author makes about cerebral palsy.

2. Write a generalization of your own about people you know. Give three details that support your generalization.

CP

You might see a person in a wheelchair and think, "That person must have hurt his legs." But that is not always the case. He may have cerebral palsy (CP).

CP is a disorder that happens when the brain is damaged before or during birth. It might also happen when a child is very young. This brain damage leads to problems with moving, and sometimes with speaking, seeing, hearing, or learning.

In general, people with CP do not have full control of their muscles. In some cases, muscles may move when the person does not want them to. Some people with CP have quick, jerky body movements. Others have smaller, slower movements of the face, neck, arms, and legs. In some cases, muscles may not move at all. That's why some people with CP must use wheelchairs.

We don't have a cure for cerebral palsy. However, there are treatments that can help. Many children and adults with this disorder live full, complete, and happy lives.

Skill Look for clue words in this next paragraph that signal the author is making a generalization.

Strategy What kinds of details do you predict you will read about next?

Strategy What other problems can you predict for people without full control of their muscles?

Skill In the final paragraph, what generalization does the author make about people with CP?

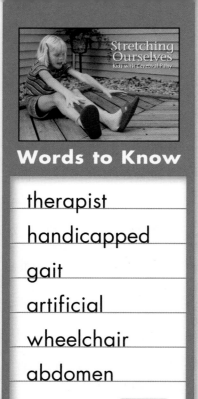

Stretching
Ourselves
Kids with Cerebral Palsy

Words to Know

therapist

handicapped

gait

artificial

wheelchair

abdomen

Remember

Try the strategy. Then, if you need more help, use your glossary or dictionary.

Vocabulary Strategy
for Unfamiliar Words

Context Clues When you find a word you do not know in a text, look for clues to its meaning. The situation the author is describing or the words of a character may suggest the unknown word's meaning.

1. Read the words around the unknown word. Do they suggest a meaning for this word?

2. If not, then read the sentences around the word. Look for examples, comparisons, or contrasts that suggest the meaning of the word.

3. Think of a meaning and test it. Does this meaning make sense?

4. If you cannot find the meaning quickly, look it up in a dictionary or talk with a friend about it.

As you read "Physical Therapists," look for clues to the meaning of each unknown word in the words and sentences around it.

Physical Therapists

The work of a physical therapist can be very rewarding. This person works with people who are hurt or have problems moving because of a physical condition. Sports players with hurt muscles or bones may visit a therapist. People who suffer from diseases that make it hard to move also see a therapist regularly. They may be handicapped by sickness, but exercise and training can help them move more easily.

A person who has had a broken leg needs to use it as it heals. The body learns how to move again after resting a long time. The muscles have become shorter. They need to be stretched and trained. This can mean the difference between walking with a limp or with a smooth gait.

Watch a therapist at work. You may see him or her helping a person with an artificial leg learn how to walk again. It is a very different job from walking on two whole legs. The therapist may be massaging and stretching the muscles of someone who must use a wheelchair. A person who cannot move much needs to work the muscles of arms, legs, abdomen, and back. Otherwise, they become very weak and small. Everyone wants to be able to move well!

Write a journal entry telling what you think it would be like to have a disorder such as cerebral palsy. Use as many words from the Words to Know list as you can.

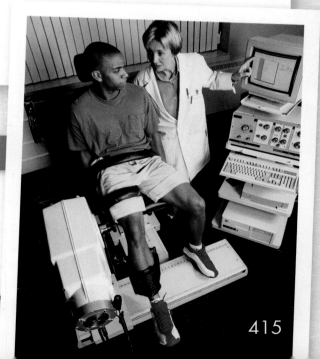

415

BY ALDEN R. CARTER   PHOTOGRAPHS BY CAROL S. CARTER

Stretching Ourselves
Kids with *Cerebral Palsy*

How do Emily, Nic, and Tanner adapt to cerebral palsy?

Bedtime always comes too soon at Emily's house. After snack and medicine, her dad helps her stretch her arms, hands, and legs.

"Sassafras!" she growls. "Rhubarb!"

"You okay, Emmers?" he asks.

"Yep," Emily says, because even if stretching hurts, it helps her to move better.

Emily has cerebral palsy (CP). Most people with CP have tight muscles and tendons. Tendons are the thin, stretchy cords that connect muscles to bones. Our bodies move when muscles contract and relax, pulling or releasing tendons that move the bones of our arms, legs, hands, or spines. Stretching helps the muscles and tendons to work more freely.

Emily has CP because her brain did not receive enough oxygen while she was in her mother's womb. The brain

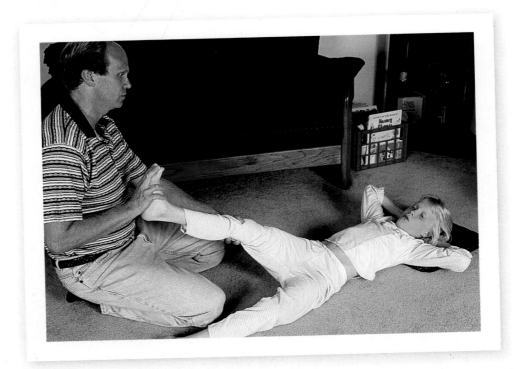

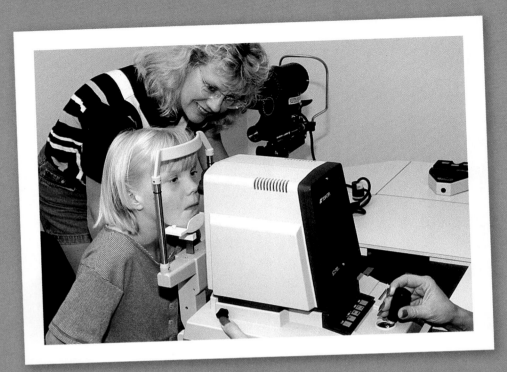

"I'm not 'sweetie,' I'm soury,"
Emily says, but she has to grin.

controls how we move, speak, see, smell, hear, and learn. People with CP can have trouble with any or all of these things. There is no cure for CP, and they must work hard to learn things that come easily to others. Emily practiced a whole summer with her mom and her brother Andrew, learning how to skate.

Because the muscles and tendons in her legs are tight, Emily's movements are stiff, and she walks slightly bent forward. Twice a week, Emily's mom takes her to see a physical therapist.

"I'm real bossy with my legs," she tells the therapist.

"That's good!" Ms. Park says. "But this morning, just relax. We're going to do a gait test to see how your legs are working with each other. Then we'll know the best exercises for you."

Emily's had operations on the muscles of her feet, bladder, and eyes. They've helped, but she's impatient. "Radishes!" she mutters, when she has to have another test to see how well her eyes are working together.

Emily's mom says, "Try again, sweetie."

"I'm not 'sweetie,' I'm *soury*," Emily says, but she has to grin.

Having CP is tough. Emily used to get upset a lot. But she practices staying calm by mothering her dolls and caring for her dogs. Bole and Zuko don't always do what she wants, but she's learned to talk firmly instead of yelling.

Cerebral palsy can affect how much and how fast a person can learn. Tasks that are simple for most people can be big challenges for people with CP. At school, Emily attends a special class for kids who need extra help. Today Mrs. Bauer is teaching them how to take better care of their hair, teeth, and skin. Emily grumbles about a snarl in Lizzy's hair.

"Celery!" Lizzy yelps.

"No vegetables!" Mrs. Bauer says. "Just keep at it. And, Emily be gentle."

Emily also gets extra help for reading and math and then goes to regular classes for art, social studies, and music. She's especially good at art, and never minds getting paint all over herself. "I'm like flowers and a rainbow!" she says.

Emily and Nic are friends at Grant School. Nic has CP because his brain was badly damaged during birth. He spends most of his time in a wheelchair and can speak only a few words. But no one likes playing ball, making jokes, or teasing the teachers more than Nic.

Every day Nic practices simple words with Ms. Larson, a speech therapist. She also helps him learn the buttons on his computer, which has an artificial voice. Nic's favorite button is "Give me a big bear hug!"

A lot of the other kids think his computer is pretty cool. At recess, Nic shows them how to use it. He makes it say "Let's play ball" and "Let's swing."

At the end of the school day, Nic rides the handicapped bus home. When Gale, his bus driver, starts the elevator, Nic likes to make crashing sounds. "Oh, my gosh, you're breaking the elevator again!" Gale yells.

While his mom gets supper ready, Nic reads books with his cousin Shylo. Turning the pages is pretty good practice for his hands. He particularly likes books about bulldozers, farms, and football.

"I'm like flowers and a rainbow!" she says.

"Way to go, Nic!" And Nic's grin says everything he needs to say.

Nic, his mom, and his cousins go bowling some Friday nights. It's not easy for Nic because his hands won't always do what he wants them to do. When he gets a good roll, his mom yells, "Way to go, Nic!" And Nic's grin says everything he needs to say.

Just like at Emily's, bedtime always comes too soon at Nic's house. Nic and his mom add a few sentences to a letter for his dad, who is way across the ocean in the army. "Is there anything more you want to say?" his mom asks. Nic hugs himself, sending his dad a very big bear hug.

Saturdays are great days. At swimming class, Nic can kick, splash, and go under the water as much as he wants. (His mom yells if he does too much kicking, splashing, or diving in the bathtub.)

"Lie back and relax, Tiger," Mr. Scheuer says. "We're going to practice floating."

Like Emily, Nic takes medicine for his CP. Last year, the doctors put a tiny pump in his abdomen. All day and all night, the pump delivers a small amount of medicine to help his muscles work better. Along with exercise and practice, the medicine may someday make it possible for Nic to walk on his own.

Nic feels loose after swimming. He practices with his walker. It's hard and frustrating. "Need some help, Nicky?" his mom calls. Nic shakes his head, growls "Self," and takes another step.

Tanner, too, would rather do things himself—even when they take longer. Tanner has milder CP than Nic or Emily, and many people don't notice his limp or his weak left arm.

Tanner had bleeding in the brain—what's called a stroke—before he was born. Every day he practices to make his arm stronger and his fingers more nimble.

Tanner loves to play ball, especially football. "I'm going to be a fullback someday," he tells his brother, Anthony.

"You bet!" Anthony says. "Just keep practicing."

Tanner is looking forward to having an operation to help his left arm. But first he must train it to move more freely. The doctors have given him a special brace to exercise his arm. "How does that feel?" his stepdad asks.

"Heavy, but I can handle it," Tanner says.

While his mom is busy, Tanner takes care of his new brother, Cole. "Slide the rings, Cole!" he tells him. Tanner could show him better using his right arm, but he practices using his left instead.

Tanner has a lot on his mind, and sometimes he falls behind in school. But he asks questions and gets help from friends. Pretty soon he's caught up again.

"Arithmetic takes practice, practice, practice," Ms. Johnson tells the class.

"You bet!" Tanner says. After all, he knows lots about practicing.

No one in class—except maybe Ms. Johnson—reads stories better than Tanner. He does lots of different voices and can always make kids laugh. Next year maybe he'll try out for the football team *and* the school play.

"I'm going to be a fullback someday," he tells his brother, Anthony.

427

Tanner loves recess. But sometimes friends shout "Hurry up, Tanner!" when he's already hurrying as fast as he can. And that makes him sad and a little mad.

But he remembers what his mom says: "You're way ahead on learning to be brave, Tanner."

People with CP *are* brave. Leslie Martin has had four operations for her CP.

"Last time they sort of tossed me in a blender and poured a new kid out the other side," she likes telling people.

Almost every Sunday, Leslie rides her horse, Annie. This summer she's going to teach Emily to ride.

"Ready to trot, Em?" she asks.

"You bet your broccoli!" Emily says.

Adults with CP work at many different jobs. Greg Kucjek, a friend of Tanner and his stepdad, schedules routes for a big fleet of trucks.

"Let me take it for a cruise, Greg," Tanner says.

Greg laughs. "In a few years, Tan my man."

Tom Hilber, who works as a welcomer and guide at the Marshfield Clinic, is a special friend to Nic and a lot of kids who come to the clinic for help.

"Give a five and you'll get a ten back every time," he often says.

Like many people with CP, Tom is married. He and his wife, Jenny, have two grown children and two grandchildren.

Having CP means working hard at simple things. Tanner explains it this way: "Kids with CP are always trying. It can be tough when our bodies don't do what we want them to do. Some of us can't even talk to ask for something or to tell how we feel. But we keep working to do as much as we can."

Emily says, "Sometimes people are scared or shy because we move or talk funny. But you don't have to be. We like the same things you like. So, as Nic says—

"Give us a bear hug!"

"Let me take it for a cruise,
Greg," Tanner says.

Reader Response

Open for Discussion Imagine that Emily, Nic, and Tanner were part of your life. How would you interact with them?

1. The photos and words in *Stretching Ourselves* work together to give you facts, ideas, and feelings. Choose one photo and the text that goes with it. Explain how they work together.

2. Make a generalization about the daily lives of the kids in *Stretching Ourselves*. Support it with details from the text.

3. Extend the generalization you made in #2. Predict other details that are not in the text that you think would fit your generalization.

4. *Stretching Ourselves* shows that dealing with CP can be a difficult task. Use words from the Words to Know list to tell why.

Look Back and Write
Stretching Ourselves begins with a photo of Emily stretching. But it's about more than just Emily stretching her arms and legs. How does the title apply to the rest of the selection? Write your explanation.

Read more books by Alden and Carol Carter.

Alden and Carol Carter worked as a team to write *Stretching Ourselves*. Mr. Carter says, "We knew a little girl (Emily in the book) with cerebral palsy. Our son and her brother played on the same basketball team, giving us quite a few opportunities to observe her."

Mr. Carter says that after getting the idea and approval from a publisher, "We looked for ways to provide a larger picture of CP. Through the school system and the Marshfield Clinic, we recruited several more people with CP for the project. Most important were, of course, Tanner and Nic. We also recruited a teenager and two adults to show how people with CP can live happy and productive lives."

The next step was to make a layout because the pictures and text had to work together. After they had a tentative layout, Mr. Carter wrote copy. It took five or six drafts before they could start taking the photographs.

At this point, Mrs. Carter took photographs. "Photo shoots are hard work and are also very exciting because we never know exactly what's going to happen. There are also opportunities that arise unexpectedly. For example, the picture of Tanner reading to his classmates was a chance opportunity."

I'm Tougher Than Diabetes!

I'm Tougher Than Asthma!

433

Expository Nonfiction

Genre

- Expository nonfiction can explain helpful technological devices.

- The author explains how these devices work, who uses them and why.

Text Features

- Headings name the devices, and photos help explain them.

- Look over the headings and photos to see what the selection will explain.

Link to Science

Selections that deal with new technologies are important in a world like ours, with so many new inventions designed to help people. Research other helpful new technologies. Find a device that seems especially helpful and report on it to the class.

helpful tools

by Sally Hobart Alexander

Slowly, between the ages of twenty-four and twenty-six, Sally Hobart Alexander lost her sight. She went on to become an award-winning author of books for young people. In one of these books she describes tools that helped her adapt to blindness. One of these tools is Braille, a writing system that uses raised dots to stand for letters and numbers.

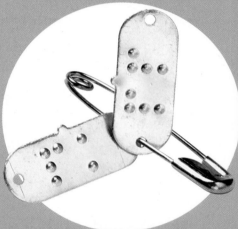

BRAILLE CLOTHING TAG

About the size of a fingernail, these metal tags have holes at either end for pinning or sewing onto labels. They tell me colors: "YW" for yellow, "PK" for pink, and "PP" for purple. When clothes are multicolored, I pin several tags onto the labels at once.

TALKING CLOCK

These clocks come in many varieties. The most common is pocket-sized, but I've had talking clocks inside ballpoint pens and key chains. You simply push a button, and a robot voice calls out the time.

BRAILLE WATCH

Imagine a life without clocks or watches, and you'll have an idea of my life when I first became blind. I dialed the phone number for the exact time so often I memorized it. I'd always taken telling time for granted, and I felt lost. I developed a good sense of how long it took to do things, but my estimates could be off by ten minutes. Without a watch, I could miss a bus or an appointment. I could arrive at work late.

A Braille watch saved me. It looks like a regular wristwatch, except that the crystal pops up when you push a button, usually the winder. You can feel that the hour hand is shorter and sits below the minute hand. All the numbers have raised dots beside them. The numbers 3, 6, and 9 have two raised dots, and the 12 has three.

BRAILLE TIMER

Usually three inches high and two inches wide, this device has raised dots by each number and works just like any other timer. I also use Braille labels on spices and cans. My microwave has a Braille pad.

Reading Across Texts

What helpful technological devices are mentioned in *Stretching Ourselves* and "Helpful Tools," and what are they used for?

Writing Across Texts Display your answers in a two-column chart.

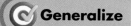 **Generalize** Why have these devices been invented?

435

Comprehension

Skill
Graphic Sources

Strategy
Monitor and
Fix Up

Skill

Graphic Sources

- A graphic source, such as a picture, diagram, or chart, organizes information and makes it easy to see.

- Preview the graphic sources in a selection to help you predict what you will be reading about.

- As you read, compare the information in the text with the graphic source.

Strategy

Strategy: Monitor and Fix Up

Good readers make sure they understand what they read. If a graphic source is part of a text, you can use it to help you understand. You can also use other references to help you. If you do not understand a word, you can look it up in a dictionary. If you need more information about a subject, you can check an encyclopedia.

1. Read "Ant Facts." Use both the text and the diagram to write a paragraph about an ant's antennae. Tell what they look like and what they are for. Include how to pronounce the word.

2. Use the diagram to write a description of the legs of an ant.

Ant Facts

Have you ever observed an ant crawling across a sidewalk lugging food back to its colony? To you, the food is the tiniest scrap. But to the ant, its size and weight are tremendous. Ants can carry objects that weigh several times more than they do. That is only one of the amazing facts about ants.

There are thousands of different species of ants. Some harvest their own food. Some wage war. Some take slaves. Yet all ants share certain characteristics.

An ant's body is divided into three sections: the head, the thorax, and the abdomen. An ant's head is large with two antennae, which are used for smelling and feeling. Its mouth has two sets of mandibles. One set is for carrying. The other is for chewing. The thorax is the middle part of the ant. It's connected to the abdomen by a small, waistlike section. The abdomen is large and oval-shaped.

Skill Preview the title and the diagram. What do you think you will be reading about ants?

Strategy What are antennae? If you don't know, look at the diagram. If you want to find out how to pronounce the word *antennae*, in which reference source would you look?

Strategy What is a mandible? If you don't know, where could you look to find out?

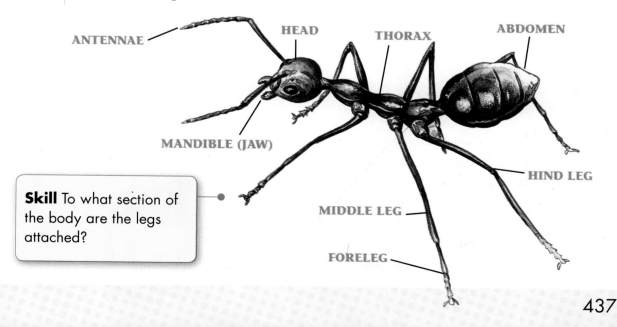

ANTENNAE HEAD THORAX ABDOMEN

MANDIBLE (JAW)

HIND LEG

MIDDLE LEG

FORELEG

Skill To what section of the body are the legs attached?

437

exploding
ants

Words to Know

enables

scarce

specialize

critical

mucus

sterile

Remember

Try the strategy. Then, if you need more help, use your glossary or dictionary.

Vocabulary Strategy
for Synonyms

Context Clues Synonyms are different words that mean almost the same thing. Sometimes an author writes a synonym near a difficult word to help readers understand the word.

1. Read the words and sentences around the unknown word. Is there a synonym?

2. To help find synonyms, look for *or* or *like*, or look for a word set off by commas.

3. Try using the synonym in place of the unknown word. Does this meaning make sense?

4. If these tips do not help, look up the unknown word in the dictionary or talk with a friend about it.

As you read "Small But Mighty," check the context of words you don't know. See if a nearby synonym gives a clue to a word's meaning.

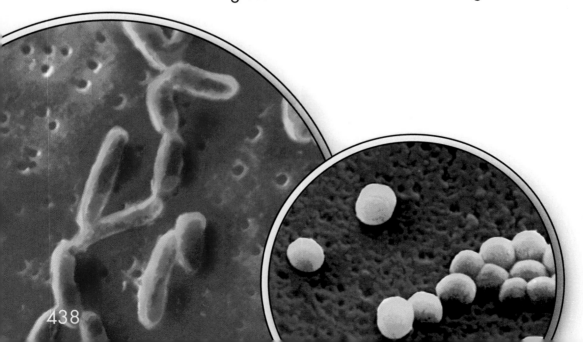

Small But MIGHTY

Bacteria are made up of just one cell. However, they adapt just like all living things. In fact, their size enables them to do this more quickly than larger animals. We have medicines to kill harmful bacteria. However, bacteria have changed so that they can stand up to many medicines. Medicines that still work against them are becoming scarce, or rare. Doctors use these medicines less often so bacteria will not "learn" how to live with them.

Different bacteria specialize in different ways. Some live in your gut and help you digest your food. Some change milk into cheese or sour cream. Still others are critical, or important, to the making of soil. They break down dead plant and animal matter.

Most bacteria are helpful, but a few kinds can harm us. One kind causes the disease called pneumonia. The bacteria get inside the body and reproduce quickly. They give off poisons, or wastes, in the body. The body fights back. It raises its temperature. It produces more mucus to protect the lining of organs. It is best to keep surfaces as sterile as possible so you do not touch harmful bacteria.

Write

Choose an animal in the photographs or artwork from *Exploding Ants*. Write about what seems to make the animal special. Use as many words from the Words to Know list as you can.

exploding ants

by Joanne Settel, Ph.D.

Amazing **Facts** About How Animals Adapt

Expository nonfiction explains what certain things are and how they came to be or behave. As you read, notice how the author explains insect behavior.

x

440

**How do insects
adapt to find food,
shelter, and safety?**

Why animals do gross things

Animals often do things that seem gross to us. They eat foods that people would find nauseating. They make their homes in disgusting places and feed on mucus and blood. They swell or blow up their body parts.

But while these behaviors are nasty to us, they are critical to life on earth. They make it possible for many kinds of living things to find food, shelter, and safety. Different species make use of every possible space and gobble down every nutritious crumb of food in the natural world. If every species of animal ate the same kind of food, or lived in the same place, there simply wouldn't be enough to go around. It would become impossible for all of the species to survive. So instead, animals

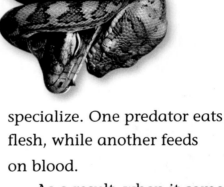

specialize. One predator eats flesh, while another feeds on blood.

As a result, when it comes to eating, nothing is wasted. Almost every part of every living animal, from skin to dung to mucus, can provide food for some other species. All of these things contain good nutrients. An animal that has the right digestive organs and chemicals can easily break them down.

Similarly, when it comes to finding shelter, animals make use of any hole or space or building material that they can find. For example, the smelly, slimy holes and organs inside the body of a bigger animal can often provide a warm, protective home for small animals like insects.

Finally, animals often put their body parts to good use. Animals don't have bags to carry things around, tools to open things, knives to cut things, or weapons to defend themselves. Instead, they use their own bodies in ways that seem gross to us. By stretching, swelling, and bursting open, they can trick predators, store food, swallow big gulps, and defend their nests.

Swelling, expanding and exploding Bodies

Living honey jars

The swollen sacs of nectar that hang from the roof of a honey ant nest are actually alive. They're the fat bodies of ants that have turned themselves into living honey jars.

The "honey jars" are worker ants that store food and are known as *repletes*. Repletes spend their lives hanging upside down from the roof of their nest waiting to feed or be fed. Their bodies provide sterile, airtight food containers.

It is when the colony has lots of extra food that the repletes get fed. Each replete receives regurgitated, or spit-up, food from hundreds of ordinary worker ants. The food consists of a golden liquid filled with a predigested mix of termite parts and plant nectar.

As they take in more and more food, the repletes swell. Soon their rear ends or abdomens are as large

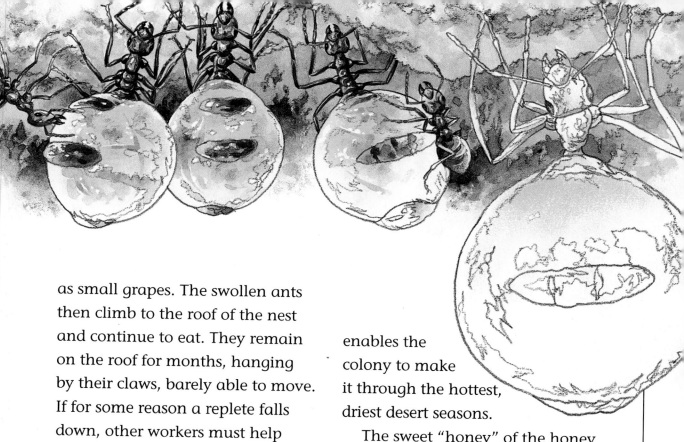

as small grapes. The swollen ants then climb to the roof of the nest and continue to eat. They remain on the roof for months, hanging by their claws, barely able to move. If for some reason a replete falls down, other workers must help drag its large, balloonlike body back up to the ceiling.

When food supplies outside the nest run low, the repletes become the feeders. Hungry nest mates now gather round for food. They touch the repletes' antennae with their own. The repletes then regurgitate big drops of golden honey.

The extra food provided by the repletes is important to the colony survival. Honey ants live in large colonies in dry desert regions of North America, Africa, and Australia, where food is often scarce. Storing food in their living honey jars enables the colony to make it through the hottest, driest desert seasons.

The sweet "honey" of the honey ant repletes is not only food for other ants, but also for some people. The aborigines in Australia consider the swollen honey ants to be sweet treats and pop them into their mouths like candy.

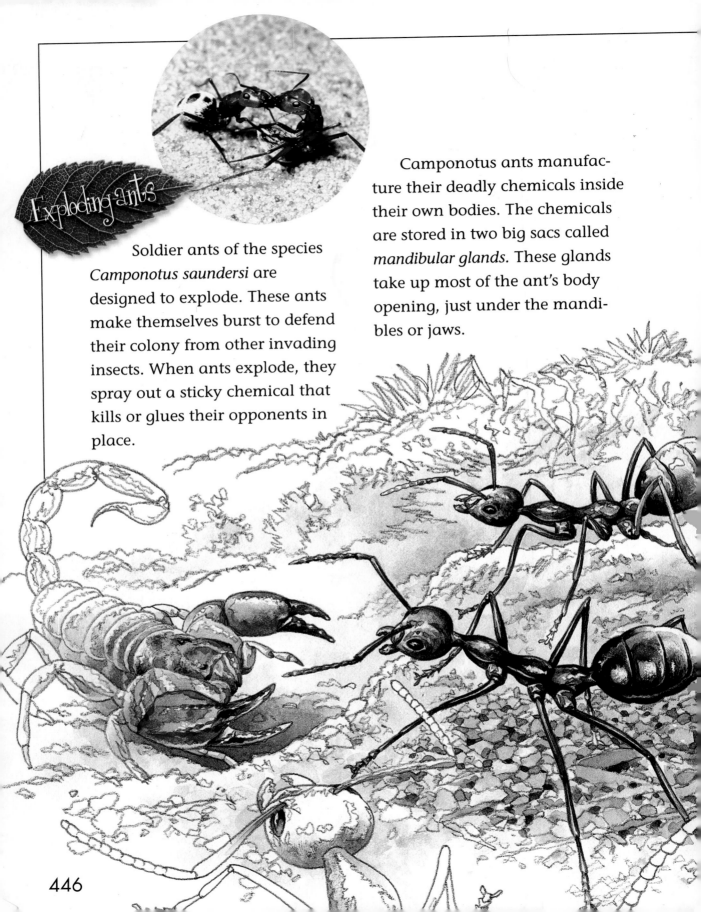

Exploding ants

Soldier ants of the species *Camponotus saundersi* are designed to explode. These ants make themselves burst to defend their colony from other invading insects. When ants explode, they spray out a sticky chemical that kills or glues their opponents in place.

Camponotus ants manufacture their deadly chemicals inside their own bodies. The chemicals are stored in two big sacs called *mandibular glands*. These glands take up most of the ant's body opening, just under the mandibles or jaws.

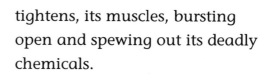

MANDIBULAR
GLANDS

EXPLODING
ABDOMEN

When an intruder approaches, the *Camponotus* ant will release small amounts of its special chemical to warn away the invader. If the intruder actually attacks, however, the *Camponotus* ant takes the next step. It violently contracts, or

tightens, its muscles, bursting open and spewing out its deadly chemicals.

Camponotus ants aren't the only insect with this unusual behavior. It turns out that soldiers of the termite species *Globitermes sulfureus* are also exploders, bursting open when threatened and spraying a sticky yellow liquid all over their opponents.

Getting it down

A ball of bones

Every evening before it goes off to hunt, an owl spits up a few balls of fur and bones. The balls, or pellets, are what's left of the owl's last meal. An owl preys on small animals, such as mice, moles, shrews, birds, and insects. When the feathered predator captures its prey, it doesn't take the time to kill its victim and then pick out the fleshy, nutritious parts. It simply swallows the animal whole. Then the owl digests all the soft stuff, the muscles and organs. The rest, the fur, feathers, teeth, and bones, are wastes. The owl gets rid of these by regurgitating a pellet.

Owls normally spit up two pellets a day. Over time the pellets pile up and form large heaps under the owl's roosting, or resting, site. By examining these

OWL PELLETS

pellets, scientists can learn all about an owl's diet. A pellet of a barn owl, for example, usually contains entire skeletons of two or three mammals, lots of fur, and insect parts. That means that a barn owl gulps down around six small mammals a day.

Six small mammals at two to six ounces each seems like a lot of meat for a bird that weighs less than one pound. The twelve-ounce owl, however, doesn't get fat on this feast. Most of its food is just the fur and bones that get chucked up as round pellets.

Big, big gulps

Gulping down a whole pig or chicken may sound like an impossible task for a snake. But it's no big deal for a twenty-foot python. In fact, many snakes often swallow food much bigger than their own heads. Even very small snakes may feast on mice, rats, birds, frogs, and whole eggs.

The snake's ability to swallow big prey results from the special design of its jaw. The bones of its mouth are loosely joined to its skull. A stretchy strip of tissue called a *ligament* holds together the two halves of the lower jaw. When the snake swallows its dinner, its mouth can stretch wide open. The lower jaw-bones spread apart and each bone moves separately to pull the prey into the mouth.

Snakes generally try to gulp down their food headfirst. This causes the prey's legs to fold back as the snake swallows. In addition, the snake's sharp teeth are curved

backward, preventing the squirming prey from wiggling back out. As the snake works its food down its throat, it pushes its windpipe out of its mouth. This means that it doesn't have to stop breathing as it swallows.

Because snakes eat such big meals, they don't need to eat every day. Most snakes only have to grab a meal once a week, and some only eat once every month. Large pythons hold the record, however. After feasting on a pig or chicken, these huge snakes can go for more than a year without any other food!

Reader Response

Open for Discussion This selection may not be appropriate for dinner table conversation. But would a true scientist call it gross? What is your opinion?

1. *Exploding Ants* begins with a general idea: "Why animals do gross things." Then the author gives specific examples that show why. Is this the way you would organize a selection like this, or do you have other ideas?

2. The title includes the words "Amazing Facts About How Animals Adapt." Look at the illustrations and discuss how they help explain the title.

3. Why do barn owls eat six small mammals a day, and how can they accomplish this amazing feat? Reread pages 448–449 and discuss the details.

4. The author states that animals *specialize* in what they eat. How does this specialization help them? What would happen if they did not specialize? Use words from the Words to Know list to answer these questions.

Look Back and Write Exactly how do soldier ants operate? Review the facts on pages 446–447. Then write a task list for a loyal soldier ant.

Joanne Settel

Read more books by Joanne Settel.

How did Dr. Joanne Settel come to write *Exploding Ants*? She says, "I am a biologist with a specialty in zoology. I have been collecting journal articles with interesting animal facts for over 30 years. Every few years I pull out the ones that are the most interesting and put them together in a book. This time, I was particularly looking for items with a wow factor. Things that would make kids go 'wow,' or 'gross,' or 'yuk.' I wanted a book that would stand out from the crowd."

She says that tracking down the photos was the most difficult part about writing this book, but it was also the most fun. She used the Internet to locate researchers. Then she had to get permission, and often pay, to use the photos.

Dr. Settel says, "I love making science exciting and accessible for others. There are so many amazing things going on in the natural world. It's tremendous fun letting people know about them." Her daughters, now grown, were excited about science, and they helped to inspire her.

Her advice to young people interested in writing is to pursue their passion. She says, "Talk to experts in the field. They will give you tidbits and unknown details that will make the writing interesting."

Why Does My Nose Run?

Why Do Cats' Eyes Glow in the Dark?

453

Experiment

Genre

- **Experiments tell how to perform a trial or test to find out about something.**

- **Most experiments deal with some kind of science.**

Text Features

- **The author begins by stating the purpose of the experiment and the materials needed to perform it. Then come step-by-step instructions, from start to finish.**

- **Scan the steps to get an idea of what the experiment is about.**

Link to Science

Experiments are at the heart of science. Scientists use them to discover and test new ideas. Perform the experiment yourself and share your results with the class.

THE CREATURE FROM THE

Adapting Lagoon

from www.nasa.gov

This science experiment is from the National Aeronautics and Space Administration (NASA). It's intended for fifth-grade students in a science class, but anyone can do it. All you need is thought and imagination.

PURPOSE

To design an animal with adaptations to a specific environment

MATERIALS

pencil, colored pencils, or markers

construction or drawing paper

science journal

PROCEDURE

1. Read over the criteria and background information.
2. Brainstorm possible creature designs that would meet the criteria listed. Check off the criteria that can be incorporated into the design.
3. Select the design that best meets the criteria.
4. Illustrate your creature in the science journal and describe each appendage and how it is used.

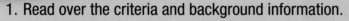

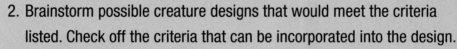

Graphic Sources How do the illustrations help you imagine the experiment?

455

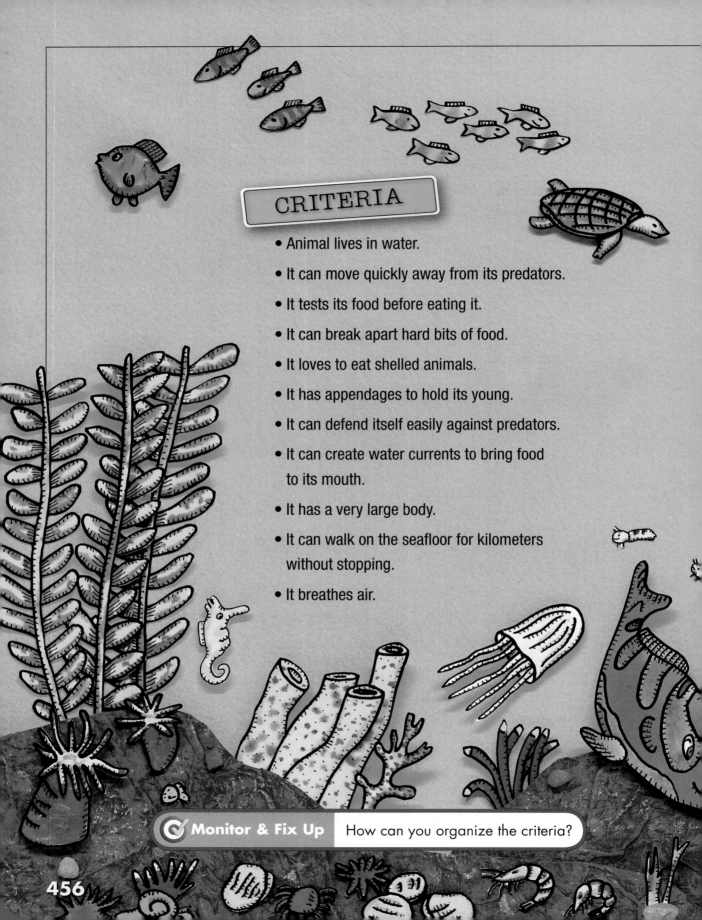

CRITERIA

- Animal lives in water.
- It can move quickly away from its predators.
- It tests its food before eating it.
- It can break apart hard bits of food.
- It loves to eat shelled animals.
- It has appendages to hold its young.
- It can defend itself easily against predators.
- It can create water currents to bring food to its mouth.
- It has a very large body.
- It can walk on the seafloor for kilometers without stopping.
- It breathes air.

Monitor & Fix Up How can you organize the criteria?

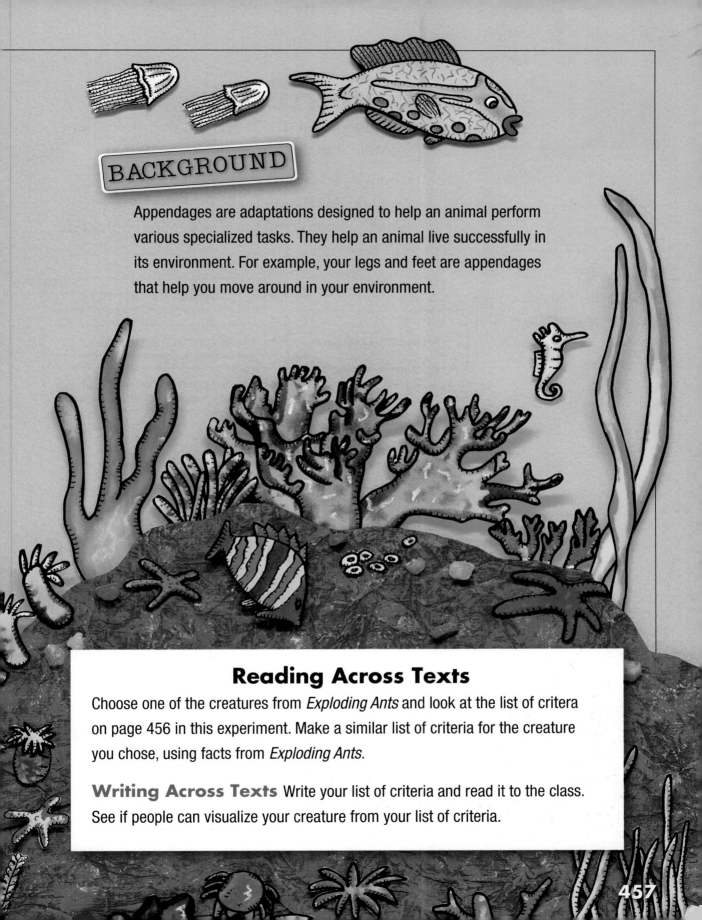

Appendages are adaptations designed to help an animal perform various specialized tasks. They help an animal live successfully in its environment. For example, your legs and feet are appendages that help you move around in your environment.

Reading Across Texts

Choose one of the creatures from *Exploding Ants* and look at the list of critera on page 456 in this experiment. Make a similar list of criteria for the creature you chose, using facts from *Exploding Ants*.

Writing Across Texts Write your list of criteria and read it to the class. See if people can visualize your creature from your list of criteria.

Comprehension

Skill
Generalize

Strategy
Story Structure

 # Generalize

- To generalize is to make a broad statement or rule that applies to several examples.

- Active readers pay close attention to what authors tell them about story characters and make generalizations about those characters as they read.

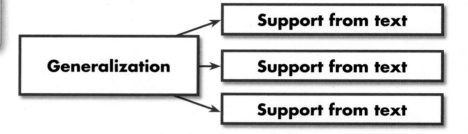

| Generalization | → | **Support from text** |

 # Strategy: Story Structure

Active readers notice story structure. They note the problem characters must deal with and the rising action, climax, and outcome. Generally, authors identify the problem at the start. They work through the problem as the action rises in the middle, and then solve it with the climax and outcome.

1. Read "Thirty Pounds of Trouble." Make a graphic organizer similar to the one above about the story's main character, Tag.

2. Use your graphic organizer to decide whether you would like a dog like Tag and tell why.

458

Thirty Pounds of Trouble

A new canine member in the family can bring joy. It can also bring trouble. Tag was our new dog, a mutt with the silliest grin. He weighed thirty pounds—thirty pounds of genuine trouble.

Tag commenced to wailing like a wolf whenever the moon came up, which kept us up all night. When he was inside, he whined to be let outside. When he was outside, he whimpered to get back in. He would crouch behind the couch and come hurtling out at Mother, and when Father was on the phone, Tag would seize the cord and yank the receiver away.

Finally, Mother and Father had absolutely no patience left. "Tag has got to go," they said.

"No," I cried. I adored that canine rascal, even if he did make munchies of my homework and conceal my socks in the rose bushes. I just had to find a way to keep Tag!

I know it sounds incredible, but six weeks later Tag graduated Obedience School at the head of his class. I think Tag was as surprised as we were. Now he is quiet and polite pretty much all the time. He still has that silly grin though, and he still hides my socks in the rose bushes.

Strategy Generally, the story's problem is told at the start. What is the problem here?

Skill Which generalization can you make?
a) Tag likes people.
b) Tag upsets people.
c) Tag is expensive.

Strategy Generally, the action rises in the middle. What is the high point of the story so far?

Skill What generalization can you make about the narrator's feelings for Tag? How does the text support it?

Words to Know

episode

demonstrates

profile

cavities

strict

combination

Remember

Try the strategy. Then, if you need more help, use your glossary or dictionary.

Vocabulary Strategy
for Unfamiliar Words

Context Clues Sometimes when you are reading, you come across a word you do not know. You can use the context—the words and sentences around the word—to find clues to its meaning.

1. Reread the sentence in which the unknown word appears. Does the author give you a clue, such as a synonym?

2. If not, read the sentences around the sentence with the unknown word. Does the author give you clues, such as examples or explanations?

3. Put the clues together and decide what you think the word means.

4. Try the meaning in the sentence. Does it make sense?

As you read "Trouble in TV Land," look for context clues that help you figure out the meanings of the vocabulary words.

TROUBLE IN TV LAND

Can a TV show teach you how to win friends in the real world? Most sitcoms solve problems in thirty minutes flat, minus about eight minutes of commercials. They present an extremely simple and reassuring view of the world. A single episode demonstrates how to teach a bully the value of kindness or how to overcome your worst fears. Nice-looking young people have a high profile in these shows, and they almost always solve their problems by the end. Plus, the commercials tell you things like how to prevent cavities and whiten your teeth. These commercial messages claim they can save you from tooth decay and so much more. If you will only buy the right clothes and choose the right cell phone, everyone will love you and you will be happy.

In the real world, problems aren't so easily solved. Things you don't enjoy, like having a strict teacher or parent, may actually be good for you. Everyone has problems. Some are as simple as forgetting a locker combination, but others are tough. You can't just make a wish and watch a failing grade go away, for example. To solve problems in the real world, you must be honest and willing to try hard, sometimes for a long time.

Write

Write a letter to your favorite fictional TV character about the way he or she solves problems. Are that character's shows realistic? State your opinion and give reasons to support it. Use words in the Words to Know list if you can.

461

The Stormi Giovanni Club

by Lydia R. Diamond

illustrated by R. Gregory Christie

How will Stormi do
in her new school?

Characters

David

**Stormi
Giovanni Green**

Hannah

**Mom
Dad**

Marsha

Ajitha

Joseph

Penelope

Mrs. Moon

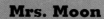

Class/Audience

SETTINGS: *The stage is divided into three areas. (1) Stormi's new home. (2) Stormi's new school: the classroom, Stormi's locker, the cafeteria. (3) Chicago, where Stormi's old friends live. Each area has a table and chairs and a computer.*

464

SCENE I

SETTING: *Stormi's new home. There are unpacked boxes everywhere.*
MOM *holds Stormi's backpack.*

MOM: Stormi, hurry up.

STORMI *(off stage):* Coming, Mom.

MOM: You don't want to be late on your first day.

STORMI *(entering):* No. Wouldn't want that. *(to AUDIENCE)* I would rather not go at all.

MOM: Honey, don't frown. You've started at a new school before. It'll be OK.

STORMI: Yeah. *(to AUDIENCE)* OK like a book report due and you haven't read the book. OK like a trip to the dentist with five cavities. OK like walking over hot coals with bare feet.

(MOM hands STORMI her backpack and exits.)

SCENE II

STORMI *(to* AUDIENCE*):* Hi. I'm Stormi Giovanni Green. I'm named after Nikki Giovanni, the famous poet. I am not a happy camper! See, Mom and Dad move around a lot with their jobs, and since I'm the kid, I go too. They're college professors. Dad teaches philosophy. Philosophers try to figure out how you know what's true and what's not true, and why some things are right and some things are wrong. I only kind of understand. Mom teaches teachers how to teach. Oops, lost my train of thought. Mom says I'm distressed. . . .

MOM: No, Stormi, you've **digressed.**

*(*MOM *exits.)*

STORMI: Digressed, right. Got off the topic. OK. I just moved here from Chicago where I had great friends, played basketball, and was on the speech team. Moving is for the birds. So this time, no new friends. In fact, no anything that I'll just have to say goodbye to. From now on it's the Stormi Giovanni Club, and I'm the only member. When I told Marsha and Penelope I was moving they said:

MARSHA & PENELOPE: NOOO!!!!

STORMI: And I said, "Yes." And they said:

MARSHA & PENELOPE: NOOO!!!!

STORMI: And I said, "Yes." And they said:

MARSHA & PENELOPE: NOOO!!!

STORMI: And David said:

466

DAVID: Stop! Don't say "no" again. It'll be OK.

MARSHA: Sure, we can e-mail.

PENELOPE: And telephone.

DAVID: And send letters.

PENELOPE: But it won't be the same!

STORMI (*to* AUDIENCE): That didn't make me feel better.

(*In Chicago,* DAVID *and* MARSHA *exit. In classroom,* MRS. MOON *enters.*)

STORMI: So, here I am, in homeroom, on the first day of school, keeping a low profile.

MRS. MOON: Welcome, Stormi. Please tell us about yourself.

STORMI (*to* CLASS): I'm Stormi Giovanni. From Chicago.

MRS. MOON: Please tell us about Chicago.

STORMI: It's called the Windy City (*pause*) because it's windy.

MRS. MOON: All right. Let's welcome Stormi Giovanni, class. On the count of three. One, two, three . . .

(MRS. MOON *gestures for the class to speak.*)

CLASS: WELCOME, STORMI GIOVANNI!

(MRS. MOON *exits classroom.* STORMI *sits at classroom computer.*)

STORMI: Well, I lived through homeroom. Things were OK until study hall, when I went online to check my e-mail.

(In Chicago, PENELOPE sits at computer and types.)

PENELOPE: Dear Stormi, I miss you so much. Fifth grade is definitely better than fourth. Everyone says hi. Write to me about your new friends. Love, Penelope.

(In Chicago, PENELOPE exits. In classroom, HANNAH enters and stands behind STORMI. Pens stick out of Hannah's hair, from behind her ears, and hang on a string around her neck.)

STORMI *(typing):* Dear Penelope, FYI, I won't be making friends. Love, Stormi G.

HANNAH *(tapping STORMI on the shoulder):* Do you have a pen? Maybe a roller ball or a ballpoint? Black or blue is best. I don't really go in for the funky colors, you know, the greens and pinks.

STORMI: Oh, I'll look.

(STORMI searches through her backpack.)

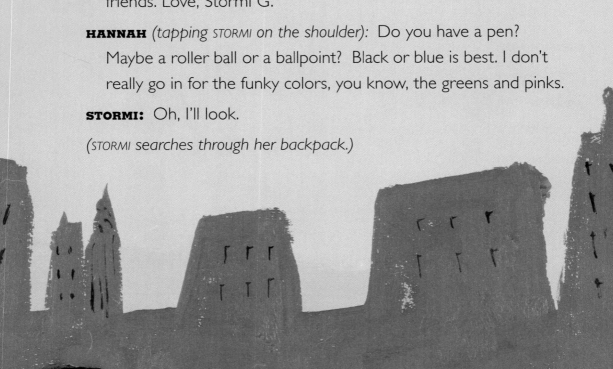

HANNAH: We aren't allowed to use school computers for e-mail. Mr. Morgan is very strict about that. *(pause)* A mechanical pencil might be all right.

STORMI: I have a yellow #2 pencil.

HANNAH *(examining Stormi's pencil and frowning):* No, thanks. *(handing pencil back)* So, you're the new girl?

STORMI: I guess so.

HANNAH: What brings you here?

STORMI: I don't want to talk about it.

HANNAH: OK. *(pause)* My friends Ajitha and Joseph and I sit together at lunch. If you want, tomorrow you can—

STORMI: I always bring a book.

HANNAH: Oh. Don't let Mr. Morgan see you on e-mail— it's a guaranteed detention.

STORMI: Thanks. Gotta go.

SCENE III

SETTINGS: *STORMI is in her new home. In Chicago, MARSHA is at the computer with DAVID looking over her shoulder.*

STORMI *(to audience):* Well, I made it through my first day. There's never much homework on the first day so I read a story in my creative writing class and made book covers. Marsha taught me this really cool way to make covers out of the funny papers. I finished and decided to check e-mail. I can go online for an hour after homework as long as Mom checks it first.

MARSHA *(typing):* Dear Stormi, Lunch was a drag without you. But David told us a stupid joke and before we knew it we were laughing anyway. Oh, wait, David wants to say hi.

DAVID *(typing):* Hey, what do you call a cross between a television and a pizza? A really bad idea. You can do it with any two things. Funny, huh? Get it? *(MARSHA pokes DAVID's shoulder.)*

MARSHA *(typing):* Me again. Isn't that the silliest thing? I bet you're making lots of new friends. OK. Later, Alligator.

(MARSHA and DAVID exit.)

STORMI *(typing):* Hey guys. I miss you. School is OK. *(to AUDIENCE)* OK like you forget your permission slip and miss the field trip. OK like your Dad's playoff game's on TV the same night as the "to be continued" episode of your favorite show. OK like vegetarian meatloaf. *(typing)* Not much to write about. Bye.

(STORMI shuts off computer and sits on the floor, legs crossed, looking sad and lonely.)

STORMI: In my old house there was this little room under the stairs. Probably a closet, but it sloped down so there really wasn't enough room in it for anything. I hung a flashlight in there, and put a rug on the floor and made some pillows. I would go there anytime I was sad, or even just needed to think. Here I just have my room.

(DAD enters.)

DAD: How was school?

STORMI: OK I guess, Dad. *(to AUDIENCE)* OK like . . . never mind . . . you get it. It was not OK.

DAD: Make any new friends?

STORMI: No.

DAD: Could you try to make just one new friend? For me?

STORMI: You should make your own friends, Dad.

DAD *(laughs):* Could you try to make just one friend for *you*, then?

STORMI: I make no promises. Could you try to raise my allowance?

DAD: I make no promises, Pumpkin.

(DAD starts to leave.)

DAD: Take a look at the bay window in the living room. I thought we could hang a curtain from the ceiling and let that be your own private space.

STORMI: Thanks, Dad. I'll look at it.

(DAD exits.)

SCENE IV

SETTINGS: STORMI's *locker in the hallway of her new school. Later, the school cafeteria.*

STORMI *(to AUDIENCE while removing things from her backpack):* The second day was worse than the first. I lost the little piece of paper that had my locker number on it, and I had to go to the office to get a new one. Then I had to dump everything out of my backpack to find the other little piece of paper that had the combination on it. Then I had to figure out how to make the combination lock work.

(HANNAH, JOSEPH, and AJITHA enter.)

HANNAH: Do you always talk to yourself?

STORMI: I wasn't. I was just—

HANNAH: Whatever. I wanted you to meet Joseph. He talks to himself too.

STORMI: Hi.

JOSEPH: Hi. This is Ajitha. Ajitha, Stormi Giovanni.

AJITHA: After the poet?

STORMI *(surprised):* Yeah.

AJITHA: Are you having a hard time with your locker?

STORMI: We didn't have locks at my old school.

AJITHA: You don't have to lock it. I put tape on the side of mine to keep it open. Like this.

(AJITHA shows STORMI.)

STORMI: Cool. Hannah, did you find a pen?

HANNAH: I got a couple of interesting ones.

JOSEPH: Hannah collects pens.

HANNAH: I'm looking for the perfect pen.

STORMI: Why?

HANNAH: When I was little my grandpa gave me this old silver fountain pen. I wasn't supposed to take it out of the house, but I did, and I lost it. I keep thinking I'll find something almost as cool. It's my passion.

STORMI: That's cool. I have a friend who collects unicorns.

JOSEPH: Next period is lunch if you want. . . .

STORMI: I have a book.

(STORMI exits.)

473

AJITHA: That was audacious. *(pause)* Rude and bold.

HANNAH: She's OK.

JOSEPH: It would be hard to start a new school.

AJITHA: That's no reason to be rude. We were only trying to be hospitable and gregarious.

JOSEPH: I was just trying to be nice.

(They sit at a table in the school cafeteria and begin eating lunch. STORMI enters.)

STORMI *(to AUDIENCE):* Lunch at a new school is the worst. There's this awful time when you have your tray and you have to figure out where to sit. A book can really help. I sit alone and act like I'm reading. I have to act because it's hard to read in all of that noise. But today my plan didn't work. The cafeteria was packed.

AJITHA: Stormi, you can sit with us.

JOSEPH: What are you reading?

STORMI: *A Wrinkle in Time.*

AJITHA: That book is quite scintillating.

HANNAH: Don't mind her. She likes to use big words. She's not trying to make you feel stupid.

STORMI *(to AJITHA):* Do you write stories?

(AJITHA pulls out a dictionary.)

AJITHA: I try to learn a new word every day. *(reading from dictionary)* Scintillate: to sparkle, gleam.

JOSEPH: *A Wrinkle in Time* is sparkly?

HANNAH: You can sit here and read if you want to.

(STORMI sits.)

JOSEPH: I thought I would try out for the play.

HANNAH: If you do, I will too.

(STORMI tries to look like she's reading but is drawn into the conversation.)

HANNAH: It's *The Wizard of Oz,* right?

STORMI: We did that at my old school. I wanted to be the Lion so badly, but I was too small for the suit. I ended up designing the set.

AJITHA: I could enjoy that.

JOSEPH: I want to be the scarecrow.

(JOSEPH does a funny scarecrow imitation, with limp knees and wobbly head movements.)

STORMI *(to AUDIENCE):* Lunch was almost as much fun as listening to David's lame jokes would have been. So, I've been thinking. You know how it is when you hurt your finger? Like maybe the pointing finger on the hand you write with. *(STORMI holds up finger and demonstrates.)* All of a sudden you notice all of these things you do with that finger. It hurts to put on a glove. It hurts to sharpen your pencil. It hurts to tie your shoe. And you think, I sure will be happy when this finger is better. Then one day you notice that it's better. You almost can't remember when it stopped hurting. You just didn't notice. It's the same with moving. You can't know when you will stop missing the last place so much it hurts, but you can't stop tying your shoes either. Hey, that sounds a little philosophical. My father would be proud.

(HANNAH steps forward.)

HANNAH: Look at this.

STORMI *(pointing to AUDIENCE):* I'm talking.

(HANNAH notices AUDIENCE for the first time.)

HANNAH: Oh. Hi.

AUDIENCE: Hi.

HANNAH: Look. *(She holds up a pen.)* A limited edition, 2001 four color, ball point gel ink pen, a rare and beautiful thing. . . .

(STORMI sits at the school computer.)

STORMI *(typing):* Hey, guys. I'm sorry I haven't had much to tell you. It's silly, but I thought I would feel better if I didn't make friends. I felt worse and I think people thought I was mean. Anyway, I've met some pretty interesting people. David, you'd like Joseph. He has this funny sense of humor and likes to act in plays. There's this really odd girl who I think is my favorite. She collects pens. Like your unicorns, Penelope. . . . And Ajitha uses all of these big words, but she isn't stuck up or anything. *(to AUDIENCE)* So, I've decided to let other members into the Stormi Giovanni Club. Really, it's better that way I think.

The End

Reader Response

Open for Discussion What is this play saying about being a newcomer and about helping one? How will you perform this play so that the audience gets the message?

1. Choose a scene and imagine yourself playing a character. Decide whether the playwright's dialogue makes it easy for you to "become" the character you're playing.

2. Make a generalization about newcomers suggested by the play. Then look for details in the text that support this generalization.

3. Stormi acts differently at the start of the play than at the end. Discuss how she changes along the way and why.

4. Stormi tells the audience humorous examples of what she really means when she or her mom says that school is "OK." Write one of these examples. Then write one of your own. Use words from the Words to Know list.

Look Back and Write In this play, each character is a true individual. Take Hannah, for instance. What is her passion and why? Look back at page 473 and then write your answer.

Meet the Author and the Illustrator

Lydia Diamond and R. Gregory Christie

Read more books about family life.

Playwright **Lydia R. Diamond** said, "I think kids are a little more brave than adults sometimes." She was thinking about her own school days when she moved around a lot. The move from Mississippi to Massachusetts was especially hard. "It was cold in Massachusetts and warm in Mississippi, and that was strange. I made new friends quickly, though. I wasn't afraid." When she moves to new places now, with a husband and baby, it's different. "It's harder to leave friends when you're an adult. But my character Stormi Giovanni has taught me to have more faith, that I will make new friends, that it will be OK."

Lydia Diamond's plays have been performed in U.S. cities from New York to California. One of them, *Here I Am . . . See Can You Handle It*, is based on the writings of Nikki Giovanni. Ms. Diamond lives in Massachusetts with her husband and her son.

Illustrator **R. Gregory Christie** has won awards for his work on books of fiction and poetry for young people. One reviewer has said that his unique illustrations, which combine realism and exaggeration, "create harmony with the words."

A Family Apart
by Joan Lowery Nixon

Flip-Flop Girl
by Katherine Paterson

50¢ City & Suburbs: 75¢ Elsewhere

Newspaper Article

Genre

- A newspaper article tells readers about current events, issues, people, and places of interest.

- News articles should report facts—actual events and quotations.

Text Features

- A news article begins with a headline that gives readers an idea of what the article is about.

- A dateline, which gives the day the article appeared, often follows the headline.

- Before reading, scan the headline and illustrations to see what the article is about.

Link to Social Studies

Find out about dress codes in your school and other schools in your area. Are there differences? Why?

Think Dress codes are a drag?

by Emilie Ostrander

Special to the *Tribune*

Savvy Shoppers Can Still Look Cool for School

While shopping for new clothes, Elyse B., 13, of Mt. Prospect, Illinois, also is scouting for hot trends. Dressed in a bright pink tank top and denim capris, Elyse says she's found an outfit she likes. The catch? Her school dress code bans tank tops—and the penalty is anything but stylish. "If they catch you, you have to change into your gym uniform," she says.

For Elyse, shopping for new clothes is all about looking good without getting in trouble. "We can't wear spaghetti straps, halter tops, or tube tops," she explains. "Tank top straps must be the width of two fingers, and shorts and skirts have to be longer than 5 inches above the knee."

As we get into spring, many kids are ready to take their warm-weather clothes to school. But some school districts say certain styles are banned from the classroom, and there are consequences for kids who disobey.

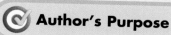 **Author's Purpose**   What is the author's purpose or purposes?

481

Paula J. Hlavacek is the principal of Elm Middle School in Elmwood Park. At her school, parents are contacted the first time a student breaks the code. A second offense means a trip to detention.

It may not seem like a lot of fun, but Hlavacek says the dress code is there for good reason. "When you come to school, you must be dressed for a work day in school," she says. "Clothes that are cut very short or expose the midriff are beachwear. School is a very different place."

While dress codes may seem unfair, Hlavacek says students can expect the same restrictions for their teachers. "Whatever rules we hold for them, we hold for ourselves," she says. So while students can't wear tank tops in scorching weather, neither can their teachers.

Ryan M., 16, of Lincolnwood says he doesn't dress like his dean [principal of a private school]. "I like to wear my pants low," he says, something his dean can't

stand. Once, Ryan's dean had him take off his belt so he could fix it. "He told me that I wouldn't have an excuse for walking around with my pants 'sagging' anymore," Ryan says.

While Ryan and Elyse wish their school dress codes were less

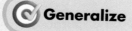 **Generalize** How is a rule a kind of generalization?

strict, Kyah K., 8, of Aurora says she thinks dress codes are a good idea. "Sometimes everyone wants to be cool, so they wear really tacky clothes," she says. "I think they should obey the rules and wear those clothes at home."

Being creative is key to still being in style and not breaking the school dress code, says Gregg Andrews, fashion director for [a department store]. "It's about creating personal style," he says.

Kyah says she has an eye for style, and thinks clothes can say a lot about a person. "My clothes say that I'm a creative person," she says. "I try to put on some mis-matchy things or things that will go together very well."

Reading Across Texts

Look back at *The Stormi Giovanni Club* and this newspaper article. Make a list of problems that the students in these selections face during a typical day at school.

Writing Across Texts Write some advice on how to successfully deal with each of these problems. Combine your results with classmates' advice. Assemble a book of advice on how to get along in school.

Comprehension

Skill
Draw Conclusions

Strategy
Visualize

Draw Conclusions

- A conclusion is a sensible decision you make after you think about facts or details that you read.

- Drawing conclusions may also be called making inferences.

- Use your prior knowledge to help you draw conclusions.

| What does the text say? |
| What do I already know? |

→ | What can I conclude? |

Strategy: Visualize

Active readers visualize as they read. They make pictures in their mind. Visualizing can help you understand what is happening in what you read. It can also help you draw conclusions about what is happening and why.

1. Read "How to Do a Cartwheel." Use a graphic organizer like the one above to draw a conclusion about which way to start a cartwheel.

2. Describe how to do a handstand, a somersault, or some other action without naming it. Exchange papers with a classmate. Try to visualize and draw a conclusion about what your classmate is describing.

How to Do a
Cartwheel

To begin a cartwheel, stand erect with one foot slightly in front of you. Use the foot of the side you feel is stronger. Let's assume you're doing a right-sided cartwheel. (To perform a left-sided cartwheel, reverse these directions. Use left for right and right for left.)

Raise both arms and lift your right foot. As you put it back down, reach to your right side and down toward the ground with your right arm. Begin lifting your left leg. Touch your right hand to the ground. Almost immediately, turn your upper body to touch your left hand to the ground beside your right hand. Your right leg should now be off the ground too. For a moment, you will be in a handstand—both hands down, both legs up.

Now bring your left foot down on the other side, lifting your right hand off the ground. Then bring your right foot down, lifting your left hand. You should be standing erect again.

The trick to performing a cartwheel is to keep your back and legs straight up, not out to the side. It sounds easy but it's not. Learning to cartwheel takes practice, practice, practice.

Skill Why do you think it's important to start out with the side you feel is stronger? (Think how you would feel starting on your weaker side.)

Strategy Visualize how you start out doing a cartwheel and what comes next.

Skill Why do you think this action is called a cartwheel?

Strategy Picture what someone looks like doing a cartwheel. Then picture the actual wheel of a cart. That can help you understand the name *cartwheel*.

The Gymnast

Words to Know

limelight

hesitation

somersault

gymnastics

cartwheels

throbbing

wincing

skidded

bluish

Remember

Try the strategy. Then, if you need more help, use your glossary or dictionary.

Vocabulary Strategy
for Suffixes

Word Structure A suffix is a syllable added to the end of a base word that changes the base word's meaning. The spelling of the base word may also change when the suffix is added. For example, when the suffix *-ion* is added to *appreciate*, the final *e* is dropped: *appreciation*. Adding this suffix adds the meaning "the act or state of being ___." The suffix *-ish* adds the meaning "somewhat" or "like," as in *brownish*. Recognizing a suffix can help you figure out the meaning of an unknown word.

1. Look at the unknown word. See if you recognize a base word in it.

2. Check to see if the suffix *-ion*, *-tion*, or *-ish* has been added to the base word.

3. Ask yourself how the suffix changes the meaning of the base word.

4. Try the new meaning in the sentence to see if it makes sense.

As you read "It's Easier in Daydreams," look for words that end with suffixes. Analyze the base words and the suffixes to figure out the meanings of words you do not know.

It's Easier in Daydreams

I love to watch Olympic gymnasts. In fact, I hope to be one myself one day. In my daydreams, I am already a star. The audience roars as I step into the limelight. Without any hesitation, I somersault across the gym. I move with terrific speed and grace. The judges smile and nod and hold up score cards with perfect 10.0's on them.

So you can understand why I was so upset after what happened. I signed up for a gymnastics class offered by the park district. The teacher showed us how to do cartwheels. "This is easy!" I thought, so

I didn't pay attention. When it was my turn, I ran to the mat, closed my eyes, and threw myself at it. The next thing I knew, I was flat on my back. My head and knees were throbbing. I couldn't help wincing in pain as I got up. On the next try, I lost my nerve and put on the brakes. I skidded several feet into a wall and thumped my shoulder. There's a nice bluish bruise there to remind me. I have a long way to go to reach the Olympics.

Write

Imagine that you are a sports writer. Write an article about a gymnastics competition or some other sporting event you just watched. Use words from the Words to Know list and as many words connected with the sport as you can.

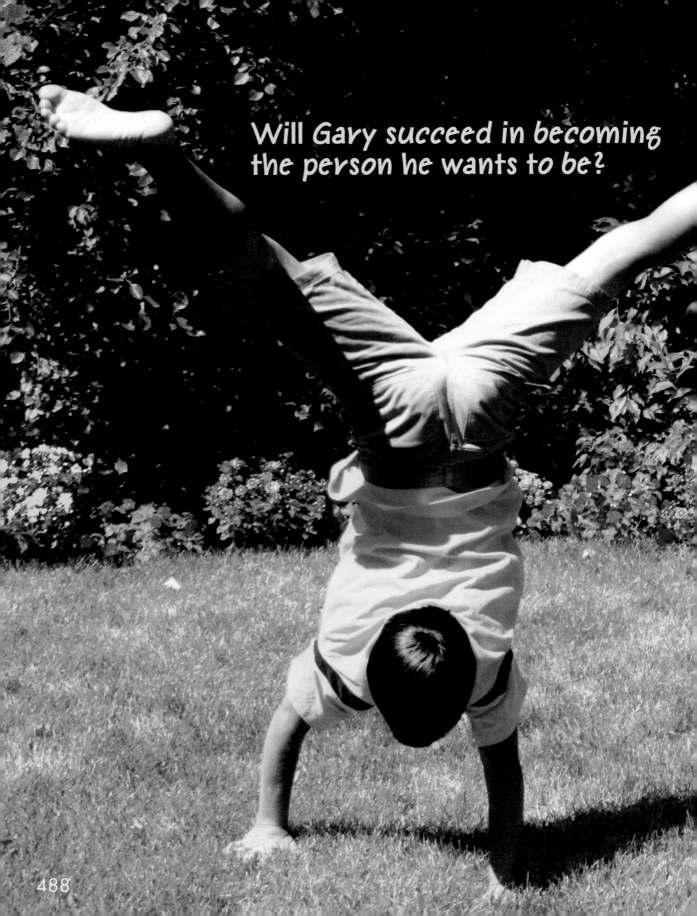

Will Gary succeed in becoming the person he wants to be?

The Gymnast

by Gary Soto

Genre

Autobiography is the story of a person's life or of a single event in it, told by the person who lived it. As you read, notice how the author looks back at himself from a humorous point of view.

For three days of my eleventh summer I listened to my mother yap about my cousin, Isaac, who was taking gymnastics. She was proud of him, she said one evening at the stove as she pounded a round steak into carne asada and crushed a heap of beans into refritos. I was jealous because I had watched my share of *Wide World of Sports* and knew that people admired an athlete who could **somersault** without hurting himself. I pushed aside my solitary game of Chinese checkers and spent a few minutes rolling around the backyard until I was dizzy and itchy with grass.

That Saturday, I went to Isaac's house where I ate plums and sat under an aluminum arbor watching my cousin, dressed in gymnastic shorts and top, do spindly **cartwheels** and back flips in his backyard while he instructed, "This is the correct way." He breathed in the grassy air, leaped, and came up smiling the straightest teeth in the world.

I followed him to the front lawn. When a car passed he did a **back flip** and looked out the side of his eyes to see if any of the passengers were looking. Some pointed while others looked ahead dully at the road.

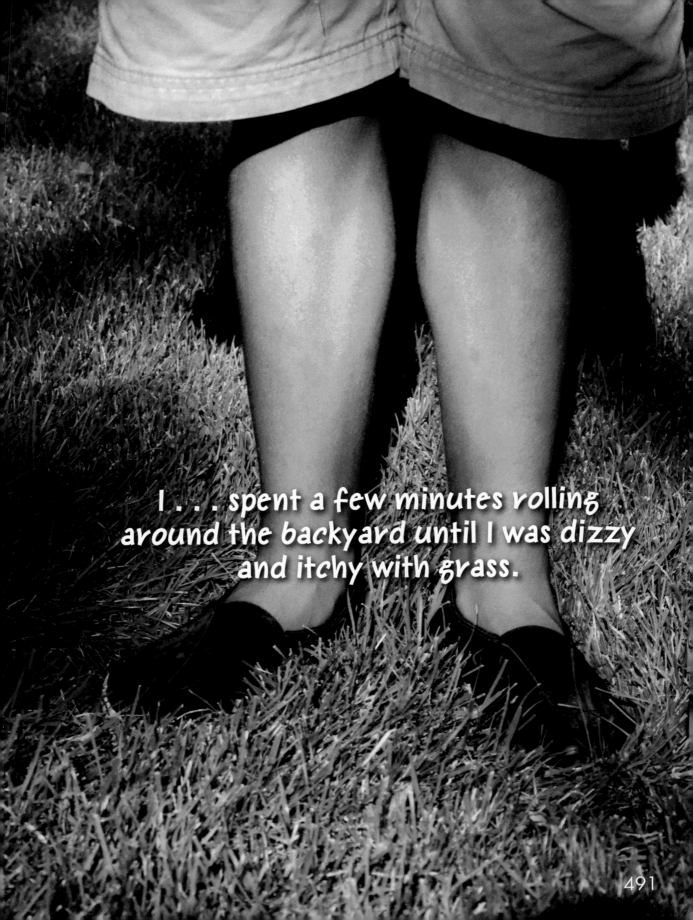

I . . . spent a few minutes rolling around the backyard until I was dizzy and itchy with grass.

But when I did a cartwheel,

the shoes flew off, along with the tape.

My cousin was a show off, but I figured he was allowed the limelight before one appreciative dog who had come over to look. I envied him and his cloth gymnast shoes. I liked the way they looked, slim, black and cool. They seemed special, something I could never slip onto my feet.

I ate the plums and watched him until he was sweaty and out of breath. When he was finished, I begged him to let me wear his cloth shoes. Drops of sweat fell at his feet. He looked at me with disdain, ran a yellow towel across his face, and patted his neck dry. He tore the white tape from his wrists—I liked the tape as well and tried to paste it around my wrists. He washed off his hands. I asked him about the white powder, and he said it kept his hands dry. I asked him why he needed dry hands to do cartwheels and back flips. He said that all gymnasts kept their hands dry, then drank from a bottle of greenish water he said was filled with nutrients.

I asked him again if I could wear his shoes. He slipped them off and said, "OK, just for a while." The shoes were loose, but I liked them. I went to the front yard with my wrists dripping tape and my hands white as gloves. I smiled slyly and thought I looked neat. But when I did a cartwheel, the shoes flew off, along with the tape, and my cousin yelled and stomped the grass.

I was glad to get home. I was jealous and miserable, but the next day I found a pair of old vinyl slippers in the closet that were sort of like gymnastic shoes. I pushed my feet into them, tugging and wincing because they were too small. I took a few steps, admiring my feet, which looked like bloated water balloons, and went outside to do cartwheels on the front lawn. A friend skidded to a stop on his bike, one cheek fat with sunflower seeds. His mouth churned to a stop. He asked why I was wearing slippers on a hot day. I made a face at him and said that they were gymnastic shoes, not slippers. He watched me do **cartwheels** for a while, then rode away doing a wheelie.

I returned inside. I looked for tape to wrap my wrists, but could find only circle bandages in the medicine cabinet. I dipped my hands in flour to keep them dry and went back outside to do cartwheels and, finally, after much hesitation, a **back flip** that nearly cost me my life when I landed on my head. I crawled to the shade, stars of pain pulsating in my shoulder and neck.

My brother glided by on his bike, smooth as a kite. He stared at me and asked why I was wearing slippers. I didn't answer him. My neck still hurt. He asked about the flour on my hands, and I told him to leave me alone. I turned on the hose and drank cool water.

. . . and, finally, after much hesitation,
a back flip that nearly cost me my life . . .

My toes cooled on the summery grass.

I walked to Romain playground where I played Chinese checkers and was asked a dozen times why I was wearing slippers. I'm taking gymnastics, I lied, and these are the kind of shoes you wear. When one kid asked why I had white powder on my hands and in my hair, I gave up on Chinese checkers and returned home, my feet throbbing. But before I went inside, I took off the slippers. My toes cooled on the summery grass. I ran a garden hose on my feet and bluish ankles, and a chill ran up my back.

Dinner was a ten-minute affair of piranha-like eating and thirty minutes of washing dishes. Once finished, I returned to the backyard, where I again stuffed my feet into the slippers and did **cartwheels by the dizzy dozens.** After a while they were easy, I had to move on. I sucked in the summer air, along with the smoke of a faraway barbecue, and tried a back flip. I landed on my neck again, this time I saw an orange burst behind my eyes. I lay on the grass, tired and sweaty, my feet squeezed in the vise of cruel slippers.

I watched the dusk settle and the first stars, pinpoints of unfortunate light tangled in telephone wires. I ate a plum and pictured my cousin, who was probably cartwheeling to the audience of one sleeping dog.

Reader Response

Open for Discussion The narrator of "The Gymnast" says, "I was jealous and miserable." Why was he jealous? What did his jealousy make him do? Do you know anyone who has had an experience like his? What was the outcome?

1. Gary Soto has taken an incident from his childhood and packed it with sensory details to bring it to life. Find details that tell how things looked and sounded and felt.

2. Young Gary draws the conclusion that his cousin Isaac is a showoff. Find details from the selection that support this conclusion.

3. Find passages that show how Gary looks in his gymnastics outfit and how his cousin looks. Discuss how the visual details help make them two very different people.

4. *Somersault* and *cartwheels* are names for gymnastic feats. What other words from the Words to Know list would go into a web with *gymnast* at the center?

Look Back and Write
The dog in "The Gymnast" acts as an audience. Find the dog on pages 493 and 497. How does the dog-as-audience change, and what does this change tell you about the gymnast? Write your answer.

Gary Soto

Read more books by Gary Soto.

Gary Soto says, "It appears these days I don't have much of a life because my nose is often stuck in a book. But I discovered that reading builds a life inside the mind. I enjoy biographies and novels and reading in Spanish. Also, I like theater, tennis, basketball, traveling (especially London) and working in the garden . . . sometimes."

Born in Fresno, California, Mr. Soto was the second of three children. Although his writing comes from his experiences growing up in a Mexican American community, he says that his stories are not all based on actual events.

Mr. Soto has taught at the University of California, but today is a full-time writer. Does Mr. Soto revise his writing? He says, "Yes, all writers revise and almost all writers have friends who look at their work. My first reader is my wife, poor thing. I bother her almost daily as I beg, 'Carolyn, could you please look at this masterpiece?' Of course it's not a masterpiece, but a way of getting her attention."

Off and Running

The Pool Party

All About Gymnastics

Online Reference Sources

Genre

- You can find reference sources, such as almanacs and dictionaries, on Internet Web sites.

- Some Web sites give you several different reference sources all in one place.

Text Features

- These electronic reference sources look a lot like printed sources, and they're organized the same way.

- Instead of turning pages by hand, you click through them with a mouse.

Link to Social Studies

Explore a topic you like. Use an encyclopedia, dictionary, and other reference sources. Write down facts you find.

After reading Gary Soto's "The Gymnast," Alice decides she might want to do gymnastics. So she goes to an online reference Web site.

This site has four reference sources: an atlas, almanac, dictionary, and encyclopedia. When Alice types the keyword "gymnastics" into the Search engine and clicks on "go," the site gives her a list of results that begins like this:

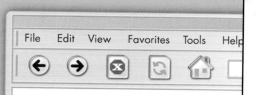

File   Edit   View   Favorites   Tools   Help

Search "gymnastics" GO!

Atlas
Almanac
Dictionary
Encyclopedia

Search Results: "gymnastics"

Gymnastics (Encyclopedia)
gymnastics, exercises for the balanced development of the body (see also aerobics).

File   Edit   View

Alice clicks on this gymnastics encyclopedia link and gets an entry for gymnastics that ends like this:

Encyclopedia

gymnastics
Women compete in the vault, floor exercises, balance beam, and uneven parallel bars, as well as in rhythmic gymnastics and on the trampoline.

 **Visualize**   Picture the steps Alice takes as she does her search.

501

She wonders what these events are like, so she types "vault" into the search engine. The results include this dictionary entry:

Dictionary

vault

Pronunciation: (vôlt) — v.i.

In gymnastics, to leap over a vaulting or pommel horse, using the hands for pushing off.

This raises another question in Alice's mind: What in the world is a pommel horse?

A dictionary search tells Alice that "pommel horse" means "a cylinder-shaped horse with handles near the center." Alice can't picture this, so she goes to another online reference site to find an image.

Her search for "pommel horse" turns up images like these:

502

She returns to the first site and types "floor exercise" into the search engine and gets the dictionary definition:

File   Edit   View   Fa

Dictionary

floor exercise
Pronunciation: floor′ ek′sər sīz
In gymnastics, a competition in which each entrant per-forms a routine of acrobatic tumbling feats and balletic movements without any appa-ratus on a specifically desig-nated floor space, usually 12 m (39 ft.) square and having a matlike covering.

File   Edit   View   Favorites   Tools   Help

Alice continues searching until she finds out all she needs to know.

Reading Across Texts

Look back at "The Gymnast" to see what kinds of moves the young Gary Soto was practicing. Compare them with the information here. Which event do you think Gary was practicing for, and why do you think so?

Writing Across Texts Describe your thinking and illustrate it with drawings.

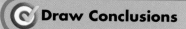 **Draw Conclusions**   A definition and picture help you understand the term.

Which Lunch Table?

by Kristine O'Connell George

Where do I sit?
All my friends
from last year
have changed;
my world is
    fractured,
    lopsided,
    rearranged.

    Where do I fit?
    Nothing is clear.
    Can already tell
    this will be
    a jigsaw year.

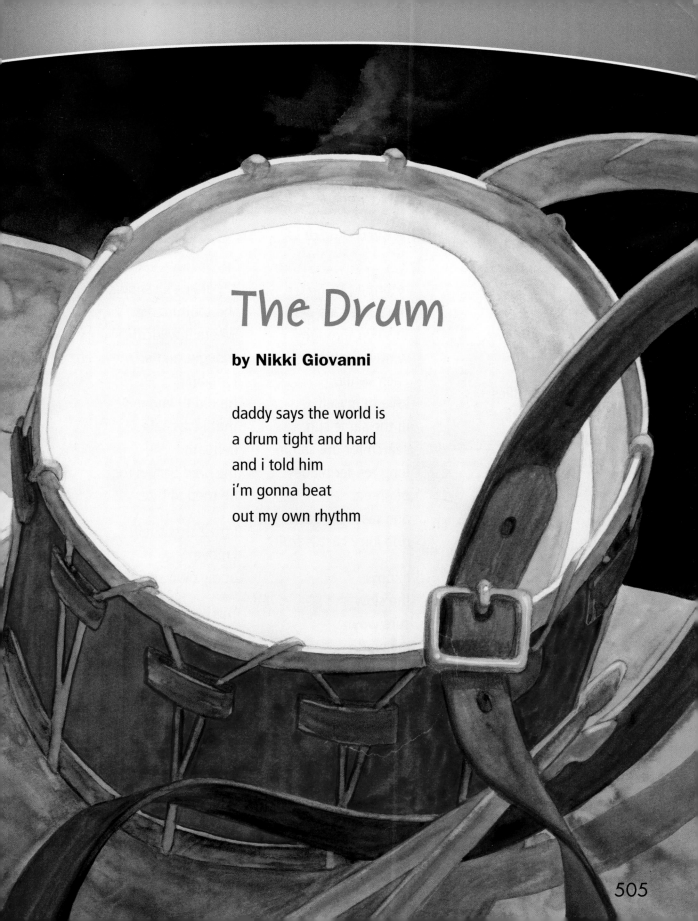

The Drum

by Nikki Giovanni

daddy says the world is
a drum tight and hard
and i told him
i'm gonna beat
out my own rhythm

Desert Tortoise

by Byrd Baylor

I am the *old* one here.

Mice
and snakes
and deer
and butterflies
and badgers
come and go.
Centipedes
and eagles
come and go.

But tortoises
grow old
and *stay.*

Our lives stretch out.

I cross
the same arroyo
that I crossed
when I was young,

returning to
the same safe den
to sleep through
winter's cold.
Each spring,
I warm myself
in the same sun,
search for the same
long tender blades
of green,
and taste the same
ripe juicy cactus fruit.

I know
the slow
sure way
my world
repeats itself.
I know
how I fit in.

My shell still shows
the toothmarks
where a wildcat
thought he had me
long ago.
He didn't know
that I was safe
beneath
the hard brown rock
he tried to bite.

I trust that shell.
I move
at my own speed.

This
is a good place
for an old tortoise
to walk.

Camel

by Lillian M. Fisher

A camel is a mammal,
A most extraordinary animal
Whose appearance is a wee bit odd.
His body is lumpy,
Knees calloused and bumpy,
And his feet are naturally shod.
His humps are fantastical,
His manner bombastical,
Due to his proud ancient past.
He feasts upon brambles
And ploddingly ambles.
His gait is not very fast.
But he carries great loads
On long dusty roads
Where many a beast cannot.
He's a tireless walker
And goes without water
In weather increasingly hot.
This strange-looking beast
Who resides in the East
And in far-off places West
Is found at the zoo
Where he's happy, it's true,
But—
Deep inside—desert is best.

Adapting Facts

connect to **WRITING**

Make a booklet of facts on adaptation that you learned in Unit 4. On each page, write a fact from one of the selections about how an animal or person adapts to a unique situation. Include an illustration to go with each fact. Add a cover with a title and illustration.

How do people and animals adapt to different situations?

Adaptation Scale

connect to
SOCIAL STUDIES

With a partner, discuss the unit selections in which humans must adapt. Then draw a number line. In boxes, write each person's name in order, from the one who must adapt the most to the one who must adapt the least. Write a short description explaining why you placed the names in this order.

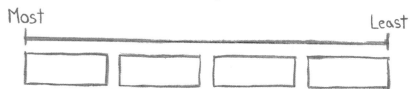

Most   Least

Keisha

Great Adaptations

connect to
SCIENCE

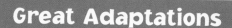

Fold a large sheet of drawing paper in half. On one half, draw a picture of Wes in Weslandia. Add at least ten labels to show ways in which he changed his environment. On the other side, draw a picture of yourself in your own environment. Add captions to show how you have adapted to your environment.

509

Adventurers

Who goes seeking adventure and why?

Comprehension

Skill
Character and Plot

Strategy
Prior Knowledge

Skill

Character and Plot

- Traits are the qualities of characters, such as bravery or shyness. We see their traits in their words and actions and how other characters treat them.

- The plot is the pattern of events in a story. Usually, the events are told in sequence, from start to finish.

- The story begins with a problem and builds through the middle with events called rising action. The character confronts the problem directly at the climax, and the story ends with the resolution.

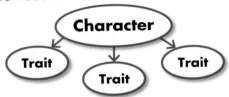

Strategy

Strategy: Prior Knowledge

Active readers use what they already know to understand what they read. As you read, think about what you already know about people and events from your own life that are similar to those in the story.

1. Read the selection "Mr. Smith." Create a graphic organizer like the one above to describe the main character.

2. Write a paragraph describing how Mr. Smith is similar to you or to someone you know.

Mr. Smith

In a quaint little town, a man named Mr. Smith lived in a big old house with his wife and family. The neighborhood kids liked and admired Mr. Smith. He was very inventive. He designed all sorts of extremely complicated and out-of-the-ordinary devices in his workshop. He also liked to get outside and have fun. One of Mr. Smith's favorite activities was playing with his kids and the rest of the kids in the neighborhood.

One day, Mr. Smith was playing a rowdy game of football with the kids. Suddenly, a downpour came, soaking them all. Everyone scurried into Mr. Smith's workshop. Mr. Smith had an idea. He convinced the kids to help him invent something that would shield them from the rain so they could continue their football game.

The kids were enthusiastic about helping! They worked feverishly all afternoon. Mr. Smith was so kindhearted that he didn't even get angry when one of his tools was broken. He said it could be replaced.

When their invention was complete, Mr. Smith carried it outside and helped the kids assemble it. It worked! It kept the kids dry while they finished their game.

Skill What do the kids like and admire about Mr. Smith? Think about what he does with them and the interesting things he makes.

Strategy Connect this to yourself. Have you ever tried to create a new invention? How did you feel while you were working on it?

Skill What adjectives would you use to describe Mr. Smith?

Strategy Based on what you know about being protected from the rain, what do you think the invention might look like?

THE THREE-CENTURY WOMAN

Words to Know

intersection

severe

spectacles

eerie

pondered

withered

Remember

Try the strategy. Then, if you need more help, use your glossary or dictionary.

Vocabulary Strategy
for Greek and Latin Roots

Word Structure When you come to a longer word you do not know, look for a familiar root in it. Greek and Latin roots are words or parts of words from the Greek and Latin languages that are used to build many English words. For example, the Latin root *spec-* means "look" or "see." It is used to build the words *inspect, spectacles,* and *spectacular.*

1. Look for a root in the word. See if you recognize the root. Do you know another word that has this root?

2. See whether the root meaning of the known word gives you a clue about the meaning of the unknown word.

3. Then check to see if this meaning makes sense in the sentence.

As you read "Happiness at Golden Times," look for Greek and Latin roots you can use to help you figure out the meanings of unknown words.

Happiness at Golden Times

The Golden Times Nursing Home is at the intersection of Pine and Second Streets. I know this because Jake and I go there every Thursday. Since birth, my dog Jake has been infected with a severe case of happiness. It is infectious. Jake has black circles around his eyes. They look like a pair of spectacles. When he is happy, his eyes close and his whole body wags.

The first time I took Jake to the nursing home, I was anxious. As we walked in, I had this spooky feeling. I thought, "It's eerie . . . too quiet." A few people sat in the lobby staring or looking distant, as though they pondered some important question. Their skin reminded me of an apple that is very old and withered.

They all turned to look at us. I wondered what to do. Then Jake took control. His tail began to wag a little. Smiles began to sprout all around. People appeared from this door and that door. They surged forward to pet Jake and make a fuss over him. Jake's whole body wagged and his eyes closed now.

Ever since, we both love our Thursdays at Golden Times.

Write

Many people volunteer to help others. Write a paragraph about what you could do as a volunteer. Use words in the Words to Know list.

THE THREE-CENTURY WOMAN

by *Richard Peck*

illustrated by *Matthew Faulkner*

Humorous fiction has characters and action that make you laugh. As you read, notice how the author creates a main character you can laugh with.

*What will Great-Grandmother
Breckenridge's fifteen minutes of fame be like?*

"I guess if you live long enough," my mom said to Aunt Gloria, "you get your fifteen minutes of fame."

Mom was on the car phone to Aunt Gloria. The minute Mom rolls out of the garage, she's on her car phone. It's state of the art and better than her car.

We were heading for Whispering Oaks to see my Great-Grandmother Breckenridge, who's lived there since I was a little girl. They call it an Elder Care Facility. Needless to say, I hated going.

The reason for Great-Grandma's fame is that she was born in 1899. Now it's January 2001. If you're one of those people who claim the new century begins in 2001, not 2000, even you have to agree that Great-Grandma Breckenridge has lived in three centuries. This is her claim to fame.

We waited for a light to change along by Northbrook Mall, and I gazed fondly over at it. Except for the Multiplex, it was closed because of New Year's Day. I have a severe mall habit. But I'm fourteen, and the mall is the place without homework. Aunt Gloria's voice filled the car.

"If you take my advice," she told Mom, "you'll keep those Whispering Oaks people from letting the media in to interview Grandma. Interview her my foot! Honestly. She doesn't even know where she is, let alone how many centuries she's lived in. The poor old soul. Leave her in peace. She's already got one foot in the—"

"Gloria, your trouble is you have no sense of history." Mom gunned across the intersection. "You got a C in History."

"I was sick a lot that year," Aunt Gloria said.

"Sick of history," Mom murmured.

"I heard that," Aunt Gloria said.

They bickered on, but I tuned them out. Then when we turned in at Whispering Pines, a sound truck from IBC-TV was blocking the drive.

"Good grief," Mom murmured. "TV."

"I told you," Aunt Gloria said, but Mom switched her off. She parked in a frozen rut.

"I'll wait in the car," I said. "I have homework."

"Get out of the car," Mom said.

If you get so old you have to be put away, Whispering Oaks isn't that bad. It smells all right, and a Christmas tree glittered in the lobby. A real tree. On the other hand, you have to push a red button to unlock the front door. I guess it's to keep the inmates from escaping, though Great-Grandma Breckenridge wasn't going anywhere and hadn't for twenty years.

When we got to her wing, the hall was full of camera crews and a woman from the suburban newspaper with a notepad.

Mom sighed. It was like the first day of school when you think you'll be okay until the teachers learn your name. Stepping over a cable, we stopped at Great-Grandma's door, and they were on to us.

"Who are you people to Mrs. Breckenridge?" the newspaperwoman said. "I want names."

These people were seriously pushy. And the TV guy was wearing more makeup than Mom. It dawned on me that they couldn't get into Great-Grandma's room without her permission. Mom turned on them.

"Listen, you're not going to be interviewing my grandmother," she said in a quiet bark. "I'll be glad to tell you anything you want to know about her, but you're not going in there. She's got nothing to say, and . . . she needs a lot of rest."

"Is it Alzheimer's?" the newswoman asked. "Because we're thinking Alzheimer's."

"Think what you want," Mom said. "But this is as far as you get. And you people with the camera and the light, you're not going in there either. You'd scare her to death, and then I'd sue the pants off you."

They pulled back.

But a voice came wavering out of Great-Grandma's room. Quite an eerie, echoing voice.

"Let them in!" the voice said.

It had to be Great-Grandma Breckenridge. Her roommate had died. "Good grief," Mom murmured, and the press surged forward. Mom and I went in first, and our eyes popped. Great-Grandma was usually flat out in the bed, dozing, with her teeth in a glass and a book in her hand. Today she was bright-eyed and propped up. She wore a fuzzy pink bed jacket. A matching bow was stuck in what remained of her hair.

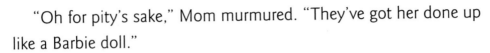

"Oh for pity's sake," Mom murmured. "They've got her done up like a Barbie doll."

Great-Grandma peered from the bed at Mom. "And who are you?" she asked.

"I'm Ann," Mom said carefully. "This is Megan," she said, meaning me.

"That's right," Great-Grandma said. "At least you know who you are. Plenty around this place don't."

The guy with the camera on his shoulder barged in. The other guy turned on a blinding light.

Great-Grandma blinked. In the glare we noticed she wore a trace of lipstick. The TV anchor elbowed the woman reporter aside and stuck a mike in Great-Grandma's face. Her claw hand came out from under the covers and tapped it.

"Is this thing on?" she inquired.

"Yes ma'am," the TV anchor said in his broadcasting voice. "Don't you worry about all this modern technology. We don't understand half of it ourselves." He gave her his big, five-thirty news smile and settled on the edge of her bed. There was room for him. She was tiny.

"We're here to congratulate you for having lived in three centuries— for being a Three-Century Woman! A great achievement."

Great-Grandma waved a casual claw. "Nothing to it," she said. "You sure this mike's on? Let's do this in one take."

The cameraman snorted and moved in for a closer shot. Mom stood still as a statue, wondering what was going to come out of Great-Grandma's mouth next.

"Mrs. Breckenridge," the anchor said, "to what do you attribute your long life?"

"I was only married once," Great-Grandma said. "And he died young."

The anchor stared. "Ah. And anything else?"

"Yes. I don't look back. I live in the present."

The camera panned around the room. This was all the present she had, and it didn't look like much.

The cameraman pulled in for a tighter shot. The anchor seemed to search his mind. You could tell he thought he was a great interviewer, though he had no sense of humor. A tiny smile played around Great-Grandma's wrinkled lips.

"But you've lived through amazing times, Mrs. Breckenridge. And you never think back about them?"

Great-Grandma stroked her chin and considered. "You mean you want to hear something interesting? Like how I lived through the San Francisco earthquake—the big one of oh-six?"

Beside me, Mom stirred. We were crowded over by the dead lady's bed. "You survived the 1906 San Francisco earthquake?" the anchor said.

Great-Grandma gazed at the ceiling, lost in thought.

"I'd have been about seven years old. My folks and I were staying at that big hotel. You know the one. I slept in a cot at the foot of their bed. In the middle of the night, that room gave me a shake, and the chiffonier walked right across the floor. You know what chiffonier is?"

"A chest of drawers?" the anchor said.

"Close enough," Great-Grandma said. "And the pictures flapped on the walls. We had to walk down twelve flights because the elevators didn't work. When we got outside, the streets were ankle-deep in broken glass. You never saw such a mess in your life."

Mom nudged me and hissed: "She's never been to San Francisco. She's never been west of Denver. I've heard her say so."

"Incredible!" the anchor said.

"Truth's stranger than fiction," Great-Grandma said, smoothing her sheet.

"And you never think back about it?"

Great-Grandma shrugged her little fuzzy pink shoulders. "I've been through too much. I don't have time to remember it all. I was on the *Hindenburg* when it blew up, you know."

Mom moaned, and the cameraman was practically standing on his head for a close-up.

"The *Hindenburg?*"

"That big gas bag the Germans built to fly over the Atlantic Ocean. It was called a zeppelin. Biggest thing you ever saw—five city blocks long. It was in May of 1937, before your time. You wouldn't remember. My husband and I were coming back from Europe on it. No, wait a minute."

Great-Grandma cocked her head and pondered for the camera.

"My husband was dead by then. It was some other man. Anyway, the two of us were coming back on the *Hindenburg*. It was smooth as silk. You didn't know you were moving. When we flew in over New York, they stopped the ball game at Yankee Stadium to see us passing overhead."

Great-Grandma paused, caught up in memories.

"And then the *Hindenburg* exploded," the anchor said, prompting her.

She nodded. "We had no complaints about the trip till then. The luggage was all stacked and we were coming in at Lakehurst, New Jersey. I was wearing my beige coat—beige or off-white, I forget. Then whoosh! The gondola heated up like an oven, and people peeled out of the windows. We hit the ground and bounced. When we hit again, the door fell off, and I walked out and kept going. When they caught up with me in the parking lot, they wanted to put me in the hospital. I looked down and thought I was wearing a lace dress. The fire had about burned up my coat. And I lost a shoe."

"Fantastic!" the anchor breathed. "What detail!" Behind him the woman reporter was scribbling away on her pad.

"Never," Mom muttered. "Never in her life."

"Ma'am, you are living history!" the anchor said. "In your sensational span of years you've survived two great disasters!"

"Three." Great-Grandma patted the bow on her head. "I told you I'd been married."

"And before we leave this venerable lady," the anchor said, flashing a smile for the camera, "we'll ask Mrs. Breckenridge if she has any predictions for this new twenty-first century ahead of us here in the Dawn of the Millennium."

"Three or four predictions," Great-Grandma said, and paused again, stretching out her airtime. "Number one, taxes will be higher. Number two, it's going to be harder to find a place to park. And number three, a whole lot of people are going to live as long as I have, so get ready for us."

527

"And with those wise words," the anchor said, easing off the bed, "we can leave Mrs. Breck—"

"And one more prediction," she said. "TV's on the way out. Your network ratings are already in the basement. It's all Web sites now. Son, I predict you'll be looking for work."

And that was it. The light went dead. The anchor, looking shaken, followed his crew out the door. When TV's done with you, they're done with you. "Is that a wrap?" Great-Grandma asked.

But now the woman from the suburban paper was moving in on her. "Just a few more questions, Mrs. Breckenridge."

"Where you from?" Great-Grandma blinked pink-eyed at her.

The Glenview Weekly Shopper.

"You bring a still photographer with you?" Great-Grandma asked.

"Well, no."

"And you never learned shorthand either, did you?"

"Well . . . no."

"Honey, I only deal with professionals. There's the door."

So then it was just Mom and Great-Grandma and I in the room. Mom planted a hand on her hip. "Grandma. Number one, you've never been to San Francisco. And number two, you never saw one of the zeppelin things."

Great-Grandma shrugged. "No, but I can read." She nodded to the pile of books on her nightstand with her spectacles folded on top. "You can pick up all that stuff in books."

"And number three," Mom said. "Your husband didn't die young. I can remember Grandpa Breckenridge."

"It was that TV dude in the five-hundred-dollar suit who set me off," Great-Grandma said. "He dyes his hair, did you notice? He made me mad, and it put my nose out of joint. He didn't notice I'm still here. He thought I was nothing but my memories. So I gave him some."

Now Mom and I stood beside her bed.

"I'll tell you something else," Great-Grandma said. "And it's no lie."

We waited, holding our breath to hear. Great-Grandma Breckenridge was pointing her little old bent finger right at me. "You, Megan," she said. "Once upon a time, I was your age. How scary is that?"

Then she hunched up her little pink shoulders and winked at me. She grinned and I grinned. She was just this little withered-up leaf of a lady in the bed. But I felt like giving her a kiss on her little wrinkled cheek, so I did.

"I'll come to see you more often," I told her.

"Call first," she said. "I might be busy." Then she dozed.

Reader Response

Open for Discussion At the mall, Megan's best friend says, "How was your visit with Great-Grandma? Did you get her to talk?" Create Megan's detailed reply.

1. Richard Peck pays close attention to the way the words fit together—their sound and rhythm. Find three phrases that are examples of Mr. Peck's use of sound and rhythm.

2. Look back at the story to see the two versions of Great-Grandma Breckenridge: the one Megan expects to see and the real one. Discuss how they differ.

3. Draw on your prior knowledge of older people such as grandparents. Did Great-Grandma Breckenridge's behavior surprise you? Why or why not? Use examples from the text to explain your answer.

4. Great-Grandma Breckenridge used disasters to make herself more interesting to reporters. What might she tell them about another disaster she "lived through"? Use words from the Words to Know list.

Look Back and Write What kind of person is the TV reporter? Use examples from the story as you discuss his character.

Richard Peck

Read books about young people and their families.

Richard Peck often writes about grandparents. One of his most memorable characters is Grandma Dowdel, who stars in his Newbery award-winning novel, *A Year Down Yonder*. Many of Mr. Peck's characters are independent people. He says that he tries to "give readers leading characters they can look up to and reasons to believe that problems can be solved." He also hopes his readers will learn that they can be different from the group.

Mr. Peck grew up in a small town in Illinois. He was a high school teacher for many years. He quit teaching to write, but he draws on his experiences with his students in his books. "Ironically, it was my students who taught me to be a writer, though I had been hired to teach *them*," he said in a speech once. "They taught me that a novel must entertain first before it can be anything else."

Mr. Peck dislikes modern technology. He does not own a computer or have his own Web site. He writes his books on a typewriter.

Fair Weather
by Richard Peck

Misty of Chincoteague
by Marguerite Henry

Genre

- A short story is narrative fiction that is short enough to be read in a single sitting.

- Short stories usually focus on a single character or event.

Link to Reading

Ask a librarian about short story collections. Read some stories and share what you learn with the class.

Understanding the Banana-Mobile

by Jeanie Stewart

Every morning as my mom leaves for work, she goes through the same routine, reminding me to brush my teeth, take out the garbage, and make my bed. She never varied a word all summer, until today.

"I want you to stay home with Grandfather today, Kenji," she added, throwing her purse strap over her shoulder.

I nearly snorted milk out my nose. "I can't, Mom! I have a ballgame this afternoon."

Mom shook her head and opened the door. "Sorry, but Grandfather needs cheering up."

There was nothing cheery about sitting around, doing boring things with Grandfather all day. He and Mom don't seem to understand that a kid wants to have some fun every now and then.

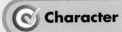

"Grandfather is upset because
I sold his car," Mom explained, "but
he shouldn't be driving—not with his failing eyesight."

She'd been threatening to sell Grandfather's car since his accident
last month, but I couldn't believe someone actually bought it. The old
monstrosity was as big as a dinosaur and the same yucky color as a
banana that should have been thrown out a day ago.

Character   What is the conflict between mother and son?

After Mom left, Grandfather entered the kitchen. Usually by this time of day, he was rushing off to the park to play Japanese chess with friends. Today, however, he just stared out the window at the oily splotch on the driveway where the banana-mobile once sat.

"Sorry about your car, Grandfather," I lied. Actually I was relieved to see the last of the banana-mobile. It was a major embarrassment, and I was always concerned that my friends would see it in front of our house, or worse, see me riding in it. Whenever Grandfather drove me places, I practically wrecked my spine, slumping in the seat, trying to be invisible.

Grandpa moaned and said, "It's not the car that I'll miss, Kenji; it's my freedom. Your grandmother and I took many exciting trips in that car. We drove across the country from the Atlantic all the way to the Pacific, stopping whenever something caught our fancy. Once we even drove to Alaska and panned for gold." He moved away from the window and sighed. "Now there will be no more adventures. It's frustrating when others control your life."

Duh! No kidding!

I didn't mean to say it aloud, but I must have, because Grandfather's wrinkled face suddenly crinkled into a grin. "Perhaps you understand," he said.

"Believe me, I *do*, Grandfather."

He clamped his arm around my shoulder in a sideways hug.

"I have an idea," I said. "It's not an Alaskan adventure, but the park isn't far, and I'm in the mood for a game of shogi. Why don't we walk over and see if your friends are still playing?"

"Let's go," he said, grabbing his hat. "And after that we'll join your friends in baseball. Do you think there are any positions open for an old man with bad eyesight?"

"Sure," I said, "you can be umpire!"

Reading Across Texts

Look at the two selections and compare the grandparents and grandchildren.

Writing Across Texts Write about what the grandchildren learned about their grandparents.

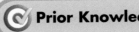 **Prior Knowledge** Think about other stories where people make friends.

Comprehension

Skill
Graphic Sources

Strategy
Ask Questions

 # Graphic Sources

- Graphic sources include charts, tables, graphs, maps, illustrations, and photographs.

- Before reading, look closely at graphic sources that accompany a selection. They will give you an idea of what you will read.

 ## Strategy: Ask Questions

Asking yourself questions before, during, and after reading and then reading to find answers to those questions can help you understand and recall what you read. For example, before reading "Shipwreck," you might ask, "What do the title and the map tell me the selection will be about?" You can also use graphic sources during and after reading to help you understand the text.

1. Read "Shipwreck." As you read, write questions you think you should ask yourself to help you remember the important information in the selection.

2. Write a paragraph telling how the map of the *Titanic*'s final resting place helped you to understand the selection.

Shipwreck

For many years, people have spent their lives trying to find certain sunken ships. Why do they want to do this? There are several reasons.

Some people want to find shipwrecks to learn exactly what caused the ships to sink. If we can find out the cause of a shipwreck, we may be able to prevent the same kind of accident from happening again.

Some scientists and explorers search for shipwrecks to learn more about the past. They want to find out how old ships were designed. They also want to see the tools people used on those ships. The study of shipwrecks is called *nautical archaeology.*

Many people who search for shipwrecks are looking for treasures, such as old jewelry. Some of these items are worth a lot of money.

When people search for shipwrecks, they use maps to help them find their way. Once people find a sunken ship, they mark its location on a map. The map here shows approximately where the ocean liner *Titanic* went down. This map will help other people locate the shipwreck for years to come.

Skill Always preview a text before reading. How do the title and map tell you what this selection will be about?

Strategy Here you could ask yourself, and answer, "What is one reason people have for searching for shipwrecks?"

Strategy Ask yourself, "What is the main idea of this selection?" Answering will help you remember it.

Skill How does this map help you understand where the Titanic sank?

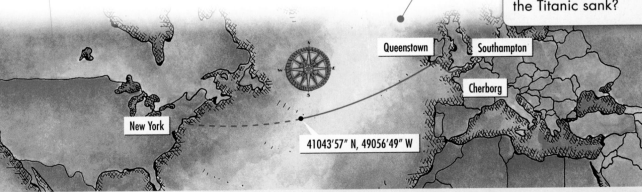

Queenstown

Southampton

Cherborg

New York

41043'57" N, 49056'49" W

Words to Know

sonar

robotic

ooze

sediment

interior

cramped

debris

Vocabulary Strategy
for Unfamiliar Words

Dictionary/Glossary Sometimes the sentences around an unfamiliar word don't have context clues to help you find its meaning. Then you should look up the word in a dictionary or glossary. Follow these steps.

1. Look to see whether the book has a glossary. If not, then use a dictionary.

2. Find the word entry. If the pronunciation is given, read it aloud. You may recognize the word when you hear yourself say it.

3. Look over all the meanings listed in the entry. Try each meaning in the sentence with the unfamiliar word.

4. Choose the meaning that makes sense in your sentence.

As you read "In the Ocean Deeps," use a dictionary or the glossary to find the meanings of words you cannot figure out from the text.

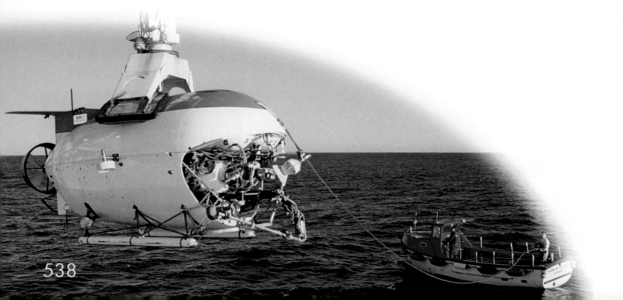

IN THE OCEAN DEEPS

What lies in the ocean deeps and who lives there? Scientists work hard to answer these questions. The ocean floor is miles deep in many places. It is very cold and dark down there. The pressure of so much water would crush divers instantly. How can they get down there to find answers?

Scientists use high-tech machines. A sonar system sends out beeps of sound that bounce off the ocean floor. Computers can use the beeps to make maps. Scientists look at the maps for areas that interest them. Then they send down submersible vehicles that can withstand the high pressure. Many of these vehicles are robotic. They carry cameras and other equipment to record what it is like down there. At great depths, they may show an ooze of melted rock coming from deep inside the Earth. They may show a "desert" of sediment or a mountain range.

Some of these deep-sea machines carry divers. The interior of one of these machines is small, so scientists are cramped. But that is a small price to pay to be able to see for themselves the wonders of deep-sea life. Strange and wonderful plants and animals have been discovered far below the surface. Sadly, so have debris, trash, and damage done by pollution.

Write

Look through the pictures in the selection. Choose one to explain and describe. Use some words from the Words to Know list.

THE UNSINKABLE
WRECK OF THE R.M.S.
TITANIC

from *Ghost Liners: Exploring the World's Greatest Lost Ships*

BY ROBERT D. BALLARD AND RICK ARCHBOLD
ILLUSTRATIONS BY KEN MARSCHALL

Genre

Narrative nonfiction tells the true story of an event. As you read, notice how the author tells why a ship sank and how he explored its wreckage.

What remains of the greatest
shipwreck of all time?

APRIL 10, 1912, 12:00 NOON

Tugboats help the *Titanic* pull away from the Southampton pier.

APRIL 14, 1912, 11:39 P.M.

As the liner enters an ice field, a large iceberg lies directly in its path.

APRIL 14, 1912, 11:40 P.M.

The iceberg scrapes along the *Titanic's* starboard side.

Inside the cramped submarine, all I could hear was the steady pinging of the sonar and the regular breathing of the pilot and engineer. I crouched on my knees, my eyes glued to the tiny viewport. The pings speeded up—that meant the wreck was close—and I strained to see beyond the small cone of light that pierced the endless underwater night.

"Come right!" I was so excited I was almost shouting, even though the two others with me inside *Alvin* were so close I could touch them. "Bingo!"

Like a ghost from the ancient past, the bow of the Royal Mail Steamer *Titanic*, the greatest shipwreck of all time, materialized out my viewport. After years of questing, I had arrived at the ship's last resting place.

Effortlessly we rose up the side of the famous bow, now weeping great tears of rust, past the huge anchor and up over the rail. We were the first in more than seventy years to "walk" on the *Titanic*'s deck! The giant windlasses used for raising and lowering the anchor still trailed their massive links of chain, as if ready to lower away. I felt as though I had walked into a dream.

◄ Our little submarine *Alvin* rests on the *Titanic's* portside boat deck while the underwater robot *Jason Junior* explores the ship's B-Deck promenade.

A 1912 poster from England advertising the new White Star Liner, *Titanic*

APRIL 15, 1912, 1:40 A.M.

Two hours after the collision, the bow of the *Titanic* is underwater.

APRIL 15, 1912, 2:17 A.M.

The *Titanic* breaks in two and the bow section begins its final plunge.

In 1912, the *Titanic* had set sail on her maiden voyage,
the largest, most luxurious ship the world had ever seen.
On board were many of the rich and famous of the day.

Then, on the fifth night out—tragedy. An iceberg, seen too late. Too few lifeboats. Pandemonium, and over 1,500 dead out of the more than 2,200 people on board.

Now the sub sailed out over the well deck, following the angle of the fallen foremast up toward the liner's bridge. We paused at the crow's nest. On the fateful night, lookout Frederick Fleet had been on duty here. It was he who warned the bridge: "Iceberg right ahead." Fleet was one of the lucky ones. He made it into a lifeboat and to safety.

The pilot set *Alvin* gently down on the bridge, not far from the telemotor control—all that remained of the steering mechanism of the ship. It was here that First Officer William Murdoch, desperate to avoid the mountain of ice that lay in the *Titanic*'s path, shouted to the helmsman, "Hard a-starboard!" Then Murdoch watched in excruciating agony as the huge ship slowly began to turn—but it was too late and the iceberg fatally grazed the liner's side. I thought of Captain E. J. Smith rushing from his cabin to be told the terrible news. Thirty minutes later, after learning how quickly water was pouring into the ship, he knew that the "unsinkable" *Titanic* was doomed.

We lifted off from the bridge and headed toward the stern. Over a doorway we could make out the brass plate with the words: 1st Class Entrance. In my mind's eye I could see the deck surging with passengers as the crew tried to keep order during the loading of the lifeboats. The broken arm of a lifeboat davit hung over the side. From this spot port-side lifeboat No. 2 was launched—barely half full. Among the twenty-five people in a boat designed to carry more than forty were Minnie Coutts and her two boys,

(Above) *Alvin* investigates the bow section of the *Titanic* wreck. The stern lies in the distance. (Below left) The telemotor control that once held the ship's wheel; (middle) the A-deck promenade; (right) a section of bow railing.

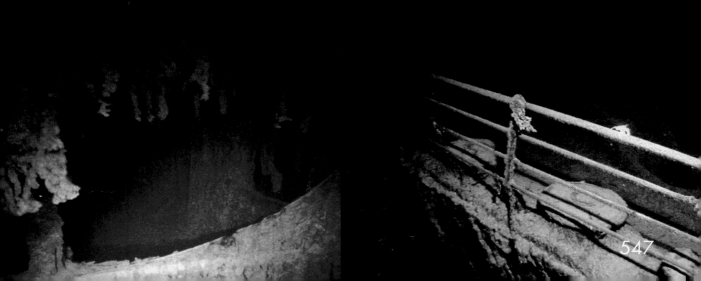

Willie and Neville. They were among the relatively few third-class passengers to survive the sinking.

As our tiny submarine continued toward the stern, we peered through the windows of first-class staterooms. The glass dome over the first-class grand staircase was long gone, providing a perfect opening for exploring the interior of the ship. But that would have to wait for a later visit, when we would bring along our robotic "swimming eyeball," *Jason Junior.* As we continued back, I wondered what we would find. We already knew the ship lay in two pieces, with the stern nearly two thousand feet (six hundred meters) away. Suddenly the smooth steel subdecking contorted into a tangle of twisted metal where the stern had ripped free. Beyond it hundreds of objects that had spilled out when the ship broke in two were lying on the ocean floor.

◄ *Jason Junior* **explores the remains of the grand staircase.**

NEARLY LOST BECAUSE OF A HAT

Willie Coutts's hat nearly cost him his life. When the *Titanic* hit the iceberg, his mother, Minnie, roused eleven-year-old Willie and his baby brother Neville (right), got them dressed, and put on their lifebelts. Through the swirl of panicking passengers, Millie led her children out of third class toward what she hoped was safety. One officer handed his own lifebelt to Minnie, saying, "If the boat goes down you'll remember me." Another crewman led them to the boat deck. Minnie and Neville got in one of the last boats—but the officer in charge held Willie back. The rule was women and children first, and the hat Willie was wearing made him look too old. Willie's mother insisted but the officer refused again. Finally, good sense prevailed and Willie, too, stepped to safety.

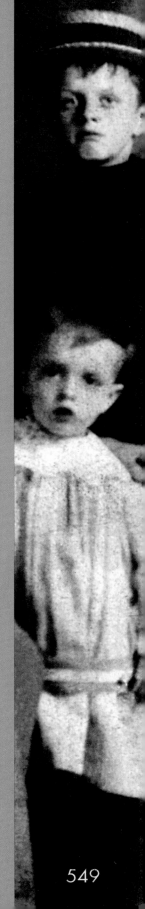

As we floated out over this debris field, I found it hard to believe that only a thin film of sediment covered plates and bottles that had lain on the bottom for seventy-four years. One of the ship's boilers sat upright on the mud with a tin cup resting on it, as if set there by a human hand. Champagne bottles lay with their corks still intact. A porcelain doll's head stared at us from its final resting place in the soft ooze. Had it belonged to little Loraine Allison, the only child from first class who didn't survive that night? Most haunting of all were the shoes and boots. Many of them lay in pairs where

HAUNTING MEMENTOS

Unlike its fairly intact bow section, the *Titanic*'s stern (page 550) literally blew apart on hitting the bottom. In the debris field between the bow and stern we saw hundreds of touching reminders of the tragedy. A porcelain doll's head (above right) is all that remains of an expensive French doll (inset). It may have belonged to Loraine Allison of Montreal (above middle with her baby brother), the only child from first class who did not survive. A tin cup (above left) has come to rest near the round furnace door of one of the ships huge boilers.

bodies had once fallen. Within a few weeks of the sinking, the corpses had been consumed by underwater creatures and their bones had been dissolved by the cold salt water. Only those shoes remain—mute reminders of the human cost of the *Titanic* tragedy.

After only two hours on the bottom, it was time for *Alvin* to begin the long ascent back to the surface ship, two and a half miles (four kilometers) above. As we headed back to the surface, I was already impatient to return to the *Titanic*. We had only begun to plumb its secrets.

551

Reader Response

Open for Discussion In this true account, you went with Robert Ballard into a silent world two-and-a-half miles beneath the ocean's surface. What did you see?

1. Like snapshots, words show you objects in the ruins: *tin cup*, *doll's head*, *shoes and boots*. Find other snapshot-like words that reveal the wreck.

2. Sometimes illustrations are meant to make readers feel certain things. What emotions do you think the illustrations on pages 549 and 551 might make readers feel? Why?

3. How did the people on the *Titanic* behave? Were they brave in the face of death? Use details from the text to explain your answers.

4. You are a news reporter chosen to dive with the crew of the *Alvin*. Write an account of what you saw of the sunken *Titanic* and how you felt about it. Use words from the Words to Know list.

Look Back and Write On a later visit Robert Ballard would bring equipment to explore inside the *Titanic*. Write what that equipment is and describe it, using page 548 to help you.

Dr. Robert Ballard

Read more books about shipwrecks.

Dr. Robert Ballard was born in Wichita, Kansas, but grew up in San Diego, California, near the water. He says that growing up he always wanted to be Captain Nemo from Jules Verne's science-fiction novel *20,000 Leagues Under the Sea*.

Dr. Ballard has led or taken part in more than one hundred deep-sea expeditions. Another of his accomplishments is founding the Jason Foundation for Education. He did this in response to the thousands of letters from schoolchildren wanting to know how he discovered the R.M.S. *Titanic*. The goal of the Jason Foundation is to help teachers, students, businesses, government, and schools work together to inspire students to use exploration and discovery in their pursuit of learning.

The Wreck of the Zanzibar
by Michael Morpurgo

The Story of the H.L. Hunley and Queenie's Coin
by Fran Hawk

Adventure Fiction

Genre

- Adventure fiction tells stories about brave and often dangerous exploits.

- The characters in this kind of fiction tend to come up against obstacles that they conquer or that conquer them.

Link to Reading

Ask a librarian about other books of fiction set on and around an ocean. What sorts of characters and adventures do you find? Share what you learn with the class.

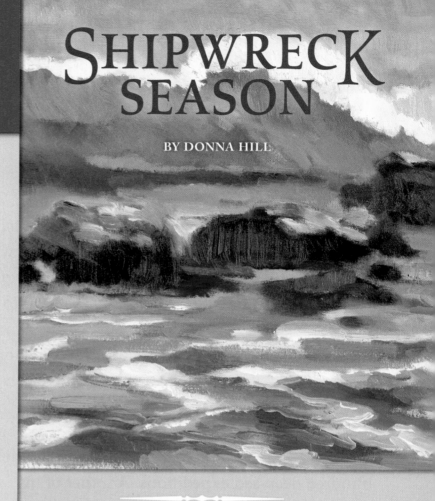

SHIPWRECK SEASON

BY DONNA HILL

It is 1880 on Cape Cod, Massachusetts. Sixteen-year-old Daniel is spending time at the lifesavers' station with the surfmen, who risk their lives to save people lost in shipwrecks along the rocky coast. Daniel has led a quiet life up until now, with very little adventure. He has rowed boats on calm rivers, never on a rough ocean. Now, with his dog, Truehart, Daniel watches from the shore as the surfmen conduct a practice lifeboat drill in the pounding seas.

The men ran along shore until the captain called, "Stop!" They sped the boat to the surf, lifted it off its carriage, and got the carriage back up on the beach. They took life belts from the boat and strapped them on. The captain put the steering oar in place. The surfmen grasped the gunwales on either side of the boat and waited tensely.

Daniel took his place at the stern beside the captain. As something on which to launch a boat, the ocean was different from what Daniel had known as a child, playing in the surf. Great mounds of water roared in toward the beach, crested, tumbled over, and came one after another in wild surges of power before turning into foam.

 **Graphic Sources** How does the picture make the sea look?

The captain was studying the sea so intently that Daniel wondered if he were doubtful about launching today.

"Rough, isn't it, sir?"

"Not bad."

"What are we waiting for?"

"The slatch." The captain did not break his attention. "Slack water followed by a backwash to sea, usually the seventh wave after the biggest."

Now Daniel saw that waves were not all the same size. Big ones rolled in one after another, then a small one followed and crested. The captain shouted, "Now!"

The men rushed the boat into the sea, with Daniel and the captain shoving from the stern. They all ran out waist deep. As each section of the boat swept free, a man scrambled aboard facing the stern and wrestled his oar into place.

The sea rose up and took the boat. The captain leaped in over the stern and seized the long steering oar.

"Pull!" he cried. "Pull!"

The boat lunged through the water. Daniel fell back. He slipped in the pushing waves but kept his eyes riveted on the rowers, their huge arms and shoulders pulling in mighty strokes as they concentrated on the captain.

The captain was standing upright at his oar in the stern. Foam crashed over his back. Spray flew high overhead. Daniel saw him steer away from the biggest waves until they broke, but when one came that he could not avoid, he called for speed and sent the boat head on. A great sea broke over the bow and drenched the men. They did not falter or even wince.

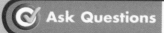 **Ask Questions** What questions do you have about the story so far?

Daniel was astounded by the surfmen's skill, power, and daring, and by the beauty of the white surfboat flying through glittering spray. He cheered, prancing, sloshing, and waving. A roaring mountain of sea came at him, ready to break over him. He saw it just in time, turned, and plunged toward shore.

The dog ran up and down the beach barking exuberantly as Daniel came splashing through the surf. She rushed at him, tail pumping madly, and nuzzled her cold nose into his hand.

"So you think I'm all right after all, do you, old girl?" Daniel laughed, roughing up her shaggy head.

Together they patrolled the beach, watching the surfboat. Out past the breakers, the boat capsized. The men bobbed in the sea. The dog stiffened and stared out intently. She did not relax until the boat was righted and the crew back at their oars.

"Ready to go to the rescue, right, old girl?" Daniel asked. He told her she was a noble dog.

Coming back with the boat looked even more hazardous than launching. The boat flew in ahead of a great swell, the captain standing in the stern, spray breaking around him.

Any oarsman, even the athletes of Daniel's club, would be impressed by this crew. The rowing Daniel and his friends did on a calm river, with nothing to think about but stroke and speed, was mere play compared to the efforts of these mighty oarsmen, which were not for sport, but in preparation to save lives.

It was no small thing to be a surfman, Daniel decided. It would be no small thing to be counted as one among them.

Reading Across Texts

Look back at the two selections and make a list of potential dangers at sea.

Writing Across Texts Write a list of safety tips for people who are planning on taking an ocean voyage. Base your tips on your list of dangers.

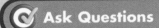 **Ask Questions** Do you have any questions after reading the story?

Comprehension

Skill
Author's Purpose

Strategy
Monitor and
Fix Up

Skill

Author's Purpose

- The author's purpose is the main reason an author writes a selection. An author may write to persuade, to inform, to entertain, or to express ideas or feelings.

- Sometimes an author may write with more than one purpose in mind.

- What the author says and details given help you figure out the author's purpose.

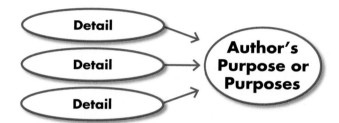

Strategy

Strategy: Monitor and Fix Up

Sometimes as you are reading you realize you've lost touch with what the author is saying. You may adjust your reading speed as you think about the author's purpose. You also might make a list of important ideas in the text.

Write

1. Read "The United States in Space." Create a graphic organizer like the one above to record the details that give clues to the purpose the author had for writing.

2. Write what you think the author's main purpose was for writing "The United States in Space" and why you think this.

The United States in Space

The space program in the United States, known to most people as NASA (the National Aeronautics and Space Administration), began in 1958. NASA was formed because the United States wanted to beat the Soviet Union in the "space race."

At first, the Soviet Union was ahead in the space race. They sent the first satellite into space in 1957. The United States didn't send a satellite into space until 1958. The Soviet Union also sent the first man to orbit Earth in 1961. The United States didn't send a man into orbit until 1962. That man was John Glenn. He orbited Earth three times.

As time passed, the United States moved ahead in the space race. President John F. Kennedy gave NASA the goal of putting a man on the moon by the end of the 1960s. NASA was able to meet that goal. In 1969, Neil Armstrong was the first man to take a step on the moon. This feat helped the United States win the space race.

APOLLO 11

Skill As you preview the article, what do you predict will be the author's main purpose for writing it—to entertain or to inform?

Strategy If you were to list main ideas in this article, what would you list for this paragraph?
a) In 1958 the Soviet Union sent up the first space satellite.
b) John Glenn orbited Earth three times.
c) The Soviet Union started the space race ahead.

Strategy What would you list as the main idea of this paragraph?

Skill What was the author's main purpose for writing this article? Was your prediction correct?

Words to Know

focus

gravity

specific

monitors

accomplishments

role

Remember

Try the strategy. Then, if you need more help, use your glossary or dictionary.

Vocabulary Strategy
for Multiple-Meaning Words

Context Clues Some words have more than one meaning. You can find clues in nearby words to decide which meaning the author is using.

1. Think about different meanings the word can have.

2. Reread the sentence in which the word appears. Which meaning fits in the sentence?

3. If you can't tell, then look for more clues in nearby sentences.

4. Put the clues together and decide which meaning works best.

As you read "To Be an Astronaut," use the context to decide which meaning a multiple-meaning word has in the article. For example, does *role* mean "a character in a play" or "a socially expected behavior"?

To Be an Astronaut

Astronauts have a special place in our history. They are people of special character too. Like all explorers, astronauts must be curious and brave. As scientists, they must be well trained in physics and math with a focus on astronomy. They are also skilled pilots.

To live in space, astronauts must be in top shape. Because there is no gravity in space, they must get used to being weightless. Each flight brings different jobs with specific assignments. One time, astronauts may build part of a space station. Another time, they may carry out dozens of tests. They may have to use a robot arm and watch what the arm is doing on monitors.

The computer screens let them adjust the arm's movements. These are only a few of the many tasks astronauts must accomplish in space.

Astronauts have many accomplishments, but none is more important than serving as role models for young people. These space explorers' courage, learning, and devotion to duty make them shining examples. They show us that people may reach for the stars.

Write

Write an essay praising a kind of worker whom you admire. Tell why you admire that person. Use words from the Words to Know list.

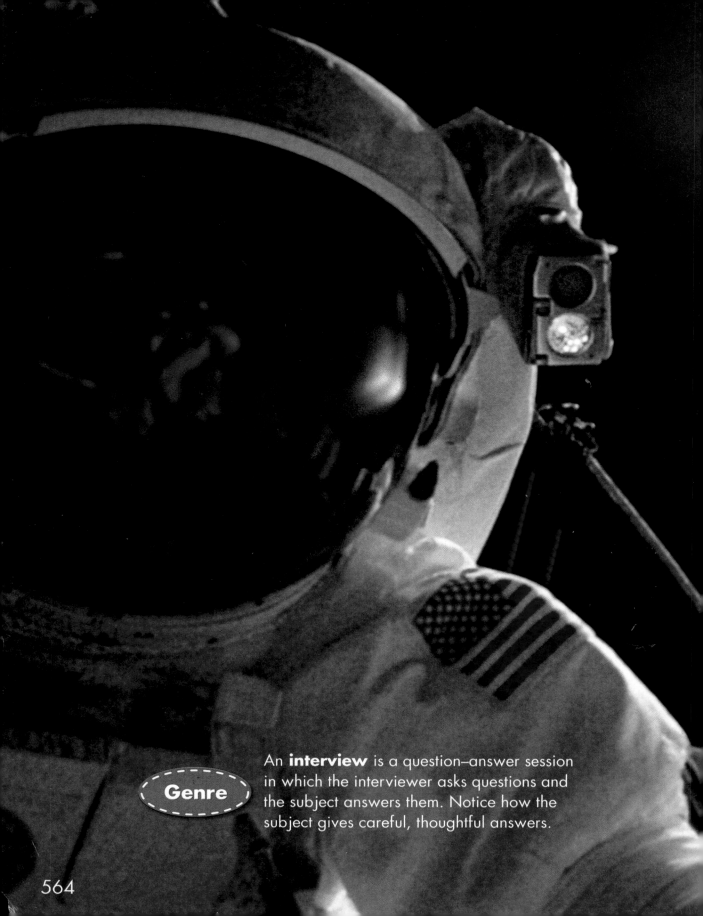

An **interview** is a question–answer session in which the interviewer asks questions and the subject answers them. Notice how the subject gives careful, thoughtful answers.

TALK WITH AN ASTRONAUT

WHAT IS IT LIKE TO FLY INTO SPACE?

Ellen Ochoa is the first Hispanic American woman to fly in space. She is also an inventor of optical and robotic devices. She was interviewed by fifth-grade students.

Q. What are your Hispanic roots? Did you speak Spanish at home when you were growing up?

A. My Hispanic roots come from my father's side. His parents were Mexican, but my father was born in this country. He was one of 12 children. My father grew up speaking both Spanish and English, but unfortunately he didn't speak Spanish with us at home. When I was growing up, my father believed, as many people did at the time, that there was a prejudice against people speaking their native language. It's really too bad, and I'm glad that things have changed in recent years.

Q. Does your being Hispanic American make you feel more pressure and more pride about your accomplishments? Do you have that in mind when you think of how well you've done in life?

A. I don't believe that being Hispanic American puts any additional pressure on me. I seem to put enough pressure on myself as it is. As for my accomplishments, being an astronaut has given me the opportunity to speak to children all over, including children with the same background as myself. I think that it's important for children to have a role model to see what they can grow up to be. It's important they know that if they work hard, they can be and accomplish whatever they want. I am proud to be an example of that.

Q. Who do you think was the most influential person in your life?

A. My mother influenced me the most. When I was a year old, she started college. She had to raise five children primarily on her own, and so she couldn't take more than one class each semester. She didn't graduate until 22 years later, but she did finish. Her primary focus was the enjoyment of learning. That's what I got from her example.

Q. What were you interested in when you were in fifth grade?

A. When I was in the fifth grade, I think I wanted to be President. I got over that by the time I was in the sixth grade. I didn't think that I would be an astronaut. But you never know how your interests will change. That's why it's important never to shut down your options. In college, I changed my major five times. I started college interested in music and business and graduated with a degree in physics. I didn't actually pursue becoming an astronaut until graduate school, when I learned about the kinds of skills NASA was looking for in potential astronauts.

Q. Why did you want to go into space?

A. I can't imagine not wanting to go into space. But I never considered being an astronaut as an option because when I was growing up there were no female astronauts. It wasn't until the first six female astronauts were selected in 1978 that women could even think of it as a possible career path.

Q. What is it like to operate a robot arm in space?

A. I have worked the robot arm on all three of my space missions, and I really love it. It's challenging to do, but lots of fun. On my last mission to the space station I worked with the help of cameras and monitors because we were docked in a way that prevented me from seeing the robot arm. This made things more difficult, but then again, everything I've done on actual missions in space has always been easier than when I first tried it during training.

Q. What is NASA training like?

A. Everything is always harder to do in training. In training, we prepare for anything that could happen on a space mission—anything that could go wrong. In training, things keep breaking, problems have to be solved. Nothing has ever gone wrong on any of my missions, and our training helps us make sure that nothing will. Each mission has its own specific purpose. For my last mission, we trained for nine months before the actual flight. I started my formal NASA training in 1990. During that period I spent about half of the time in training; the other half I spent performing other duties. I was in training for three years before my first mission, which isn't that long of a wait. Some astronauts have waited 10, even 16 years before they finally go into space!

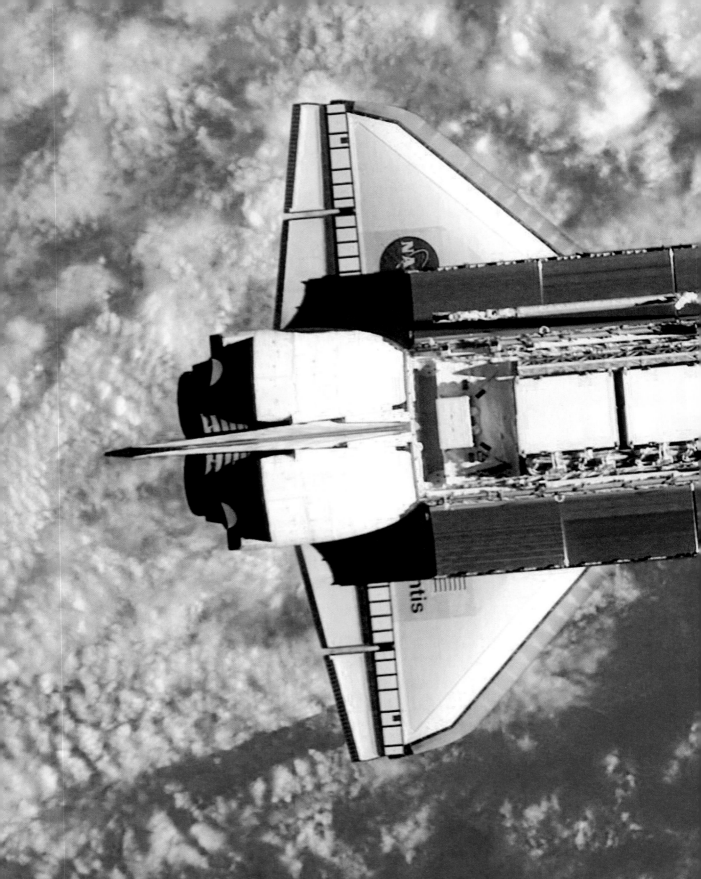

Q. What is it like to float in zero gravity?

A. Weightlessness is the fun part of the mission. There is really nothing to compare it to on Earth. I guess the closest thing would be swimming or scuba diving. It's a similar freedom of movement. What is odd is that weightlessness seems more natural. You don't have the same kinds of sensations in space as you do in the water.

Q. How do you sleep on the space shuttle? Does everyone sleep at the same time, or do you take turns? Do you have weird dreams because you're sleeping in space?

A. On my first two missions we slept in two shifts. We had sleeping compartments that looked like coffins. On my last mission we slept in a single shift. Instead of the sleeping compartments, we slept in what can best be described as a sleeping bag with hooks. You would find a place to hook on to and float in. As for my dreaming, it isn't that different in space. I tend to dream a lot, whether I'm in space or at home on Earth. I have floating dreams on Earth and non-floating dreams on a mission in space.

Q. What does Earth look like from space?

A. That's a really hard question. You have to remember that the shuttle is moving at five miles a second, so the Earth looks very different depending on where you are in space in relation to the position above Earth and what time of day it is. I have to say, though, Earth looks very much like I expected it to look. The *Imax* films are pretty close to what Earth really looks like from space. The main difference is that the colors are much more vivid when you're in space.

Q. How do you eat in space? Do you have to eat food out of a toothpaste tube? Does the food taste good?

A. Astronauts haven't eaten food out of tubes for over twenty years. Most of the food now is freeze-dried. All we do is add hot water. We eat a variety of foods, including nuts, granola, cookies, dried fruit, tortillas. We have drinks that we add water to as well.

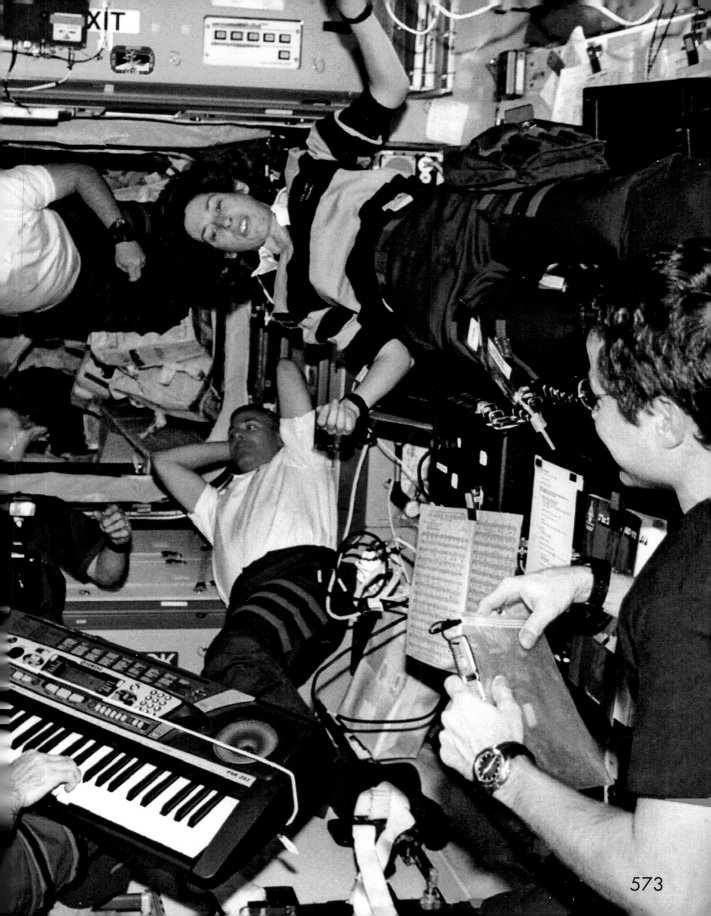

Q. Is it hard being an astronaut and a mother? Do you worry about going into space now that you're a mother? How does your son feel about your going into space?

A. I think it's hard being anything and a mother. Both are full-time jobs, and you have to work very hard at both to do a good job. Personally, I find both jobs wonderful. It is hard to be separated from my husband and son when I go on a mission, and I miss them a great deal. But lots of people have to be away from their families because of their jobs. Right now my son is only eighteen months old, so the last time I went into space, he didn't really know what was going on. I think it will be much harder the next time, since he will understand more.

Q. Can you talk to your family from space?

A. Yes, thanks to e-mail, when I am in space my husband and I are able to communicate every day—which is very nice. And on missions lasting more than ten days, we are allowed to visit with each other by having a video conference from space.

Q. What is the scariest thing that ever happened to you in space?

A. There's never really been anything for me to be scared of because nothing has ever gone wrong on any of my missions. For me, going into space is very exciting, not scary. The riskiest part of the flight is the launch because it's the phase of the flight when things are most likely to go wrong. But like I said, there have never been problems on my missions, and besides, we are trained to handle any problems that might come along.

Q. Do you think communication with extraterrestrials is possible? Do you think there are other life-forms out there?

A. I'm not really sure if communication is possible right now, with the technology we have today. Given the number of stars that have been discovered in the last couple of years, it isn't inconceivable that life exists on other planets. Though it is important to differentiate between life that is single-celled and life-forms that are intelligent and capable of communication.

Q. I love math and I want to become an astronaut. What can I start to do to prepare myself?

A. It's good that you love math, because in order to be an astronaut, a college degree in math or a technical science is very important to have. Being an astronaut isn't just the science, though. An astronaut must be both a team player and a leader as well. You should get involved in activities where you work closely with other people—because working closely with other people is an essential part of being an astronaut!

Reader Response

Open for Discussion Role models, interests, options, teamwork: Ellen Ochoa tells how each of these applies to her life. How might they apply to yours?

1. Suppose you were going to interview a famous adventurer. How might the questions in "Talk with an Astronaut" help you think up good questions for the interview?

2. One purpose of an interview is to gather facts about someone. Another purpose is to gather opinions. What are some of Ellen Ochoa's opinions? Use examples from the interview to explain your answer.

3. How is weightlessness like swimming? How is it different from swimming? Use quotes from the interview to explain your answer.

4. Write a question of your own to ask Ellen Ochoa. Use words from the Words to Know list.

Look Back and Write Why is training harder than the actual space mission? Reread page 568 to be sure of the answer. Then write it in your own words.

Ellen Ochoa

Read more about astronauts and space exploration.

Ellen Ochoa grew up in La Mesa, California. She received a degree in physics from San Diego State University and a Ph.D. from Stanford University. Some of her professors discouraged women from going into math and science, but she knew she could succeed.

At Stanford, Dr. Ochoa focused on the area where she would make her name: optical information systems. She develops ways for computers to "see" objects and analyze them. In 1987 she applied to the NASA astronaut program, but was rejected. Rather than letting this get her down, Ochoa got her pilot's license! In 1990 NASA accepted her application.

In 1993 Dr. Ochoa became the first Hispanic woman to enter outer space. In four missions in space, she has researched issues such as the effect of the sun on Earth's atmosphere and has visited the International Space Station.

Dr. Ochoa lives with her husband and their two children. In her spare time she flies planes, plays volleyball, and goes bicycling. An accomplished flutist, she has even played her flute in space!

Space Station Science: Life in Free Fall
by Marianne J. Dyson

To Space & Back
by Sally Ride

Women Astronauts

Online Directories

Genre

- Online directories list links to many Web sites about a given topic.

- You can use an online directory to learn about a topic.

Text Features

- Directories list topics as links. You may click on any topic link.

- Or you may type in keywords and click on the search button.

- Your next stop is a list of links to Web sites that are all about your topic.

Link to Science

Many astronauts do scientific studies in space. Research what they study and share your results with the class.

Let's say you want to find out more about women astronauts. You go to an Internet online directory. Here are some of the topics you find listed there.

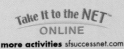

Take It to the NET™
ONLINE
more activities sfsuccessnet.com

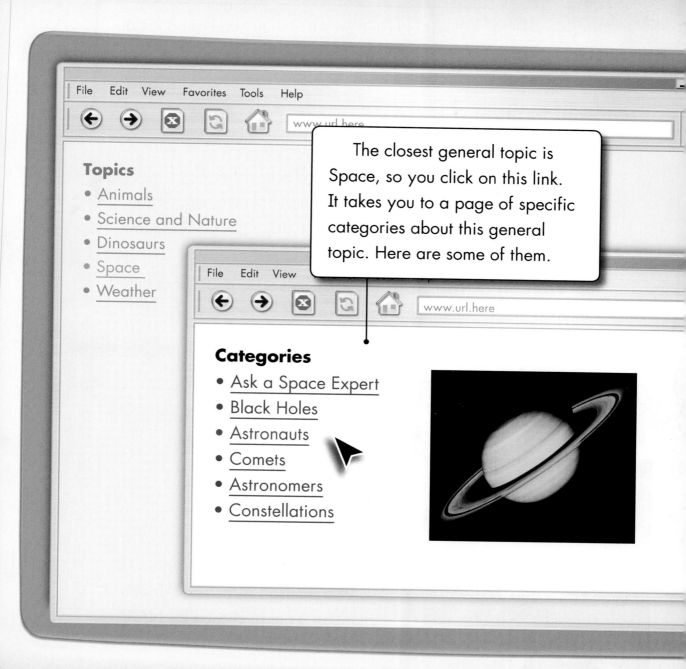

Topics

- Animals
- Science and Nature
- Dinosaurs
- Space
- Weather

The closest general topic is Space, so you click on this link. It takes you to a page of specific categories about this general topic. Here are some of them.

Categories

- Ask a Space Expert
- Black Holes
- Astronauts
- Comets
- Astronomers
- Constellations

 Author's Purpose Is information easy to find on this site?

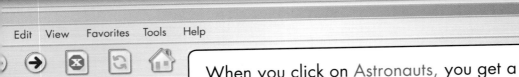

When you click on Astronauts, you get a list of Web sites. You decide to click on this one:

Jemison, Mae

Sites

1. **Astronaut Bio: Mae Jemison** - facts of her life, education, experience from the National Science Foundation.

2. **NASA: Dr. Mae Jemison** - read about the first woman of color to go into space, from NASA Quest.

3. **Women of The Hall - Mae Jemison** - read about this medical doctor, engineer, and astronaut.

Here is what you get:

Mae Jemison

Hometown:
Chicago, Illinois

Greatest Achievement:
Mae Jemison is the first African American woman chosen by NASA to be a Space Shuttle astronaut.

How She Did It:
From her earliest years, Mae planned to be a scientist. Her parents

encouraged her to do her best, and she knew she had the ability to do just about anything she wanted. She earned a degree in engineering and then in medicine. Before she became an astronaut, Mae worked as a doctor in West Africa. Mae Jemison is a strong, determined person who used school to help her become a doctor, an engineer, and an astronaut—a real science star!

What She Says:

"Don't let anyone rob you of your imagination, your creativity, or your curiosity. It's your place in the world, it's your life. Go on and do all you can with it, and make it the life you want to live."

Reading Across Texts

Look back at "Talk with an Astronaut" and make a list of qualities, such as curiosity and courage, that make a good astronaut. Do the same for "Mae Jemison."

Writing Across Texts In a paragraph, tell what makes a good astronaut.

 Monitor & Fix Up   Read Mae Jemison's advice and think about it.

Skill
Cause and Effect

Strategy
Summarize

Cause and Effect

- A cause (why something happens) may have several effects. An effect (what happens as a result of the cause) may have several causes.

- Sometimes clue words such as *since, as a result, caused, thus, therefore,* and *consequently* are used to show cause-and-effect relationships.

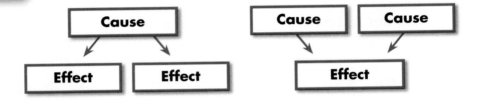

Strategy: Summarize

Summarizing, telling what a story or article is basically about, helps you understand and remember what you read. It helps you figure out main ideas and find important supporting details. It also helps you see important causes and effects.

1. Read the selection "Earth." Create graphic organizers like the ones above to show any causes and effects in the selection.

2. Write a summary of the selection "Earth." Use your graphic organizers to help you.

EARTH

Until about sixty years ago, we didn't know much about the inside of Earth. We didn't have the hi-tech equipment to reach deep down. Then we invented drills to reach into the Earth and machines called seismographs to measure movements below the surface. As scientists used these instruments to study what lies below ground, they learned more about what is inside the Earth.

Skill What did scientists use (cause) to help us learn (effect) more about what is inside the Earth?

The Earth is made up of three layers. The outer layer is the *crust,* the middle layer is the *mantle,* and the center layer is the *core.*

The crust is the thinnest layer. It is hard and can break. The crust is also the coolest layer.

Strategy What is the most important idea of the fourth paragraph? What are the important details?

The mantle is the middle layer of Earth. It is hotter and thicker than the crust. Even though the mantle does not get hot enough to melt, it does get hot enough for rocks to move. This movement causes volcanoes and earthquakes.

Skill What causes earthquakes and volcanoes? What clue word is used?

The core, which is at the center of the Earth, has two sections. The outer core is a liquid. This liquid spins as the Earth spins, causing the Earth's magnetic field. The inner core is hard rock. The core is the hottest layer of the Earth.

Strategy What are the important details to remember about the core of the Earth?

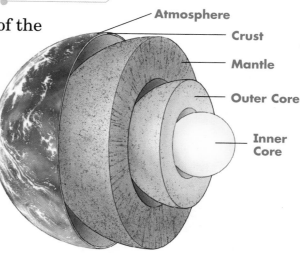

Atmosphere

Crust

Mantle

Outer Core

Inner Core

extinct

serpent

hideous

plunged

armor

encases

Try the strategy. Then, if you need more help, use your glossary or dictionary.

Vocabulary Strategy
for Unfamiliar Words

Context Clues As you read, you may come to a word you do not know. Look for clues in the context, or words and sentences around the word. They may help you figure out the meaning of the unknown word.

1. Reread the sentence in which the unknown word appears. Does the author include a synonym, antonym, or other clue to the word's meaning?

2. If you need more help, read the sentences around the one with the unknown word.

3. Put the clues together and think of a logical meaning for the word. Does this meaning make sense in the sentence?

As you read "The Land of Imagination," use the context to help you figure out the meanings of any unfamiliar words.

The Land of Imagination

The dinosaurs have been extinct for many millions of years. No human ever trembled to hear the roar of one of these prehistoric monsters. We can only imagine how the Earth quaked beneath the weight of these vanished creatures. Still, we have no trouble imagining them eating or drinking or fighting with one another.

A beast like a serpent with legs, only many times larger, stands in the shallows of a warm ocean eating immense, strange water plants. On the shore, a hideous lizard with teeth like deadly knives stands on its powerful haunches. It roars as it charges the plant eater.

Soon both are plunged beneath the water, locked in a giant struggle. When they surface, the dying plant eater's tormented cries echo through the trees.

Another dinosaur draws near. A thick, hornlike armor encases its thick body and long tail. These plates cover every square inch that the terrible lizard might attack. Angry-looking spikes bristle from its back as well. It waits to see if any dinner will be left for it.

Did it really happen like this? We will never know for sure. But in the land of our imagination, it did.

Write a description of a dinosaur you know something about. Include details about actions as well as appearance. Use words from the Words to Know list.

JOURNEY TO THE CENTER OF THE EARTH

by Jules Verne   illustrated by Marc Sasso

What strange animals await the explorers at the center of the Earth?

Genre

Science fiction is imaginary writing based upon scientific ideas. Notice how the author uses vivid and exciting sights and sounds to create a make-believe world.

In 1864, when this story was written, people did not know what the center of the Earth was made of. One science fiction writer, Jules Verne, imagined what it might be like. In Verne's story, Professor von Hardwigg discovers a crater in Finland that leads to the very center of the Earth and sets out with his nephew, Harry, and a guide, Hans, to explore it. They descend many miles downward. Finally, they reach a deep ocean and decide to explore it on a raft. Young Harry keeps a diary of their adventures.

Tuesday, August 20.

At last it is evening—the time of day when we feel a great need to sleep. Of course, in this continuing light, there is no night, but we are very tired. Hans remains at the rudder, his eyes never closed. I don't know when he sleeps: but I find I am dozing, myself.

And then . . . an awful shock! The raft seems to have struck some hidden rock. It is lifted right out of the water and even seems to be thrown some distance. "Eh!" cries my uncle. "What's happening?" And Hans raises his hand and points to where, about two hundred yards away, a great black mass is heaving. Then I know my worst fears have been realized.

"It's some . . . monster!" I cry.

"Yes," cries the Professor, "and over there is a huge sea lizard!"

"And beyond it . . . a crocodile! But who ever saw such a crocodile! Such hideous jaws! Such terrible teeth!"

"And a whale!" the Professor shouts. "See those enormous fins! And see how it blows air and water!"

And indeed two columns of water rise from the surface of the sea as he speaks, reaching an immense height before they fall back into the sea with an enormous crash. The whole cave in which this great sea is set, its walls and roof invisible to us, echoes with the sound of it. We are at the center of the most tremendous uproar! And then we see—and how tiny we feel! —

that we are in the middle of a great circle of these creatures. Here, a turtle, forty feet wide: here, a serpent even longer, its ghastly head peering out of the water. Wherever we look, there are more of them: great teeth, frightful eyes, great coiling bodies! They are everywhere! I snatch up my rifle and think at once how useless it is. What effect would a bullet have on the armor that encases the bodies of these monsters?

There seems no hope for us. Though, suddenly, most of the creatures have plunged under the surface and are no longer to be seen, they leave behind a mighty crocodile and a prodigious sea serpent: and they are making toward us, and the end seems near. I think that, useless though it is, I will fire a shot. But Hans makes a sign for me to wait. For these monsters, having come so close to the raft, suddenly turn and make a rush at each other. In their fury they appear not to have seen us. And at that moment we realize how very small we are. To their great eyes, we must seem nothing bigger than an inch or so of floating scrap.

And so, in a thunder of broken water, the battle begins. At first I think all the other creatures have come to the surface and are taking part. *There* is a whale!—*there* a lizard!—a turtle!—and other monsters for which I can find no name. I point them out to Hans. But he shakes his head.

"*Tva!*" he cries.

"*Tva?* Two? Why does he say two? There are more than two!" I cry.

"No, Hans is right," says my uncle. "One of those monsters has the snout of a porpoise, the head of a lizard, the teeth of a crocodile . . . It is the ichthyosaurus, or great fish lizard."

"And the other?"

"The other is a serpent, but it has a turtle's shell. It is the plesiosaurus, or sea crocodile."

He is right! There seem to be half a dozen monsters, or more, but the truth is there are only two!

And ours are the first human eyes ever to look at these great primitive reptiles! I am amazed by the flaming red eyes of the ichthyosaurus, each bigger than a man's head. Those eyes, I know, are of enormous strength, since they have to resist the pressure of water at the very bottom of the ocean. The creature is a hundred feet long, at least, and when I see his tail rise out of the water, angrily flicked like the hugest whip you could imagine, I can guess at his width. His jaw is larger than I'd ever dreamed a jaw could be, and I remembered that naturalists have said the jaw of the ichthyosaurus must have contained at least one hundred and eighty-two teeth. They were making their calculations, of course, from the fossilized bones of creatures they imagined had been extinct for millions of years. Now I, and Hans, and the Professor, are gazing, from our tiny raft, at a living ichthyosaurus, rising from an ocean deep inside the Earth!

The other creature is the mighty plesiosaurus, a serpent with a trunk like an immensely long cylinder, and a short thick tail and fins like the banks of oars in a Roman galley. Its body is enclosed in a shell, and its neck, flexible as a swan's, rises thirty feet above the surface of the sea.

No other human being has ever seen such a combat! They raise mountains of water, and time and again the raft seems about to be upset. Time and again we imagine we are drowned. The creatures hiss at each other—and the hissing is worse than the sound of the wildest winds you can imagine, all blowing together. Then they seize each other in a terrible grip, giant wrestlers: and then, break away again. And again comes the great hissing, the furious disturbance of the water!

And in the middle of it all, how tiny we are! We crouch on the raft, expecting that any moment it will be overturned and we shall drown in that wildly disturbed sea, hundreds of miles below the surface of the Earth: far, far from the sky, trees, the blessed fresh air!

And then, suddenly, ichthyosaurus and plesiosaurus disappear together under the waves. Their going down, in one enormous plunge, draws the sea down with them, as if a great hole had been made in the water, and we are nearly dragged down with them. For a while there is silence. The water grows calmer. And then, not far from the raft, an enormous shape appears. It is the head of the plesiosaurus.

The monster is mortally wounded. All we can make out is its neck, a serpent's. It is twisted and coiled in the agonies of death. With it the creature strikes the water as if with some great whip. Then it wriggles, as some vast worm might do, cut in two. Every dreadful movement stirs the sea violently, and we are nearly blinded as the tormented water sweeps over the raft. But bit by bit the great writhings die down, and at last the plesiosaurus lies dead on the surface.

As for the ichthyosaurus, he was surely recovering from the struggle in some deep cave. He could not have been unhurt. He must need to lick his wounds.

Or was he on his way to the surface again, to destroy us?

Reader Response

Open for Discussion "There seems no hope for us," Harry wrote in his diary. Why did he write this? What indicates that, after all, there really may be hope?

1. Jules Verne wrote *Journey to the Center of the Earth* more than a century ago, yet his science-fiction stories are still popular. Why do you think people still read his stories today?

2. Why does Harry think there are more than half a dozen monsters when there are only two? Use details from the story to support your answer.

3. Summarize the big battle at sea in your own words. Begin by telling who the fighters are and where the battle takes place.

4. Harry's diary ends with a question. Write a diary entry for the next day, August 21, which answers that question. Use words from the Words to Know list.

Look Back and Write
The two monsters in the battle are made up of many different parts. Look back at the story and then list the parts.

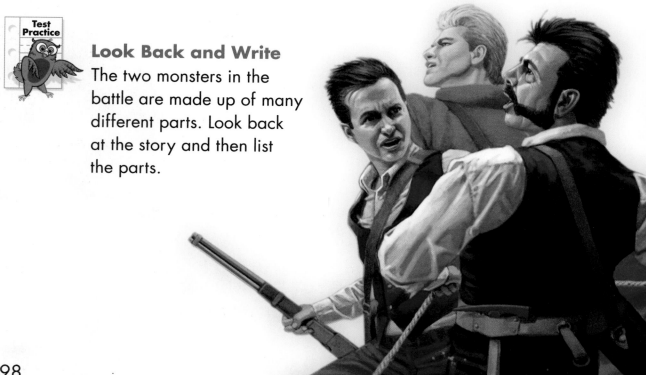

Jules Verne

Read more books of science fiction.

Jules Verne was born in France in 1828. He studied to become a lawyer, but from the beginning he knew he would be a better writer than lawyer. He is one of the most translated authors of all time, and his books are read throughout the world.

Journey to the Center of the Earth is just one of his stories about extraordinary voyages. The source of the story probably was the "hollow Earth" theory that was being talked about in France at the time. There was growing interest in geology and in the seismograph, a machine invented in 1855 to measure earthquakes.

Once, when he was asked about his work habits, Jules Verne answered that he got up at five and worked for three hours before breakfast. Although he would work another couple of hours later in the day, he said his stories had "nearly all been written when most folks are sleeping."

Mr. Verne's books are a mix of fact and fantasy. They combine science with action and adventure. He created what he called a "novel of science," or "scientific novel." Today we call the genre science fiction. In modern times, many of his books, including *Journey to the Center of the Earth,* have been made into movies.

A Wrinkle in Time
by Madeline L'Engle

20,000 Leagues Under the Sea
by Jules Verne

Science in Reading

Textbook

Genre

- Textbooks are used in classrooms to teach facts, give information, and offer explanations in a specific subject area.

- The information has been researched for accuracy.

- The material in textbooks is designed to help students learn and do well on tests.

Text Features

- In textbooks, diagrams are sometimes used to explain important information.

- Captions in pictures and diagrams add information.

Link to Science

Research more about the Earth's core and report to the class what you learn.

Crust, Mantle, Core

From *Scott Foresman Science, C*

You learned a little about the lithosphere—the hard outer shell of the Earth. Now pretend you have an imaginary ship that can move safely down into the Earth. Get ready to explore what's beneath your school. Follow along on the diagram of the Earth.

As you plunge into the Earth, you enter the outer layer, or crust. As you travel into this hard rock layer, you notice that it covers the whole Earth. It is thinner under the oceans and thicker under the continents. As you dive deeper and deeper into the crust, the temperature rises.

CRUST

The crust is about 40 kilometers thick in many places. It is solid rock. The temperature increases from the surface to the inner edge.

LITHOSPHERE

The rigid outer shell of the Earth includes all the crust and the rigid top part of the mantle.

MANTLE

The mantle is about 2,900 kilometers thick. Below the rigid, solid top, the mantle is partly melted rock. Below that the mantle is solid again. The temperature continues to increase with depth.

CORE

The distance from the outer edge of the core to the center of the core is about 3,500 kilometers. The outer part is liquid iron and nickel. The inner part is solid iron and nickel.

Summarize How do the diagram's captions help you summarize?

THREE TYPES OF ROCK FOUND ON EARTH

SEDIMENTARY
Rocks that are formed by the accumulation and consolidation of sediments

METAMORPHIC
Rocks that have been altered by intense heat or extreme pressure

IGNEOUS
Rocks that are formed when magma cools and solidifies

Banded Ironstone

Halleflinta

Feldspar Pegmatite

Echinoderm Fossil

Green Marble

Syenite

As you continue down, you eventually enter the mantle. The mantle—the middle layer of the Earth—is beneath the crust. Notice that the mantle is much thicker than the crust. The upper part of the mantle is rigid. This rigid part of the mantle, along with the whole crust, makes up the lithosphere. As you go deeper, the temperature continues to increase. Soon the mantle rock is not quite solid anymore. As you go even deeper, it becomes solid again.

As you continue to go deeper, you eventually enter the core—the center part of the Earth made of iron and nickel.

GLOSSARY

crust the top layer of the Earth, above the mantle

mantle the middle layer of the Earth, between the crust and the core

core the center part of the Earth, beneath the mantle

In the outer part of the core, the iron and nickel are melted. As you go deeper into the outer part of the core, the temperature continues to rise.

As you go still deeper, more and more of the Earth is above you. The pressure becomes so great it forces the melted iron and nickel to become solid—yet the metal is white hot! Now, you are in the inner core. Finally, you arrive at the center of the Earth. You can go down no further. All directions are up.

Reading Across Texts

Look back at the two selections to compare the two descriptions of the Earth's core.

Writing Across Texts Write a scene from a science-fiction story in which explorers descend into the Earth's true, actual core. Describe the kind of equipment they would have to use in order to survive.

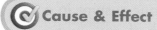 **Cause & Effect** Notice that causes and effects are clearly stated.

Generalize

- To generalize means to make a broad statement or rule that applies to several examples.

- Sometimes authors make generalizations in their writing. Clue words such as *all*, *many*, and *most* can signal generalizations.

- Active readers pay close attention to these generalizations. If they are supported by the text or logic, they are *valid generalizations*. If they are not supported by the text or by logic, they are *faulty generalizations*.

Generalization	→	Support from Article
		Support from Article
		Support from Article

Strategy: Graphic Organizers

Active readers often use graphic organizers to help them understand and remember what they read. Graphic organizers can be used before, during, or after reading a selection. You can create a graphic organizer like the one above to help you decide whether an author's generalizations are valid.

1. Read "The Gold Rush." Make a graphic organizer like the one above for the final paragraph.

2. Is the generalization in the final paragraph *valid* or *faulty*? Explain your answer in a paragraph of your own.

604

THE GOLD RUSH

Abraham Lincoln described the western United States in the mid-1800s as the "treasure house of the nation." Why? People had found abundant amounts of gold, silver, and other precious metals there.

The first large amount, or lode, of gold was found near the Sacramento River in California in 1848 by John Sutter and James Marshall. They tried to conceal their discovery to save the riches for themselves. However, word got out and thousands rushed to the area. By 1849, about 80,000 people were in the area searching for gold. Many Americans had caught gold fever and become part of the gold rush!

A lode of silver was found in 1859 in Nevada. Discovered on property owned by Henry Comstock, it became known as the Comstock Lode. Many people got rich from the Comstock Lode. Grubby miners turned into instant millionaires. George Hearst and a group of friends made $90,000 in two months. One deposit, known as "The Big Bonanza," produced more

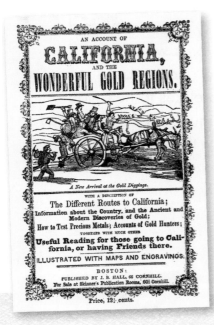

AN ACCOUNT OF
CALIFORNIA,
AND THE
WONDERFUL GOLD REGIONS.

A New Arrival at the Gold Diggings.

WITH A DESCRIPTION OF
The Different Routes to California;
Information about the Country, and the Ancient and Modern Discoveries of Gold;
How to Test Precious Metals; Accounts of Gold Hunters;
TOGETHER WITH MUCH OTHER
Useful Reading for those going to California, or having Friends there.
ILLUSTRATED WITH MAPS AND ENGRAVINGS.

BOSTON:
PUBLISHED BY J. B. HALL, 66 CORNHILL.
For Sale at Skinner's Publication Rooms, 601 Cornhill.

Price, 12½ cents.

than one million dollars worth of gold and silver.

Many towns were built and destroyed by the gold rush. Towns such as Virginia City, Nevada, and Cripple Creek, Colorado, sprang up almost overnight. While the gold or silver lasted, the towns were successful. When the gold or silver was used up, however, many towns became deserted.

Skill Notice the three examples in the last sentence. From them, what generalization did Abraham Lincoln make about the West in the mid-1800s?

Strategy Make a graphic organizer for the generalization in this paragraph. What clue word in the final sentence signals the generalization?

Skill What generalization is made in this paragraph? Is this generalization valid or faulty? How can you tell?

Strategy What details of support are used for the generalization in this paragraph?

independence

scrawled

economic

overrun

vacant

Remember

Try the strategy. Then, if you need more help, use your glossary or dictionary.

Vocabulary Strategy
for Prefixes

Word Structure A prefix is a word part added at the beginning of a base word. Each prefix has a meaning of its own. Recognizing a prefix's meaning can help you figure out the word's meaning. For example, one of the meanings for the prefix *over-* is "too much." A room that's *overcrowded* is too crowded. The prefix *in-* can mean "not." People who are *insensitive* are not sensitive.

1. Look at an unfamiliar word to see if it has a base word you know.

2. Check to see if a prefix has been added to the base word.

3. Ask yourself how the prefix changes the meaning of the base word.

4. Try the meaning in the sentence. Does it make sense?

As you read "The Sky's the Limit," find words with the prefixes *re-* and *in-*. Use the prefixes to help you figure out the meanings of the words.

The Sky's the Limit

Independence has always been an important value to people who live in the United States. It has been a cornerstone of American life ever since the founding fathers scrawled their signatures at the bottom of the Declaration of Independence.

Independence refers to people's freedoms, of course. But it also refers to their headlong way of pursuing prosperity. From all over the world, people have flocked to America in search of freedom. But many also hoped to become rich. The building of America has been based on economic success and muscle as much as on armies and governments.

This will to "make a better life" was behind the wagon trains that ventured into the West during the nineteenth century. It drove the settling of boom towns—towns that were overrun by miners. They grew quickly, died quickly, and soon became nothing but vacant buildings and empty streets. Every miner believed that he or she could strike it rich. The spread of railroads, then highways, recalled this theme. Every freight train chugged a message: "The sky's the limit!"

Write

Pretend you are a reporter covering a gold rush in the 1800s. Write an article describing what happens in a gold boom town. Use words from the Words to Know list.

WHY DID BUSY TOWNS TURN INTO GHOST TOWNS?

Expository nonfiction explains a person, a thing, or an idea. Notice how the author tries to solve the mysteries surrounding ghost towns.

Genre

GHOST TOWNS

OF THE

AMERICAN WEST

BY RAYMOND BIAL

While its neighbor, Phoenix, flourished, Goldfield, a turn-of-the-century ghost town in Arizona, did so only briefly, and then declined as a mining town. However, the collection of buildings has since been given new life—as a ghost town.

An air of mystery swirls around the ghost towns of the American West. What sad and joyous events happened within the tumbledown walls and on the wind-blown streets? Why did people settle in these lonesome places? Why did they pull up stakes and move away? What went wrong in these towns? Virtually every ghost town has untold stories of people who longed for a chance at a better life. Relics of the past, the towns now stand as evidence of high adventure, hopes of striking it rich, and the sudden loss of fortune—or life.

Although ghost towns can be found throughout the world, in the United States they are most often thought of as the mining camps, cowboy towns, and other settlements of the sprawling western frontier.

Most ghost towns were originally mining camps where men sought gold, silver, copper, and other precious minerals.

Most were once mining camps where adventurous men came to seek their fortunes. These communities boomed as miners sought gold, silver, copper, or other precious minerals but died out when all of the ore was panned from streams or blasted from rocky tunnels. In cowboy towns, cattle were driven to other towns, and then shipped to markets in the East. Many lumber camps in deep forests and farming communities on the broad prairies also enjoyed brief prosperity before they were abandoned. Along with the miners, cowboys, and farmers, merchants and bankers, as well as doctors and schoolteachers, also went west. They laid out streets and put up buildings in hopes of growth and prosperity. As one newspaper editor declared, most folks wished "to get rich if we can."

In 1848, James W. Marshall discovered gold at Sutter's Mill when he shut down the water on the millrace and glanced into the ditch. "I reached my hand down and picked it up; it made my heart thump for I felt certain it was gold," he recalled. Soon the word was out. "Gold! Gold! Gold from the American River!" shouted Sam Brannon, waving a bottle of gold dust as he strode through the San Francisco streets. Seeking pay dirt, "forty-niners" (as the prospectors came to be known) streamed into California in the first of the great American gold rushes. Yet, over time, people came to refer to the sawmill as "Sutter's Folly" as the land of John Sutter was overrun with prospectors. Everywhere, men claimed "squatter's rights," in which they settled on land without paying for it.

Towns sprang up overnight. Charles B. Gillespie, a miner who worked near Coloma, California, described the typical main streets of these towns as "alive with crowds." To him, the miners were ragged, dirty men who were otherwise good-natured. They were a mix of Americans and immigrants—Germans, French, and other Europeans,

After several hard hours of travel, these trail-weary settlers paused in the foothills of the Rocky Mountains. Unhitching their wagon, they watered their livestock, ate a noonday meal, and briefly rested.

Loading all of their possessions in Conestoga wagons with billowing canvas tops, settlers seeking independence moved westward to homestead farms, stake a mining claim, or set up storekeeping in a new town.

and gold seekers from China and Chile, along with British convicts from Australia. Mark Twain declared, "It was a driving, vigorous, restless population in those days . . . two hundred thousand *young* men—not simpering, dainty, kid-gloved weaklings, but stalwart, muscular, dauntless young braves, brimful of push and energy."

In 1851, when a Scottish artist named J. D. Borthwick arrived to try his luck as a prospector, he wrote that the main street of Hangtown, later renamed Pacerville, "was in many places knee-deep in mud, and was plentifully strewn with old boots, hats, and shirts, old sardine-boxes, empty tins of preserved oysters, empty bottles, worn-out pots and kettles, old ham-bones, broken picks and shovels, and other rubbish." Borthwick described the town as "one long

straggling street of clapboard houses and log cabins, built in a hollow at the side of a creek, and surrounded by high and steep hills." Along the creek, he said, "there was continual noise and clatter, as mud, dirt, stones, and water were thrown about in all directions, and the men, dressed in ragged clothes and big boots, wielding picks and shovels . . . were all working as if for their lives."

In the typical western town, the buildings were often skirted with a sidewalk of wooden planks, along with hitching posts and water troughs for horses. There might be a bank made of solid brick to assure depositors that their hard cash or gold dust was safe from robbers. There might also be a mercantile store, an early version of the department store, as well as a general store. The town certainly had to have a blacksmith shop and livery stable, as well as corrals for horses and cattle. Some towns had a telegraph office and their very own newspaper. The town might be lucky enough to be on a stagecoach route, a Pony Express station, or, better yet, a railroad stop.

"The Americans have a perfect passion for railroads," wrote Michel Chevalier, a French economist, in the 1830s. If the railroad bypassed the village, it quickly became a ghost town. Helen Hunt Jackson described Garland City, Colorado, where she lived: "Twelve days ago there was not a house here. Today, there are one hundred and five, and in a week there will be two hundred." However, the town lasted only a few months, at least at that site. When the railroad passed thirty miles to the west, folks moved the entire town— walls and windows, as well as sidewalks, furnishings, and goods—to the railroad tracks. Railroads laid down thousands of miles of gleaming tracks across the grasslands, with a transcontinental link completed in 1869.

COLD and WARM BATHS

None of these towns would have prospered, even briefly, and the frontier would never have become settled, without women and children. Storekeepers and farmers occasionally brought their wives and children with them, but men still outnumbered women nine to one. Most towns actively sought women. In 1860, a letter to the editor of the *Rocky Mountain News* from the new settlement of Breckenridge, Colorado, read: "A few very respectable looking women have ventured over to see us. Send us a few more." Another Colorado writer asked, "We have one lady living in Breckenridge and one on Gold Run; we would be glad to welcome many arrivals of the 'gentler' portion of the gold-seeking humanity, and can offer a pleasant country, good

locations, and peaceable neighbors . . . except for an occasional lawsuit."

The waves of western migration reached a peak between 1860 and 1880. Over time, some towns grew into large cities, such as Denver and Phoenix, while many others were abandoned and forgotten in the desert sands or mountain snows. Most went bust because of economic failure—all the gold or silver was mined or the cattle were driven to another market town. A few people got rich, but others suffered heartbreak, hunger, and plain bad luck, and then abandoned the town. Perched on mountain cliffs, tucked into a wooded valley, or baking in the desert sun, these ghost towns are so remote that they are almost impossible to find. People often have to travel to them by four-wheel-drive vehicles and then hike several miles up rocky slopes or over cactus-studded deserts. Finding the ghost towns may be as difficult as the search for gold that led to the founding of the towns.

John Steele described Washington, California, in the 1840s, just six months after it had been founded: "With a large number of vacant cabins it contained several empty buildings and quite a large hotel, closed and silent." Once ringing with the voices of cheerful people, the towns have now fallen silent. They have become little more than empty shells of their former selves. There may be a handful of old false-front buildings, weathered to a haunting gray, with open doorways and broken windows. But little else remains; few people even remember the place. Even the memories, along with the hopes and dreams of the inhabitants, have blown away, like so much dust in the wind.

ABOVE: Cabezon, New Mexico, ghost town. In ghost town cemeteries, names of the dead were sometimes scrawled on rough boards.

RIGHT: Here, a group of men have set up a mining camp at a place known as Gregory's Diggings during the early days of the gold rush in Colorado.

Reader Response

Open for Discussion Suppose you said to a ghost town, "Don't be shy. Summon up the adventures you have known." Now suppose you actually got a reply. Report it!

1. Authors of nonfiction often do more than report the facts. They also report how they feel about those facts. Read parts of this selection that reveal the author's feelings about ghost towns.

2. Make a generalization about ghost towns and use details from the selection to support it.

3. What kind of graphic organizer would best help you understand and remember the information in this selection? Why?

4. Write an obituary—a death notice—for a town that once was lively but now is abandoned. Tell why it was born and how it became a ghost town. Use words from the Words to Know list.

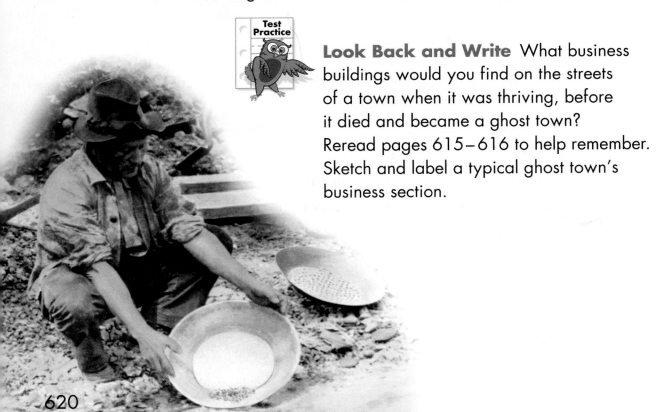

Test Practice

Look Back and Write What business buildings would you find on the streets of a town when it was thriving, before it died and became a ghost town? Reread pages 615–616 to help remember. Sketch and label a typical ghost town's business section.

620

Read more books by Raymond Bial.

Raymond Bial says about *Ghost Towns of the American West*, "I actually stayed in a ghost town with my wife, Linda, and two of my children to make photographs for this book." A photographer who works in both color and black and white, he has published more than thirty books for children and adults.

Ghost Towns of the American West is a blend of photographs and text called a photo essay. Mr. Bial says, "Whenever I ask groups of schoolchildren why photo essays should be written as stories, they always answer correctly, 'So they won't be boring.'"

Mr. Bial says his work as a writer and photographer grew out of his experiences growing up. "Having spent a good portion of my childhood in a small town in southern Indiana, I have vivid memories of those joyous years of bicycling around the neighborhood, swimming at the municipal pool, stopping for ice cream at the local hotspot, and frequently visiting our Carnegie public library."

Today he lives in an old house in Urbana, Illinois, with his wife and three children. He says, "In creating nonfiction photo essays, I now draw upon my experiences with my family as well as memories of my childhood."

Tenement: Immigrant Life on the Lower East Side

The Farms

Social Studies
in Reading

Narrative Nonfiction

Genre

- Narrative nonfiction tells the story of an event or series of events.

- Some narrative non-fiction describes events from people's lives.

Text Features

- Sometimes maps are used to make the events easier to follow.

- Interactive maps use numbers to link the events described to geographic places.

Link to Social Studies

Who were some other people who went West in search of gold? Research this topic and share your results with the class.

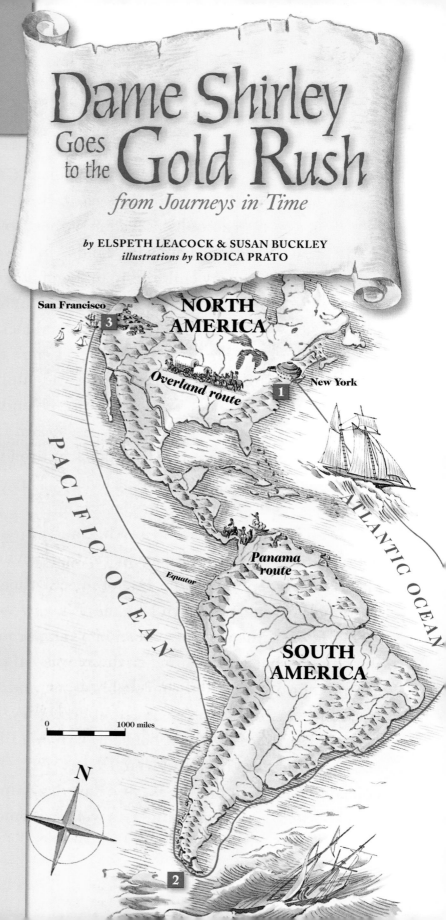

Dame Shirley Goes to the Gold Rush

from Journeys in Time

by ELSPETH LEACOCK & SUSAN BUCKLEY
illustrations by RODICA PRATO

Louise Amelia Knapp Smith Clappe was worried. Though she loved to travel, nothing had prepared her for the 18,000-mile voyage she had just begun. Louise was sailing to California with her new husband, Dr. Fayette Clappe, in 1849. Nine months earlier, President James Polk had confirmed the wild rumors that were spreading around the world. Yes, gold had been discovered in California. Now the rush for gold was on, and 30-year-old Louise was part of it.

Louise Clappe's journey began on August 20, 1849, when the sloop *Manilla* left New York Harbor. **1** After several months at sea, the *Manilla* approached the dreaded Cape Horn, **2** where violent storms tossed ships about like twigs in a tornado. Past the danger, the *Manilla* traveled north along the western coast of South America. On January 11, 1850–almost five months after she set out–Louise Clappe sailed past the Golden Gate to the busy little town of San Francisco. **3**

For a year and a half, the Clappes remained in San Francisco. But Fayette was often sick in the damp climate around the bay. By September 1851 Louise and Fayette had decided to try their luck in the mining country. Fayette left first, then Louise took a small steamboat up-river to Marysville. **4** Enchanted by the possibility of adventure, Louise was curious about the rough mining camps she had heard so much about. And she was excited, for she had a new project. At the suggestion of a newspaper editor, she was going to write about her adventures. She had even chosen a pen name–Dame Shirley.

Louise's first California adventure was the trip itself. After stopping at a ranch near Marysville, Louise set out by mule with Fayette. She soon found herself lying in the road when her saddle slipped. **5** She laughed, but Fayette insisted that she travel by wagon to the next stop. Louise felt as though she bounced along every stretch of the 39-mile trip to the settlement of Bidwell's Bar. **6** Sleeping

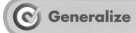

Generalize   What makes this look like a difficult journey?

623

arrangements at Bidwell's Bar were a tent on the flea-covered ground. So Louise and Fayette traveled on with the mules. But they got lost and had to sleep in the woods. **7** For 24 hours they tried to find their way up one path and down another. When they finally reached the Berry Creek House, Louise wanted to sleep for weeks!

The next morning, they rode to the Wild Yankee's inn, where California Indians crowded into the room to see them, **8** then on to the Buckeye Rancho. **9** Losing their way once more, they slept under the trees that night, unaware that the sounds in the distance were grizzly bears. **10**

The next day, they made their way through silent pine forests and across broad high plains. At last, looking down a great hill, Louise and Fayette could see Rich Bar, **11** the mining camp where they would live for the next few weeks. Louise galloped past a rattlesnake ready to strike and descended the treacherous trail.

Louise and Fayette settled into the Empire Hotel, the saloon and rooming house that was Rich Bar's best–and only–hotel. On September 13, 1851, Louise wrote her first letter from the gold mines. The 23 letters that Dame Shirley wrote from the mining country painted a picture of joy and sorrow, kindness and cruelty, good luck and bad. It was a life Louise Amelia Knapp Smith Clappe could not have imagined when she set sail on the *Manilla* just a few years before.

Reading Across Texts

Look back at the two selections and make a list of Rewards and a list of Punishments for people who moved West.

Writing Across Texts Make a poster either inviting people living in 1849 to move West or warning them not to.

 **Summarize** What main ideas would summarize this article?

GOLD RUSH FACTS

→ Between 1848 and 1854, California produced almost $350 million worth of gold. In today's dollars the gold would be worth almost $7 billion.

→ San Francisco grew from about 800 people in 1848 to 5,000 in 1849 and more than 20,000 in 1850.

→ The California Indian population dropped from 150,000 in 1845 to less than 30,000 by 1870.

Rich Bar

Buckeye Rancho

North Fork

Middle Fork

South Fork

Berry Creek House

Bidwell's Bar

Feather River

Yuba River

Marysville

0   10   20   30 miles

625

Your World

by Georgia Douglas Johnson

Your world is as big as you make it.
I know, for I used to abide
In the narrowest nest in a corner,
My wings pressing close to my side.

But I sighted the distant horizon
Where the sky line encircled the sea
And I throbbed with a burning desire
To travel this immensity.

I battered the cordons around me
And I cradled my wings on the breeze
Then soared to the uttermost reaches
With rapture, with power, with ease!

Share the Adventure

by Patricia and Fredrick McKissack

Pages and pages
A seesaw of ideas—
Share the adventure

Fiction, nonfiction:
Door to our past and future
Swinging back and forth

WHAM! The book slams shut,
But we read it together
With our minds open

627

A Path to the Moon

by bp Nichol

From my front door there's a path to the moon
that nobody seems to see
tho it's marked with stones & grass & trees
there's nobody sees it but me.

    You walk straight ahead for ten trees or so
    turn left at the robin's song
    follow the sound of the west wind down
    past where the deer drink from the pond.

    You take a right turn as the river bends
    then where the clouds touch the earth
    close your left eye & count up to ten
    while twirling for all that you're worth.

And if you keep walking right straight ahead
clambering over the clouds
saying your mother's & father's names
over & over out loud

you'll come to the place where moonlight's born
the place where the moonbeams hide
and visit all the crater sites
on the dark moon's secret side.

From my front door there's a path to the moon
that nobody seems to see
tho it's marked with stones & grass & trees
no one sees it but you & me.

Great-Grandma Was There

connect to **WRITING**

Suppose you rewrote "The Three-Century Woman," in which Great-Grandma pretends she took part in important events in the past. Think of two real-life events from the past 100 years that you could add to the story. Rewrite parts of the story to weave in these two additional adventures as a part of Great-Grandma's pretend past.

Who goes seeking adventure and why?

Treasure Map

connect to
SCIENCE

Think of all the adventures from this unit. Then create your own adventure. Make a treasure map for it. Show some of the people, places, and events an adventurer will encounter. For the "treasure" part of the map, show something valuable that the adventurer will discover along the way.

Space Dream Team

connect to
SCIENCE

Suppose that you were leading an expedition into outer space. Assemble a team that will work together and make the adventure a success. What kinds of skills will team members need to succeed? What kinds of training? Discuss your plan with a partner. Then complete a chart like the one below.

Team Members	Needed Skills	Training

The Unexpected

What can we learn from encounters with the unexpected?

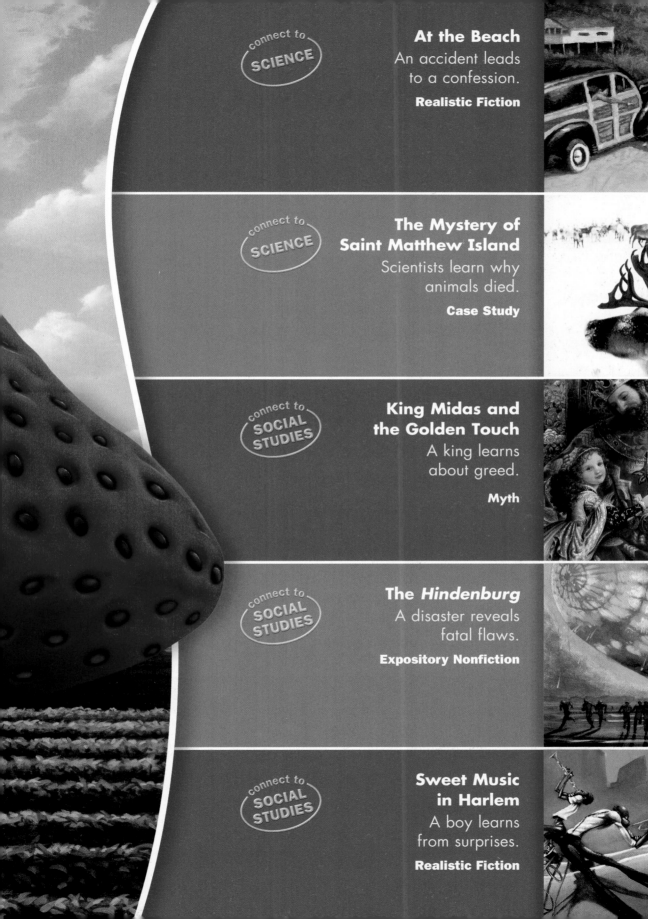

At the Beach
An accident leads
to a confession.
Realistic Fiction

connect to
SCIENCE

**The Mystery of
Saint Matthew Island**
Scientists learn why
animals died.
Case Study

connect to
SCIENCE

**King Midas and
the Golden Touch**
A king learns
about greed.
Myth

connect to
SOCIAL
STUDIES

The *Hindenburg*
A disaster reveals
fatal flaws.
Expository Nonfiction

connect to
SOCIAL
STUDIES

**Sweet Music
in Harlem**
A boy learns
from surprises.
Realistic Fiction

connect to
SOCIAL
STUDIES

Comprehension

Skill
Drawing
Conclusions

Strategy
Visualize

Drawing Conclusions

- Active readers draw logical conclusions, or make decisions, based on information in the text and on their own knowledge.

- Examine your own conclusions as you read. Ask yourself, "Can I support them with information from the text or with facts I already know?"

- Authors also draw conclusions in their writing. Good readers ask themselves: "Are this author's conclusions logical? Are they based on facts?"

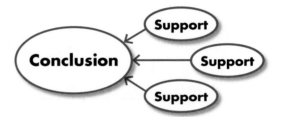

Strategy: Visualize

When you visualize, you make mental images from what you read. Visualizing may involve all the senses: sight, sound, taste, touch, and smell. As you add new details to your mental pictures, you can draw new conclusions about the text.

1. Read "Making Tortillas." Make a graphic organizer similar to the one above. Use visualizing to help you. What conclusions can you draw from reading this article?

2. Use your organizer to make a list of Dos and Don'ts for making good tortillas.

MAKING TORTILLAS

Authentic Mexican tortillas are made by hand. First, corn is boiled with slaked limestone. This causes the corn's skin to separate from the kernel. The skins are discarded, and the remaining corn is ground using a *metate*, or grinding stone. Water is added periodically. This time-consuming step can take up to an hour, depending on the number of tortillas being made.

The resulting dough is shaped into balls, and then skillfully patted into flat tortillas. This is no small feat. The tortilla must be thin and round. It must retain its moisture. The tortilla can be neither too wet nor too dry. There is little time to create a perfect tortilla. The longer the dough is handled, the drier it becomes. Tortillas are baked on a hot griddle for 30 to 60 seconds on each side. Many things can go wrong during this step. If the dough is too wet, too dry, or air bubbles form in the dough, the tortilla will be ruined.

Today, tortillas can be made in factories by large machines. But factory-made tortillas cannot be as good as handmade tortillas. They are not lovingly prepared, one by one, by experts. If you want a fresh, authentic tortilla, it must be prepared by an expert tortilla-maker.

Skill The author has already drawn this conclusion, or made this decision, from her experience. Look for details that will support it.

Strategy Can you imagine grinding the corn with a *metate*? What do you see, smell, hear? Is it hard to grind the corn? What does it taste like?

Strategy Visualize each step of making tortillas. What conclusion can you draw about making tortillas by hand?

Skill Do you agree with the conclusion the author has drawn here? Do you think the author has made a logical conclusion based on facts?

driftwood

sea urchins

algae

concealed

tweezers

hammocks

sternly

lamented

Vocabulary Strategy
for Unfamiliar Words

Dictionary/Glossary Dictionaries and glossaries list words and their meanings in alphabetical order. A dictionary lists most of the words in a language. A glossary lists only the important words in the book where they appear.

A dictionary entry may also give the pronunciation, part of speech, and spellings of different forms of a word. You may need to look at a dictionary or glossary to get the meaning of an unknown word.

1. First, look at the words around the unknown word to see if they help.

2. If not, then look up the word in a glossary or dictionary.

3. If the word has several meanings, try the one that seems to fit best.

4. If that meaning doesn't make sense, try other meanings until you find one that does make sense.

As you read "My Special Island," use a dictionary or glossary to find the meanings of words when other strategies do not work.

My Special Island

I like to daydream about my special island. It has the most beautiful beach for exploring. I walk along the sand and admire the wild driftwood shapes, polished by the waves and sun. I pause beside a tidal pool and watch crabs, sea urchins, and other strange animals.

Standing in the water, I look at a forest of algae stretching as far as I can see. I wonder what strange and beautiful creatures lie concealed in that underwater forest. In my dream I am a world-famous scientist. Armed with my microscope, tweezers, and diving equipment, I learn all the secrets of the ocean world.

After a long day of amazing discoveries, I head for one of the hammocks under the palm trees. There I store my treasures and lie down, letting a gentle breeze rock me to sleep.

"Martin!" Ms. Smith says sternly. "Wake up and get to work!" Oh, well. Back to arithmetic. I have often lamented my bad habit of daydreaming during classes!

Write

Imagine that you are at the beach in the picture. Write about what you see, hear, taste, smell, and touch there. Use words from the Words to Know list.

At The Beach
Abuelito's Story

by Lulu Delacre
paintings by Michael Sterinagle

Genre

Realistic fiction deals with characters and actions that seem real but come from the author's imagination. As you read, notice how the author uses words to paint a realistic picture of Guanabo Beach.

How can an unexpected
event lead to a very
difficult decision?

I remember those evenings well when I was a young boy
in Cuba, those balmy island nights before a trip to Guanabo
Beach. The spicy aroma of *tortilla española* that Mami had left
to cool would waft through the house as I lay in my bed. But I
was always too excited to sleep. All I could think about was the
soft white sand, the warm foamy water, and Mami's delicious
tortilla. Ahhh. A day at the beach. It was full of possibilities.

One Saturday in May, I was awakened at the crack of dawn
by sounds of laughter. My aunts, Rosa and Olga, had arrived with
hammocks, blankets, and an iron kettle filled with Aunt Rosa's
steaming *congrí*. And best of all, they had arrived with my cousins:
Luisa, Mari, and little Javi. Uncle Toni had come too.

When we were ready to leave, Papi, the only one in the family who owned a car, packed his Ford woody wagon with the nine of us. No one cared that we children had to squeeze into the back along with the clutter of pots and plates, food and bags, towels and blankets and hammocks. Soon the engine turned, and the car rumbled down the road into the rising sun.

Along the way, we drove past sugarcane fields and roadside markets. My cousins and I shouted warnings to the barking dogs and laughed at the frightened hens that scurried in every direction at the sight of our car. It seemed like a long time until the cool morning breeze that blew into the windows turned warm. And the growing heat made the aroma of Mami's tortilla all the more tempting.

"Lick your skin, Fernando," my older cousin Luisa told me. "If it tastes salty, that means we'll be there any time now."

She was right. My skin tasted salty. And soon—almost magically—the turquoise ocean appeared as we rounded a bend in the road. Papi pulled into the familiar dirt lot and parked under the pine trees. While the grown-ups unloaded the car, we eagerly jumped out and ran toward the sea, peeling off our clothes along the way.

"Remember, don't go too far!" Mami and Aunt Olga warned us sternly from the distance. I turned to see them picking up our scattered clothing.

When we reached the edge of the ocean, the water felt cold. I waded farther in and went under to warm up quickly. When I emerged I saw Luisa, Mari, and little Javi, all standing still in the clear water. They were watching the schools of tiny gold-and-black striped fish rush between their legs. Then they swam over to join me, and together we rode the big waves.

Later, Uncle Toni came in to play shark with us. We splashed and swallowed the stinging seawater as he chased us above and under the waves. But after a while, we tired him out, and he went back to sit with the grown-ups.

I was getting very hungry, and for a moment I thought of returning with him to sneak a bite of Mami's tortilla. But then I had a better idea.

"Let's explore the reef!" I said.

"¡Sí!" everyone agreed. "Let's go!"

We all splashed out of the water and ran, dripping wet, across the sand. High above, the sun beat down on us.

When we got to the marbled rocks, Luisa looked concerned. "Our moms told us not to come this far," she said.

"I know the way well," I replied. "Besides, nobody will notice. They're too busy talking."

I looked in the distance and saw Mami and my two aunts in the shady spot they had picked. They had set up a nice camp. The hammocks were tied to the pine trees, the blankets were spread over the fine sand. Papi and Uncle Toni played dominoes, while they sipped coffee and shared the *cucurucho de maní* they had purchased from the peanut vendor. They were having fun. No one would miss us for a long time.

"**W**atch out for sea urchins!" I warned as I led the group on our climb. The spiny black sea urchins hid inside the crevices and crannies of the rough boulders. It was very painful if you stepped on one. Luisa and Mari followed behind me. They were careful to only step on the rocks I stepped on. Little Javi came last. He stopped constantly to look at the *cobitos,* the tiny hermit crabs that scurried around on the rocks, and at the iridescent tropical fish that were concealed in the deepest tide pools. I had to keep checking behind me to make sure he didn't stray from our path.

Just then, I turned around to watch helplessly as Javi slipped on an algae-covered rock. "*¡Cuidado!*" I warned. But it was too late. "*¡Ay!*" he shrieked, and then began to cry uncontrollably.

Cautiously, we all hurried back to help Javi. Luisa and Mari crouched down to examine his foot.

"He stepped on a sea urchin!" Mari cried. "Now what are we going to do?"

"We should have never followed you," Luisa lamented. "We'll all be punished."

At that moment I did not want to think of what the punishment would be. What if we couldn't have any of Mami's tortilla? All I knew was that we had to help Javi right away. I looked around and found a piece of driftwood.

"Luisa," I ordered. "Hold his leg still while I remove the urchin from his foot."

Luisa held Javi's leg still as Mari held his hand and tried to comfort him. But Javi's desperate cries were now drowning out the sound of the sea.

I pulled and tugged, but the urchin wouldn't budge. It was stuck to Javi's foot by the tips of its spines. Javi was scared and in pain. And we were too far from our parents to ask for help. What if we couldn't get Javi back? I struggled relentlessly until I was finally able to remove the spiny creature from his foot.

Gently, Luisa poured some seawater over Javi's foot. That was when she noticed there was still a piece of the sea urchin's spine lodged in it. Javi wasn't going to be able to walk back, and he was much too heavy for us to carry. We had to remove that piece of spine so that he could walk on his own.

The sun burnt our backs as we all took turns trying to dislodge the sea urchin's spine.

"I have an idea," said Luisa suddenly. She removed her hair barrettes and held them like tweezers. Then, with the smallest movement, she pulled the broken spine out. With that solved, we started back.

I helped Javi walk on his sore foot. He wept and limped with every step. Our walk back seemed endless. As we got closer I realized that we would have to explain how it was that we went to the reef in the first place. I would surely end up with no tortilla if we told the truth.

"What will we do now?" Mari asked.

"We'll have to tell our parents what happened," said Luisa matter-of-factly.

"No!" I said emphatically. "We'll be punished for sure."

We walked the rest of the way in silence. The sound of crashing waves, children playing, and seagulls' calls became a background drone to Javi's cries.

When we finally reached our parents, Javi was crying louder than ever. Aunt Olga took one look at him and gasped. *"¡Niños!* Children! What's happened to Javi?"

Mari looked at Luisa. Luisa looked at me. Javi cried even louder.

"Well. . . ," I hesitated. By now everyone was staring at me. "We were walking along the beach looking for cockles and urchin shells," I began, "when I found a live sea urchin attached to a piece of driftwood. So I called the others. Javi came running so fast that he stepped on it by accident."

Luisa and Mari stared at me in disbelief. I didn't think they liked my story.

"Let me see your foot, Javi," Aunt Olga said, kneeling next to her son.

Mami and Aunt Rosa looked on as Aunt Olga examined Javi's foot closely. Then she gave him a big hug and a kiss. "He's fine," she said at last. "It looks like the children were able to pull it out."

And at this good news, Javi's tears disappeared and were replaced by a big broad smile. "I'm hungry," he said.

"Then let's have lunch," Aunt Olga suggested.

I was dumbfounded. Not only had they believed me, but we were also going to eat Mami's tortilla!

The men went back to their domino game. The women went back to their conversation as they busied themselves serving everybody. No one but me seemed to notice how quiet Luisa and Mari had grown.

Mami handed me a plate filled with my favorite foods. The tortilla smelled delicious. But I was unable to eat. I looked up at Luisa and Mari who were quietly picking at their food. I watched Mami as she served herself and sat next to my aunts. I looked at my plate again. How could I enjoy my food when I knew I had done something I wasn't supposed to do? There was only one thing I could do now. I stood up, picked up my plate, and went right over to Mami.

"What's wrong, Fernando?" Mami asked.

I looked back at Luisa and Mari and swallowed hard. Then, I handed Mami my untouched plate.

"You wouldn't have given me this if I had told you the truth," I said.

Mami looked puzzled. The whole group grew silent and watched me struggle. I was very embarrassed.

"It was my fault," Luisa said. "I should have stopped them."

"And I went along," said Mari.

"No, no, it was my idea to go to the reef," I said. Then I told everyone about our adventure at the reef. When I was finished, Mami looked at me with tear-filled eyes.

"You are right, Fernando," she said. "I should punish you for doing something you knew not to do. Somebody could have been seriously hurt."

"I know," I whispered, "and I'm sorry." But then the glimmer of a smile softened Mami's expression. She slid her arm over my shoulders as she said, "You know, Fernando, anyone can make a mistake. But not everyone has the courage to admit it. *Gracias*. Thank you for telling the truth."

That afternoon, under the shade of the pine trees, the nine of us sat down on the old blankets for lunch. We had congrí, bread, and Mami's famous tortilla española. And do you know something? That day it tasted better than it ever had before.

Reader Response

Open for Discussion Some day Fernando may tell his children about this day at Guanabo Beach. What do you think he will say he learned?

1. Experience the setting of "At the Beach." Read examples to show how the author helps you see, feel, and taste things.

2. Both the grown-ups and the children are partly responsible for Javi getting hurt. Explain how this is so. Use details from the story to explain your answer.

3. Pick the moment in the story that you remember best. Close your eyes and visualize it. Then describe it. Afterward, reread that moment to see how accurate your mental picture was.

4. *Driftwood* is a word that helps us "see" the setting. What other words from the Words to Know list and the selection added to your sense of place as you read?

Look Back and Write Why didn't Mami punish Fernando? Look at the ending of the story and write your answer.

Meet the Author

Lulu Delacre

Read more
books by
Lulu Delacre.

Lulu Delacre grew up in Puerto Rico and is the daughter of two professors. Today she lives in Maryland and writes and illustrates books about Latin America.

For her story "At the Beach," Ms. Delacre says, "I wanted to write about an adventure at the beach. When I was a child I went to the beach with my father and sister most weekends. One of my fondest memories is walking carefully on the big boulders, sidestepping sea urchins to reach the deepest pools where colorful fish hid." Like the boy in the story, Ms. Delacre has actually stepped on a sea urchin! "It is indeed very painful," she says.

"Growing up on the island was a fun-filled experience, where climbing up a tamarindo tree with a friend to eat its fruit was as commonplace as hunting for tiny brown lizards. I used to gently open their mouths and hang them from my earlobes as earrings!"

Salsa Stories

Arroz con Leche: Popular Songs and Rhymes from Latin America

651

Legend

Genre

- A legend is a story handed down from the past.

- Some legends deal with heroic deeds. Others explain something in nature.

- What do the title and drawings lead you to expect the selection will be about?

Link to Writing

Think of a memorable feature of an animal, such as a giraffe's neck or a bat's wings. Write a "legend" that explains how that feature came to be.

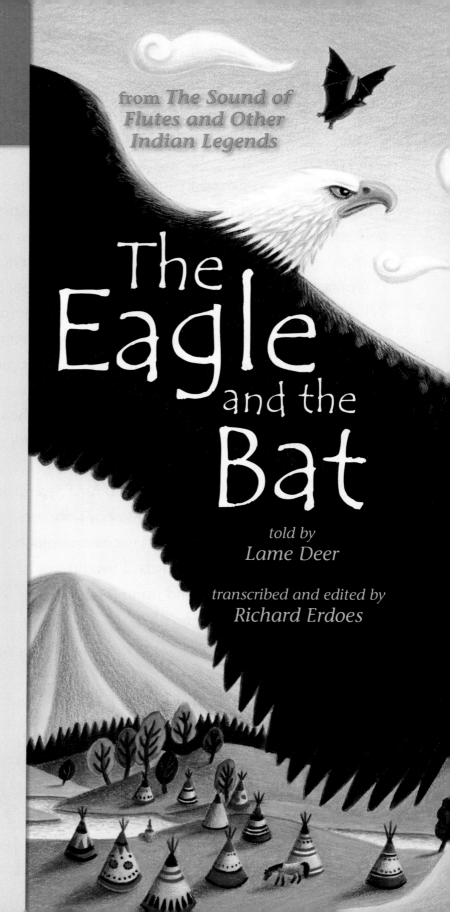

from *The Sound of Flutes and Other Indian Legends*

The Eagle and the Bat

told by
Lame Deer

transcribed and edited by
Richard Erdoes

Once all the birds came together in a big powwow. They played games to see who could fly the fastest and had other contests. At the end they said, "Now let's see which of us can fly higher than all the others." The kite, the hawk, the falcon, the wild goose, the crane—they all flew so high that they almost disappeared from sight. But then Wanblee, the eagle, spread his mighty wings and soared up into the air, higher than any other bird, almost all the way to the sun.

When Wanblee finally came down again, all the birds set up a trilling, high-pitched honoring cry, saying, "The eagle beat us all. He can fly the highest!"

But just then a little bat popped up from out of the plumes on the top of Wanblee's head, flapping its puny leather wings and yelling, "No, no, I flew higher than Wanblee, hiding myself on top of his head. Being on top of Wanblee, naturally I was higher up than he or anybody else."

For this presumption and trickery, the birds transformed the bat into a mouse, taking away his wings. "From now on," said the eagle, "you'll stay in a hole beneath the earth, and the owl will watch so that you won't dare come out of your hole until you learn how to behave yourself."

Reading Across Texts

Think about this selection and "At the Beach." Imagine that each one tries to teach a lesson about telling the truth and lying. What would those lessons be?

Writing Across Texts Write a poem about telling the truth and lying inspired by the two selections.

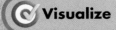 **Visualize** How could "becoming" one character help you visualize?

Comprehension

Skill
Main Idea
and Details

Strategy
Text Structure

 Skill

Main Idea
and Details

- The main idea of a selection is the most important idea about the topic of that selection.

- Sometimes the author states the main idea in a single sentence. When the author does not state the main idea, the reader must figure it out.

- Active readers ask, "What is this selection all about?" To check your main idea, ask, "Does it cover all the important details?"

 Strategy

Strategy: Text Structure

Text structure is the way a writer organizes a selection. For example, the piece may describe events in a start-to-finish sequence, or may use a cause-and-effect pattern or a series of main ideas and details. Active readers use text structure to help them understand the selection's main idea. As you read, look for text structure.

1. Read "Works of Art or Works of Aliens?" Make a graphic organizer to record the main idea and details.

2. Use your graphic organizer to write a short summary of the selection.

Works of ART or Works of ALIENS?

In the farm fields of southern England during the 1970s, simple designs, called crop circles, were formed from flattened stalks of grain. Some were only a few feet in diameter. Others were as big as 1,500 feet across. How did they get there? Who or what was responsible for them?

Some scientists claimed these mysterious designs were caused by the weather. Other people believed they were caused by outer-space aliens or perhaps by humans here on Earth. No one knew for sure. More designs appeared in fields each year, and crop circles appeared in other countries as well.

In 1991, two men calling themselves crop artists admitted they were responsible for some of the crop circles. Crop artists think of their designs as art. Each one takes up to two weeks to finish, but crop artists hardly ever take credit for their designs. They believe that the mystery and folklore is part of their art.

The relationship between crop artists and farmers sometimes benefits both parties. While farmers provide the "canvas," the artists bring in the tourists. Farmers often charge tourists a small fee to see the circles. Are farmers concerned about the origin of the crop circles? Many feel that as long as they are well made, people can believe whatever they want to believe.

Strategy Think about these two questions. Do they help you determine the text structure—how the author is organizing the text?

Skill Based on this paragraph, what do you predict the main idea of this selection will be?
a) The causes of crop circles
b) Aliens from outer space
c) Tourism in England

Skill What three details can be added to your graphic organizer from this paragraph?

Strategy What has been the effect of crop circles on farmers?

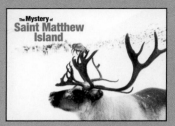

Words to Know

carcasses

scrawny

suspicions

starvation

parasites

tundra

decay

bleached

Remember

Try the strategy. Then, if you need more help, use your glossary or dictionary.

Vocabulary Strategy
for Endings

Word Structure An ending is a letter or letters added to the end of a base word that changes how the word is used. For example, the endings *-s* and *-es* make singular nouns plural. Recognizing an ending may help you figure out a word's meaning.

1. Look at the unknown word to see if it has a base word you know.

2. Check to see if the ending *-s* or *-es* has been added.

3. Ask yourself how the ending changes the meaning of the base word.

4. See if the meaning makes sense in the sentence.

As you read "Cleanup by Mother Nature," look for words with the ending *-s* or *-es*. Use the endings to help you figure out the meanings of the words.

CLEANUP BY
MOTHER NATURE

All living things die. This is not a pleasant fact to investigate, so we don't think about it often. However, the carcasses of animals hit on the road are a startling reminder. Some animals die to provide food for other animals. Perhaps you have seen a scrawny wild animal. This arouses suspicions in your mind. It is unhealthy. It may die from starvation, sickness, or parasites, such as worms, that have been living off its tissues. Still other living things pass through their whole life cycle and die of old age. What happens to the bodies of animals when they die?

Mother Nature has a plan so that nothing is wasted. From the frozen tundra to the steaming jungles, the bodies of dead animals are broken down. Through the process of decay, their tissues are changed into simpler chemicals. These go into the soil and are used by plants. Soon all that can be seen is bleached bones. In time, these, too, break down and disappear.

Write

Look at the pictures in the selection. Choose a picture to write about. Use as many words from the Words to Know list as you can.

The Mystery of Saint Matthew Island

by SUSAN E. QUINLAN

Genre

In **case studies,** investigators detail how they found answers to difficult questions or solutions to difficult problems. As you read, notice how scientists go about solving a mystery.

Why did all
the reindeer
die?

659

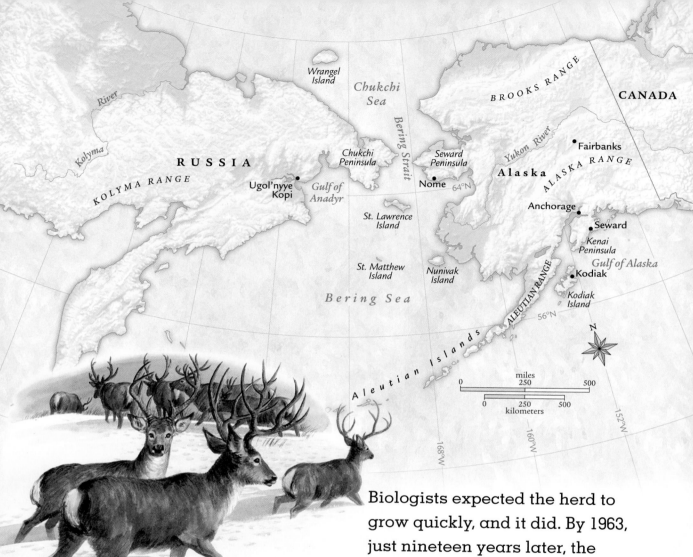

Biologists expected the herd to grow quickly, and it did. By 1963, just nineteen years later, the herd numbered more than six thousand animals.

Then something went terribly wrong. Sailors who visited Saint Matthew to hunt reindeer in 1965 found the island littered with reindeer skeletons. They saw only a few live reindeer.

When the sailors' disturbing report reached Dr. David Klein, a scientist who had studied the herd, he immediately made

When twenty-nine reindeer were released on Saint Matthew Island in 1944, the future of the herd seemed bright. This island in the midst of the Bering Sea offered plenty of plants and lichens for the reindeer to eat. No wolves, bears, or other large predators lived on the island.

plans to investigate. Arranging transportation to the remote island was difficult. Located halfway between Alaska and Siberia, this American island is so far from anywhere that it is nearly impossible to reach. No one lives there, so the island has no airports, and it is too far offshore for small planes to venture. For most of the year, it is surrounded by polar sea ice and thus unreachable even by boat. So it was over a year before Klein and two co-workers were able to reach the island by Coast Guard ship. With camping gear, food, and a promise that they would be picked up within two weeks, the investigators were left on the lonely shore.

The first step of their investigation was to determine if the disaster report was true. On his two previous visits to Saint Matthew years before, Klein had seen small groups of reindeer everywhere. But now the island was strangely still. The bleached skeletons of reindeer lay scattered across the tundra. Klein had a few suspicions about the disaster based on his earlier trips to the island. But to solve the mystery, he needed to conduct a thorough investigation.

As a first step, the researchers explored the mountainous island. After several days of difficult hiking, they found that only forty-two live animals remained on the entire island. All of these were adult females, except one scrawny adult male. There were no calves. The absence of calves meant that the lone male was unable to sire young. So the herd was doomed to disappear completely someday. When and how had the other six thousand animals perished? And why had such a disaster happened to this once healthy herd?

Perhaps there was a clue in the reindeer skeletons. Klein noticed that nearly all of the

skeletons were in the same state of decay. That meant the entire herd had died at about the same time. Based on the moss growing on the bones and their bleached condition, Klein estimated that the carcasses had lain around for at least three years. Klein had counted six thousand animals when he visited the island in summer 1963, so he concluded that the reindeer had died sometime between that summer and the summer of 1964.

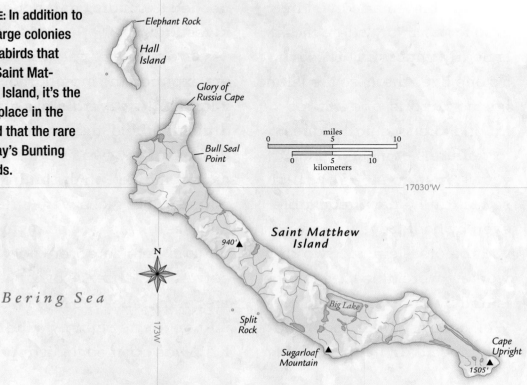

ABOVE: In addition to the large colonies of seabirds that use Saint Matthew Island, it's the only place in the world that the rare McKay's Bunting breeds.

Elephant Rock

Hall Island

Glory of Russia Cape

Bull Seal Point

miles

kilometers

17030'W

Saint Matthew Island

940'

Bering Sea

173W

Big Lake

Split Rock

Sugarloaf Mountain

Cape Upright

1505'

RIGHT: Part of the Saint Matthew herd when it was six thousand strong, silhouetted against a stormy sky in 1963.

Klein examined the skeletons more carefully, hoping to find more clues about the date of the die-off. He soon found the tiny, newly formed bones of baby reindeer that had died while still inside their mothers. These tiny bones told Klein that the female reindeer had died in late winter when their calves were still developing.

With the time of death narrowed down to late winter 1963–1964, Klein searched for clues about the cause of death. No predators lived on the island, and people rarely visit it. So neither of these potential killers were suspects in the case.

LEFT: The vole that lives on Saint Matthew Island has developed into its own species, having arrived more than 10,000 years ago when the oceans were lower and the island was connected to the mainland.

During the winter, the reindeer fed off vegetation such as lichen (TOP LEFT), sedge (TOP RIGHT), and willow (RIGHT), which grew on the windswept areas of the island where the snow is often blown free.

Klein ruled out diseases and parasites because he had found almost no signs of disease or parasites on his earlier visits to Saint Matthew. And it was not possible that an infected animal from somewhere else had brought in any disease or parasite. Saint Matthew Island is too remote.

Klein found skeletons from animals of all ages. Therefore old age was not the cause of the die-off either. That left weather and starvation as possible causes.

Weather seemed likely to be involved. The 1963–64 winter included some of the deepest snows and the coldest temperatures ever recorded in the Bering Sea area. But Klein thought a severe winter alone should not have caused such a massive die-off. Reindeer are arctic animals. As long as they have enough food, most healthy reindeer should be able to survive, even in a severe winter.

Thus Klein suspected that the Saint Matthew Island reindeer had been unhealthy or had run out of food during the winter of 1963–64. With this

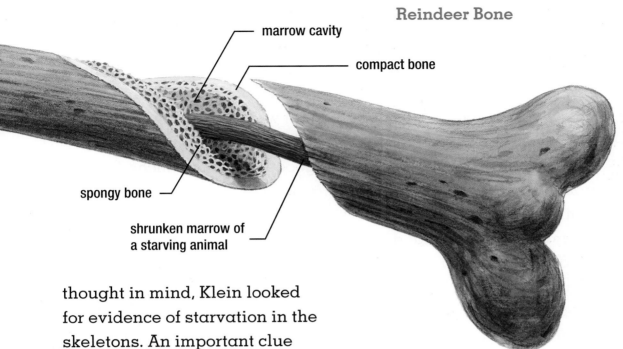

marrow cavity

compact bone

spongy bone

shrunken marrow of
a starving animal

thought in mind, Klein looked for evidence of starvation in the skeletons. An important clue lay hidden inside the bones. A well-fed animal has fat in its bone marrow. This fatty marrow remains in the bones for five years or more after an animal dies. Knowing this, Klein cracked open the leg bones of the skeletons to examine the marrow. Bone after bone, skeleton after skeleton, the marrow was completely gone. None of the animals had fat in their bone marrow when they died. This was clear evidence that the herd had starved to death.

When Klein visited the island three years earlier, he had noticed that some important winter food plants of the reindeer looked overgrazed. When he looked around this time, he noticed more severe damage. Many of the small plants looked as if they had been clipped back. And lichens, mosslike organisms that once carpeted the island, were now absent from many areas. Klein observed that the most serious damage was on hilltops and ridges, where winds keep the ground snow-free in winter. Such places would have been used heavily by reindeer during winter.

The damaged plant life led Klein to suspect that the reindeer had run out of nutritious food. Knowing that a lack of healthy food would show up in the weights of the reindeer, Klein reviewed the records from his earlier visits to Saint Matthew. The animals he had examined in 1957 weighed 199 to 404 pounds—more than most reindeer elsewhere. Clearly, the animals had plenty of food then. In contrast, the reindeer Klein had weighed in 1963 averaged 50 to 120 pounds less in weight. These lower weights showed that when the herd had numbered six thousand animals, many of the reindeer were not getting enough to eat. Klein next weighed a few of the live reindeer that remained on the island. These animals still weighed less than normal. They were not getting enough good food. That clinched the case. Klein was now certain what had happened.

Without predators or disease to limit its numbers, the small reindeer herd had grown quickly. Many young were born, and all the animals had plenty to eat. But after a few years, there were too many animals. The reindeer ate and trampled the tundra plants and lichens faster than these could grow. Crowded onto the windswept

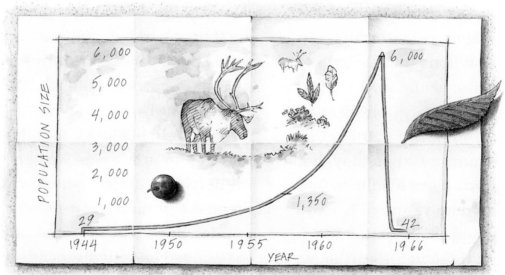

Assumed population of the Saint Matthew Island reindeer herd.
Actual counts are indicated on the population curve.

RIGHT: View of Bull Seal Point, Saint Matthew Island.

BELOW: The very last reindeer. She was last seen in 1982.

ridges in winter, the large herd destroyed the lush lichen carpet. When the most nutritious plants and lichens became scarce, the reindeer began to lose weight. In poor condition, and with little food to sustain them, disaster was inevitable. The harsh winter of 1963–64 spelled the end for the once healthy herd. The Saint Matthew Island reindeer had literally eaten themselves out of house and home. By their numbers alone, they had destroyed their island home and their future.

When Klein and his co-workers left Saint Matthew Island, they brought with them an important understanding of the connections between animals and their environment. Populations of all living things can skyrocket in numbers, like the reindeer herd. Usually, however, animal numbers are kept in check by predators, parasites and diseases, or other factors. The mystery of the Saint Matthew Island reindeer showed that in the absence of these natural checks, a growing population eventually destroys its own environment. And disaster strikes.

Reader Response

Open for Discussion What was the mystery of Saint Matthew Island? What was the solution? What were the clues? What now?

1. Dr. David Klein did not guess at answers. He searched for them and found them. How has the author portrayed Dr. Klein as a scientist rather than a guesser?

2. Think of the main idea of the selection as a piece of advice for both animals and humans. What would the advice be? Use details from the selection to support your answer.

3. The selection can be seen as a series of clues that add up to a solution. Look back and list the clues, from start to finish. Then discuss how they add up to the solution.

4. Imagine that you are Dr. Klein on the island investigating the reindeers' deaths. Describe what you see and how you feel. Use words from the Words to Know list.

Look Back and Write Page 665 cites "clear evidence" showing why the reindeer died. Write what this clear evidence was.

Meet the Author

Susan E. Quinlan

Read more books by Susan E. Quinlan.

Susan E. Quinlan loves wildlife. She says, "It's hard to draw a line between what I do for a living and what I do for hobbies." As a biologist and naturalist guide, she has explored environments in many parts of the world. "The Mystery of Saint Matthew Island" is one of fourteen accounts in *The Case of the Mummified Pigs and Other Mysteries in Nature*. To write the book, she followed up on "wisps of knowledge" she had collected from her experiences in the field and from interviewing scientists.

Ms. Quinlan says, "My primary career interest is to share my fascination with nature and science with other people. Through my years of education and work as a wildlife biologist, I gradually realized that people who are trained as biologists look at nature differently from other people. This different way of looking at things results from acquired nature observation skills and from learning about the research of other scientists. One of my goals as a writer is to help others learn to look at nature in the ways that a biologist might. I also want to interpret the research work of scientists in ways that children and non-scientists can understand and enjoy."

The Case of the Monkeys That Fell from the Trees and Other Mysteries in Tropical Nature

The Case of the Mummified Pigs and Other Mysteries in Nature

Science
in Reading

Narrative Nonfiction

Genre

- **Narrative nonfiction tells the story of an event or a series of events.**
- **Narrative nonfiction may be written by the person who lived the event or by another person who reports it.**

Text Features

- **Narrative nonfiction usually deals with things in time order, from start to finish.**
- **Narrative nonfiction may include sidebars. Sidebars are like mini-articles within an article. These chunks of text are presented separately, usually in a column along the outside of the page.**

Link to Science

Investigate lead on your own. Find out where else it shows up and how it can be a threat to human health. Report your results.

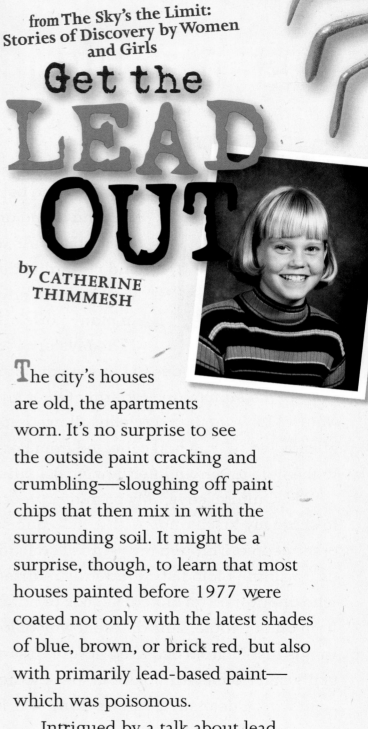

from **The Sky's the Limit: Stories of Discovery by Women and Girls**

Get the LEAD OUT

BY CATHERINE THIMMESH

The city's houses are old, the apartments worn. It's no surprise to see the outside paint cracking and crumbling—sloughing off paint chips that then mix in with the surrounding soil. It might be a surprise, though, to learn that most houses painted before 1977 were coated not only with the latest shades of blue, brown, or brick red, but also with primarily lead-based paint—which was poisonous.

Intrigued by a talk about lead poisoning given at an Earth Day celebration at her local zoo (she

June 12: Planted plants in lead contaminated soil.

would later write in her logbook: *Saw exhibit on lead. Very Dangerous! Decided to do science project . . .*), Katie Murray took it upon herself to search out more information and explore the hazards of lead poisoning. Katie was just eleven years old when, in 1998, she decided to formulate and test an original hypothesis about lead poisoning in vegetables. Through her efforts, Katie discovered that potentially harmful levels of lead could find their way into home-grown vegetables— vegetables that people would probably eat.

"My dad works with a man who plants vegetables in the inner city, in community gardens," Katie said, as she explained how she came up with her idea. "Ms. Maher, a health department nurse at the zoo, had talked about inner cities—how bad lead poisoning is there—and so I wanted to see if those plants that were planted in the lead-contaminated soil, if when you ate them, you would be poisoned."

Katie's love of science had really taken hold the previous year. When she was a fifth grader, she did a science project, "Paper or Plastic?" about which type of grocery bag was better from an environmental standpoint. She won several awards. (As with her lead project, Katie did her fifth-grade project and entered it in science fairs on her own because her school didn't offer science-fair opportunities.) Now, armed with a small spiral notebook to log her progress, Katie began to find out about lead poisoning. Getting the lead—which is unavailable to the general public—proved to be a challenge.

Veggies that survived

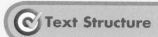 **Text Structure**   How has the author organized her writing?

671

But after several phone calls, she was finally able to obtain it with the help of her sixth-grade science teacher. She first planted six different vegetables in both lead-contaminated soil and regular potting soil. But in the lead-contaminated soil, only two plants—the tomatoes and green peppers—survived.

"I called around to see if anyone could test them for me, because I didn't have the equipment. Finally, I called the FDA, and a man there named Mr. Hughes said that he would test them," explained Katie. "So I brought the plants to him and he cut them up—it was a long process he had to go through—and then he used a spectrograph test, and that's how he found out how much lead was in them."

Mr. Hughes, a chemist at the Food and Drug Administration (FDA), was stunned. His tests showed that Katie's green peppers had a lead content of .131 parts per million, while the tomatoes contained .06 parts of lead per million. The established safety standard for children is .08; anything above that is considered dangerous.

"Although the tomato was under the limit," Katie said, "it was under by such a small amount that Mr. Hughes said if children were to eat it, they would probably get lead poisoning. So it's still an unsafe amount."

What shocked the experts was that Katie's vegetables survived at all. It had always been assumed that plants containing high levels of lead would simply die before producing tempting, edible vegetables.

Katie Murray's discovery of potentially harmful lead levels in home-grown vegetables earned her nine awards, including a First Place Plaque at the Greater Kansas City Science and Engineering Fair and selection as a finalist for the "Discovery Young Scientist Challenge." Her discovery also prompted a prominent toxicologist to encourage Katie to publish her work in scientific journals, and he is helping her to do just that.

According to the Centers for Disease Control and Prevention, the number-one environmental health problem for children in the United States is lead poisoning. Young children (babies to preschoolers) are the ones most affected. Exposure to low levels of lead may cause learning disabilities, hearing loss, delayed growth, and a lower IQ. Exposure to higher lead levels may cause anemia, kidney problems, convulsions, coma, and even death.

Reading Across Texts

The scientists in both selections learned something about life and death. Think about what they learned.

Writing Across Texts Explain what each scientist learned. Write your explanations as a short speech to an audience of young children.

Main Idea What main ideas become the summary of this article?

 February 2: Finished project with tomato and pepper results. 673

Comprehension

Skill
Compare
and Contrast

Strategy
Answer Questions

 Skill

Compare and Contrast

- Writers sometimes use comparisons and contrasts to organize their writing. Clue words such as *same*, *also*, *before*, *although*, and *however* signal comparisons and contrasts.

- Good readers notice the author's comparisons and contrasts and make their own as they read.

Advantages	Disadvantages

 Strategy

Strategy: Answer Questions

Good readers know where to find the answers to questions about what they read. To answer questions about comparisons and contrasts, look for clue words and use your prior knowledge. You may find an answer in just one sentence. Other times you will find it in several different places.

1. Read "Lucky Winners?" List the advantages and disadvantages of winning the lottery in a graphic organizer like the one above.

2. Use your graphic organizer to help you describe how you might feel if you won the lottery.

674

LUCKY WINNERS?

What if you won the lottery? Wouldn't you be happy? Aren't all lottery winners happy? It may seem hard to believe, but while many lottery winners are happy, others are unhappy.

Winning a huge amount of money can be truly life-changing. It can buy the winners freedom from having to work. It can give them the time and resources to actually do the things they only dreamed of doing before, such as traveling to faraway places. However, not all winners' lives change for the better.

Psychologists who specialize in "sudden wealth syndrome" have found that some lottery winners feel an enormous letdown after the shock of winning passes. They become stressed as scores of people start asking them to share their wealth. They feel guilty and depressed because they have so much more than others have.

According to psychologists, rich people are not necessarily a great deal happier than the average person. Often both are equally happy. In a short time, a lottery winner's level of happiness may fall back to its former level. Within five years, many winners have spent, given away, or lost nearly all their winnings. It seems that large amounts of wealth do not always bring more happiness over time. Maybe the old saying is true: Money can't buy happiness.

Strategy What is the author comparing and contrasting? Find the answer in this paragraph.

Skill Find a clue word near the end of this paragraph that signals that a contrast is coming.

Strategy In which two paragraphs would you look to find reasons why some lottery winners end up happy and others do not?

Skill What similarities does this paragraph show between people who are rich and people who are not?

lifeless

cleanse

realm

spoonful

adorn

precious

Remember

Try the strategy. Then, if you need more help, use your glossary or dictionary.

Vocabulary Strategy
for Suffixes

Word Structure A suffix is a word part added to the end of a base word that changes the base word's meaning. Sometimes the spelling of the base word also changes when a suffix is added. Knowing the meaning of a suffix can help you figure out the meaning of a word.

1. Look at an unfamiliar word to see if it has a base word you know.

2. Check to see if the suffix *-less* or *-ful* has been added.

3. Decide how it changes the base word's meaning. The suffix *-less* can mean "without," as in *harmless*. The suffix *-ful* can mean "the amount that will fill," as in *handful*.

4. Try this meaning in the sentence to see if it makes sense.

As you read "Hospital for Wild Animals," look for words with the suffix *-less* or *-ful*. Use the suffixes to help you figure out the meanings of the words.

Hospital for Wild Animals

There are places around us where magic happens. I learned about one when I found an injured owl in my backyard. It had been shot in the wing. My heart sank as I bent over its apparently lifeless form. Then it moved! What could I do to save the owl?

My mom told me to call the wildlife rehabilitation center. They told us how to carefully wrap and carry the owl to them. The worker on duty was careful to cleanse the wound. She said the owl was weak, but it might live.

Over the next few weeks, I visited this magic realm every day and saw kind people helping foxes, raccoons, and birds of all kinds. Soon the owl was ravenous and ate its first spoonful of meat. I saw that complex patterns of color adorn its feathers.

There was a special kind of enchantment about the place. I felt lucky to see these wild creatures up close and to be able to help them get well. It is good to know there are people who realize that the lives of wild things are precious.

Write

Write about a place you think is wonderful or special. Be sure to tell why. Use several words from the Words to Know list.

WILL THE KING
GET HIS WISH?

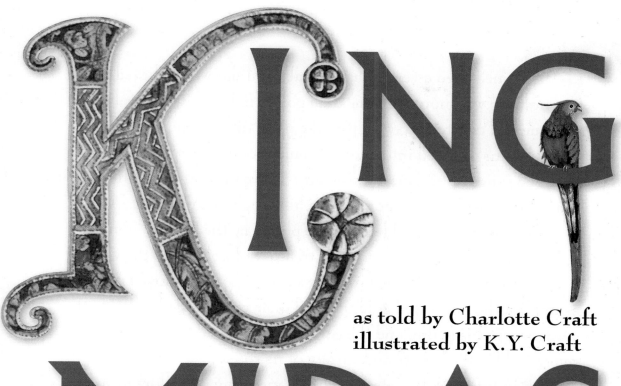

KING MIDAS

as told by Charlotte Craft
illustrated by K.Y. Craft

MIDAS

and the

GOLDEN TOUCH

Genre

Myths are tales handed down by word of mouth for generations. They tell about nature and human behavior. As you read, notice that the author points out how the king's behavior leads to tragedy.

There once lived a very rich king called Midas who believed that nothing was more precious than gold. He loved its soft yellow hue and comforting weight in the palm of his hand. The chink of gold coins dropped into a leather purse sounded sweeter to him than the songs of his finest musicians. There was only one thing that Midas loved more, and that was his daughter, Aurelia.

"Aurelia," he often told her as she played by the throne, "someday I shall bequeath to you the greatest treasury of gold in all the world."

There had been a time, however, when King Midas loved roses as much as he now loved gold. He had once called together the best gardeners in his realm, and the garden they created for him became renowned for the beauty and variety of its roses.

But in time the delicate fragrances and exquisite colors meant nothing to Midas. Only Aurelia still loved the garden. Every day she would pick a bouquet of the most perfect roses to adorn the king's breakfast table. But when Midas saw the flowers, he would think, Their beauty lasts but a day. If they were gold, it would last forever!

One day the king's guards found an old man asleep under the rosebushes and brought him before King Midas.

"Unbind him," Midas ordered. "Without my gold, I would be as poor as he. Tonight he shall dine with me!"

So that night the old man sat at the king's table, where he was well fed and entertained by the king himself. And after a good night's sleep, the old man went on his way.

That morning, as he often did, Midas went down into his dungeon. With a large brass key, he unlocked the door to the secret chamber where he kept his gold. After carefully locking the door behind him, he sat down to admire his precious wealth.

"Ah, I do love it so," he sighed, gazing at his riches. "No matter how hard I work, no matter how long I live, I will never have enough."

He was lost in these thoughts when the chamber suddenly filled with light. King Midas looked up and was amazed to behold the glowing figure of a young man. Since there was no way into the room but through the locked door, Midas knew that he was in the presence of magic.

"Do you not recognize me, friend?"

Midas shook his head. The mysterious stranger smiled at him, and it seemed that all the gold in the dungeon glittered even brighter.

"I am the old man from the rose garden. Instead of punishing me for trespassing, you entertained me at your table. I had thought to reward you for your kindness, but with so much gold, you must surely want for nothing."

"That's not true," cried Midas. "A man can never have enough gold."

The stranger's smile broadened. "Well, then, what would make you a happier man?"

Midas thought for only a moment. "Perhaps if everything I touched would turn to gold," he said.

hat is your wish?"

"Yes, for then it would always be at my fingertips," Midas assured him.

"Think carefully, my friend," cautioned the visitor.

"Yes," replied Midas. "The golden touch would bring me all the happiness I need."

"And so it shall be yours."

With that, the mysterious figure became brighter and brighter, until the light became so intense that Midas had to close his eyes. When he opened them, he was alone once again.

Had the enchantment worked?

Midas eagerly rubbed the great brass door key but was greatly disappointed. There was no gold in his hands. Bewildered, he looked around the dim room and wondered if perhaps he had been dreaming.

But when King Midas awoke the next day, he found his bedchamber bathed in golden light. Glistening in the morning sun, the plain linen bedcovers had been transformed into finely spun gold!

Jumping out of bed, he gasped with astonishment. The bedpost turned to gold as soon as he touched it. "It's true," he cried. "I have the golden touch!"

Midas pulled on his clothes. He was thrilled to find himself wearing a handsome suit of gold—never mind that it was a bit heavy. He slid his spectacles onto his nose. To his delight, they too turned to gold—never mind that he couldn't see through them. With a gift as great as this, he thought, no inconvenience could be too great.

Without wasting another moment, Midas rushed out of

the room, through the palace, and into the garden.

The roses glistened with the morning dew, and their scent gently perfumed the air. Midas went from bush to bush, touching each of the blossoms.

"How happy Aurelia will be when she sees these roses of gold!" he exclaimed. He never noticed how the perfect golden blossoms drooped and pulled down the bushes with their weight.

Soon it was time for breakfast. Midas sat down just as Aurelia entered the room, clutching a golden rose, her face wet with tears.

"Father, Father, a horrible thing has happened," she said, sobbing. "I went to the garden to pick you a flower, but all of the roses have become hard and yellow."

"They are golden roses now, my love, and will never fade."

"But I miss their scent, Father," cried Aurelia.

"I am sorry, my dear. I thought only to please you. Now we can buy all the roses you could ever wish for." Midas smiled at his daughter to comfort her. "Please wipe your eyes, and we'll have our breakfast together."

Midas lifted a spoonful of porridge to his mouth, but as soon as the porridge touched his lips it turned into a hard golden lump.

689

Perhaps if I eat quickly, he thought, puzzled, and snatched a fig from a bowl of fruit. It turned to solid gold before he could take a bite. He reached out for some bread, but his fingertips had no sooner brushed against the loaf than it, too, turned to gold. He tried cheese and even a spoonful of jam, but all to no avail. "How am I to eat?" he grumbled.

"What's wrong, Father?" asked Aurelia.

"Nothing," he answered, wishing not to worry her. "Nothing at all, my child."

But Midas began to wring his hands. If he was hungry now, he imagined how much more hungry he would be by dinner. And then he began to wonder: Will I ever eat again?

Aurelia, who had been anxiously watching her father all this time, slipped out of her chair and went to comfort him, "Please don't cry," she said. Midas smiled and took her hand in his. But suddenly he recoiled in horror.

His daughter stood before him, an expression of concern frozen on her face, a teardrop clinging to her golden cheek. His cursed touch had turned Aurelia into a lifeless statue.

Midas howled in anguish and tore at his hair. He couldn't bear to look at the statue, but neither could he bear to leave her side.

"Well, King Midas, are you not the happiest of men?" Midas wiped his eyes and saw the mysterious stranger standing before him once again.

"Oh, no, I am the most miserable of men!" he cried.

"What? Did I not grant your wish for the golden touch?"

"Yes, but it is a curse to me now." Midas wept. "All that I truly loved is now lost to me."

"Do you mean to say," asked the young man, "that you would prefer a crust of bread or a cup of water to the gift of the golden touch?"

"Oh, yes!" Midas exclaimed. "I would give up all the gold in the world if only my daughter were restored to me."

"Then make your way to the river that flows past the borders of your kingdom. Follow the river upstream until you reach its source. As you cleanse yourself in the foaming spring, the golden touch will be washed away. Take with you a vase so that you may sprinkle water over any object you wish to change back to its original form." With those words, the young man vanished.

As soon as Midas reached the spring, he plunged in without removing even his shoes. As the water washed the gold from his clothes, he noticed a pretty little violet growing wild along the banks and gently brushed his finger against it. When he saw that the delicate purple flower continued to bend with the breeze, he was overjoyed.

Midas made his way back to the palace, where the first thing he did was to sprinkle the water over his beloved Aurelia. No sooner did the water touch her cheek than she was restored, laughing at her father's game and remembering not a moment of being a golden statue.

Together, the two went out to the rose garden. Midas sprinkled each frozen rose with a little river water, and Aurelia clapped her hands when she saw them cured of their golden blight.

Joyfully, then, Midas restored all else he had transformed— except for a single rose, kept forever as a reminder of the golden touch.

Reader Response

Open for Discussion Take the part of the mysterious stranger. Why did he do what he did? Why, for instance, did he come back twice?

1. This story originated long ago—no one is sure when. No one is sure why, either. Why do you think the story originated, and why do you think it is still alive today?

2. The king is restless at the start of the story and content at the end. What brought about this transformation? Use details from the story to explain the change.

3. "King Midas" is known as a cautionary tale. It warns us against something. What is the warning in this cautionary tale? Use details from the story to support your answer.

4. Certain words are commonly used in myths. Make a list of words from the Words to Know list and the story that fall into this category.

Test Practice

Look Back and Write Sometimes people mention "the Midas touch." Reread pages 683–684 and then write what "the Midas touch" must mean.

Read more books illustrated by Kinuko Craft.

Kinuko Craft, illustrator of *King Midas and the Golden Touch*, says, "I feel that, throughout time, each generation has a person with a 'golden touch' who learns the same lesson Midas did." In her paintings for some of the scenes in the book, she used geometric patterns. These come from the designs on small objects found at a burial site believed to be that of the real King Midas. Archaeologists found the objects during a dig at the site in Turkey.

Kinuko Craft is one of the most widely respected illustrators of fantasy in the United States today. In an interview, she said, "From grade school through my high school days, my effort was to imitate nature—anything natural." Later, she worked in the world of commercial art, where she used a large variety of styles and mediums. About ten years ago, she began creating paintings for picture books using oil over watercolor.

Sleeping Beauty

The Adventures of Tom Thumb

Charlotte Craft is the daughter of illustrator Kinuko Craft. She lives in Scotland with her family. Her inspiration for the story of *King Midas and the Golden Touch* was Nathaniel Hawthorne's retelling of the Greek myth.

Genre

- **A poem is a composition arranged in lines. Some poems have rhyme.**

- **Some poems are written in the voice of a first-person narrator who tells the reader a story. Sometimes this story is humorous and fantastic.**

- **Look at the drawings and ask yourself: "What clues tell me this poem will be funny and fantastic?"**

Link to Writing

Think about how it might feel to be Jimmy Jet. Write a poem from his point of view telling what he sees and how he feels.

by Shel Silverstein
from *Where the Sidewalk Ends*

JIMMY JET AND HIS TV SET

I'll tell you the story of Jimmy Jet—
And you know what I tell you is true.
He loved to watch his TV set
Almost as much as you.

He watched all day, he watched
      all night
Till he grew pale and lean,
From "The Early Show" to
      "The Late Late Show"
And all the shows between.

He watched till his eyes were frozen wide,
And his bottom grew into his chair.
And his chin turned into a tuning dial,
And antennae grew out of his hair.

And his brains turned into TV tubes,
And his face to a TV screen.
And two knobs saying "VERT." and "HORIZ."
Grew where his ears had been.

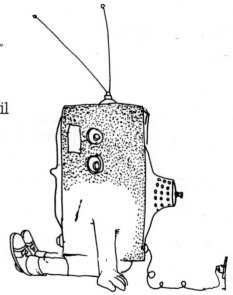

And he grew a plug that looked like a tail
So we plugged in little Jim.
And now instead of him watching TV
We all sit around and watch him.

Reading Across Texts

Think about the mistakes that King Midas and Jimmy Jet made.

Writing Across Texts Write a dialogue between King Midas and Jimmy in which they explain their mistakes to each other.

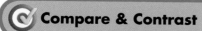 **Compare & Contrast**   Do you know people who overdo one activity?

THE HINDENBURG

Comprehension

Skill
Fact and Opinion

Strategy
Ask Questions

Skill

Fact and Opinion

- Statements of fact are objective, not personal. They can be proved true or false. Statements of opinion are personal judgments or beliefs. They cannot be proved true or false.

- Statements of opinion can be valid or faulty. Valid statements can be supported by facts and common sense. Faulty statements cannot.

- Examine statements of opinion by using your prior knowledge. Based on what you have seen or read or what you know, ask, *Is the statement valid or faulty?*

Statement of Opinion	Support	Valid or Faulty?

Strategy

Strategy: Ask Questions

Active readers ask questions before, during, and after reading. Asking and answering questions can help you recall important ideas and decide whether opinions are valid or faulty.

1. Read "How Blimps Are Used." Make a graphic organizer like the one above to keep track of statements of opinion.

2. Use your graphic organizer to help you write an answer to one of your questions about blimps.

How Blimps Are Used

There is no better outdoor advertisement than the blimp. These flying billboards carry advertising messages hundreds and thousands of feet in the air, where they can be viewed by hundreds and thousands of people at once. These brightly colored, lighter-than-air craft of many different shapes and sizes have appeared in the skies for more than 80 years.

In 1925, the American tire company Goodyear built its first blimp. It was a huge success. Goodyear went on to build more than 300 blimps, all promoting their products. They are often seen on TV sports programs, where audiences watch them floating above stadiums. Cameras on board give viewers aerial shots of the action. The Goodyear blimps are some of the most famous aircraft in history.

These airborne blimps are faster than most ocean-going ships. In fact, the U. S. Navy used them during the Second World War. Large enough to carry equipment and stay in the air for days at a time, they are also used by law enforcement officers.

Because blimps have the best safety record of any type of flying vehicle today, they are used to cover many special events. Today, tourists also use them. There is no better way to see the African plains or follow a river in a rain forest than by floating above them. A ride in a blimp is truly a unique, one-of-a-kind adventure.

Strategy Think of what you already know about blimps. List any questions you have about them that this article might answer.

Skill One of the sentences in the first paragraph is a statement of opinion. Which one? Why?

Strategy Have you found answers to any of your questions? What other questions have you thought of as you read?

Skill Based on your own knowledge, would you say this statement of opinion is valid or faulty?

cruised

hydrogen

explosion

drenching

era

criticizing

Remember

Try the strategy. Then, if you need more help, use your glossary or dictionary.

Vocabulary Strategy
for Unfamiliar Words

Context Clues As you read, you may see a word you do not know. Often the author has given clues to help you figure out the meaning of an unknown word. Check the words and sentences around the unknown word for these clues.

1. Reread the sentence where the unknown word appears.

2. Is there a specific clue to the word's meaning?

3. For more help, read the sentences around the sentence with the unknown word. Look for words or phrases that suggest a reasonable meaning.

4. Try the meaning in the sentence with the unknown word. Does it make sense?

As you read "The Birth of the Automobile," use the context to help you figure out the meanings of unfamiliar words.

IN THE MARIPOSA BIG TREE GROVE   4595

YOSEMITE NATIONAL PARK, CALIFORNIA   89629

The Birth of the Automobile

The automobile may well have been the most important invention in transportation history. However, it took many people many years to come up with an engine that worked well. In 1771 a Frenchman invented a three-wheeled sort of tractor. It ran on steam power, and it cruised along at 2½ miles per hour. (Get a horse!) It crashed into a stone wall. Don't worry—all the riders survived! In 1807 a Swiss fellow invented an engine that used a mix of hydrogen and oxygen for fuel. (Can you imagine the explosion?) Neither of these succeeded.

Not until the 1880s did inventors come up with an engine that was practical. A gas engine was mounted on an open coach. (If it rained, the driver and guests got a drenching.) This four-wheeled vehicle had a top speed of 10 miles per hour.

Improvements happened fast after that. The era of the automobile had begun. This age has continued to the present time and shows no signs of stopping. Instead of criticizing the early cars, we should admire them for pointing the way.

Imagine you are traveling long ago. Write about the transportation you are using. See how many words from the Words to Know list you can use.

Expository nonfiction explains what certain things are and how and why they came to be. As you read, notice how the author explains the origins of the *Hindenburg*—and its disastrous end.

THE HINDENBURG

PATRICK O'BRIEN

Could a tiny spark lead to
a gigantic explosion?

Hugo Eckener piloting the Graf Zeppelin

In Germany in 1900, the first dirigible was successfully flown. This mammoth airship consisted of several giant, gas-filled balloons inside a hard, hollow structure that was moved along by motors and steered by fins. In 1931 the most advanced dirigible yet, the *Graf Zeppelin*, began flying from Germany across the Atlantic and back, carrying twenty passengers in dreamy luxury. Meanwhile, its designer, Hugo Eckener, had even grander plans in mind.

The Graf Zeppelin over Tokyo

While the *Graf Zeppelin* was busy with these transatlantic
flights, Eckener planned another airship that was soon taking
shape at the Zeppelin Company in Germany. A bigger and better
ship. The perfect airship. The *Hindenburg*.

The new zeppelin was to be so big that a giant new hangar
had to be made to house it.

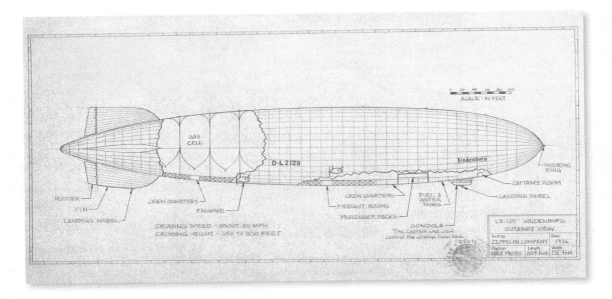

The gas cells in the *Hindenburg* were filled with hydrogen. Hydrogen can be extremely dangerous because it will explode if it comes into contact with a spark or a flame. All the German zeppelins ever made had been filled with hydrogen, but the zeppelin workers were very careful and they had an excellent safety record. In the early days there had been a few accidents in which crew members were killed, but no paying passenger had ever been hurt or killed in a German zeppelin accident.

The designers of the *Hindenburg* included all the latest safety measures in their new zeppelin. An American naval officer examined the ship and reported, "I consider all possibilities of danger in the new zeppelin eliminated."

In the 1930s, the Nazis came into power in Germany. Eckener did not like their brutal ways. He resisted their control whenever he could, and he made speeches criticizing the Nazi party. Eckener thought that transatlantic travel could help create better understanding between different countries. He said that he wanted "to be of service to mankind in the development of air travel." But the Nazis wanted zeppelins only to glorify Germany and to symbolize Nazi power.

The Nazis did not like Eckener, so they made him a
"nonperson." This meant that his name could not be mentioned
in newspapers, and no one was allowed to print a picture of
him. Eckener was forced to put the Nazi symbol, the swastika,
on the *Hindenburg*. His dream airship would have to fly the
Atlantic with the hated swastika displayed on the tail fins.

The *Hindenburg* made its first flight to America in May of 1936. The takeoff was so smooth that passengers did not even know the ship was airborne unless they were looking out the windows. The ride was perfectly steady and quiet as the ship cruised at 80 miles per hour over the Atlantic Ocean.

Only the rich could afford to travel by airship. The tickets were $400, about the price of a small car in those days. The passengers had their own rooms with beds and sinks, and there was even a shower on board. The kitchen was well stocked with the finest foods. On Atlantic crossings, the chefs used 440 pounds of meat and poultry, 800 eggs, and 220 pounds of butter.

When the airship arrived in America, cruising low over New York City, thousands of people filled the rooftops, window-sills, and streets, cheering wildly as the huge zeppelin floated overhead. Eckener later tried to explain the strange appeal of his giant soaring ships. A zeppelin, he said, was "like a fabulous silvery fish, floating quietly in the ocean of air. . . . It seemed to be coming from another world and to be returning there like a dream."

The *Hindenburg* made nine more round-trip flights to the United States in 1936. The landing spot was in Lakehurst, New Jersey, about an hour south of New York City. During the winter of that year, the *Hindenburg* made seven trips down to Rio de Janeiro.

The first flying season was a huge success, and eighteen trips to the United States were scheduled for the next year. At the same time, the Zeppelin Company's other ship, the *Graf Zeppelin,* was still keeping a schedule of regular flights from Germany to Rio de Janeiro.

Because of the success of the *Hindenburg,* Hugo Eckener was able to make an agreement with an American company. The Americans would build two big airships, and the Zeppelin Company in Germany would build two more. There would be four new airships flying the Atlantic. Eckener's dream of regular transatlantic travel was beginning to come true.

On May 3, 1937, sixty-one crew members and thirty-six passengers boarded the *Hindenburg* for the flight to America. Fourteen-year-old Werner Franz was thrilled to be a cabin boy on the famous airship. He was the youngest member of the crew. Two of the passengers were even younger—Werner and Wallace Doehner, ages six and eight. Somewhere over the Atlantic, a steward politely took away Werner's toy truck. It made sparks when it rolled. In an airship filled with explosive hydrogen, sparks could mean disaster.

The *Hindenburg* cruised low over the icebergs of the North Atlantic, close to the spot where the *Titanic* had gone down twenty-five years before. At four o'clock on the afternoon of May 6, the *Hindenburg* arrived over the landing field in Lakehurst, New Jersey.

There were thunderstorms in the area, so it cruised south over the beaches of the Atlantic coast to wait out the storms.

Shortly after seven o'clock, the *Hindenburg* returned to the landing field and slowed to a stop about 250 feet above the ground. The crew dropped ropes from the ship's nose so the men below could help bring the ship in. Everything was done according to plan. It was a routine landing. There was no warning of what was about to happen.

In thirty-two seconds, the mighty airship *Hindenburg*
was a mass of flaming wreckage on the ground.

Amazingly, of the ninety-seven people on board, sixty-seven survived the explosion. One person on the ground was killed, and five survivors died later in the hospital.

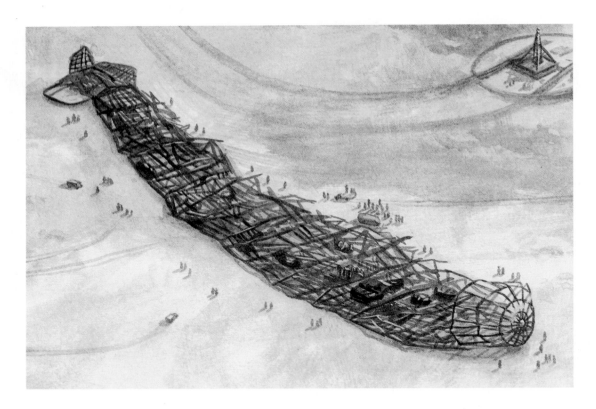

One passenger who was an acrobat was able to hang on outside a window of the burning airship until it was low enough that he could drop off onto the sandy ground below. He stood up, brushed himself off, and limped away. One older couple walked down the steps of the slowly falling ship as if it was a normal landing. They escaped, injured but alive. The Doehner brothers survived when their mother threw them out of a window into the arms of the rescuers below.

Werner Franz, the fourteen-year-old cabin boy, rode the flaming airship almost all the way to the ground. A large water tank in the ship above his head burst, drenching him with water. He jumped to the ground as the flaming airship was falling around him and dashed out, soaking wet but unharmed.

The cause of the *Hindenburg* explosion is still a mystery. Hugo Eckener felt that there was static electricity in the air because of the thunderstorms in the area, and that this electricity might have ignited some hydrogen that was leaking near the back of the airship. Some people believe, however, that a bomb caused the explosion. There was no evidence of a bomb, but the swastikas on the tail of the ship might have made the *Hindenburg* a target for people who wanted to destroy a symbol of Nazi power.

Millions of people around the world watched newsreels of the *Hindenburg* explosion and heard reports about it on the radio. Zeppelins were now seen as death traps, and all interest in building more of them died with the *Hindenburg*. Eckener wrote that "it appeared to me the hopeless end of a great dream, a kind of end of the world."

Over the years, airplanes have been developed to be much faster and bigger than they were before. People now fly in airplanes instead of airships. Even Hugo Eckener had to admit that "a good thing has been replaced by a better." The mighty zeppelins no longer cruise through the ocean of air on grand voyages to distant lands. Like the *Hindenburg,* the era of the great airships is gone forever.

◀ The *Hindenburg* made the trip from Germany to America in two and a half days. The only other way to cross the Atlantic was by ship, and the fastest ships needed five days to make the trip.

On one return trip from Rio de Janeiro, someone sneaked five monkeys on board the *Graf Zeppelin.* They soon got loose and were seen swinging through the girders inside the airship. Pets were shipped on the *Hindenburg*—dogs, birds, fish, and even a deer. ▼

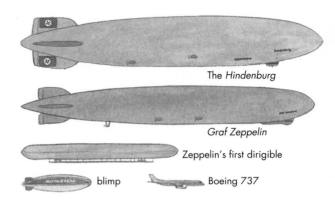

The *Hindenburg*

Graf Zeppelin

Zeppelin's first dirigible

blimp   Boeing 737

▲ The *Hindenburg* was the biggest thing that ever flew.

The *Hindenburg* was ▶ named for a former president of Germany, Paul von Hindenburg.

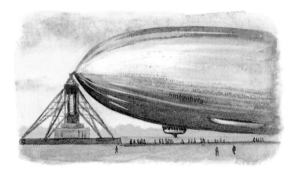

The tower on the top of the Empire State Building was built as a mooring mast. It was never used. ▼

▲ Airships docked at mooring masts. A ring on the front of an airship was attached to the top of the mast. This allowed the ship to swing with the wind while moored.

◄ Play stopped at a baseball game between the Brooklyn Dodgers and the Pittsburgh Pirates in Brooklyn when the *Hindenburg* flew over on its way to a landing. Everyone wanted to watch the airship.

Eckener went to a party in New York City to celebrate the *Hindenburg*'s first flight. In the middle of the table was a mound of ice cream in the shape of a zeppelin. ►

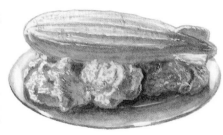

Reader Response

Open for Discussion Someone says, "Unexpectedly, the history of flight changed in just thirty-two seconds!" Explain in detail what that person must mean.

1. Nonfiction authors often include human-interest tidbits to help readers identify with the people and situations in their writing. What are some human-interest tidbits in *The Hindenburg*?

2. One word on page 715 strongly signals an opinion. What is that word and the opinion it signals? Is this opinion valid or faulty? Use details from the page to support your answer.

3. Reread the naval officer's statement on page 708. Then reread the first paragraph on page 712 and ask yourself how it contradicts the officer's statement. Answer the question with details from the text.

4. You are a reporter for the *Lakehurst Gazette*. You happen to be at the field when the *Hindenburg* makes its final landing. Write an account for your paper, using words from the Words to Know list and from the selection.

Test Practice

Look Back and Write
Reread the last sentence on page 717. Is it a statement of fact or of opinion? Do you agree or disagree with it? Write your reaction.

The Graf Zeppelin over Tokyo

Read more
books by
Patrick O'Brien.

Patrick O'Brien has been working as an illustrator since the 1980s, specializing in animal and historical illustrations. He also does freelance art for advertising agencies, providing illustrations for video boxes, posters, stickers, and refrigerator magnets. In 1998 Mr. O'Brien began writing and illustrating children's books.

Mr. O'Brien says, "I began working on *The Hindenburg* after my editor asked me if I would be interested. I did a lot of research. I went up to Lakehurst, New Jersey, where the crash site was. I bought a plastic model of the *Hindenburg* and photographed that to get the different angles and do it accurately. I often use models if I can find them. I had to order it from Germany on the Internet. For the explosions, I watched historical films of the actual event and other movies with big explosions."

Mr. O'Brien says the main thing about writing the story was deciding which part to focus on. "I decided to use the most famous character in the story, Mr. Hugo Eckener, as the main character. He was involved in making airships since the beginning and was a strong anti-Nazi."

Duel of the Ironclads

The Great Ships

Reading Online

Earthquakes and Primary Sources

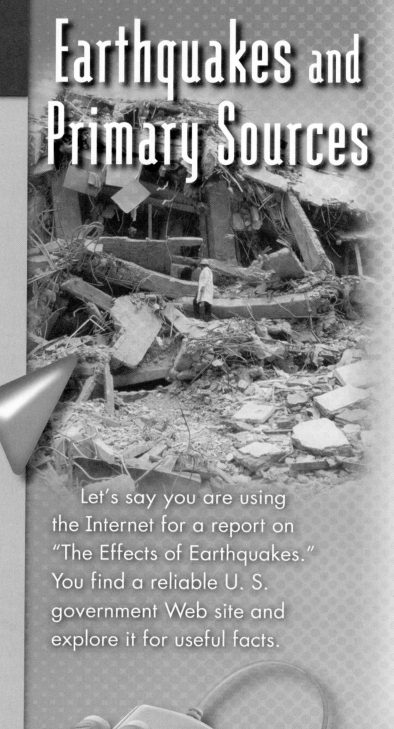

Evaluating Sources

Genre

- You can find information fast on the Internet, but only some of it will be reliable and useful.

- On government and reference Web sites, such as NASA and Fact Monster, you'll find facts you can rely on.

Text Features

- The addresses of these reliable Web sites often end in .gov, .edu, or .org.

- Web sites that end in other ways, such as .com or .net, may be reliable. Use what you know and other sources to decide.

Link to Social Studies

Search through nonfiction books and magazines. Do the authors tell you where they got their facts?

Let's say you are using the Internet for a report on "The Effects of Earthquakes." You find a reliable U. S. government Web site and explore it for useful facts.

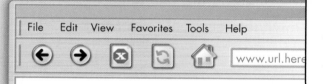

Which of the "Cool Earthquake Facts" from the Web site are useful for your report?

Cool Earthquake Facts

1. The world's deadliest recorded earthquake occurred in 1557 in central China. It struck a region where most people lived in caves carved from soft rock. These dwellings collapsed during the earthquake, killing an estimated 830,000 people.

2. Moonquakes ("earthquakes" on the moon) do occur, but they happen less frequently and are smaller than earthquakes on the Earth.

3. Florida and North Dakota have the smallest number of earthquakes in the United States.

4. In 1663 the European settlers experienced their first earthquake in North America.

5. It is thought that more damage was done by the resulting fire after the 1906 San Francisco earthquake than by the earthquake itself.

You decide that only the first and last facts are useful, since they alone deal with your topic, the effects of earthquakes.

 **Ask Questions**   Why are facts 2, 3 and 4 not useful?

Then you find another useful site. This one is from a university. It contains primary source materials. These are firsthand documents that were written during the time an event happened. This is an eyewitness account from Mark Twain's nonfiction book *Roughing It*:

Mark Twain and the October 8, 1865, San Francisco Earthquake

As I turned the corner, around a frame house, there was a great rattle and jar, and it occurred to me that here was an item!—no doubt a fight in that house. Before I could turn and seek the door, there came a terrific shock; the ground seemed to roll under me in waves, interrupted by a violent joggling up and down, and there was a heavy grinding noise as of brick houses rubbing together. . . . The entire front of a tall four-story brick building on Third Street sprung outward like a door and fell sprawling across the street, raising a great dust-like volume of smoke!

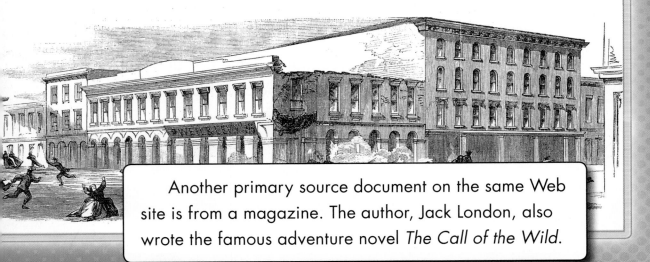

Another primary source document on the same Web site is from a magazine. The author, Jack London, also wrote the famous adventure novel *The Call of the Wild*.

Jack London and the April 1906 San Francisco Earthquake

San Francisco is gone. Nothing remains of it but memories and a fringe of dwelling-houses on its outskirts. Its industrial section is wiped out. Its business section is wiped out. Its social and residential section is wiped out.

Within an hour after the earthquake shock the smoke of San Francisco's burning was a lurid tower visible a hundred miles away. And for three days and nights this lurid tower swayed in the sky, reddening the sun, darkening the day, and filling the land with smoke.

You make notes on these primary sources and then continue looking for more facts on the effects of earthquakes.

Reading Across Texts

Compare the earthquakes described by Mark Twain and Jack London with the airship disaster in *The Hindenburg*. Which event, one of the earthquakes or the *Hindenburg* crash, would make a more exciting movie?

Writing Across Texts Give your opinion in a persuasive paragraph or two. Be specific. Use facts from the selections to back up your opinion.

Fact & Opinion   Do the authors use facts in exciting ways?

Comprehension

Skill
Sequence

Strategy
Prior Knowledge

Sequence

- Sequence is the order of events in a selection. Dates and times of day or clue words such as *first, next,* and *then* can help you follow the sequence of events.

- Clue words such as *meanwhile* or *during* signal events happening at the same time.

First Event	Second Event	Third Event	Fourth Event

Strategy: Prior Knowledge

Prior knowledge is what you already know about a topic. Active readers connect their prior knowledge to the text to help them understand it. They add to and revise their prior knowledge as they read and think about the text. When the author does not give the sequence in exact dates and times, use your prior knowledge to decide when events in the selection take place.

1. Read "What Do You Know About Harlem?" Create a time line like the one above. Use clues from the story to put the events in sequence.

2. Make another time line showing important events in your school or community. Use it to write a paragraph describing the events.

WHAT DO YOU KNOW ABOUT HARLEM?

I had to write a report for school about Harlem. Before I did my research, all I knew about Harlem was that it was part of New York City.

Harlem was founded in 1658 as a Dutch settlement, and through the 1700s it was a farming area. Later, high-class houses and apartments were built there, but the hard times of the panic of 1893 left many of these places empty. Soon the white owners were willing to rent to African Americans. Many African Americans had moved to the North to find jobs. Some settled in Harlem. Before World War I, Harlem had become the largest African American neighborhood in the United States. It was poor in terms of money but rich in terms of culture.

In the 1920s, music, literature, and arts began to blossom in a time known as the Harlem Renaissance. Harlem offered amazing music in the form of jazz, blues, and ragtime. Shows at the Apollo Theater and the Cotton Club helped relations in America. They brought crowds of white and black people together who had never spent time together before.

The books, poems, and art showed a strong sense of pride. This was the first time that African American arts gained attention from the whole country. The Great Depression brought an end to the Harlem Renaissance, but not before America had been changed forever.

Strategy Based on this paragraph, what prior knowledge did the author have about Harlem? What is your own prior knowledge of Harlem?

Skill As you read, what clues help you determine the order of events, or sequence, of the selection?

Strategy How does your prior knowledge about race relations in America in the 1920s help you understand this paragraph?

Skill The dates of the Great Depression are not given. Do you need the actual dates to place it in time order? Why or why not?

Vocabulary Strategy
for Homographs

Context Clues Homographs are words that are spelled the same but have different meanings and histories. Some homographs also have different pronunciations. For example, *minute* (MIN-it) means "60 seconds," while *minute* (my-NOOT) means "tiny." Use the words and sentences around a homograph to figure out which word (and meaning) is being used.

1. Read the words and sentences around the homograph.

2. Think about its possible meanings.

3. Reread the sentence and put in one of the meanings.

4. See if the meaning makes sense in the sentence. If not, try another meaning for the homograph.

As you read "Jazz in Harlem," use the words and sentences around a homograph to decide which meaning the author is using.

Jazz in Harlem

No history of black Harlem would be complete without talking about culture. In writing, art, and music, its African American creators shone. In no area was that light brighter than in jazz. It grew out of the blues and ragtime. It was wild and free and toe-tapping. In the 1920s in Harlem, the nighttime was alive with this music.

Great musicians such as Louis Armstrong and Duke Ellington jammed far into the night. The sounds of trumpet, drums, clarinet, and bass spilled from night clubs. The jazz they played had big muscles and a big heart. It wanted to dance. Never mind that some of the instruments were secondhand and the musicians didn't make as much money as they deserved. Big crowds listened with rapt attention. From the most forgetful old-timer to the most fidgety baby, people soaked up the music as if it were sunshine. Harlem in the 1920s was a place for African Americans to show their culture and their spirit.

Write

Imagine you can hear the group in the picture on page 728 playing. Write a description of their music. Use words from the Words to Know list.

Will C. J. ever find
what he's looking for?

BY DEBBIE A. TAYLOR
ILLUSTRATED BY FRANK MORRISON

Sweet Music in Harlem

Genre

Realistic fiction has characters, settings, and actions that seem real, but the author has made them up. As you read, look for details that make the story seem realistic.

"C. J., where can my hat be?" called Uncle Click from the bathroom. "That photographer from *Highnote* magazine will be out front in an hour, and I've got to look good. It's not every day a Harlem trumpet player gets his picture taken."

C. J. smiled at the old poster on the wall. A young Uncle Click with a snappy black beret blew a gleaming trumpet. C. J. looked at that poster every morning and dreamed of standing onstage, blowing his own sweet music for a roomful of admiring folks.

During the four years he had lived with Uncle Click, C. J. had learned to hold his clarinet just right, to practice every day, and to keep a penny in his shoe for good luck. When he blew out the candles on his birthday cake next week, he'd wish that one day his own picture would be on a poster too. But for now C. J. just tried to make his notes ring out clear and strong from his dented, secondhand clarinet.

Uncle Click chuckled as he walked into the room. "Those were the days," he said, nodding at the poster. "Back then I played the meanest trumpet in Harlem. Now all I do is lose things."

"Don't worry, Uncle Click. I'll find your hat," C. J. said. "Where could you have left it?"

"Well," said Uncle Click as he looked behind the couch. "Last night I stopped at the barbershop and the diner. Later on I jammed at the Midnight Melody Club . . ." Uncle Click's voice trailed off as he searched under the cushion of his favorite chair.

When music was on Uncle Click's mind, he forgot everything else. He could have left his hat anywhere, and there wasn't much time to find it.

C. J. ran down the street. The striped pole outside Garlic's Barbershop glistened like a candy cane. Inside, the place buzzed as everyone talked at once. At Garlic's, neighborhood news traveled faster than a subway train speeding downtown.

"Did you see that Kansas City drummer cut loose at the Midnight Melody last night?" one of the men shouted.

"Yeah, he was cool, but it sure was hot in there!" someone else replied.

Mr. Garlic talked louder than anyone. A toothpick jutting from the corner of his mouth bounced up and down as he scolded a fidgety customer.

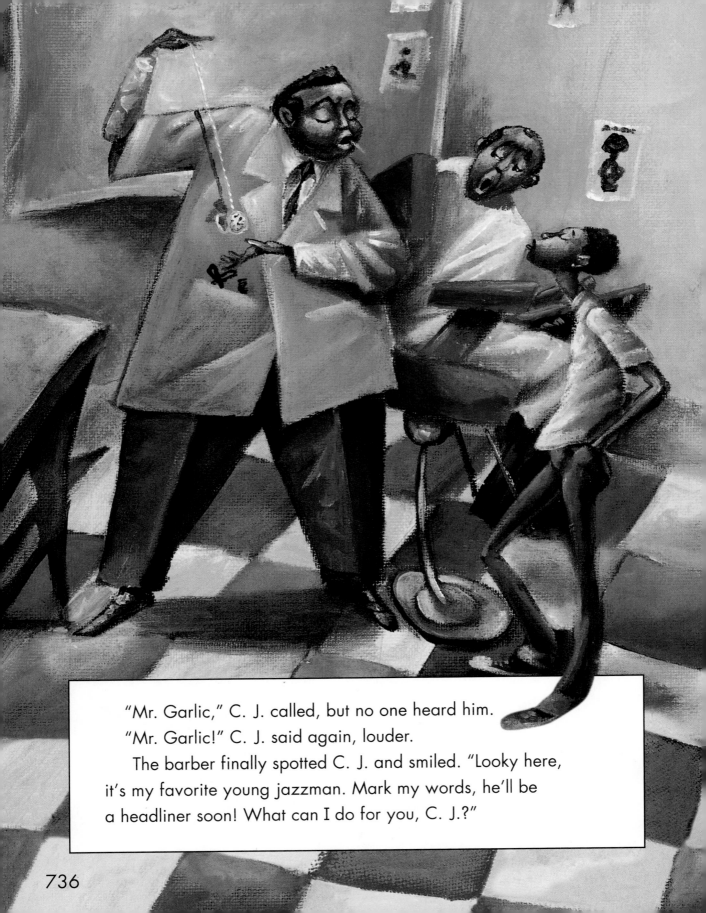

"Mr. Garlic," C. J. called, but no one heard him.

"Mr. Garlic!" C. J. said again, louder.

The barber finally spotted C. J. and smiled. "Looky here, it's my favorite young jazzman. Mark my words, he'll be a headliner soon! What can I do for you, C. J.?"

"A photographer from *Highnote* magazine is coming soon," C. J. blurted out, "and Uncle Click lost his hat. Did he leave it here?"

"Your uncle didn't leave his hat, but he did leave this," said Mr. Garlic, holding up a shiny watch. "When Click blows his horn that barber pole spins, but he *is* a little forgetful."

C. J. thanked Mr. Garlic and slipped the watch into his pocket.

"You say some photographer is coming from *Highnote*?" Mr. Garlic said. "Well, a photo without big Charlie Garlic wouldn't be much of a picture, right folks?"

As C. J. hurried away, he could hear the people in the barbershop buzzing about the photographer. "I've got to find that hat," C. J. muttered to himself.

C. J. rushed around the corner and into the jam-packed Eat and Run Diner. Just inside the door he jumped back as a waitress zipped past, balancing plates of ham and eggs on one arm and home fries and sausage on the other.

The waitress grinned at C. J., her apron still swaying from her dash across the room. "Hey, C. J.," she said.

"Hi, Mattie Dee," said C. J. "Did Uncle Click leave his hat here? A photographer from *Highnote* magazine is coming to take his picture in a few minutes, and Uncle Click needs his hat."

"Honey, Click didn't leave his hat, but he did leave this," said Mattie Dee. She pulled a handkerchief from her pocket and dropped it into C. J.'s hand.

"Your uncle leaves his things all over Harlem, but when he wails on his trumpet, the saltshakers bounce! And if you keep practicing, one day you'll make them bounce too."

"Thanks for the hankie, Mattie Dee," C. J. said.

"Did you say a photographer from *Highnote* is coming?" Mattie Dee asked. "I'd love to be in the picture—especially if I can stand right next to your handsome uncle."

As C. J. left the diner, he could hear Mattie Dee telling her customers about the photographer. "But I've still got to find Uncle Click's hat!" C. J. moaned.

C. J. raced down the block, then bounded down the stairs of the Midnight Melody Club. Even though the club was closed, eight musicians were crowded onto the small stage, playing as if it were still show time. The bass player's eyes glistened as he plucked his instrument. The vibraphone player tapped the keys with his eyes closed.

"C. J.!" the drummer shouted without losing the beat. "We're saving a spot for you here. I reckon you'll be joining us in a few years."

A woman strolled toward C. J. from the back of the club. She didn't seem to notice that it wasn't nighttime. She still wore a fancy dress, and rings glittered on her fingers.

"Miss Alma!" C. J. called. "A photographer from *Highnote* magazine is coming to take Uncle Click's picture, and he can't find his hat. Did he leave it onstage last night?"

Canary Alma shook her head. "Your uncle didn't leave his hat here, but he did leave this," she said, and plucked a bow tie from the piano bench. "He's forgetful, but when Click blows his trumpet the wallpaper curls."

C. J. thanked Canary Alma and slid the tie over his wrist.

"A photographer from *Highnote*!" Canary Alma exclaimed, smoothing her dress. "My face next to your uncle's will give that photo a touch a class."

C. J.'s shoulders drooped as he left the Midnight Melody Club. He didn't want to disappoint Uncle Click, but he just couldn't find that hat anywhere.

C. J. dragged his feet up the steps of the brownstone where his uncle waited. A lump like a sour ball wedged in C. J.'s throat.

"Uncle Click," C. J. said. "I didn't find your hat, but I did find these." He held out the watch, the handkerchief, and the bow tie.

Uncle Click looked at C. J., and a huge smile spread across his face. "Looks like you found something else too," he said, pointing behind C. J.

C. J. turned around. Big Charlie Garlic, Mattie Dee, and Canary Alma were walking down the street toward them. But they weren't alone! They were followed by men from the barbershop, people from the diner, and musicians from the Midnight Melody Club. There were also folks C. J. had never seen before and people he'd only seen on posters or record covers.

"Hey, Click," called Charlie Garlic. "You sure know how to gather a crowd."

"Wasn't me," said Uncle Click, winking at C. J.

C. J. could hardly believe his eyes. Here were some of the greatest musicians and singers in Harlem. It was like seeing the sun, the moon, and the stars all shining at once.

"Your nephew drew a crowd without even blowing a note!" said Charlie Garlic. "He won't have any trouble packing them in at the Apollo in a few years."

"I've never seen so many jazzy folks in one place, and right in front of my very own home!" said Uncle Click, a twinkle in his eyes. "This really is something special. Who needs a hat to appreciate that?"

"The photographer's here!" someone yelled.

Everyone scrambled to get a good spot on the steps. There were so many people, some ended up sitting on the curb and standing on the sidewalk.

The photographer laughed from behind his camera. "Guess I'd better use a wider lens!" he called.

As the photographer adjusted his camera, the crowd settled into position for the picture.

"Smile!" the photographer finally shouted, and then *POP!*, a bright light flashed.

Laughter and clapping filled the air.

That night as C. J. lay in bed, light from the hallway crept into his room. Uncle Click stood in the doorway with a large box wrapped in bright red paper.

"I know your birthday's not until next week," said Uncle Click, "but I wanted to give you this before all the magic of today wears off."

C. J. opened the box and lifted out a black case. His eyes widened as he raised the lid. Inside, nestled in velvet, was a brand-new clarinet.

"It's perfect!" C. J. said, cradling the horn gently in his hands.

C. J. hugged his uncle tightly. Then he noticed something else in the box. "Uncle Click, your hat!"

"Well, look at that!" said Uncle Click. "It must have fallen in there last night when I was wrapping your present."

"You know, a jazzman like you is going to need a good hat," said Uncle Click as he placed the beret neatly on C. J.'s head. "Besides, I'm getting used to not wearing one."

C. J. adjusted the hat and put the clarinet to his lips. He started to blow while his fingers danced over the keys. Uncle Click beamed and nodded to the beat as C. J.'s own sweet music rang out clear and strong for the most admiring audience in all of Harlem.

747

Reader Response

Open for Discussion Why call this story *Sweet Music in Harlem* instead of *The Lost Hat* or *A Gift for C. J.*? How does the actual title help you focus on what's most important in this story?

1. With just a few words, the author makes you see a character: Charlie Garlic with his toothpick, Canary Alma's "touch of class." Find other examples that bring this story's characters to life.

2. Early in the story the author gives the reader an idea of where C. J. will be going for the rest of the story. Look back at page 733 to find these places. Where is C. J. going and why?

3. Think about the way you feel about the music you like. How does it compare with the way C. J. and the other characters in the story feel about music? How are their feelings and yours alike and different?

4. The sweet music in Harlem was jazz. Make a web with *jazz* at the center. Around it, place the names of instruments that jazz musicians use. Include words from the Words to Know list and from the selection.

Look Back and Write Where was Uncle Click's hat? Reread the last two pages of the story. Then write about where the hat was finally found and whether it got there by accident.

Frank Morrison

Read more books about performers.

Frank Morrison is a noted painter whose works are collected for their artistic value. He brings a canvas alive with beauty. He is known for his special style with its long, thin, dramatic figures. Although he had an interest in art early in life, he didn't know that was to be his calling. While visiting the Louvre Museum in Paris, he suddenly realized he wanted to paint.

Comedian Bill Cosby, who takes pride in discovering the artistic talents of African Americans, is a collector of his paintings. Mr. Morrison's works have been seen on television shows, and he was commissioned to create a work for the annual music festival sponsored by *Essence* magazine. This work is titled *Duet*.

Mr. Morrison gets inspiration from his mother and his grandparents. He was born in Massachusetts but now lives with his wife, Connie, and their three children in New Jersey.

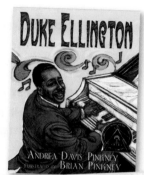

Duke Ellington
by Andrea Davis Pinkney

M is for Music
by Kathleen Krull

Author's Note

Genre

- In an author note, the author of a selection fills the reader in on how or why he or she wrote it.

- An author note is written in the first person. It consists of the author's personal memories and observations.

Text Features

- Author notes often contain anecdotes, short accounts of interesting events. Some anecdotes tell what inspired the author to write the selection.

- Look at the illustrations and ask yourself: "What will the author be telling me about?"

Link to Social Studies

The Harlem District of New York has produced many great artists, including painters, writers, and musicians. Research some of these artists.

SWEET MUSIC IN HARLEM: Author's Note

BY DEBBIE A. TAYLOR

Sweet Music in Harlem was inspired by a photograph on a T-shirt my husband was wearing one day. In the photograph a crowd of famous jazz musicians poses on the steps of a brownstone in Harlem, New York, while children sit on the curb. I wondered who those children were and what they might have thought about seeing all those people gathered on their street.

Months later, on the way to a hotel in St. Louis, I passed nightclubs, restaurants, and streets with jazz-related names. They reminded me of that picture of jazz musicians. As I sat in the hotel eating breakfast the next morning, the plot of the story evolved clearly. A boy named C. J. started racing through Harlem, trying to find his uncle's missing hat in time for a photo shoot for a jazz magazine.

The picture on that shirt was taken in 1958 by Art Kane, a young photographer on his first assignment for *Esquire* magazine. He had invited some musicians to a photo shoot in Harlem, not knowing if anyone would show up. Magically, the news spread quickly, and fifty-seven of the greatest men and women of jazz gathered, as well as some curious neighborhood children!

Sequence What events inspired the author?

75

The jazz greats in the historic photograph above are numbered for your reference:

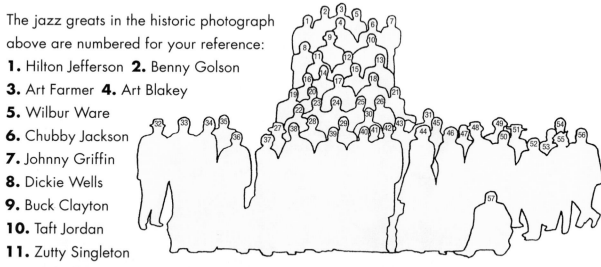

1. Hilton Jefferson **2.** Benny Golson

3. Art Farmer **4.** Art Blakey

5. Wilbur Ware

6. Chubby Jackson

7. Johnny Griffin

8. Dickie Wells

9. Buck Clayton

10. Taft Jordan

11. Zutty Singleton

12. Red Allen **13.** Tyree Glenn **14.** Sonny Greer **15.** Jimmy Jones

16. Miff Mole **17.** Jay C. Higginbotham **18.** Charles Mingus

19. Jo Jones **20.** Gene Krupa **21.** Osie Johnson

22. Max Kaminsky **23.** George Wettling **24.** Bud Freeman
25. Pee Wee Russell **26.** Buster Bailey **27.** Jimmy Rushing
28. Scoville Brown **29.** Bill Crump **30.** Ernie Wilkins
31. Sonny Rollins **32.** Gigi Gryce **33.** Hank Jones **34.** Eddie Locke
35. Horace Silver **36.** Luckey Roberts **37.** Maxine Sullivan **38.** Joe
Thomas **39.** Stuff Smith **40.** Coleman Hawkins **41.** Rudy Powell
42. Oscar Pettiford **43.** Sahib Shihab **44.** Marian McPartland
45. Lawrence Brown **46.** Mary Lou Williams **47.** Emmett Berry
48. Thelonious Monk **49.** Vic Dickenson **50.** Milt Hinton **51.** Lester
Young **52.** Rex Stewart **53.** J. C. Heard **54.** Gerry Mulligan
55. Roy Eldridge **56.** Dizzy Gillespie **57.** Count Basie

Reading Across Texts

Both selections are about inspiration. Think about what
inspired C. J. and what inspired Debbie Taylor.

Writing Across Texts Explain what inspired C. J. and
Debbie and why. Then tell about something that inspires
you and explain why.

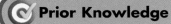 **Prior Knowledge**   Have you heard of some of these musicians?

Limericks

There was an Old Man with a beard,
Who said, "It is just as I feared!
   Two Owls and a Hen,
   Four Larks and a Wren,
Have all built their nests in my beard!"
Edward Lear

A bridge engineer, Mister Crumpett,
Built a bridge for the good River Bumpett.
   A mistake in the plan
   Left a gap in the span,
But he said, "Well, they'll just have to jump it."
   Anonymous

Sunflakes

by Frank Asch

If sunlight fell like snowflakes,
gleaming yellow and so bright,
we could build a sunman,
we could have a sunball fight,
we could watch the sunflakes
drifting in the sky.
We could go sleighing
in the middle of July
through sundrifts and sunbanks,
we could ride a sunmobile,
and we could touch sunflakes—
I wonder how they'd feel.

Almost Human

by Pat Moon

Come and see the people, dear.
Oh, look how they sit!
Aren't they sweet
The way they laugh?
I really must admit
That they seem quite intelligent.
Just hear the sounds they make;
You could almost believe
They're trying to communicate.

They're very easily trained
And respond to simple rules.
Just watch how they point and wave
As we swim around the pool.
See how they stand and clap
When we dive through the hoop?
And the noise they make
When we walk on our tails
Or leap the bar in one swoop!

Just watch how they jump and shout
In my favorite part of the shows
When we dive and splash the water
All over the front few rows.

It's time to leave them now, dear,
They've had enough for one day.
It's quite amazing what people can do
If you treat them in the right way.

The Bat

by Theodore Roethke

By day the bat is cousin to the mouse.
He likes the attic of an aging house.

His fingers make a hat about his head.
His pulse beat is so slow we think him dead.

He loops in crazy figures half the night
Among the trees that face the corner light.

But when he brushes up against a screen,
We are afraid of what our eyes have seen:

For something is amiss or out of place
When mice with wings can wear a human face.

Be Careful What You Wish For

King Midas learned to be careful what he wished for. Work with a small group. Plan a skit about another character who yearns for something that leads to unexpected consequences. Make simple costumes or gather props. Practice your skit and then present it to the class.

The Girl Who Wanted to Live Underwater

What can we learn from encounters with the unexpected?

Unexpected Results

connect to
SCIENCE

"The Mystery of Saint Matthew Island" shows a chain of events that leads to a tragedy. Research another event where a new, non-native species is introduced with disastrous results—for example, rabbits in Australia or the African honey bee in South America. Draw a cause-and-effect diagram to explain the disaster that resulted. Use illustrations in your diagram.

Causes and Effects of The Mystery of Saint Matthew Island

Observation Log

connect to
WRITING

Unexplained events are all around you. Pay close attention to an event in your own life or in the news. Make entries in a log about your observations. Record your thoughts about possible causes of the event, clues that help point to an answer, and, if possible, the actual causes or results, once they become known.

Tuesday, Back Yard

There are two small sets of footprints leading up to the garden. They suddenly stop under the bird feeder and walk around in one

Answering Questions Well

Different Kinds of Questions

As a student, you must answer many questions.

- Your teacher asks you questions.
- Your textbooks contain questions.
- Practice books and workbooks contain questions.
- The tests you must take are full of questions.

Some tests have one kind of question. Other tests have more than one kind of question.

You might find multiple-choice or fill-in-the-blank questions. You might be asked to write your answers. If you write, your answers might have to be short or long.

To help you answer questions and take tests, read the pages that follow. You will learn strategies to help you read questions and find the answers. You can also use these strategies when you take tests. Some pages ask you to try to find the answers yourself. Write your answers on a separate sheet of paper.

Remember, you can develop the skills you need to do well.

A Lifelong Skill

The skills you are learning will help you do well on tests while you are in school. They will also help you after you finish school.

Throughout your life, you will have to answer questions that come from many sources. You may need to answer questions on a job. You will need to understand what you are being asked and to answer the best you can.

Tips for Tests
Study for a test, but don't worry ahead of time. Get a good night's rest. Eat a good breakfast. Then, believe in yourself. Help yourself take a test by knowing you can do it. You have studied. You have learned test-taking skills. You are prepared!

Understand the Question

Key Words

Before you can answer a question in a book or on a test, you must understand it. One way is to find key words. These tips will help you.

Read the question slowly. Ask yourself, "Who or what is this question about?" The words that tell who or what the question is about are **key words.**

Look for other key words in the question. Often the first word of the question is another key word. The first word might be *who, what, where, when,* or *how.*

Read the sentence and the sample question. Notice the key words.

> Look for **key words** in the question. The question often uses words that are clues to the answer.

The first bicycle appeared in Europe in the late 1700s.

1 *When* did the first bicycle appear in Europe?

Turn the question into a statement. Use the key words in a sentence that begins "I need to find out. . . ." After you read a question that begins with *when*, you might think to yourself, "I need to find out *when*. . . ." You might think, "I need to find out *when* the first bicycle appeared in Europe." Then look back at the text. The answer is "the late 1700s."

Here is a sample text.

A dolphin uses sonar to guide itself through the water. Sonar tells the dolphin how far away an object is.

Here is a sample question about the text. See how one student makes sure she understands the question.

Test Question

1 What does a dolphin use to guide itself through the water?

I've read the question. What is it about? Well, it's talking about a dolphin and what it uses to guide itself through water. **Dolphin** and **guide** must be key words.

Okay, I'm going to read the question again. There's the key word **what**, and there's the key word **guide**. I need to find out what a dolphin uses to guide itself through water.
The answer must be "sonar."

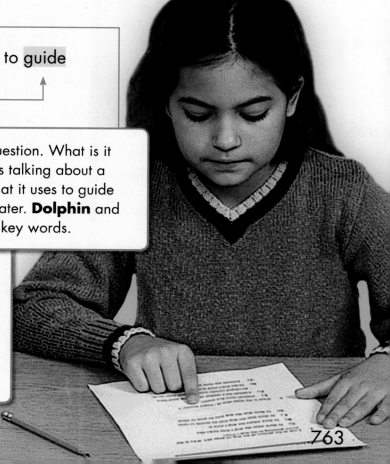

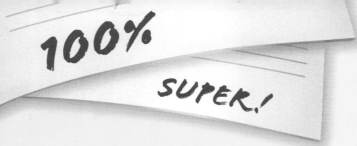

100%

SUPER!

Here are strategies that will help you when you answer questions anytime. Think about each one. Which have you tried before? Which are new to you?

In the Book

Sometimes the answer to a question is **in the book.** You can find these answers right there in the text.

Right There

- The answer is RIGHT THERE in one spot in the text.

- The answer is usually easy to find.

- You can put your finger on the answer.

Think and Search

- The answer IS in the text, but NOT in one spot.

- You need to SEARCH for the answer in different parts of the text.

- You need to THINK how to put the information together.

In My Head

Sometimes the answers to questions are **in your head.**
The answers are NOT right there in the text.

Author and Me

- The answer is NOT written in the text.

- The AUTHOR gives you clues about the answer.

- You also must use what YOU already know.

- You put all this together to find the best answer.

On My Own

- The answer is NOT in the text at all.

- You must think about what you already know.

- You need to use your background knowledge to answer the question.

I Can Find the Answer

In the Book

Right There

When you answer questions, sometimes you can find the answer RIGHT THERE in the text. It may be in one sentence.

Read this selection and the test question. Notice that the answer is RIGHT THERE in the text. You can find it in one sentence and put your finger on it. The answer is highlighted for you.

The answer is **right there.**

George Washington is best known for being the first president of the United States. What many people don't know about Washington is that he was a very shy man. During his lifetime, he refused many honors. One honor he refused was a plan to **build a monument** to him. It was not until 34 years after his death that plans were finally made to build a monument in his honor.

1 What did Washington think of the plan to **build a monument** to him?

- (A) He died before he knew about the plan.
- (B) He refused the honor.
- (C) He said no president could accept an honor.
- (D) He said it was too soon to honor him.

When you read a question in a book or for a test, decide what the key words are. Then look for the key words in the text. The key words in this question are marked for you in bold type. Find the answer near the key words in the text.

Try It!

Now you decide the correct answers. Read this selection and the questions. Look for key words in the questions and in the text. Find the answers RIGHT THERE in the text.

Ferdinand Magellan, a sea captain, said he could find a shorter way to the Spice Islands by traveling west instead of east. On September 20, 1519, he sailed from Spain with five ships and 241 crew members. They crossed the Atlantic Ocean to the coast of South America, where they looked for a passage to the Pacific Ocean. At the tip of South America they found a narrow waterway, now known as the Strait of Magellan. Magellan sailed through this strait to the Pacific on November 28, 1520.

> Read carefully. Look for key words in the question. Then look for them in the text.

> Remember: Sometimes you can find the answer to a test question **right there** in the text. The answer is often near the key words in the text.

1 Why did Magellan travel west instead of east?

- (A) to find the tip of South America
- (B) to find the Spice Islands in South America
- (C) to sail along the South American coast
- (D) to find a shorter way to the Spice Islands

2 What is the Strait of Magellan?

- (F) a land route across South America
- (G) the name of Magellan's expedition
- (H) a narrow waterway at the tip of South America
- (J) a paper given to Magellan from the king of Spain

767

Think and Search

Sometimes when you take a test or write answers in class, you cannot put your finger right on the answer. You may need to SEARCH for the answer in two or more places in the text or a graphic source. Then you need to THINK how to put the information together for your answer.

Read this selection and study the circle graph. Notice that the key words are in bold type in the question, in the selection, and in the graph. To find the answer, you need to combine information from *both* the selection and the graph.

Amelia Earhart was an amazing pilot whose life was cut short. In 1937, **Amelia Earhart** disappeared **without a trace** on a flight over the Pacific Ocean.

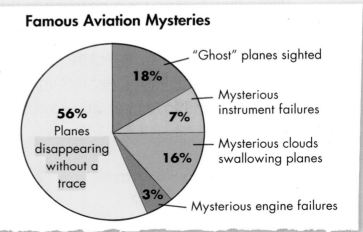

Famous Aviation Mysteries

- 18% — "Ghost" planes sighted
- 7% — Mysterious instrument failures
- 16% — Mysterious clouds swallowing planes
- 3% — Mysterious engine failures
- 56% Planes disappearing without a trace

1 What **percentage** of planes **disappeared** in the same way as **Amelia Earhart's**?

- (A) 7%
- (B) 16%
- (C) 18%
- (D) 56%

The text tells you that "Amelia Earhart disappeared without a trace." Almost the same words appear in the circle graph, along with a percentage figure. Put together the information from both places to find answer D.

768

Try It!

Now you decide the correct answers. Read this selection and these test questions. Remember that you may have to SEARCH in more than one place to find the answers. Then THINK about how the information fits together.

Earth and Mars are alike in some ways and different in others. Mars is 142 million miles from the sun. Mars has a reddish color, while Earth is blue. A Martian day is $24\frac{1}{2}$ hours long. No vegetation has yet been discovered on Mars. A great deal of land on Earth is covered with vegetation.

CATEGORY	EARTH
Distance from the sun	93 million miles
Color	blue
Length of day	almost 24 hours

Decide what the key words are. Look for them in the text and chart.

Remember: You may have to **search** for information in both the text and the chart. **Think** how the information fits together.

1 Compared with Mars, how many miles closer to the sun is Earth?

- (A) 39 million
- (B) 49 million
- (C) 50 million
- (D) 142 million

2 In which category are Mars and Earth alike?

- (F) length of day
- (G) color
- (H) distance from the sun
- (J) amount of ice

In My Head

Author and Me

Sometimes your reading does not give you every part of the answer to a question. You have to find the answer by putting together what the author tells you and what you already know. YOU and the AUTHOR work together.

Read the text and the question. Notice how the author gives you some of the information you need to answer the question. A sample answer is written for you.

> Once upon a time there was a princess who lived in a very nice castle. She had many things, but she was bored. She wanted a friend to play with. She decided to hold a friendship contest. Three sisters entered the contest. The first sister brought the princess many fine toys. The second sister brought delicious food. But the third sister brought nothing. Instead she told the princess stories and riddles, taught her new games, and made her laugh. When the sisters left, the princess knew what to do.

To answer the question, you need to predict an outcome. Use the clue the **author** tells you and what **you** already know about how people will probably act.

1 What will the princess do?

I think the princess will choose the third sister. The princess was bored. She wanted someone to play with. The first two sisters brought gifts, but the third sister played with the princess. The princess wasn't bored anymore.

Try It!

Now you decide the best answers. Read the text and the questions. Think about what the AUTHOR tells you and what YOU know.

Laura's knees shook as she sat down on the chair in the center of the stage and tuned her guitar. She looked out into the audience and saw her parents sitting in the front row. Laura was afraid she had forgotten every note. Then she took a deep breath and began to play. She forgot everything but the music. She could feel each note she played. When Laura finished, she heard the sound of applause. She saw her mother smiling. Her father was wiping a tear from his eye.

Read carefully. Look for clues from the author about how the characters feel.

Remember: Sometimes you and the author work together. Information from the **author** + information from **me** = the best answer.

1 Which sentence best tells how Laura's parents probably feel after Laura performs?

(A) Laura's mother feels happy but her father feels sad.

(B) Both parents feel relieved that the recital is over.

(C) Both parents feel happy and proud of Laura.

(D) Laura's father feels happier than her mother does.

2 Which phrase best describes the change in Laura from the time she sits down to the time she plays?

(F) from fear to calm

(G) from worry to doubt

(H) from sadness to joy

(J) from happiness to pride

I Can Find the Answer

In My Head

On My Own

Sometimes the answer to a test question or a question in a book is *not* in the selection. It is in your head. You have to think about what you already know. For this kind of question, you can answer ON YOUR OWN.

Sometimes a test will ask you to write about a topic. Your answer should give details that tell what you know about the topic. Read this selection, test directions, and one student's answer.

> The key words are highlighted. They tell the *topic* to write about.

Sheila and Mike were talking about time capsules. They each wrote a list of things to put into a time capsule if they could. Sheila's list included her first pair of baby shoes and her fifth-grade report card. Mike's list included his father's wedding ring and a poster from the Olympics.

Directions: What would you put into a time capsule so that people in later years will know about you? You might include objects that tell about your family, your favorite things, or anything else you like. Write about what you would put into a time capsule and why the objects have meaning for you.

> Notice that the answer came from the student's personal ideas and experiences.

My time capsule would contain the postcards my grandmother sent me. I like to collect pictures of different places. I would put my mother's photo album inside too. It shows how close our family is. I like flags, so I would include my state flag and a flag of the United States.

772

Try It!

Read the text below. Notice that you do not need the text to write your answer. Remember that sometimes you need to write an answer ON YOUR OWN.

Tennis is the best sport to learn. First of all, it's an inexpensive sport. All you need for tennis is a racket, tennis balls, and the right shoes. Also, it's a fun way to get good exercise. And it's a great way to get out of doors into the fresh air. Finally, it is a sport that can be enjoyed by people of all ages. Everyone should play tennis.

Read the directions carefully. Find key words that tell you what topic to write about.

Directions: What is your favorite sport or activity? Is it one that you can play, or one you like to watch other people play, like baseball? Tell about your favorite sport or activity and why you enjoy it more than other sports or activities. Write your answer on a separate sheet of paper.

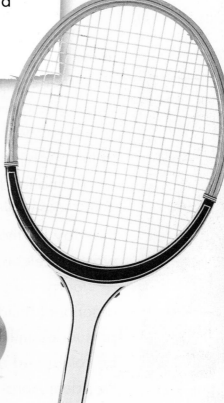

Remember to think about the topic before you write so you can give clear details about your own ideas.

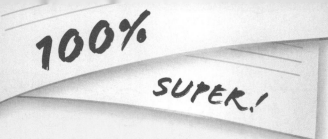

Practice Test

100% SUPER!

In the Book	In My Head
Right There	Author and Me
Think and Search	On My Own

Directions: Read this selection. Then answer the questions that follow. Write the correct letter of each answer. **Use a separate sheet of paper.**

The summer of 1621 was a successful one for the Pilgrims in the Massachusetts Bay Colony. The corn harvest was large. Governor Bradford called for a three-day feast to celebrate. A thanksgiving feast to which both Pilgrims and Native Americans came was held on July 30, 1623. This custom of holding a day of thanksgiving spread to other colonies.

The national holiday began years later. On November 26, 1789, George Washington asked Americans to give thanks on that day for their new freedom. Although successful, the holiday was not celebrated nationwide again for some time.

Today we give Sarah Hale credit for making Thanksgiving a national holiday. As the editor of *Godey's Lady's Book,* she persuaded millions of Americans that Thanksgiving Day should be celebrated as a national holiday every year. In 1863, President Abraham Lincoln spoke with Sarah Hale about her idea. After their meeting, Lincoln declared the last Thursday of

774

November to be the day set aside for a national Thanksgiving.

Then, in 1941, Congress officially declared the fourth Thursday of November to be Thanksgiving Day in the United States. This declaration remains official today.

1 Today, who is given credit for making Thanksgiving a national holiday?

(A) George Washington
(B) Abraham Lincoln
(C) Congress
(D) Sarah Hale

2 What can you conclude about *Godey's Lady's Book*?

(F) It was written for members of Congress.
(G) Millions of Americans read it in the mid-1800s.
(H) Godey was the editor.
(J) Abraham Lincoln never heard of it.

3 For what did Americans give thanks in 1789?

(A) their new freedom
(B) the large harvest
(C) a nationwide holiday
(D) George Washington

4 Which is the most likely reason to hold Thanksgiving in November?

(F) The Pilgrims had Thanksgiving in November.
(G) November is a cold month.
(H) The first nationwide Thanksgiving was in November.
(J) Corn is harvested in the autumn months.

5 When did Congress officially make Thanksgiving the fourth Thursday of November?

(A) 1863
(B) 1940
(C) 1941
(D) 1931

6 Write about your favorite holiday. Tell why it is important to you and how you celebrate the holiday.

Glossary

How to Use This Glossary

This glossary can help you understand and pronounce some of the words in this book. The entries in this glossary are in alphabetical order. There are guide words at the top of each page to show you the first and last words on the page. A pronunciation key is at the bottom of every other page. Remember, if you can't find the word you are looking for, ask for help or check a dictionary.

The entry word is in dark type. It shows how the word is spelled and how the word is divided into syllables.

The pronunciation is in parentheses. It also shows which syllables are stressed.

Part-of-speech labels show the function or functions of an entry word and any listed form of that word.

ad·vise (ad vīz′), **1.** *V.* to give advice to; offer an opinion to; counsel: *I shall act as you advised.* **2.** *V.* to give notice; inform: *We were advised that a storm was approaching, so we didn't go sailing.* ❑ *V.* **ad·vised, ad·vis·ing.**

Sometimes, irregular and other special forms will be shown to help you use the word correctly.

The definition and example sentence show you what the word means and how it is used.

Aa

ab·do·men (ab′də mən), *N.* the part of the body containing the stomach, the intestines, and other important organs; belly.

ab·o·rig·i·ne (ab′ə rij′ə nē), *N.* one of the earliest known inhabitants of Australia. ❑ *N. PL.* **ab·o·rig·i·nes.**

ab·sence (ab′səns), *N.* condition of being without; lack: *Darkness is the absence of light.*

ac·com·plish·ment (ə kom′plish mənt), *N.* something that has been done with knowledge, skill, or ability; achievement: *The teachers were proud of the pupils' accomplishments.*

a·chieve (ə chēv′), *V.* to carry out to a successful end; accomplish; do: *Have you achieved your purpose?* ❑ *V.* **a·chieved, a·chiev·ing.**

ac·quaint (ə kwānt′), *V.* to make aware; let know; inform: *Let me acquaint you with your new duties.* ❑ *V.* **ac·quain·ted, ac·quain·ting.**

ad·mir·ing·ly (ad mīr′ing lē), *ADV.* With wonder, pleasure, and approval: *We gazed admiringly at the beautiful painting.*

a·dorn (ə dôrn′), *V.* to add beauty to; put ornaments on; decorate: *She adorned her hair with flowers.* ❑ *V.* **a·dorned, a·dorn·ing.**

ad·vice (ad vīs′), *N.* opinion about what should be done; suggestion: *My advice is that you study more.*

ad·vise (ad vīz′), **1.** *V.* to give advice to; offer an opinion to; counsel: *I shall act as you advised.* **2.** *V.* to give notice; inform: *We were advised that a storm was approaching, so we didn't go sailing.* ❑ *V.* **ad·vised, ad·vis·ing.**

a·gree·ment (ə grē′mənt), *N.* harmony in feeling or opinion: *The coaches are in complete agreement that she will be a superb gymnast.*

air·time (âr′tīm), *N.* specific amount of time in a television, radio, or any broadcast media program.

al·gae (al′jē), *N. PL.* group of related living things, mostly living in water.

Alz·heim·er's (älts′hī mərz), *N.* disease of the brain that causes confusion and gradual loss of memory.

a·nat·o·my (ə nat′ə mē), *N.* structure of a living thing: *the anatomy of an earthworm.*

ap·pre·ci·ate (ə prē′shē āt), *V.* to think highly of; recognize the worth or quality of; value; enjoy: *Almost everybody appreciates good food.* ❏ *V.* **ap·pre·ci·at·ed, ap·pre·ci·at·ing.**

ar·chi·tect (är′kə tekt), *N.* person who designs and makes plans for buildings. (*Architect* comes from two Greek words, *archi* meaning "chief" and *tekton* meaning "builder.")

ar·mor (är′mər), *N.* any kind of protective covering. The steel plates of a warship and the bony shell of an armadillo are armor.

armor

ar·ti·fi·cial (är′tə fish′əl), *ADJ.* made by human skill or labor; not natural: *Plastics are artificial substances that do not occur in nature.*

as·cent (ə sent′), *N.* act of going up; upward movement; rising: *The sudden ascent of the elevator made us dizzy.*

as·sign·ment (ə sīn′mənt), *N.* something assigned, especially a piece of work to be done: *Today's assignment in arithmetic consists of ten problems.*

as·ton·ish (ə ston′ish), *V.* to surprise greatly; amaze: *We were astonished by the child's remarkable memory.* ❏ *V.* **as·ton·ished, as·ton·ish·ing.**

au·da·cious (ȯ dā′shəs), *ADJ.* rudely bold; impudent: *The audacious waiter demanded a larger tip.*

Bb

back·flip (bak′ flip), *N.* backward somersault performed in the air. ❏ *N. PL.* **back·flips.**

back·ground (bak′ ground), *N.* the part of a picture or scene toward the back: *The cottage stands in the foreground with the mountains in the background.*

bar·ber (bär′bər), *N.* person whose business is cutting hair and shaving or trimming beards.

bass¹ (bās), **1.** *N.* the lowest male voice in music. **2.** *N.* the largest, lowest sounding stringed instrument in an orchestra or band.

bass² (bas), **1.** *N.* North American freshwater or saltwater fish with spiny fins, used for food.

be·hav·ior (bi hā′vyər), *N.* manner of behaving; way of acting: *Her sullen behavior showed that she was angry.*

bel·fry (bel′frē), *N.* space in a tower in which a bell or bells may be hung.

a	in hat	ō	in open	sh	in she
ā	in age	ȯ	in all	th	in thin
â	in care	ô	in order	ᴛʜ	in then
ä	in far	oi	in oil	zh	in measure
e	in let	ou	in out	ə	= a in about
ē	in equal	u	in cup	ə	= e in taken
ėr	in term	u̇	in put	ə	= i in pencil
i	in it	ü	in rule	ə	= o in lemon
ī	in ice	ch	in child	ə	= u in circus
o	in hot	ng	in long		

ben·e·fac·tor (ben′ə fak′tər), *N.* person who has given money or kindly help. (*Benefactor* comes from two Latin words, *bene* meaning "well" or "good" and *facere* meaning "do.")

be·queath (bi kwēth′), *V.* to give or leave by means of a will when a person dies: *He bequeathed his fortune to his children.* ❑ *V.* **be·queathed, be·queath·ing.**

bleach (blēch), *V.* to whiten by exposing to sunlight or by using chemicals: *animal skulls bleached by the desert sun.* ❑ *V.* **bleached, bleach·ing.**

blen·der (blen′dər), *N.* an electric kitchen appliance for grinding, mixing, or beating various foods.

blu·ish (blü′ish), *ADJ.* somewhat blue; somewhat like the color of the clear sky in daylight.

bluish

blun·der (blun′dər), *N.* a stupid mistake: *Misspelling the title of a book is a silly blunder to make in a book report.* ❑ *N. PL.* **blun·ders.**

bound·ar·y (boun′dər ē), *N.* a limiting line or thing; limit; border: *the boundary between Canada and the United States.* ❑ *N. PL.* **bound·aries.**

brack·ish (brak′ish), **1.** *ADJ.* slightly salty. Coastal marshes often have brackish waters. **2.** *ADJ.* bad-tasting.

brand (brand), **1.** *N.* a certain kind, grade, or make: *Do you like this brand of flour?* **2.** *V.* to mark by burning the skin with a hot iron: *The cowboys branded the cows.* ❑ *V.* **brand·ed, brand·ing.**

break·fast (brek′fəst), *V.* to eat the first meal of the day. ❑ *V.* **break·fast·ed, break·fast·ing.**

bronze (bronz), *N.* a dark yellow-brown alloy of copper and tin.

Cc

ca·ble (kā′bəl), *N.* a message sent through wires by electric current or electronic signals.

cal·cu·la·tion (kal′kyə lā′shən), *N.* careful thinking; deliberate planning: *The success of the expedition was the result of much calculation.* ❑ *N. PL.* **cal·cu·la·tions.**

cam·e·o (kam′ē ō), *N.* a semiprecious stone carved so that there is a raised design on a background, usually of a different color.

can·non (kan′ən), *N.* a big gun, especially one that is mounted on a base or wheels.

can·tan·ker·ous (kan tang′kər əs), *ADJ.* ready to make trouble; ill-natured; quarrelsome.

car·cass (kär′kəs), *N.* body of a dead animal. ❑ *N. PL.* **car·cass·es.**

cart·wheel (kärt′wēl′), *N.* a sideways handspring with the legs and arms kept straight. ❑ *N. PL.* **cart·wheels.**

cat·er·pil·lar (kat′ər pil′ər), *N.* the wormlike larvae of insects such as butterflies and moths.

cav·i·ty (kav′ə tē), *N.* hollow place; hole. Cavities in teeth are caused by decay. ❑ *N. PL.* **cav·i·ties.**

ce·re·bral pal·sy (ser′ə brəl pȯl′zē), *N.* paralysis caused by damage to the brain before or at birth. Persons suffering from cerebral palsy have trouble coordinating their muscles.

choir (kwīr), *N.* group of singers who sing together, often in a church service.

cir·cum·stance (sėr′kəm stans), **1.** *N.* condition that accompanies an act or event: *Unfavorable circumstances such as fog and rain often delayed us in our trip to the mountains.* **2.** *N.* the existing condition or state of affairs: *He was forced by circumstances to resign.* □ *N. PL.* **cir·cum·stanc·es.**

civ·i·li·za·tion (siv′ə lə zā′shən), *N.* the ways of living of a people or nation: *The civilizations of ancient Egypt and ancient Greece had many contacts over the centuries.*

clar·i·net (klar′ə net′), *N.* a woodwind instrument, having a mouthpiece with a single reed and played by means of holes and keys.

cleanse (klenz), **1.** *V.* to make clean: *cleanse a wound before bandaging it.* **2.** *V.* to make pure: *cleanse the soul.* □ *V.* **cleansed, cleans·ing.**

close-up (klōs′up′), *N.* picture taken with a camera at close range.

cock·le (kok′əl), *N.* any of several kinds of saltwater clams with two-ridged, heart-shaped shells. □ *N. PL.* **cock·les.**

close-up of chimpanzee

co·coon (kə kün′), *N.* case of silky thread spun by the larvae of various insects, to live in while they are developing into adults. Most moth larvae form cocoons.

com·bi·na·tion (kom′bə nā′shən), *N.* series of numbers or letters dialed in opening a certain kind of lock: *Do you know the combination of the safe?*

com·plex (kom′pleks), *ADJ.* hard to understand: *The instructions for building the radio were complex.*

con·ceal (kən sēl′), *V.* to put out of sight; hide: *The murky water concealed the crabs.* □ *V.* **con·cealed, con·ceal·ing.**

con·fi·dence (kon′fə dəns), *N.* firm belief in yourself; self-confidence: *Years of experience at her work have given her great confidence.*

con·ser·va·tion (kon′sər vā′shən), *N.* preservation from harm or decay; protection from loss or from being used up: *Conservation of energy saves fuel.*

con·struct (kən strukt′), *V.* to put together; fit together; build: *construct a bridge.* □ *V.* **con·struct·ed, con·struct·ing.**

con·tri·bute (kən trib′yüt), *V.* to help bring about: *A poor diet contributed to the child's bad health.* □ *V.* **con·tri·but·ed, con·tri·but·ing.**

cove (kōv), *N.* a small, sheltered bay; inlet on the shore.

cramp (kramp), *V.* to shut into a small space; limit: *Living in only three rooms, the family was cramped.* □ *V.* **cramped, cramp·ing.**

a	in hat	ō	in open	sh	in she
ā	in age	ȯ	in all	th	in thin
â	in care	ô	in order	ᴛʜ	in then
ä	in far	oi	in oil	zh	in measure
e	in let	ou	in out	ə	= a in about
ē	in equal	u	in cup	ə	= e in taken
ėr	in term	u̇	in put	ə	= i in pencil
i	in it	ü	in rule	ə	= o in lemon
ī	in ice	ch	in child	ə	= u in circus
o	in hot	ng	in long		

cran·ny (kran′ē), *N.* a small, narrow opening; crack; crevice: *She looked in all the nooks and crannies of the house for the misplaced book.* ❑ *N. PL.* **cran·nies.**

crit·i·cal (krit′ə kəl), *ADJ.* being important to the outcome of a situation: *Help arrived at the critical moment.*

crit·i·cize (krit′ə sīz), *V.* to find fault with; disapprove of; blame: *Do not criticize him until you know all the circumstances.* ❑ *V.* **crit·i·cized, crit·i·ciz·ing.**

cruise (krüz), *V.* to travel in a car, airplane, boat, etc. at the speed at which the vehicle operates best. ❑ *V.* **cruised, cruis·ing.**

Dd

dain·ti·ly (dān′ti lē), *ADV.* with delicate beauty; freshly and prettily: *She daintily wiped her mouth with her napkin.*

deaf·en·ing (def′ən ing), *ADJ.* very loud; amazingly noisy.

de·bris (də brē′), *N.* scattered fragments; ruins; rubbish: *The street was covered with broken glass, stone, and other debris from the storm.*

debris in a landfill

de·cay (di kā′), *N.* process of rotting: *The decay in the tree trunk proceeded so rapidly that the tree fell over in a month.*

dem·on·strate (dem′ən strāt), *V.* to show how a thing is done; explain by using examples. ❑ *V.* **dem·on·strates, dem·on·strat·ed, dem·on·strat·ing.**

de·pressed (di prèst′), *ADJ.* gloomy; low-spirited; sad. (*Depressed* comes from the Latin word *depressum* meaning "pressed down.")

de·vas·ta·tion (dev′ə stā′shən), *N.* the act of laying waste, destroying.

die-off (dī′ òf), *N.* to die one after another until all are dead: *The entire herd experienced a die-off during the drought.*

dig·ni·tar·y (dig′nə ter′ē), *N.* person who has a position of honor: *We saw several foreign dignitaries when we visited the United Nations.* ❑ *N. PL.* **dig·ni·tar·ies.**

di·gress (dī gres′), *V.* to turn aside from the main subject in talking or writing: *I lost interest in the book because the author digressed too much.* ❑ *V.* **di·gressed, di·gres·sing.**

dip·lo·mat (dip′lə mat), *N.* person whose work is to manage the relations between his or her nation and other nations.

dir·i·gi·ble (dir′ə jə bəl), *N.* an airship made with a rigid framework. It is filled with gas that is lighter than air.

dis·lodge (dis loj′), *V.* to drive or force out of a place, position, etc.: *She used a crowbar to dislodge a heavy stone.* ❑ *V.* **dis·lodged, dis·lodg·ing.**

dis·re·spect (dis′ri spekt′), *V.* to show a lack of respect; to be rude. ❑ *V.* **dis·re·spect·ed, dis·re·spect·ing.**

dis·tri·bu·tion (dis′trə byü′shən), *N.* the act of giving some of to each, of dividing and giving out in shares.

drench (drench), *V.* to wet thoroughly; soak: *A sudden, heavy rain drenched us.* ❏ *V.* **drenched, drench·ing.**

drift·wood (drift′wůd′), *N.* wood carried along by water or washed ashore from the water.

du·o (dü′ō), *N.* pair.

Ee

e·co·nom·ic (ek′ə nom′ik), *ADJ.* of or about the management of the income, supplies, and expenses of a household, government, etc.

eer·ie (ir′ē), *ADJ.* causing fear because of strangeness or weirdness: *a dark and eerie old house.*

el·bow (el′bō), **1.** *N.* joint between the upper and lower arm. **2.** *V.* to push with the elbow; make your way by pushing: *Don't elbow me off the sidewalk.* ❏ *V.* **el·bow·ed, el·bow·ing.**

e·merge (i mèrj′), *V.* to come into view; come out; come up: *The sun emerged from behind a cloud.* ❏ *V.* **e·merged, e·mer·ging.**

em·phat·i·cal·ly (em phat′i cal lē), *ADV.* said or done forcefully; strongly.

en·a·ble (en ā′bəl), *V.* to give ability, power, or means to; make able: *The airplane enables people to travel great distances rapidly.* ❏ *V.* **en·abled, en·a·bling.**

en·case (en kās′), *V.* to cover completely; enclose: *A cocoon encased the caterpillar.* ❏ *V.* **en·cases, en·cased, en·cas·ing.**

en·thu·si·as·tic (en thü′zē as′tik), *ADJ.* full of enthusiasm; eagerly interested: *My little brother is very enthusiastic about going to kindergarten.*

en·vi·ron·ment (en vi′rən ment), *N.* condition of the air, water, soil, etc.: *working for a pollution-free environment.*

en·vy (en′vē), *N.* feeling of discontent, dislike, or desire because another person has what you want: *The children were filled with envy when they saw her new bicycle.*

ep·i·sode (ep′ə sōd), *N.* one part of a story that is published or broadcast in several parts, one at a time.

er·a (ir′ə), *N.* a period of time or history: *We live in the era of space exploration.*

e·rect (i rekt′), *V.* to put up; build: *That house was erected 40 years ago.* ❏ *V.* **e·rec·ted, e·rec·ting.**

es·sen·tial (ə sen′shəl), *ADJ.* absolutely necessary; very important: *Good food and enough rest are essential to good health.*

ex·pand (ek spand′), *V.* to make or grow larger; increase in size; enlarge: *The balloon expanded as it was filled with air.* ❏ *V.* **ex·pan·ded, ex·pan·ding.**

ex·plo·sion (ek splō′zhən), *N.* act of bursting with a loud noise; a blowing up: *The explosions of the bombs shook the whole city.*

a	in hat	ō	in open	sh	in she
ā	in age	ȯ	in all	th	in thin
â	in care	ô	in order	ᵺ	in then
ä	in far	oi	in oil	zh	in measure
e	in let	ou	in out	ə	= a in about
ē	in equal	u	in cup	ə	= e in taken
ėr	in term	ů	in put	ə	= i in pencil
i	in it	ü	in rule	ə	= o in lemon
ī	in ice	ch	in child	ə	= u in circus
o	in hot	ng	in long		

ex·qui·site (ek′skwi zit, ek skwiz′it), *ADJ.* very lovely; delicate: *These violets are exquisite.*

ex·tinct (ek stingkt′), *ADJ.* no longer existing.

ex·tra·ter·res·tri·al (ek′strə tə res′trē əl), *N.* a creature from outer space.

an **exquisite** pattern

Ff

fash·ion (fash′ən), *V.* to make, shape, or form: *He fashioned a whistle out of wood.* ❑ *V.* **fash·ioned, fash·ion·ing.**

fast·ball (fast′bȯl′), *N.* a pitch thrown at high speed with very little curve.

fate (fāt), *N.* what becomes of someone or something: *The Revolutionary War decided the fate of the United States.*

fear·less (fir′lis), *ADJ.* without fear; afraid of nothing; brave; daring.

fidg·et·y (fij′ə tē), *ADJ.* restless; uneasy: *That fidgety child keeps twisting and moving.*

flee (flē), *V.* to run away; get away by running: *The robbers were fleeing, but the police caught them.* ❑ *V.* **fled, flee·ing.**

fo·cus (fō′kəs), **1.** *N.* the correct adjustment of a lens, the eye, etc., to make a clear image: *If the camera is not brought into focus, the photograph will be blurred.* **2.** *N.* the central point of attraction, attention, activity, etc.: *The new baby was the focus of attention.*

foot·man (fût′mən), *N.* a uniformed male servant who answers the bell, waits on the table, goes with a car or carriage to open the door, etc. ❑ *N. PL.* **foot·men.**

for·get·ful (fər get′fəl), *ADJ.* apt to forget; having a poor memory: *When I get too tired, I become forgetful.*

foun·da·tion (foun dā′shən), *N.* part on which the other parts rest for support; base: *the foundation of a house.* ❑ *N. PL.* **foundations.**

Gg

gait (gāt), *N.* the kind of steps used in moving; manner of walking or running: *A gallop is one of the gaits of a horse.*

ges·ture (jes′chər), *V.* to make a movement to help express an idea or feeling. ❑ *V.* **ges·tured, ges·tur·ing.**

glim·mer (glim′ər), *N.* a faint, unsteady light.

gnaw (nȯ), *V.* to bite at and wear away: *A mouse has gnawed the cover of this box.* ❑ *V.* **gnawed, gnaw·ing.**

gos·pel (gos′pəl), *N.* religious music with much emotion and enthusiasm, including features of spirituals and jazz.

grat·i·tude (grat′ə tüd), *N.* kindly feeling because of a favor received; desire to do a favor in return; thankfulness. (*Gratitude* comes from the Latin word *gratia* meaning "favor.")

grav·i·ty (grav′ə tē), *N.* the natural force that causes objects to move or tend to move toward the center of the earth. Gravity causes objects to have weight.

green·horn (grēn′hôrn′), *N.* person without training or experience.

gren·a·dier (gren′ə dir′), *N.* a member of a specially chosen unit of foot soldiers. ❑ *N. PL.* **gren·a·diers.**

guar·an·tee (gar′ən tē′), *V.* to make certain that something will happen as a result: *Not studying for a test is a guaranteed way to make a poor grade.* ❑ *V.* **guar·an·teed, guar·an·tee·ing.**

gym·nas·tics (jim nas′tiks), *N.* a sport in which very difficult exercises are performed.

girl doing **gymnastics**

Hh

ham·mock (ham′ək), *N.* a hanging bed or couch made of canvas, cord, etc. It has cords or ropes at each end for hanging it between two trees or posts. ❑ *N. PL.* **ham·mocks.**

hand·i·capped (han′dē kapt′), *ADJ.* having a physical or mental disability.

Ha·nuk·kah (hä′nə kə), *N.* a yearly Jewish festival that lasts eight days, mostly in December. It celebrates the rededication of the temple in Jerusalem after a victory over the Syrians in 165 B.C. Candles are lighted on each of the eight days of Hanukkah.

head·land (hed′lənd), *N.* narrow ridge of high land jutting out into water; promontory.

hes·i·ta·tion (hez′ə tā′shən), *N.* act of failing to act promptly; doubt; indecision.

hid·e·ous (hid′ē əs), *ADJ.* very ugly; frightful; horrible: *a hideous monster.*

hu·mane (hyü mān′), *ADJ.* not cruel or brutal; kind; merciful: *We believe in the humane treatment of animals.*

hus·tle (hus′əl), **1.** *V.* to push or shove roughly or hurriedly; jostle rudely: *Guards hustled the demonstrators away from the mayor's office.* **2.** *V.* to hurry along: *He had to hustle to get the lawn mowed before dinner.* **3.** *V.* INFORMAL. get or sell in a hurried or illegal way. ❑ *V.* **hus·tled, hus·tling.**

hy·dro·gen (hī′drə jən), *N.* a colorless, odorless gas that burns easily. Hydrogen is a chemical element that weighs less than any other element. It combines with oxygen to form water and is present in most organic compounds.

Ii

ich·thy·o·sau·rus (ik′thē ə sôr′əs), *N.* large, fishlike reptile, now extinct, that lived in the sea. It had a long beak, paddlelike flippers, and a tail with a large fin.

a in hat	ō in open	sh in she
ā in age	ȯ in all	th in thin
â in care	ô in order	ŦH in then
ä in far	oi in oil	zh in measure
e in let	ou in out	ə = a in about
ē in equal	u in cup	ə = e in taken
ėr in term	u̇ in put	ə = i in pencil
i in it	ü in rule	ə = o in lemon
ī in ice	ch in child	ə = u in circus
o in hot	ng in long	

im·mi·grant (im′ə grənt), *N.* someone who comes into a country or region to live there: *Canada has many immigrants from Europe.* ❏ *N. PL.* **im·mi·grants.**

in·con·ceiv·a·ble (in′kən sē′və bəl), *ADJ.* hard to imagine or believe; incredible: *It is inconceivable that two nations so friendly for centuries should now be at odds.*

in·con·ven·ience (in′kən vē′nyəns), *N.* something inconvenient; cause of trouble, difficulty, or bother.

in·de·pend·ence (in′di pen′dəns), *N.* freedom from the control, influence, support, or help of others: *The American colonies won independence from England.*

in·no·va·tion (in′ə vā′shən), *N.* change made in the established way of doing things: *The principal made many innovations.* ❏ *N. PL.* **in·no·va·tions.**

in·spire (in spīr′), *V.* to fill with a thought or feeling; influence: *A chance to try again inspired her with hope.* ❏ *V.* **in·spired, in·spir·ing.**

in·tact (in takt′), *ADJ.* with nothing missing or broken; whole; untouched; uninjured: *The missing money was found and returned to the bank intact.*

in·ter·i·or (in tir′ē ər), *N.* inner surface or part; inside: *The interior of the house was beautifully decorated.*

theater **interior**

in·ter·sec·tion (in′tər sek′shən), *N.* point, line, or place where one thing crosses another: *a dangerous intersection.*

in·ves·ti·ga·tion (in ves′tə gā′shən), *N.* a careful search; detailed or careful examination: *An investigation of the accident by the police put the blame on the drivers of both cars.*

i·ras·ci·ble (i ras′ə bəl), *ADJ.* easily made angry.

is·sue (ish′ü), *V.* to send out; put forth: *The government issues money and stamps.* ❏ *V.* **is·sued, is·su·ing.**

Jj

jam (jam), **1.** *V.* to press or squeeze tightly between two surfaces: *The ship was jammed between two rocks.* **2.** *V.* to make music with other musicians without having practiced (*SLANG*). ❏ *V.* **jammed, jamm·ing. 3.** *N.* preserve made by boiling fruit with sugar until thick: *strawberry jam.*

Kk

kelp (kelp), *N.* any of various large, tough, brown seaweeds.

Ll

lair (lâr), *N.* den or resting place of a wild animal.

la·ment (lə ment′), **1.** *V.* to feel or show grief for; mourn aloud for: *We lament the dead.* **2.** *V.* to say sadly, with grief: *She lamented his absence.* ❏ *V.* **la·ment·ed, la·ment·ing.**

land·scape (land′ skāp), *N.* 1 view of scenery on land. 2 picture showing a land scene.

life·less (līf′lis), *ADJ.* without life: *a lifeless statue.*

lime·light (līm′līt′), *N.* center of public attention and interest: *Some people are never happy unless they are in the limelight.*

lin·ger (ling′gər), *V.* to stay on; go slowly, as if unwilling to leave: *He lingers after the others leave.* ❏ *V.* **ling·ered, ling·er·ing.**

log·ger (lȯ′gər), *N.* a person whose work is cutting down and removing trees. ❑ *N. PL.* **log·gers.**

lul·la·by (lul′ə bī), *N.* song for singing to a child in a cradle; soft song to lull a baby to sleep.

lux·ur·y (luk′shər ē), **1.** *N.* use of the best and most costly food, clothes, houses, furniture, and amusements: *The movie star was accustomed to luxury.* **2.** *N.* something pleasant but not necessary: *Candy is a luxury.*

Mm

mag·ni·fy (mag′nə fī), *V.* to cause something to look larger than it actually is; increase the apparent size of an object: *A microscope magnifies bacteria so that they can be seen and studied.*
❑ *V.* **mag·ni·fied, mag·ni·fy·ing.**

match·mak·er (mach′mā′kər), *N.* person who arranges, or tries to arrange, marriages for others.

mer·can·tile (mėr′kən til), *ADJ.* of merchants or trade; commercial: *a mercantile company.*

midst (midst), *N.* in the middle of.

mi·grant (mī′ grənt), *ADJ.* migrating; roving: *a migrant worker.*

min·i·a·ture (min′ē ə ch·r, min′ə chər), *ADJ.* a reduced image or likeness: *miniature furniture for a dollhouse.*

mock (mok), *V.* to laugh at; make fun of: *The student was punished for mocking the kindergartner.*
❑ *V.* **mocked, mock·ing.**

mold¹ (mōld), *N.* a hollow shape in which anything is formed, cast, or solidified, such as the mold into which melted metal is poured to harden into shape, or the mold in which gelatin is left to stiffen.

mold² (mōld), *N.* loose or broken earth.

mon·i·tor (mon′ə tər), **1.** *N.* a television set connected to a computer. ❑ *N. PL.* **mon·i·tors. 2.** *V.* to listen to and check radio or television transmissions, telephone messages, etc., by using a receiver.
❑ *V.* **mon·i·tored, mon·i·tor·ing.**

mon·u·men·tal (mon′yə men′tl), *ADJ.* very great: *monumental ignorance.*

mu·cus (myü′kəs), *N.* a slimy substance produced in the nose and throat to moisten and protect them.

Nn

nau·se·at·ing (nȯ′shē āt ing), *ADJ.* sickening; causing nausea.

Na·zi (nä′tsē *or* nat′sē), *N.* member of the National Socialist Party, a fascist political party in Germany, led by Adolf Hitler. ❑ *N. PL.* **Nazis.**

new·com·er (nü′kum′ər), *N.* person who has just come or who came not long ago.

news·reel (nüz rēl′), *N.* a short news story for a movie audience. ❑ *N. PL.* **news·reels.**

night·time (nīt′tīm′), *N.* time between evening and morning.

nu·tri·tious (nü trish′əs), *ADJ.* valuable as food; nourishing.

a in hat	ō in open	sh in she
ā in age	ȯ in all	th in thin
â in care	ô in order	ᴛʜ in then
ä in far	oi in oil	zh in measure
e in let	ou in out	ə = a in about
ē in equal	u in cup	ə = e in taken
ėr in term	u̇ in put	ə = i in pencil
i in it	ü in rule	ə = o in lemon
ī in ice	ch in child	ə = u in circus
o in hot	ng in long	

Oo

oc·ca·sion (ə kā′zhən), *N.* a special event: *The jewels were worn only on great occasions.*

on·stage (on′stāj′), *ADV.* on the part of a stage that the audience can see: *walk onstage.*

ooze (üz), *N.* a soft mud or slime, especially at the bottom of a pond or river or on the ocean bottom.

out·field (out′fēld′), **1.** *N.* the part of a baseball field beyond the diamond or infield. **2.** *N.* the three players in the outfield.

o·ver·run (ō′vər run′), *V.* to spread over: *Vines overran the wall.* ❑ *V.* **o·ver·ran, o·ver·run·ning.**

Pp

par·a·pet (par′ə pet), *N.* a low wall at the edge of a balcony, roof, or bridge.

par·a·site (par′ə sīt), *N.* any living thing that lives on or in another, from which it gets its food, often harming the other in the process. Lice and tapeworms are parasites. ❑ *N. PL.* **par·a·sites.**

parapet

pa·vil·ion (pə vil′yən), *N.* a light building, usually somewhat open, used for shelter, pleasure, etc.: *The swimmers took shelter from the sudden storm in the beach pavilion.*

ped·dler (ped′lər), *N.* person who travels about selling things carried in a pack or in a truck, wagon, or cart.

per·mit (pər mit′), **1.** *V.* to let; allow: *My parents will not permit me to stay up late.* ❑ *V.* **per·mit·ted, per·mit·ting. 2.** *N.* license or written order giving permission to do something: *Do you have a permit to fish in this lake?*

phi·los·o·pher (fə los′ə fər), *N.* a person who attempts to discover and understand the basic nature of knowledge and reality. (*Philosopher* comes from a Greek word *philosophia* meaning "love of wisdom.")

pitch (pich), **1.** *V.* to throw or fling; hurl; toss: *They were pitching horseshoes.* ❑ *V.* **pitched, pitch·ing. 2.** *N.* thick, black, sticky substance made from tar or turpentine, used to fill the seams of wooden ships, to cover roofs, to make pavements, etc.

ple·si·o·saur·us (plē′sē ə sôr′əs), *N.* any of several large sea reptiles that lived about 200 million years ago. They had long necks and flippers instead of legs.

plesiosaurus

plunge (plunj), *V.* to fall or move suddenly downward or forward: *The sea turtle plunged into the water.* ❑ *V.* **plunged, plung·ing.**

pon·der (pon′dər), *V.* to consider carefully; think over: *ponder a problem.* ❑ *V.* **pon·dered, pon·der·ing.** (*Ponder* comes from a Latin word *pondus* meaning "weight.")

post·hu·mous·ly (pos′chə məs lē), *ADV.* happening after death: *The author was honored posthumously.*

pot·hole (pot′hōl′), *N.* a deep hole in the surface of a street or road. ❏ *N. PL.* **pot·holes.**

pre·cious (presh′əs), *ADJ.* having great value; worth much; valuable. Gold, platinum, and silver are often called the precious metals. Diamonds, rubies, and sapphires are precious stones.

pred·a·tor (pred′ə tər), *N.* animal or person that lives by killing and eating other animals.

pre·his·tor·ic (prē′hi stôr′ ik), *ADJ.* Of or belonging to periods before recorded history: *Some prehistoric people lived in caves.*

pro·ce·dure (prə sē′jər), *N.* way of proceeding; method of doing things: *What is your procedure in making bread?* ❏ *N. PL.* **pro·ce·dures.**

pro·ces·sion (prə sesh′ən), *N.* something that moves forward; persons marching or riding: *The opening procession started at noon.*

pro·file (prō′fīl), **1.** *N.* a side view, especially of the human face. **2.** *N.* low profile; moderate attitude or position, deliberately chosen in order to avoid notice (*IDIOMATIC*).

pro·por·tion (prə pôr′shən), *N.* a proper relation among parts: *The dog's short legs were not in proportion to its long body.*

pros·per·i·ty (pro sper′ə tē), *N.* prosperous condition; good fortune; success: *a time of peace and prosperity.*

pro·to·type (prō′ tə tīp), *N.* the first or primary type of anything: *A modern ship has its prototype in the hollowed log used by primitive peoples.*

push·cart (pùsh′kärt′), *N.* a light cart pushed by hand. ❏ *N. PL.* **push·carts.**

Rr

ra·vine (rə vēn′), *N.* a long, deep, narrow valley eroded by running water.

realm (relm), *N.* kingdom.

re·as·sem·ble (rē′ə sem′ bəl), *V.* come or bring together again. ❏ *V.* **re·as·sem·bled, re·as·sem·bling.**

rec·om·mend (rek′ə mend′), *V.* to speak in favor of; suggest favorably: *The teacher recommended him for the job.* ❏ *V.* **rec·om·men·ded, rec·om·men·ding.**

ref·u·gee (ref′yə jē′ *or* ref′yə jē′), *N.* person who flees for refuge or safety, especially to a foreign country, in time of persecution, war, or disaster: *Refugees from the war were cared for in neighboring countries.* ❏ *N. PL.* **refugees.**

re·lease (ri lēs′), *V.* to permit to be published, shown, sold, etc. ❏ *V.* **re·leased, re·leas·ing.**

re·li·gious (ri lij′əs), *ADJ.* much interested in the belief, study, and worship of God or gods; devoted to religion: *He is very religious and prays often.*

a	in hat	ō	in open	sh	in she
ā	in age	ȯ	in all	th	in thin
â	in care	ô	in order	ŦH	in then
ä	in far	oi	in oil	zh	in measure
e	in let	ou	in out	ə	= a in about
ē	in equal	u	in cup	ə	= e in taken
ėr	in term	ù	in put	ə	= i in pencil
i	in it	ü	in rule	ə	= o in lemon
ī	in ice	ch	in child	ə	= u in circus
o	in hot	ng	in long		

Ren·ais·sance (ren′ə säns′ *or* ren′ə säns), *N.* the great revival of art and learning in Europe during the 1300s, 1400s, and 1500s; the period of time when this revival occurred.

rep·re·sent·a·tive (rep′ri zen′tə tiv), *N.* person appointed or elected to act or speak for others: *She is the club's representative at the convention.* ❏ *N. PL.* **rep·re·sent·a·tives.**

re·proach·ful·ly (ri prōch′fəl lē), *ADV.* with disapproval.

rep·u·ta·tion (rep′yə tā′shən), *N.* what people think and say the character of someone or something is; character in the opinion of others; name; repute: *This store has an excellent reputation for fair dealing.*

re·source·ful (ri sôrs′fəl), *ADJ.* good at thinking of ways to do things; quick-witted: *The resourceful children mowed lawns to earn enough money to buy new bicycles.*

ri·val (ri′vəl), *N.* person who wants and tries to get the same thing as another or who tries to equal or do better than another; competitor: *The two girls were rivals for the same class office.*

ro·bo·tic (rō bot′ik), *ADJ.* of or for a machine with moving parts and sensing devices controlled by a computer: *robotic design.*

role (rōl), **1.** *N.* an actor's part in a play, movie, etc.: *She played the leading role in the school play.* **2.** *N.* role model, a person whose patterns of behavior influence someone else's actions and beliefs: *Parents are important role models for children.*

rus·tle (rus′əl), *V.* to make or cause to make a light, soft sound of things gently rubbing together: *The leaves were rustling in the breeze.* ❏ *V.* **rus·tled, rus·tling.**

Ss

sa·cred (sā′krid), **1.** *ADJ.* worthy of reverence: *the sacred memory of a dead hero.* **2.** *ADJ.* not to be violated or disregarded: *a sacred promise.* (*Sacred* comes from a Latin word *sacrare* meaning "holy.")

scarce (skârs), *ADJ.* hard to get; rare: *Water is becoming scarce.*

scin·til·late (sin′tl āt), *V.* to sparkle; flash: *Her brilliant wit scintillates.* ❏ *V.* **scin·til·lat·ed, scin·til·lat·ing.**

scoun·drel (skoun′drəl), *N.* an evil, dishonorable person; villain; rascal: *The scoundrels who set fire to the barn have been caught.*

scrawl (skrôl), *V.* to write or draw poorly or carelessly. ❏ *V.* **scrawled, scrawl·ing.**

scraw·ny (skrô′nē), *ADJ.* having little flesh; lean; thin; skinny: *Turkeys have scrawny necks.*

sea ur·chins (sē′ ėr′chəns), *N.* any of numerous small, round sea animals with spiny shells.

sec·ond·hand (sek′ənd hand′), **1.** *ADJ.* not new; used already by someone else: *secondhand clothes.* **2.** *ADV.* from other than the original source; not firsthand: *The information came to us secondhand.*

sed·i·ment (sed′ə mənt), *N.* material that settles to the bottom of a liquid: *A film of sediment covered the underwater wreck.*

seed·ling (sēd′ling), *N.* a young plant grown from a seed. ❏ *N. PL.* **seed·lings.**

sem·i·pro (sem′ī prō′), *N.* a part-time professional athlete.

ser·pent (sėr′pənt), *N.* snake, especially a big snake.

se·vere (sə vir′), *ADJ.* serious; grave: *a severe illness.*

shell·fish (shel′fish′), *N.* a water animal with a shell. Oysters, clams, crabs, and lobsters are shellfish.

shut·down (shut′doun′), **1.** *N.* act of closing of a factory, or the like, for a time: *The factory had a partial shutdown last week to fix some faulty equipment.* **2.** *N.* a stopping; a checking of (*INFORMAL*): *His reply was a real shutdown to her negative comment.*

side·track (sīd′trak′), *V.* to draw someone's attention away from something: *Don't sidetrack me with pointless questions.* ❑ *V.* **side·tracked, side·track·ing.**

sin·ew (sin′yü), *N.* tendon.

sketch (skech), *V.* to draw roughly and quickly. ❑ *V.* **sketched, sketch·ing.**

skid (skid), *V.* to slip or slide sideways while moving: *The car skidded on the slippery road.* ❑ *V.* **skid·ded, skid·ding.**

slav·er·y (slā′vər ē), *N.* the condition of being owned by another person and being made to work without wages.

sol·i·tar·y (sol′ə ter′ē), *ADJ.* without companions; away from people; lonely.

som·ber (som′bər), **1.** *ADJ.* having deep shadows; dark; gloomy: *A cloudy winter day is somber.* **2.** *ADJ.* sad; gloomy; dismal: *His losses made him somber.*

som·er·sault (sum′ər sôlt), *V.* to run or jump, turning the heels over the head. ❑ *V.* **som·er·saul·ted, som·er·saul·ting.**

*a **somber** picture (def. 2)*

so·nar (sō′när), *N.* device for finding the depth of water or for detecting and locating underwater objects. Sonar sends sound waves into water, and they are reflected back when they strike the bottom or any object.

So·vi·et (sō′vē et), *N.* a person belonging to or fighting for the former Soviet Union. ❑ *N. PL.* **So·vi·ets.**

spe·cial·ize (spesh′ə līz), *V.* to develop in a special way: *Animals and plants are specialized to fit their surroundings.* ❑ *V.* **spe·cial·ized, spe·cial·iz·ing.**

spe·cif·ic (spi sif′ik), *ADJ.* definite; precise; particular: *There was no specific reason for the party.*

spec·ta·cles (spek′tə kəlz), *N. PL.* eyeglasses. (*Spectacles* comes from a Latin word *spectare* meaning "to watch.")

spec·tac·u·lar (spek tak′ yə lər), *ADJ.* making a great display or show; very striking or imposing to the eye: *a spectacular storm.*

spin·dly (spind′lē), *ADJ.* very long and slender; too tall and thin: *a spindly plant.*

spir·i·tu·al (spir′ə chü əl), *N.* a religious song which originated among African Americans of the southern United States. ❑ *N. PL.* **spir·i·tu·als.**

a in hat	ō in open	sh in she
ā in age	ò in all	th in thin
â in care	ô in order	ᴛʜ in then
ä in far	oi in oil	zh in measure
e in let	ou in out	ə = a in about
ē in equal	u in cup	ə = e in taken
ėr in term	ù in put	ə = i in pencil
i in it	ü in rule	ə = o in lemon
ī in ice	ch in child	ə = u in circus
o in hot	ng in long	

spoon·ful (spün′fúl), *N.* as much as a spoon can hold.

star·va·tion (stär vā′shən), *N.* suffering from extreme hunger; being starved: *Starvation caused his death.*

stealth·y (stel′thē), *ADJ.* done in a secret manner; secret; sly: *The cat crept in a stealthy way toward the bird.*

steed (stēd), *N.* horse, especially a riding horse.

ster·ile (ster′əl), *ADJ.* free from germs: *Bandages should always be kept sterile.*

stern·ly (stėrn′ lē), *ADV.* strictly; firmly: *The teacher frowned sternly.*

strat·e·gy (strat′ə jē), *N.* the skillful planning and management of anything.

strict (strict), *ADJ.* very careful in following a rule or in making others follow it: *The teacher was strict but fair.*

stroke (strōk), *N.* a sudden attack of illness, especially one caused by a blood clot or bleeding in the brain; apoplexy.

sub·ject (sub′jikt), **1.** *N.* something that is thought about, discussed, investigated, etc.; topic: *The subject for our composition was "An Exciting Moment."* **2.** *N.* person under the power, control, or influence of another: *subjects of the king.*

su·per·i·or (sə pir′ē ər), *N.* person who is higher in rank, position, or ability: *A captain is a lieutenant's superior.* ❑ *N. PL.* **su·per·i·ors.**

sus·pend·ers (sə spen′dərz), *N. PL.* straps worn over the shoulders to hold up the trousers.

sus·pi·cion (sə spish′ən), *N.* belief; feeling; thought: *I have a suspicion that the weather will be very hot today.* ❑ *N. PL.* **sus·pi·cions.**

Tt

tape·worm (tāp′wėrm′), *N.* any of the numerous long, flat worms that live during their adult stage as parasites in the intestines of human beings and other animals. ❑ *N. PL.* **tape·worms.**

teen·ag·er (tēn′ā′jər), *N.* person in his or her teens.

ther·a·pist (ther′ə pist), *N.* person who specializes in the treatment of diseases, injuries, or disorders.

thieve (thēv), *V.* to steal. ❑ *V.* **thieved, thiev·ing.**

throb (throb), *V.* to beat rapidly or strongly: *My injured foot throbbed.* ❑ *V.* **throb·bed, throb·bing.**

ti·dy (tī′dē), *V.* to put in order; make neat: *I tidied the room.* ❑ *V.* **ti·died, ti·dy·ing.**

to·ga (tō′gə), *N.* a loose, outer garment worn in public. ❑ *N. PL.* **to·gas.**

tra·di·tion (trə dish′ən), *N.* custom or belief handed down from generation to generation: *According to tradition, Betsy Ross made the first American flag.* ❑ *N. PL.* **tra·di·tions.**

trans·at·lan·tic (tran′sət lan′tik), *ADJ.* crossing the Atlantic: *a transatlantic liner.*

tum·ble·down (tum′bəl doun′), *ADJ.* ready to fall down; not in good condition; dilapidated: *a tumbledown shack in the mountains.*

tun·dra (tun′drə), *N.* a vast, level, treeless plain in the arctic regions. The ground beneath its surface is frozen even in summer.

tweez·ers (twē′zərz), *N.* small pincers for pulling out hairs, picking up small objects, etc.

Uu

u·nique (yü nēk′), *ADJ.* having no like or equal; being the only one of its kind: *a unique specimen of rock, a unique experience.*

un·screw (un skrü′), *V.* to loosen or take off by turning: *Can you help me unscrew this tight lid?* ❑ *V.* **un·screwed, un·screw·ing.**

Vv

va·cant (vā′kənt), *ADJ.* not occupied: *a vacant chair, a vacant house.*

var·mint (vär′mənt), *N.* an objectionable animal or person (*DIALECT*).

vein (vān), *N.* **1.** membranous tubes forming part of the system of vessels that carry blood to the heart. **2.** a small natural channel within the earth through which water trickles or flows. ❑ *N. PL.* **veins.**

vi·bra·phone (vī′brə fōn), *N.* musical instrument similar to the xylophone, with metal bars and artificially increased vibration; vibraharp.

view·port (vyü′pôrt), *N.* small window in a small vessel, such as a space capsule or mini-submarine.

vi·sa (vē′zə), *N.* an official signature or endorsement upon a passport, showing that it has been examined and approved. A visa is granted by the consul or other representative of the country to which a person wishes to travel.

Ww

wai·tress (wā′tris), *N.* woman who serves or brings food to people in a restaurant.

weak·ness (wēk′nis), *N.* a weak point; slight fault: *Putting things off is her weakness.*

weight·less·ness (wāt′lis nis), *N.* the condition of being free from the pull of gravity: *weightless travelers in space.*

wheel·chair (wēl′châr′), *N.* chair on wheels, used especially by people who are sick or unable to walk. It can be moved by the person who is sitting in the chair.

wince (wins), *V.* to draw back suddenly; flinch slightly: *I winced when the dentist's drill touched my tooth.* ❑ *V.* **winced, winc·ing.**

wind·up (wind′up′), *N.* (in baseball), a swinging movement of the arms while twisting the body just before pitching the ball.

with·er (wiTH′ər), *V.* to lose or cause to lose freshness; make or become dry and lifeless; dry up; fade; shrivel: *Age had withered the old woman's face.* ❑ *V.* **with·ered, with·er·ing.**

work·shop (wėrk′shop′), *N.* space or building where work is done.

wor·ship (wėr′ship), *V.* to pay great honor and reverence to: *to worship God.* ❑ *V.* **wor·shipped, wor·ship·ping.**

worth·less (wėrth′lis), *ADJ.* without value; good-for-nothing; useless: *Throw those worthless, broken toys away.*

a in hat	ō in open	sh in she
ā in age	ȯ in all	th in thin
â in care	ô in order	ŦH in then
ä in far	oi in oil	zh in measure
e in let	ou in out	ə = a in about
ē in equal	u in cup	ə = e in taken
ėr in term	u̇ in put	ə = i in pencil
i in it	ü in rule	ə = o in lemon
ī in ice	ch in child	ə = u in circus
o in hot	ng in long	

English/Spanish
Selection Vocabulary List

Unit 1
Frindle

English	Spanish
acquainted	conocer (gente)
assignment	trabajo
essential	esencial
expanded	ampliado
guaranteed	garantiza
procedures	procedimientos
reputation	reputación
worshipped	adoraba

Thunder Rose

English	Spanish
branded	marcados
constructed	construyó
daintily	con elegancia
devastation	devastación
lullaby	nana
pitch	brea
resourceful	ingeniosa
thieving	(hábitos de) robar
veins	venas

Island of the Blue Dolphins

English	Spanish
gnawed	royeron
headland	promontorio
kelp	algas
lair	guarida
ravine	barranco
shellfish	mariscos
sinew	tendón

Satchel Paige

English	Spanish
confidence	confianza
fastball	bola rápida
mocking	burlón
outfield	jardines
unique	único
weakness	debilidad
windup	movimiento para lanzar

Shutting Out the Sky

English	Spanish
advice	consejos
advised	aconsejó
circumstances	circunstancias
elbow	ábrete paso
hustled	estafaba
immigrants	inmigrantes
luxury	lujo
newcomer	recién llegado
peddler	mercachifle

Unit 2
Inside Out

English	Spanish
caterpillar	oruga
cocoon	capullo
disrespect	falté el respeto
emerge	emerger
migrant	migratorio
sketched	esbocé
unscrewed	desenrosqué

Passage to Freedom

English	Spanish
agreement	acuerdo
cable	cable
diplomat	diplomático
issue	asunto
refugees	refugiados
representatives	representantes
superiors	superiores
visa	visa

The Ch'i-lin Purse

English	Spanish
astonished	asombrada
behavior	comportamiento
benefactor	benefactora
distribution	distribución
gratitude	gratitud
procession	procesión
recommend	recomendar
sacred	sagrado
traditions	tradiciónes

Jane Goodall's 10 Ways to Help Save Wildlife

English	Spanish
conservation	conservación
contribute	contribuyen
enthusiastic	entusiastas
environment	medio ambiente
investigation	investigación

The Midnight Ride of Paul Revere

English	Spanish
fate	destino
fearless	intrépido
glimmer	destello
lingers	se entretiene
magnified	ampliado
somber	sombrías
steed	corcel

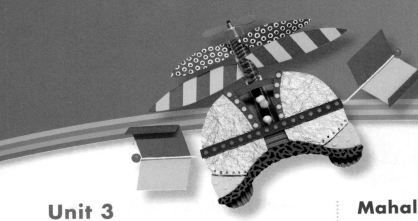

Unit 3

Wings for the King

English	Spanish
admiringly	con admiración
permit	permítame
scoundrel	canalla
subject	súbdita
worthless	inútiles

Leonardo's Horse

English	Spanish
achieved	logrado
architect	arquitecto
bronze	bronce
cannon	cañón
depressed	deprimido
fashioned	elaboró
midst	(en) medio (de)
philosopher	filósofo
rival	rival

The Dinosaurs of Waterhouse Hawkins

English	Spanish
erected	erigió
foundations	cimientos
mold	molde
occasion	ocasión
proportion	proporción
tidied	ordenó
workshop	taller

Mahalia Jackson

English	Spanish
appreciate	apreciar
barber	barbero
choir	coro
released	se publicó
religious	religiosa
slavery	esclavitud
teenager	adolescente

Special Effects in Film and Television

English	Spanish
background	fondo
landscape	paisaje
miniature	miniatura
prehistoric	prehistórico
reassembled	reensamblados

Unit 4
Weslandia

English	Spanish
blunders	tropezones
civilization	civilización
complex	complejo
envy	envidia
fleeing	huir
inspired	inspiró
rustling	susurrando
strategy	estrategia

Stretching Ourselves: Kids with Cerebral Palsy

English	Spanish
abdomen	abdomen
artificial	artificial
gait	manera de caminar
handicapped	discapacitado
therapist	terapeuta
wheelchair	silla de ruedas

Exploding Ants: Amazing Facts About How Animals Adapt

English	Spanish
critical	críticos
enables	permite
mucus	mucus
scarce	escaso
specialize	se especializan
sterile	estériles

The Stormi Giovanni Club

English	Spanish
cavities	caries
combination	combinación
demonstrates	demuestra
episode	episodio
profile	(mantenerse en) segundo plano
strict	estricto

The Gymnast

English	Spanish
bluish	azulados
cartwheels	volteretas laterales
gymnastics	gimnástica
hesitation	duda
limelight	centro de atención
skidded	patinó
somersault	dar saltos mortales
throbbing	latía
wincing	haciendo una mueca de dolor

Unit 5

The Three-Century Woman

English	Spanish
eerie	escalofriante
intersection	intersección
pondered	reflexionó
severe	serio
spectacles	gafas
withered	marchita

The Unsinkable Wreck of the R.M.S. *Titanic*

English	Spanish
cramped	estrecho
debris	restos
interior	interior
ooze	limo
robotic	robótico
sediment	sedimento
sonar	sonar

Talk with an Astronaut

English	Spanish
accomplishments	logros
focus	atención
gravity	gravedad
monitors	monitores
role	ejemplo
specific	específico

Journey to the Center of the Earth

English	Spanish
armor	armadura
encases	reviste
extinct	extintas
hideous	horroroso
plunged	sumergido
serpent	serpiente

Ghost Towns of the American West

English	Spanish
economic	económico
independence	independencia
overrun	rebosante
scrawled	garabateó
vacant	vacantes

Unit 6
At the Beach

English	Spanish
algae	algas
concealed	ocultado
driftwood	madera flotante
hammocks	hamacas
lamented	lamentó
sea urchins	erizos de mar
sternly	severamente
tweezers	pinzas

The Mystery of Saint Matthew Island

English	Spanish
bleached	decolorados
carcasses	animales muertos
decay	descomposición
parasites	parásitos
scrawny	escuálido
starvation	inanición
suspicions	sospechas
tundra	tundra

King Midas and the Golden Touch

English	Spanish
adorn	adornar
cleanse	(te) bañas
lifeless	inanimada
precious	precioso
realm	reino
spoonful	cucharada

The *Hindenburg*

English	Spanish
criticizing	criticando
cruised	navegó
drenching	empapándolo
era	era
explosion	explosión
hydrogen	hidrógeno

Sweet Music in Harlem

English	Spanish
bass	bajo
clarinet	clarinete
fidgety	inquieto
forgetful	olvidadizo
jammed	improvisé
nighttime	noche
secondhand	segunda mano

Acknowledgments

Text

22: From *Frindle* by Andrew Clements. Text ©1996 by Andrew Clements. Reprinted by permission of Simon & Schuster Books for Young Readers, an imprint of Simon & Schuster Children's Publishing Division; **36:** *Punctuation Takes a Vacation* by Robin Pulver. Text ©2003 by Robin Pulver. All rights reserved. Reprinted by permission of Holiday House, Inc.; **46:** *Thunder Rose*, text ©2003 by Jerdine Nolen. ©2003 by Kadir Nelson. Reprinted by permission of Harcourt, Inc.; **66:** "Measuring Tornadoes" from *Storm Chasers* by Trudi Strain Trueit. ©2002 Franklin Watts, a Division of Scholastic, Inc. Used by permission of Scholastic Library Publishing; **72:** From *Island of the Blue Dolphins.* ©1960, renewed 1988 by Scott O'Dell. Reprinted by permission of Houghton Mifflin Company. All rights reserved; **86:** "7 Survival Questions," by Buck Tilton. Used with permission of Buck Tilton and *Boys' Life*, April 2001. Published by the Boy Scouts of America; **94:** From *Satchel Paige* by Lesa Cline-Ransome, paintings by James E. Ransome. Text ©2000 Lesa Cline-Ransome. Illustrations ©2000 James E. Ransome. Reprinted with the permission of Simon & Schuster Books for Young Readers, an imprint of Simon & Schuster Children's Publishing Division; **110:** From "The Girls of Summer" by Ellen Klages. Adapted with permission, © Exploratorium, www.exploratorium.edu. Used by permission; **116:** From *Shutting Out the Sky* by Deborah Hopkinson. Published by Orchard Books, a division of Scholastic Inc. ©2003 by Deborah Hopkinson. Reprinted by permission of Scholastic Inc.; **130:** "The Immigrant Experience" from *Tenement Tid-Bits*, e-mail newsletter of The Lower East Side Tenement Museum, November 2003. Reprinted by permission of The Lower East Side Tenement Museum at www.tenement.org/immigrantexperience; **134:** "The Microscope" by Maxine W. Kumin. ©1968 by Maxine W. Kumin. Used by permission of The Anderson Literary Agency Inc; **136:** "Full Day" from *Come With Me: Poems For A Journey* by Naomi Shihab Nye. Text ©2000 by Naomi Shihab Nye, Greenwillow Books. Used by permission of HarperCollins Publishers; **146:** From "Inside Out," from *The Circuit* by Francisco Jiménez. ©1997 by Francisco Jiménez. Reprinted by permission of the University of New Mexico Press; **160:** "Random Acts of Kindness" from the Random Acts of Kindness Web site. Reprinted by permission of The Random Acts of Kindness Foundation at www.actsofkindness.org; **166:** *Passage to Freedom: The Sugihara Story.* Text ©1997 by Ken Mochizuki. Illustrations ©1997 by Dom Lee. Afterword ©1997 by Hiroki Sugihara. Permission arranged with Lee & Low Books Inc., New York, NY 10016; **180:** From "I Wanted My Mother," from *Hiding to Survive: Stories of Jewish Children Rescued from the Holocaust.* ©1994 by Maxine B. Rosenberg. Reprinted by permission of Clarion Books/Houghton Mifflin Company. All rights reserved; **190:** "The Ch'i-lin Purse" from *The Ch'i-lin Purse* by Linda Fang. ©1963 by Linda Fang. Reprinted by permission of Farrar, Straus & Giroux, LLC; **206:** "Lion and the Mouse" from *The Fables of Aesop* retold by Ruth Spriggs. ©1975 by Eurobook Limited, Oxfordshire, England. Used by permission; **212:** "Jane Goodall's 10 Ways to Help Save Wildlife," from *National Geographic KIDS*, April 2003. ©2003 National Geographic Society. Reprinted by permission; **226:** "Why Some Animals Are Considered 'Bad' or 'Scary'" from SanDiegoZoo.org. Used by permission of the Zoological Society of San Diego; **234:** Illustrations from *The Midnight Ride of Paul Revere* by Henry Wadsworth Longfellow, graved and painted by Christopher Bing, ©2001 Christopher Bing. Reproduced with permission of the publisher, Handprint Books, Inc.; **250:** "Deborah Sampson" by Michael Zullo from www2.1hric.org. Used by permission of Michael Zullo; **254:** "For Peace Sake" by Cedric McClester ©1990 by Cedric McClester. Used by permission of the author; **256:** "Two People I Want to Be Like" from *If Only I Could Tell You* by Eve Merriam. ©1983 Eve Merriam. Used by permission of Marian Reiner; **257:** "Strangers" from *Good Luck Gold and Other Poems* by Janet S. Wong. ©1994 by Janet S. Wong. Reprinted with the permission of Margaret K. McElderry Books, an imprint of Simon & Schuster Children's Publishing Division. All rights reserved; **266:** From *Wings for the King* by Anne Sroda from

Plays, November 2000, Vol. 60, No.2. Reproduced with permission of Sterling Partners, Inc./PLAYS, P. O. Box 600160, Newton, MA 02460; **282:** "Becky Schroeder: Enlightened Thinker" from *Brainstorm! The Stories of Twenty American Kid Inventors* by Tom Tucker, illustrated by Richard Loehle. ©1996 by Tom Tucker. Reprinted by permission of Farrar, Straus & Giroux, LLC; **292:** *Leonardo's Horse* by Jean Fritz and illustrated by Hudson Talbott. Text ©Jean Fritz, 2001. Illustrations ©Hudson Talbott, 2001. Published by arrangement with G. P. Putnam's Sons, a division of Penguin Young Readers Group, a member of Penguin Group (USA) Inc. All rights reserved; **312:** "Humans with Wings," from *HumanPower* by Roger Yepsen. ©1992 Roger Yepsen. Reprinted with the permission of Simon & Schuster Books for Young Readers, an imprint of Simon & Schuster Children's Publishing Division; **320:** From *The Dinosaurs of Waterhouse Hawkins* by Barbara Kerley Kelly. Text ©2001 by Barbara Kerley Kelly. Illustrations ©2001 by Brian Selznick. Reprinted by permission of Scholastic, Inc; **340:** "A Model Scientist" adapted from *OWL Magazine*, Oct. 2002. Used by permission of Bayard Canada Inc.; **350:** "Mahalia Jackson" from *The Blues Singers* by Julius Lester. ©2001 Julius Lester. Illustrated by Lisa Cohen. Reprinted by permission of Hyperion Books for Children; **360:** From *Perfect Harmony* by Charles Smith. ©2002 Charles Smith. Reprinted by permission of Hyperion Books For Children; **368:** From *Special Effects in Film and Television* by Jake Hamilton. ©1998 Dorling Kindersley. Reprinted by permission; **380:** Adaptation of "A Trick of the Eye" by Brian Sibley from http://ww.bfi.org.uk. Used by permission of Sheil Land Associates Ltd.; **384:** "Chemistry 101" from *Carver: A Life In Poems* by Marilyn Nelson. ©2001 by Marilyn Nelson. Used by permission of Front Street, a division of Boyds Mill Press, Inc; **385:** "The Bronze Horse" by Beverly McLoughland, *Cricket*, November 1990. Used by permission of the author; **386:** "The Termites" from *Insectlopedia*, ©1998 by Douglas Florian, reprinted by permission of Harcourt, Inc. This material may not be reproduced in any form or by any means without the prior written permission of the publisher; **387:** "Stairs" from *Excuse It Please* by Oliver Herford, J. B. Lippincott Company, 1929; **396:** *Weslandia* by Paul Fleischman. Text ©1999 by Paul Fleischman. Illustrations ©1999 by Kevin Hawkes. Reproduced by the publisher Candlewick Press, Inc., Cambridge, MA; **410:** "Under the Back Porch" by Virginia Hamilton. ©1992, 2004 by Virginia Hamilton. Reprinted by permission of Arnold Adoff, 750 Union St., Yellow Springs, OH 45387; **411:** "Keziah," from *Bronzeville Boys and Girls* by Gwendolyn Brooks. ©1956 by Gwendolyn Brooks Blakely. Used by permission of HarperCollins Publishers; **416:** From *Stretching Ourselves* by Alden R. Carter, Photographs by Carol S. Carter. ©2000 Alden R. Carter. Reprinted by permission of John Hawkins & Associates, Inc.; **434:** "Helpful Tools" from *Do You Remember the Color Blue?* by Sally Hobart Alexander, ©2000 by Sally Hobart Alexander. Used by permission of Viking Children's Books, A Division of Penguin Young Readers Group, A Member of Penguin Group (USA) Inc., 345 Hudson Street, New York, NY 10014, the Author and BookStop Literary Agency. All rights reserved; **440:** From *Exploding Ants* by Joanne Settel, Ph.D. Text ©1999 by Joanne Settel. Reprinted with the permission of Atheneum Books for Young Readers, an imprint of Simon & Schuster Children's Publishing Division; **480:** "Think Dress Codes Are a Drag?" by Emilie Ostrander from the *Chicago Tribune*, April 15, 2003. Copyrighted 4/15/2003, Chicago Tribune Company. All rights reserved. Used with permission; **488:** "The Gymnast" by Gary Soto from *A Summer Life* ©1990 by University Press of New England. Reprinted with permission; **501:** From "Gymnastics" from *The Columbia Electronic Encyclopedia*, 6th ed. ©2003, Columbia University Press. Used by permission; **502:** *Random House Webster's Unabridged Dictionary.* New York: Random House, 1991. **504:** "the drum" from *Spin A Soft Black Song* by Nikki Giovanni. ©1971, 1985 by Nikki Giovanni. Reprinted by permission of Hill and Wang, a division of Farrar, Straus & Giroux, LLC; **505:** "Which Lunch Table?" from *Swimming Upstream: Middle Grade Poems* by Kristine O'Connell George. Text ©2002 by Kristine O'Connell

Illustrations

Photographs

Glossary

The contents of this glossary have been adapted from *Thorndike Barnhart Advanced Dictionary.* Copyright ©1997, Pearson Education, Inc.

Tennessee

State Performance Indicators

SPI#	State Performance Indicators
Content	
5.1.5	Identify setting, character, and plot in a passage.
5.1.10	Identify sequence of events in fiction and nonfiction selections.
5.1.15	Select the appropriate summary statement for a given passage.
5.1.18	Distinguish among various literary genres (e.g., poetry, drama, letters, ads, historical fiction, biographies, and autobiographies).
5.1.19	Identify and interpret the main incidents of a plot, their causes, how they influence future actions, and how they are resolved.
5.1.20	Recognize that a story is told from the first-person point of view.
5.1.21	Identify the author's purpose(s) (i.e., to inform or entertain).
5.1.22	Determine whether the theme is stated or implied within a passage.
5.1.27	Identify, using a graphic organizer, placement of events in a given plot.
Grammar Conventions	
5.3.1	Recognize usage errors occurring in the writing process (e.g., double negatives, troublesome words: *to, too, two; there, their, they're; lie, lay; sit, set*).
5.3.3	Identify the correct use of nouns (i.e., singular/plural, possessives, predicate nouns, nouns as objects), pronouns (i.e., agreement, subject, object), verbs (i.e., action/linking, regular/irregular, agreement, tenses), adjectives (i.e., common/proper, comparative forms, predicate adjectives), and adverbs (i.e., comparative forms, negatives) within context.
5.3.4	Identify sentences with correct subject-verb agreement (person/number).
5.3.5	Identify the correct use of commas (i.e., series, dates, addresses, friendly letters, compound sentences, coordinating conjunctions, introductory words) within context.
5.3.6	Choose the correct use of quotation marks and commas in direct quotations.
5.3.8	Identify the correct spelling of plurals and possessives.
5.3.10	Choose the most appropriate interjection to complete a sentence.
5.3.11	Identify the correct use of colons (i.e., in business letters and preceding a list of items).
Meaning	
5.1.7	Select questions used to focus and clarify thinking before, during, and after reading the text.
5.1.11	Select stated or implied main idea and supporting details within context.
5.1.12	Identify stated or implied cause-and-effect relationships within context.
5.1.13	Distinguish between elements of fact/opinion and reality/fantasy.
5.1.14	Determine inferences from selected passages.
5.1.17	Recognize reasonable predictions of future events within a given context.
Techniques and Skills	
5.1.4	Select and use common text to make meaning from text (e.g., headings, key words, graphics, captions, sidebars).
5.1.16	Locate information using available text features (e.g., maps, charts, graphics, indexes, glossaries, and tables of content).

5.1.23	Identify similes, metaphors, personification, and hyperbole in context.
5.1.24	Identify the effect of sound within context (e.g., onomatopeia, alliteration, rhymes, and repetition).
5.1.25	Identify information to support opinions, predictions, and conclusions.
5.2.10	Identify the most reliable sources of information for preparing a report or project.
5.3.7	Identify correctly (or incorrectly) spelled words in context.

Vocabulary

5.1.1	Recognize root words, prefixes, suffixes, and syllabication as aids in determining meaning within context.
5.1.2	Select appropriate synonyms, antonyms, and homonyms within context.
5.1.3	Identify compound words, contractions, and common abbreviations within text.
5.1.6	Recognize and use grade-appropriate vocabulary within context.
5.1.8	Determine the correct meaning/usage of multiple-meaning words within context.
5.1.9	Determine word meanings within context.
5.1.26	Select a logical word choice to complete an analogy using synonyms, antonyms. categories, and subcategories.

Writing/Organization

5.2.2	Rearrange sentences to form a sequential, coherent paragraph.
5.2.5	Select details that support a topic sentence.
5.2.8	Rearrrange paragraphs in a narrative writing selection in a sequential or chronological order.
5.2.9	Select appropriate time-order or transitional words/phrases to enhance the flow of a writing sample.
5.2.12	Select the best title for a written selection.
5.2.14	Supply a missing piece of information in an outline.
5.2.21	Arrange a multi-paragraphed work of expostion (e.g., persuasion, comparison/contrast) in a logical and coherent order.
5.2.23	Select an appropriate concluding sentence for a well-developed paragraph.

Writing Process

5.2.1	Complete a graphic organizer (i.e., clustering, listing, mapping, webbing) to group ideas for writing.
5.2.3	Identify the purpose for writing (i.e., entertain, inform, report).
5.2.4	Identify the audience for which a piece of text is written.
5.2.6	Choose vivid and active words.
5.2.11	Select the best way to combine sentences to provide syntactic variety within context.
5.2.13	Choose the supporting sentence that best fits the context and flow of ideas in a paragraph.
5.2.22	Identify the sentence irrelevant to a paragraph's theme or flow.
5.3.2	Select the best way to correct incomplete sentences within context.
5.3.9	Identify within context a variety of appropriate sentence-combining techniques (i.e., comma + coordinating conjunction, use of semicolon, introductory phrases and/or clauses).
5.3.12	Select the most appropriate method to correct a run-on sentence (i.e., conjunctions, semicolons, and periods to join or separate elements) within context.

Tennessee

Reading and Writing Accomplishments

READING Accomplishments
Content Standard 1.0

The student will develop the reading and listening skills necessary for word recognition, comprehension, interpretation, analysis, evaluation, and appreciation of print and nonprint text.

5.1.01   **Continue to develop oral language and listening skills.**

　　a.　Listen attentively by facing the speaker, asking questions, and paraphrasing what is said.

　　b.　Use established rules for conversation (e.g., do not interrupt, do ask questions, do provide appropriate feedback).

　　c.　Understand, follow, and give oral multistep directions that may include illustrations.

　　d.　Formulate and respond to questions from teachers and other group members.

　　e.　Participate in creative responses to text (e.g., choral reading, discussion, dramatization, and oral presentations).

　　f.　Summarize orally what has been learned or accomplished after completing an activity or assignment.

　　g.　Create and deliver an oral presentation that includes an introduction and conclusion.

　　h.　Create and deliver an oral presentation that uses visual aids or props and incorporates several sources.

　　i.　Use different voice levels and speech patterns for small groups, informal discussions, and reports.

　　j.　Interpret and use a variety of nonverbal communication techniques (e.g., gestures, facial expression, posture).

k. Present and/or perform original or published literary work with a group and/or individually.

l. Participate in recitations of assigned/self-selected passages.

5.1.02   Demonstrate knowledge of concepts of print.

a. Use parts of text (e.g., title, title page, table of contents, chapter titles, glossary, appendix, and index).

b. Use common text features to enhance understanding (e.g., headings, keywords, graphics, captions, side bars, footnotes).

c. Recognize different forms of text (e.g., poems, plays, drama, letters, ads, journalism, historical fiction, biographies, autobiographies).

5.1.03   Expand reading skills through phonemic awareness.

a. Develop awareness of the sounds of language through repeated exposure to a variety of auditory experiences (e.g., poetry, music lyrics, sound effects, books on tape, read alouds).

b. Understand rhyming patterns in printed materials.

c. Respond and analyze the effects of sound in language (e.g., alliteration, onomatopoeia, rhythm, beat).

5.1.04   Use decoding strategies to read unfamiliar words.

a. Continue to use knowledge of letter-sound correspondence knowledge and structural analysis to decode words.

b. Expand understanding and use of root words, prefixes, and suffixes to decode words.

c. Use syllabication to decode words.

d. Understand, recognize, and use spelling patterns and word families to decode words.

e. Decode unknown grade-level words utilizing learned strategies and verify word meanings within the context.

5.1.05 **Read to develop fluency, expression, accuracy, and confidence.**

    a. Increase confidence and poise in reading aloud (e.g., paired reading, shared reading, choral reading, echo reading, and Readers' Theater).

    b. Read with fluency and confidence from a variety of text (e.g., poetry, drama, newspapers, novels, textbooks).

    c. Participate in guided oral reading.

    d. Read orally using appropriate pronunciation, expression, and rate.

    e. Adjust speed based on the purpose for reading and reading level.

    f. Read independently daily.

5.1.06 **Expand reading vocabulary.**

    a. Build vocabulary by listening to literature, participating in discussions, and reading self-selected texts.

    b. Build vocabulary through frequent read alouds.

    c. Infer word meanings using roots, prefixes, and suffixes.

    d. Determine the meaning of unfamiliar words using context clues, dictionaries, glossaries, and other resources.

    e. Use appropriate synonyms, antonyms, and homonyms.

    f. Foster word consciousness (e.g., word play, word walls, and word sorts).

    g. Use context clues and pronunciation cues when appropriate to determine the correct meaning/usage of multiple-meaning words.

    h. Select the correct word to complete an analogy.

    i. Explore the impact of vocabulary in evaluating ideas, information, and experiences.

    j. Use word origins to determine the meaning of unknown words (e.g., Latin and Greek roots, meanings of commonly-used foreign words).

    k. Build vocabulary by reading from a wide variety of text and literary genres.

5.1.07 **Employ prereading strategies to facilitate comprehension.**

    a. Set a purpose for reading (e.g., to understand, to interpret, to enjoy, to solve problems, to locate specific information/ facts, to discover models for writing).

    b. Utilize reference sources to build background for reading.

    c. Organize prior knowledge using a variety of strategies (e.g., webbing, mapping, brainstorming, listing, outlining).

    d. Explore significant words to be encountered in selected/ assigned text.

    e. Preview text using text features (e.g., illustrations/pictures, captions, graphs, diagrams, and headings).

    f. Make predictions about text using text features (e.g., title, author, illustrations, and text format).

    g. Relate text to prior personal and historical experiences, current events, as well as previously read print and nonprint media.

5.1.08 **Use active comprehension strategies to derive meaning while reading and to check for understanding after reading.**

    a. Derive meaning while reading by

        1. formulating clarifying questions.

        2. predicting outcomes based upon prior knowledge and adjusting appropriately.

        3. using metacognitive and self-monitoring reading strategies to improve comprehension (e.g., rereading, identifying miscues, reading ahead, asking for help, and drawing on earlier reading).

        4. creating mental images.

        5. expressing reactions and personal opinions to a selection or relating the selection to a personal experience.

        6. making inferences and recognizing unstated assumptions.

        7. verifying or modifying the prereading purpose.

        8. drawing conclusions based on evidence gained.

    b. Check for understanding after reading by

        1. indicating sequence of events in fiction and nonfiction text.

        2. selecting main idea and supporting details from text.

        3. identifying the author's purpose (e.g., to entertain, to inform, to explain, to persuade).

4. discussing similarities and differences in events and/or characters using evidence cited in three or more texts.

5. selecting, prioritizing, and organizing information to meet a specific purpose.

6. stating reasonable generalizations in reference to two or more pieces of text on a similar topic.

7. locating information to support opinions, predictions, and conclusions.

8. identifying cause-and-effect relationships.

9. distinguishing between fact/opinion and reality/fiction.

10. identifying and interpreting figurative language (e.g., idioms, similes, metaphors, hyperboles, personification, imagery).

11. recognizing a common theme between two passages.

12. reflecting upon comprehension strategies utilized to make meaning from text.

5.1.09 Develop appropriate informational skills and study skills to facilitate learning.

a. Use and discern appropriate reference sources in various formats (e.g., interviews with family, community leaders and government leaders; encyclopedias; card/electronic catalogs; almanacs; newspapers; and periodicals).

b. Use media (e.g., photographs, videos, films, the arts, on-line catalogs, nonfiction books, encyclopedias, CD-ROM references, Internet) to view, read, and represent information.

c. Use current technology as a research and communication tool for personal interest, research, and clarification.

d. Understand a variety of informational texts which include primary sources (e.g., autobiographical sketches, letters, and diaries; directions; and Internet sites).

e. Utilize the dictionary, glossary, thesaurus, and other word-referenced materials.

f. Skim materials to develop a general overview of content or to locate specific information.

g. Retrieve, organize, and represent information (e.g., charts, maps, graphs, forms, timelines, and outlines).

h. Develop notes that include important concepts, paraphrases, summaries, and identification of reference sources.

i. Develop an awareness of the effects of media (e.g., television, print materials, radio, Internet, newspapers, periodicals) on daily life.

j. Identify the techniques of propaganda (i.e., bandwagon, loaded words, testimonials).

k. Gather and record information on a research topic using three or more sources.

5.1.10 Develop skills to facilitate reading to learn in a variety of content areas.

a. Develop and maintain vocabulary specific to content and to current events.

b. Locate information using available text features (e.g., maps, charts, graphics, indexes, glossaries, and tables of contents).

c. Apply comprehension skills and strategies to informational text (e.g., prereading and active comprehension).

d. Use self-correction strategies while reading (e.g., pausing, rereading, consulting other sources, asking for help).

e. Determine and evaluate the reliability of sources on a given topic (e.g., editorials, newspapers, magazines, biographies, news reports, and films).

5.1.11 Read independently for a variety of purposes.

a. Read for literary experience.

b. Read to gain information.

c. Read to perform a task.

d. Read for enjoyment.

e. Read to expand vocabulary.

f. Read to build fluency.

5.1.12 Experience various literary and media genres.

a. Read and recognize various literary (e.g., poetry, novels, historical fiction, nonfiction) and media (e.g. photographs, the arts, film, video) genres.

b. Predict and determine the sequence of events in a story including possible problems and solutions.

c. Identify the conflict of the plot.

d. Interpret a character's feelings and identify his motives.

e. Trace changes in the main character and describe how this affects the plot.

f. Make inferences about print and nonprint text.

g. Identify how culture, ethnic, and historical eras are represented in print and nonprint texts.

h. Compare and contrast events and characters using evidence cited from print and nonprint text(s).

i. Compare and contrast different versions of the same stories/events that reflect different cultures and/or different perspectives.

j. Summarize selected passages.

k. Retell a story from a different point of view.

l. Understand the way in which figurative language is used to derive meaning from text (e.g., personification, simile, metaphor, imagery, hyperbole).

5.1.13 Develop and sustain a motivation for reading.

a. Visit libraries/media centers and book fairs to explore books.

b. Use personal criteria to select reading material (e.g., personal interest, knowledge of authors, text difficulty, text, genres, recommendation of others).

c. Read daily from self-selected materials.

d. Relate literary experiences (e.g., book discussions, literacy circles, writing, oral presentations, artistic expressions).

e. Maintain a personal reading list or reading log/journal to reflect reading progress and accomplishments.

f. Experience and develop an awareness of literature that reflects a diverse society.

g. Choose to read as a leisure activity.

WRITING Accomplishments
Content Standard 2.0

The student will develop the structural and creative skills of the writing process necessary to produce written language that can be read, presented to, and interpreted by various audiences.

5.2.01   **Engage in prewriting using a variety of strategies.**

     a.   Generate and focus ideas through brainstorming and peer discussions.

     b.   Use print and nonprint materials along with prior knowledge to provide background for writing.

     c.   Arrange ideas by using graphic organizers (e.g., listing, clustering, using story maps, and using webs).

     d.   Develop notes that include important concepts.

     e.   Construct an outline with main ideas and supporting details.

     f.   Select and refine a topic.

     g.   Determine appropriate audience.

     h.   Establish a purpose for writing.

5.2.02   **Write for a variety of audiences and purposes.**

     a.   Compose narratives (e.g., to entertain, to inform, to report).

     b.   Write frequently in the narrative mode.

     c.   Write in response to a standard prompt and/or select a prompt from a varied group.

     d.   Write to inform a particular audience about a specific issue.

     e.   Write a descriptive paragraph to create a visual image.

     f.   Explore and experience frequent opportunities for writing in the expository mode.

     g.   Write to acquire knowledge (e.g., clarify thinking, take notes, synthesize information, enhance communication).

5.2.03   **Show evidence of drafting and revision with written work.**

     a.   Select format based on purpose.

     b.   Write with a sense of audience.

     c.   Develop a paragraph with a topic sentence, supporting details, and a concluding sentence.

d. Maintain focus of topic with specific relevant supporting details.

e. Explain and/or illustrate key ideas.

f. Demonstrate syntactic variety.

g. Arrange multiparagraph work in a logical and coherent order.

h. Write using appropriate time-order words or transitional words/phrases.

i. Use correct page format (e.g., paragraphs, margins, indentations, and titles).

j. Revise to clarify thought, to refine ideas, and to distinguish between important and unimportant information.

k. Use precise language including vivid words and figurative language.

l. Produce multiple drafts.

5.2.04 Include editing before the completion of finished work.

a. Edit for elements of language.

b. Proofread using reference materials and technology.

c. Create readable documents.

5.2.05 Evaluate own and others' writing.

a. Develop and use classroom rubrics for written work.

b. Use the state assessment rubric to make appropriate suggestions for improvement.

c. Participate in peer review and editing.

d. Review personal collection to determine progress.

e. Acknowledge and discuss diversity of individual writing styles.

5.2.06 Experience numerous publishing opportunities.

a. Produce a variety of written works (e.g., literature response, essays, "published" books, literary collections).

b. Incorporate photos, illustrations, charts, tables, or graphs.

c. Use technology for publishing individual and group work.

d. Identify and explore opportunities for publication (e.g., local and national contests, Internet Web sites, newspapers/periodicals).

5.2.07   **Write narrative accounts.**

a. Write in response to narrative prompts, including frequent opportunities for timed writing.

b. Write with developed characters, setting, and plot.

c. Write with well-developed organizational structure, sequence of events, and details.

d. Maintain focus of topic with specific relevant supporting details.

e. Elaborate through the use of sensory details, vivid words, and figurative language to establish a context that enables readers to visualize an event or experience.

f. Explain and/or illustrate key ideas.

g. Demonstrate syntactic variety (i.e., vary sentence structure).

h. Demonstrate facility in use of language (i.e., unique word choice).

i. Develop an identifiable voice.

j. Use classroom/state rubric as a guide for writing narrative accounts.

5.2.08   **Write frequently across all content areas.**

a. Produce a variety of creative works utilizing knowledge from the content areas (e.g., journals, letters to the editor, historical fiction).

b. Compose and respond to original questions and/or problems from all content areas.

c. Explain procedures used to solve problems encountered in content areas (e.g., science experiments, math problems, map and globe activities).

d. Investigate content-specific topics to gather information and write.

e. Use experiences from the arts to write creatively and expressively.

5.2.09 **Write expressively using original ideas, reflections, and observations.**

    a.   Express thoughts and feelings using colorful, fully elaborated descriptions.

    b.   Incorporate vivid words and figurative language.

    c.   Write poems and stories based upon personal reflections, observations, and experiences.

    d.   View, read, or listen to examples of various writing styles.

5.2.10 **Write in response to literature.**

    a.   Write a letter to/as a character in a written work.

    b.   Create an optional ending for a story.

    c.   Retell a story from a different point of view.

    d.   Compare and contrast literary works.

    e.   Write a reader's response to a literary work.

    f.   Write creative, imaginative, and original responses to literature (e.g., poems, raps, songs, stories).

5.2.11 **Write in a variety of modes and genres.**

    a.   Write narratives with vivid, sensory details.

    b.   Write descriptive papers which include vivid words and figurative language.

    c.   Write expository paragraphs that include multiple steps or examples to support explanation.

    d.   Write an essay to compare/contrast two or more people, places, things, or ideas.

    e.   Create a variety of poems.

    f.   Write a research report using multiple sources and notes taken from those sources citing titles and authors.

    g.   Write friendly and business letters.

    h.   Write journalistic articles.

    i.   Use journal entries to demonstrate level of understanding.

    j.   Write an autobiographical account.

ELEMENTS OF LANGUAGE Accomplishments
Content Standard 3.0

The student will use standard English conventions and proper spelling as appropriate to speaking and writing.

5.3.01   Demonstrate knowledge of standard English usage.

   a.   Use nouns appropriately (e.g., common/proper, singular/plural, possessives, predicate nouns).

   b.   Use verbs appropriately (e.g., action/linking, regular/irregular, *be/have,* verb phrases, agreement with subject in person and number).

   c.   Use pronouns appropriately (e.g., agreement with antecedent, reflexive, possessive, correct pronoun case).

   d.   Use adjectives appropriately (e.g., common/proper, predicate adjectives, demonstrative adjectives, proper comparative forms).

   e.   Use prepositions appropriately (e.g., place prepositional phrases in correct location within the sentence).

   f.   Use adverbs appropriately (e.g., proper comparative forms, adverbs of degree *{too, very}*).

   g.   Use conjunctions appropriately (e.g., coordinating).

   h.   Use interjections appropriately.

   i.   Recognize usage errors (e.g., double negatives, troublesome words *{affect/effect, sit/set, lie/lay, may/can, leave/let, teach/learn}*).

   j.   Recognize and appreciate cultural and regional differences signaled by word usage and vocabulary.

5.3.02   Demonstrate knowledge of standard English mechanics.

   a.   Capitalize correctly sentence beginnings, proper nouns and adjectives, titles, abbreviations, quotations, parts of friendly letters and business letters.

   b.   Use correct end of sentence punctuation (e.g., period, question mark).

c. Demonstrate knowledge of rules for commas, colons (between the hour and minute and after the greeting of a business letter), semicolons (in combining sentences), and quotation marks in titles.

d. Demonstrate the correct use of quotation marks in conversation, including their use with capitalization, end marks, and explanatory material.

e. Form contractions and possessives using apostrophes.

f. Abbreviate words correctly.

g. Continue to write legibly.

5.3.03 Demonstrate knowledge of standard English spelling.

a. Spell high-frequency words correctly.

b. Spell correctly commonly misspelled words as appropriate to grade level.

c. Spell correctly words commonly used in content-specific vocabulary.

d. Recognize misspelled words in the context of sentences.

e. Spell plurals and possessives correctly.

f. Use knowledge of root words, prefixes, suffixes, and structural analysis to spell words correctly.

g. Determine correct spelling of words utilizing electronic and print tools (e.g., spell checkers, dictionaries, lists, word walls, charts).

h. Identify correctly spelled homonyms within the context of sentences or phrases.

i. Proofread and edit for accuracy of spelling using appropriate strategies to confirm spelling and to correct errors.

j. Develop a consciousness toward correct spelling across all subject areas.

5.3.04   **Demonstrate knowledge of correct sentence structure.**

    a.   Use appropriate language structure in oral and written communication (e.g., subject-verb agreement in simple and compound sentences, correct word order, correct placement of modifiers).

    b.   Recognize and edit incomplete sentences and run-on sentences.

    c.   Combine simple sentences into compound sentences.

    d.   Combine sentences using compound subjects and/or predicates.